Contemporary Olson

edited by
DAVID HERD

Manchester University Press

Copyright © Manchester University Press 2015

While copyright in the volume as a whole is vested in Manchester University Press, copyright in individual chapters belongs to their respective authors, and no chapter may be reproduced wholly or in part without the express permission in writing of both author and publisher.

Published by Manchester University Press
Altrincham Street, Manchester M1 7JA, UK
www.manchesteruniversitypress.co.uk

British Library Cataloguing-in-Publication Data
A catalogue record for this book is available from the British Library

Library of Congress Cataloging-in-Publication Data applied for

ISBN 978 07190 8971 8 *hardback*

First published 2015

The publisher has no responsibility for the persistence or accuracy of URLs for external or any third-party internet websites referred to in this book, and does not guarantee that any content on such websites is, or will remain, accurate or appropriate.

Typeset in Sabon by
Koinonia, Manchester
Printed and bound in Great Britain by
TJ International Ltd, Padstow

Contents

List of illustrations	page vii
Notes on contributors	ix
Acknowledgements	xiv
Abbreviations	xvi
Introduction: Contemporary Olson *David Herd*	1

Section I: Knowledge

1 Myth and document in Charles Olson's *Maximus Poems* *Miriam Nichols*	25
2 Discoverable unknowns: Olson's lifelong preoccupation with the sciences *Peter Middleton*	38
3 'Empty Air': Charles Olson's cosmology *Reitha Pattison*	52
4 A reading of 'In Cold Hell, in Thicket' *Ian Brinton and Michael Grant*	64

Section II: Poetics

5 From Olson's breath to Spicer's gait: spacing, pacing, phonemes *Daniel Katz*	77
6 Poetic instruction *Michael Kindellan*	89
7 Reading Blackburn reading Olson: Paul Blackburn reads Olson's 'Maximus, to Gloucester: Letter 15' *Simon Smith*	103
8 From Weymouth back: Olson's British contacts, travels and legacy *Gavin Selerie*	113
9 A fresh look at Olson *Elaine Feinstein*	127

Section III: Gender

10 Olson and his *Maximus Poems* *Rachel Blau DuPlessis*	135
11 'When the attentions change': Charles Olson and Frances Boldereff *Robert Hampson*	149
12 'The pictorial handwriting of his dreams': Charles Olson, Susan Howe, Redell Olsen *Will Montgomery*	163

Section IV: History

13 The contemporaries: a reading of Charles Olson's
   'The Lordly and Isolate Satyrs'   *Stephen Fredman*   181
14 Futtocks   *Anthony Mellors*   195
15 Death in life: the past in 'As the Dead Prey Upon Us'
   Ben Hickman   209
16 'To Gerhardt, There, Among Europe's Things of Which
   He Has Written Us in His "Brief an Creeley und Olson"':
   Olson on history, in dialogue   *Sarah Posman*   221
17 'Moving among my particulars': the 'negative dialectics' of
   The Maximus Poems   *Tim Woods*   233
18 A note on Charles Olson's 'The Kingfishers'
   Charles Bernstein   252

Section V: Space

19 Transcultural projectivism in Charles Olson's
   'The Kingfishers' and Clifford Possum Tjapaltjarri's
   Warlugulong   *Peter Minter*   257
20 The view from Gloucester: Open Field Poetics and the
   politics of movement   *David Herd*   272
21 Why Olson did ballet: the pedagogical avant-gardism of
   Massine   *Karlien van den Beukel*   286
22 On the back of the elephant: riding with Charles Olson
   Iain Sinclair   297
23 Charles Olson's first poem   *Ralph Maud*   308

Bibliography   311
Index of writings by Charles Olson   322
Index   324

Illustrations

1 'I have been an ability 11' (1966), Charles Olson (1910–70). Previously unpublished works by Charles Olson are copyright of the University of Connecticut Libraries. Used with permission. *page* 94

2 'I have been an ability 12' (1966), Charles Olson (1910–70). Previously unpublished works by Charles Olson are copyright of the University of Connecticut Libraries. Used with permission. 95

3 Cover of *Evergreen Review* 1:4 (Spring 1958). Author's private collection. 187

4 'Indianapolis' (1956), Robert Frank (1924–). Author's private collection. 188

5 'Rosa Mundi' (1965), Charles Olson (1910–70). Previously unpublished works by Charles Olson are copyright of the University of Connecticut Libraries. Used with permission. 202

6 'Sea Poppy 1 (collaboration with Alistair Cant)' (1966), Ian Hamilton Finlay (1925–2006). Photo credit: © Tate, London 2014. 203

7 *Warlugulong* (1977), Clifford Possum Tjapaltjarri (1932–2002). Synthetic polymer paint on canvas, 202 x 337.5 cm. National Gallery of Australia, Canberra. Purchased with the generous assistance of Roslynne Bracher and the Paspaley Family, David Coe and Michelle Coe, Charles Curran and Eva Curran 2007. Copyright © the estate of the artist, licensed by Aboriginal Artists Agency Ltd. 262

Contributors

Charles Bernstein is author of *Recalculating* (University of Chicago Press, 2013), *Attack of the Difficult Poems: Essays and Inventions* (Chicago, 2011), and *All the Whiskey in Heaven: Selected Poems* (Farrar, Straus and Giroux, 2010). He is Donald T. Regan Professor of English and Comparative Literature at the University of Pennsylvania. More info at epc.buffalo.edu.

Ian Brinton co-edits two contemporary poetry magazines, *Tears in the Fence* and *SNOW*. His most recent publications include an edited collection of essays on the poetry of J.H. Prynne and two books on the poetry and prose of Andrew Crozier. His translations of poems by Yves Bonnefoy (co-written with Michael Grant) appeared in two volumes from Oystercatcher Press in 2013.

Rachel Blau DuPlessis is the author of the long poem *Drafts*, begun in 1986. The newest book, *Surge: Drafts 96–114*, was published by Salt in 2013, thus bringing this twenty-six-year long poem to a temporary fold. Earlier volumes of *Drafts* are available from Wesleyan University Press and Salt Publishing. Her recent *Purple Passages: Pound, Eliot, Zukofsky, Olson, Creeley and the Ends of Patriarchal Poetry* (University of Iowa Press, 2012) is part of a trilogy of works about gender and poetics that includes *The Pink Guitar: Writing as Feminist Practice* and *Blue Studios: Poetry and its Cultural Work*, both from University of Alabama Press. She has published three other critical books on modern poetry, fiction and gender, eight other books of poetry, and three co-edited anthologies as well as editing *The Selected Letters of George Oppen*. DuPlessis is Professor Emerita at Temple University.

Elaine Feinstein has written fifteen novels, many radio plays, television dramas, and five biographies, including lives of Marina Tsvetaeva (1987), Pushkin (1998), Ted Hughes (2001) and Anna Akhmatova (2005). *Bride of Ice*, an extended edition of her versions of the poems of Marina Tsvetaeva, first published in 1971, came out from Carcanet in 2009. *It Goes with the Territory: Memoirs of a Poet* came out from Alma Books in 2013. Her debut novel *The Circle* was longlisted for the 'lost' Man Booker Prize, a one-off award honouring books published in 1970 that were not eligible for consideration for the Booker Prize.

Stephen Fredman is Professor of English and Concurrent Professor of American Studies, University of Notre Dame. He is the author of *Poet's Prose* (1983, 1990),

The Grounding of American Poetry (1993), *A Menorah for Athena* (2001), and *Contextual Practice* (2010). He has edited *A Concise Companion to Twentieth Century American Poetry* (2005) and, with Steve McCaffery, *Form, Power, and Person in Robert Creeley's Life and Work* (2010). His edition, *How Long Is the Present: Selected Talk Poems of David Antin*, is due out in 2014.

Michael Grant was born in 1940. He studied English at Cambridge, where he numbered amongst his teachers Donald Davie and Jeremy Prynne. He subsequently taught English at the University of Kent. He went on to become Senior Lecturer in Film Studies until his retirement. Amongst his publications are: *T.S. Eliot: The Critical Heritage* (1982, as editor), *Dead Ringers* (1997), *The Poetry of Anthony Barnett* (1993, as editor), *The Modern Fantastic: The Cinema of David Cronenberg* (2000, as editor), and *The Raymond Tallis Reader* (2007, as editor). He has also published a number of articles on cinema and on modern poetry. Of his books of poetry, the most recent is *The White Theatre* (2011).

Robert Hampson is Professor of Modern Literature at Royal Holloway, University of London, where he is a member of the Poetics Research Centre and teaches on the MA in Modernism and Contemporary Literature and the MA in Poetic Practice. His recent publications include *Frank O'Hara Now* (Liverpool University Press, 2010), co-edited with Will Montgomery; *Conrad's Secrets* (Palgrave Macmillan, 2012); a book-art book, *out of sight* (Crater Press, 2012); and two volumes of poetry, *an explanation of colours* (Veer Books, 2010) and *reworked disasters* (Knives Forks and Spoons, 2013).

David Herd is Professor of Modern Literature at the University of Kent, where he directs the Centre for Modern Poetry. His collections of poetry include *All Just* (Carcanet, 2012) and *Outwith* (Bookthug 2012). He is the author of two critical monographs: *John Ashbery and American Poetry* and *Enthusiast! Essays on Modern American Literature*. His recent writings on poetry and politics have appeared in *PN Review, Parallax* and *Almost Island*.

Ben Hickman is Lecturer in Modern Poetry at the University of Kent, having studied at Kent and University College, London. His *John Ashbery and English Poetry* was published by Edinburgh University Press in 2012, and his new book, entitled *Poetry and Real Politics: Crisis and the US Avant-Garde*, will be published next year, also with EUP. His poems have appeared in *Poetry Review, Tears in the Fence, Shearsman, Blackbox Manifold* and elsewhere.

Daniel Katz is Professor of English and Comparative Literary Studies at the University of Warwick. He is the author of *Saying I No More: Subjectivity and Consciousness in the Prose of Samuel Beckett* (Northwestern University Press, 1999), *American Modernism's Expatriate Scene: The Labour of Translation* (Edinburgh University Press, 2007; paperback re-issue, 2014), and *The Poetry of Jack Spicer* (Edinburgh University Press, 2013), as well as many articles on twentieth and twenty-first century poetry and prose. Forthcoming work includes contributions to *The Cambridge Companion to American Poetry* and *The Cambridge Companion to the American Modernist Novel*.

Michael Kindellan is an Alexander von Humboldt postdoctoral researcher at the Universität Bayreuth, where he is working on the late cantos of Ezra Pound. In 2012 he was a teaching fellow at the University of Sussex in nineteenth and twentieth century Anglo-American literature. In 2011 he was an EMMA postdoctoral researcher at the Université Paul-Valéry, Montpellier III, where he worked on the poetry of William Wordsworth and J.H. Prynne. In 2010 he completed a DPhil thesis on Walt Whitman, Ezra Pound and Charles Olson at the University of Sussex.

Ralph Maud is Professor Emeritus at Simon Fraser University and founder of the Charles Olson Literary Society. He is the author of *Charles Olson Reading* (1996), *What Does Not Change: The Significance of Charles Olson's 'The King-Fishers'* (1997) and *Charles Olson at the Harbour* (2008). He is the editor of *The Selected Letters of Charles Olson* (2000) and *Muthologos: Lectures and Interviews* (2010). Beyond his work on Olson, he is a world-renowned expert on the work of Dylan Thomas, and on the ethnographers of the Pacific Northwest.

Anthony Mellors is Reader in Poetry and Poetics at Birmingham City University. He has published widely in modernism, literary theory, and contemporary British and American poetry and is the author of *Late Modernist Poetics from Pound to Prynne* (Manchester University Press, 2005; 2010).

Peter Middleton is the author of *Distant Reading*, and a forthcoming book on American poetry and science in the Cold War, as well as a number of articles on poetry and science, including one on mid-century poetry and physics in the Jan 2014 *Modernism/Modernity*. He teaches poetry and modern literature at the University of Southampton.

Peter Minter is a leading Australian poet, poetry editor and poetics theorist. His poetry books include *blue grass* and *Empty Texas* and his poetry is widely published and regularly anthologised in Australia and internationally. He has edited journals and anthologies such as *Cordite, Calyx: 30 Contemporary Australian Poets, Meanjin, Overland, Angelaki: Journal of the Theoretical Humanities*, the *Macquarie PEN Anthology of Aboriginal Literature* and *The Literature of Australia* (Norton). He is a senior lecturer in English at the University of Sydney where he works in Australian literature, contemporary poetry and poetics.

Will Montgomery is a senior lecturer in contemporary poetry and poetics in the English department at Royal Holloway, University of London. He is the author of *The Poetry of Susan Howe* (2010) and the co-editor, with Robert Hampson, of the essay collection *Frank O'Hara Now*. He has published many articles on contemporary poetry. He co-runs London's POLYply reading and performance series and has an interest in the relationships between sound and literature.

Miriam Nichols is an Associate Professor at the University of the Fraser Valley where she teaches modernism and literary theory in the Department of English. Her publications include editions of Robin Blaser's *The Fire: Collected Essays* and *The Holy Forest: Collected Poems* (University of California Press, 2006). She has also published a collection of critical essays on the New American poetry titled *Radical Affections: Essays on the Poetics of Outside* (University of Alabama Press, 2010) and her edition of Robin Blaser's *The Astonishment Tapes* is also forthcoming from the University of Alabama Press. She is currently working on a literary biography of Blaser.

Reitha Pattison is a critic and poet. Her latest book of poetry, *A Droll Kingdom*, was published by Punch Press in 2013. She wrote her doctoral thesis on Edward Dorn, co-edited Dorn's *Collected Poems* (Carcanet, 2012), and her monograph, *Edward Dorn: The Cosmology of Capitalism*, is forthcoming from Peter Lang. She works for Cambridge University Press.

Sarah Posman is a postdoctoral researcher (FWO) at Ghent University. Her research concentrates on modernist and avant-garde poetry. She has co-edited *The Aesthetics of Matter: Modernism, the Avant-Garde and Material Exchange* (De Gruyter, 2013) and *Gertrude Stein's Europe: Talking and Listening* (forthcoming).

Gavin Selerie was born in London, where he still lives. He taught at Birkbeck, University of London for many years and edited the Riverside Interviews. His books include *Azimuth* (1984), *Roxy* (1996) and *Le Fanu's Ghost* (2006)—all long sequences with linked units. A *Selected Poems, Music's Duel*, was published by Shearsman Books in 2009. His work has appeared in anthologies such as *The New British Poetry* (1988), *Other: British and Irish Poetry since 1970* (1999) and *The Reality Street Book of Sonnets* (2008). He has written extensively about London, layering voices through history and landscape. *Hariot Double* (forthcoming) engages with early English settlement of the New World.

Iain Sinclair writes fiction, poetry and non-fiction, and has collaborated on a number of film projects including *The Falconer* (1998). His early work was poetry, published by his own Albion Village Press, and included the collections *Lud Heat: A Book of the Dead Hamlets* (1975) and *Suicide Bridge: A Mythology of the South and East* (1979). He also edited the 1996 poetry anthology, *Conductors of Chaos*. His novels include *Downriver* (1991), which tells of a UK under the rule of 'The Widow', a grotesque version of Margaret Thatcher; *Landor's Tower* (2001); *White Goods* (2002); and *Dining on Stones* (2004). His most recent book is *American Smoke: Journeys to the End of the Light* (2013).

Simon Smith's fifth collection of poetry is *11781 W. Sunset Boulevard* from Shearsman Books. His translations, reviews and essays have appeared in *New Statesman*, *Poetry Review*, *PN Review*, and *Stand*, among other magazines. *The Books of Catullus* will be published soon, and he is presently working on *The Paul Blackburn Reader*. He is a Senior Lecturer in Creative Writing at the University of Kent.

Karlien van den Beukel is Senior Lecturer of Creative Writing at London South Bank University.

Tim Woods is Professor of English and American Literature at Aberystwyth University, where he is also the Director of the Institute for Education, Graduate and Professional Development. Among numerous books and articles, he is the author of *Beginning Postmodernism* (1999); with Peter Middleton, *Literatures of Memory: Time, Space and History in Postwar Writing* (2000); *The Poetics of the Limit: Ethics and Politics in Modern and Contemporary American Poetry* (2002); and *African Pasts: History and Memory in African Literature* (2007). He is currently writing a book on post-apartheid South African Literature, and has recently published articles on US poetry magazines, AIDS in South African literature, and Cid Corman.

Acknowledgements

From the beginning this book has been the work of many hands. It was in 2009 that the Modern Poetry Reading Group in the Centre for Modern Poetry at the University of Kent embarked on a collective reading of Charles Olson's writing. A rich conversation quickly emerged among regular members of the group (Luke Currie, Laurie Duggan, Kate Fox, Nancy Gaffield, Michael Grant, Edward Greenwood, Ben Hickman, Brian Madden, Jan Montefiore, Todd McEwen, Kat Peddie, Simon Smith and Juha Virtanen) and it was as a result of that conversation that the plan to hold an Olson centenary conference was hatched. Preparation for that British-based re-assessment of Olson's work was greatly assisted by the generous advice of Steve Collis, who was already in the process of arranging a centenary event in Vancouver. It is a great pleasure to thank Steve here, for his ongoing friendship and commitment to intellectual exchange. Thanks are also due to all the speakers and delegates at the conference for making that occasion a moment for such serious reflection, not only on Olson's work but on the work of those with whom he was in dialogue. Particular gratitude is due to those who gave keynotes lectures at the event: Elaine Feinstein, Stephen Fredman, Ralph Maud, Peter Middleton and Iain Sinclair.

Stephen Fredman and Peter Middleton have acted as editorial advisors on the book throughout its preparation and I am very grateful to them for the generosity with which they have given their time and expertise. Many others have also contributed to the book's shape and intellectual approach and I am glad to be able to thank the following people for their conversation and writing: David Ayers, Vincent Broqua, Olivier Brossard, Anthony Caleshu, Michael Farrell, Peter Gizzi, Fiona Green, Robert Hampson, Daniel Kane, Daniel Katz, Kristen Kreider, Miriam Nichols, Redell Olsen, Sarah Posman, Will Montgomery, Lytle Shaw, and Ann Vickery.

As the editor of *Contemporary Olson* I am extremely grateful to the book's contributors, not just for the quality of their work but for the time and attention they have given to the project as a whole. There has been a shared sense that the moment is right to re-consider Olson's contribution to postwar poetry and culture and it been a great pleasure to be in conversation about the questions and possibilities his work brings in to view. It is worth underlining that this conversation is international, the book bringing together writers and scholars from Australia, Belgium, Britain, Canada and the USA. The fact that the book's

Acknowledgements

contributions come from this range of intellectual contexts shows that Olson's aesthetic continues to speak well beyond its immediate setting.

Funding for the original conference, and for related research activities, was generously provided by the British Academy, the Kent Institute of Advance Studies in the Humanities (KIASH) and the School of English. This is an appropriate place also to recognize the ongoing support that the University of Kent has given to the study and development of modern poetry, not least through its support for such collaborative ventures as the Sounds New Poetry festival, the performance series Free Range and the poetry collective Zone. Works by Charles Olson published during his lifetime are held in copyright by the Estate of Charles Olson. Previously unpublished works by Charles Olson are copyright of the University of Connecticut Libraries. Permission for the reproduction of such work is gratefully acknowledged here, as is the generous assistance of Melissa Watterworth, Curator of Archives and Special Collections at the University of Connecticut's Thomas J. Dodd Research Center.

As on previous occasions, I am very grateful to Manchester University Press for the care and commitment with which they have prepared the volume. In particular I am glad to be able to thank Matthew Frost (a great friend to poetry) for commissioning and sustaining the project.

My personal thanks go, as always, to Abi, Lily and Eli, with whom it is my great good fortune to share a life. The book is dedicated to my parents, whose life-long commitment to state education chimes deeply with the values of Olson's own teaching.

David Herd
University of Kent

Abbreviations

CP   Charles Olson, *The Collected Poems of Charles Olson (excluding the Maximus poems)*, ed. George F. Butterick (Berkeley, Los Angeles & London: University of California Press, 1997)

CPr   Charles Olson, *Collected Prose*, ed. Donald Allen and Benjamin Friedlander, intro. Robert Creeley (Berkeley, Los Angeles & London: University of California Press, 1997)

GMP   George F. Butterick, *A Guide to the Maximus Poems of Charles Olson* (Berkeley: University of California Press, 1980)

MP   Charles Olson, *The Maximus Poems*, ed. George F. Butterick (Berkeley, Los Angeles & London: University of California Press, 1983)

MUTH Charles Olson, *Muthologos: Lectures and Interviews*, revised second edition, ed. Ralph Maud (Vancouver: Talonbooks, 2010)

SL   Charles Olson, *Selected Letters*, ed. Ralph Maud (Berkeley, Los Angeles & London: University of California Press, 2000)

SW   Charles Olson, *Selected Writings*, ed. and intro. Robert Creeley (New York: New Directions, 1966)

Introduction: Contemporary Olson

David Herd

Composition by field

When Charles Olson published the essay 'Projective Verse' in *New York Poetry* in the Spring of 1950, he issued a set of findings that had been long in development. Although with only one slim volume of poetry, *Y & X*, to his name, and with his first major poem, 'The Kingfishers', still awaiting publication, by the time he laid out the principles of what he variously termed (in his subsequent 'Letter to Elaine Feinstein') 'Projective Open or Field Verse', Olson had given extensive thought to the situation of contemporary poetry (*CPr*, 250).[1] In part circumstantially, but also characteristically, Olson's thinking about poetry had crossed and been informed by various intersecting practices and disciplines. As a graduate student at Harvard in the 1930s he had altered the field of Melville studies, both as archivist (re-assembling Melville's library) and through his radical re-contextualisation of *Moby-Dick*.[2] The resulting book, *Call Me Ishmael*, published in 1947, dug deep into the political economy of mid-nineteenth-century New England, presenting Melville's novel as the period's focal point, what Ezra Pound would call a vortex.[3] Between graduate study and the publication of his research, Olson was politically engaged in the war effort, working in the Foreign Language Division of the Office of War Information and rising to a position of seniority in Roosevelt's Democratic Party. For two years after the war he visited Pound at St Elizabeth's.[4] In October 1948 he was appointed visiting lecturer at the experimental arts institute, Black Mountain College. *Y & X*, published in 1949, was a co-publication with the artist Corrado Cagli, to whose drawings of Buchenwald Olson's poems issued a response. Written and revised in collaboration with Robert Creeley and Frances Boldereff, 'Projective Verse' appeared in *New York Poetry* on 3 April 1950. Noting the essay's moment of publication in his introduction to Olson's *Selected Writings*, Creeley observed, 'The date is significant' (*SW*, 6).

In insisting on the significance of the date, Creeley, writing in 1965, was in part underlining Olson's own assertion in correspondence with Donald Allen that the year 1950 (not some earlier modernist moment) was the appropriate start date for what Allen called the New American Poetry.[5] Indebted as it undoubtedly was to modernist models, Olson's view was that poetry after the war had to be understood to be irrevocably different from what had gone before. There were continuities but unquestionably, also, there had been a rupture, to describe which Olson coined the term 'post-modern'.[6] But when Creeley wrote, without qualification or explanation, that the publication date of 'Projective Verse' was significant, it was not primarily to underscore a literary historical narrative. What mattered, as he saw it, was simply that with the appearance of the essay a change had been effected; that the possibilities of poetry, and creative thought more generally, had been decisively altered.

Looking back from the present vantage point, after the many readings and counter-readings generated by the essay's welter of terms, with knowledge of the major body of work that emerged out of it, and also with the poet's personality clearly in view, it can be difficult to get a fix on Olson's central findings, on what he was really introducing when he announced his new approach. It is useful, therefore, to go back to the central term itself, to the 'field', the metaphor on which all of Olson's innovations hinged. A glance at the dictionary gives a series of partly overlapping, partly disconnected meanings that in the combination of their relatedness and un-relatedness speak to Olson's aesthetic intent. A field, to work from the ground up, is an 'area of open land', though one might note immediately that the designation of a given 'area' is on some level at odds with the definition's basic assertion of openness.[7] An important sub-meaning of this first definition, stepping away from the term's pastoral implication, is that of land 'rich in a natural product such as oil, or gas'. A second meaning of the term is that of 'a branch of study or sphere of activity'. A third meaning indicates 'the space or range within which objects are visible from a viewpoint or through a particular apparatus'. In sport, not to be disregarded, the field means 'all the participants in a given event'. In physics the term defines the region in which 'a force such as gravity or magnetism is effected'. In mathematics it points to 'a system subject to two binary operations analogous to those for the multiplication and addition of real numbers, and having similar commutative and distributive laws'.

When Olson used the term 'field', when he spoke of 'the moment' that the poet 'ventures into FIELD COMPOSITION' (Olson's emphasis), all of the above meanings were, in some measure, in play (*CPr*, 240). As in his book about Melville, in which he presented it as the 'central fact', he meant to make space (the space of the page and the space of the person inscribing the page) central to the new poetics, both as a common property but also as a site of potential conflict.[8] He meant to signal diverse spheres of practice and knowledge and, more particularly, their connections and intersections. He meant to raise the limitations and difficulty registered by the fact of a framing view. He wanted to emphasize the idea of shaping forces, drawing on the term's meaning in physics. He wanted, crucially, to establish the poem as a means of attending to 'all participants'. To say it in a single sentence: what Olson set out in 'Projective Verse', following the catastrophic disregard for human society that constituted the Second World War, and building on his profoundly cross-disciplinary study of political and economic space in nineteenth-century literature, was a conception of the poem grounded in relations; an aesthetic that made relatedness (of people, objects and ideas) axiomatic to the poem's form and creative practice. As he says in the essay:

> let me indicate this, that every element in an open poem (the syllable, the line, as well as the image, the sound, the sense) must be taken up as participants in the kinetic of the poem just as solidly as we are accustomed to take what we call the objects of reality; and that these elements are to be seen as creating the tensions of a poem just as totally as do those other objects create what we know as the world.
>
> (*CPr*, 243)

One of the premises of this book, one of its primary arguments for re-visiting Olson, is that the suppleness and scale with which he is able to figure the complexity of inter-relations (whether between people, between people and the world, or between areas of knowledge) makes him necessary reading in our own politically and economically conflicted moment. It will be necessary later to consider why, as is the case, his thought and writing slipped from critical view in the decades following his death in 1970, an evolution that tells us something about Olson but also something about the history we have lived and are living through. It will be important also, in presenting a contemporary Olson, to indicate how, and with what degrees of reservation and respect, he should now be read. Before setting those literary historical issues out, however, I want briefly to consider how the question of relations and inter-relatedness developed in his thought and writing, from his first major poem 'The Kingfishers', through his spoken and written poetics, to his epic of human labour and engagement, *The Maximus Poems*.

As several writers in this volume, including Charles Bernstein and Peter Minter, observe, 'The Kingfishers' remains a poem of great historical and aesthetic charge. Completed in 1949, though not published until late 1950, the poem is composed as if from the ruins, presenting a series of fragments that in their heft on the page read like the abandoned monumental stones with which the poem concludes. The poet hunts among stones, but so does the reader, trying to make sense of a situation whose meaning is not readily disclosed. As both acts imply (both the poet's hunting and the reader's), a central question for 'The Kingfishers' is the question of human agency. We need to be careful about the phrasing, however, because 'The Kingfishers' is not concerned with human agency in the externalized way a philosophical essay might be. Instead the poem dramatizes the issue, or, more fully perhaps, affords it form. From the opening line and its quotation from Heraclitus ('What does not change / Is the will to change'), the matter of agency is entirely integral to the poem's procedure, to its mode of expression, its way of being (*CP*, 86).

Again, the phrasing needs to be qualified. All reading involves agency, some measure of intellectual re-assembly; the act of reading, in this respect, was hardly introduced by any version of the avant-garde. The matter of agency was, however, emphasized by modernist innovators, such that *The Waste Land* calls on the reader to engage more actively than, say, 'In Memoriam' in its process. The further difference between the agency implied by Eliot's poem and Olson's, however, is not so much a matter of degree as a matter of kind. To clarify what this means, whereas in Eliot the question of readerly engagement is framed by, but also subordinate to, the poem's over-riding interest in the value of the tradition, in 'The Kingfishers' the question of agency is itself the writing's animating concern. What Olson wants to know, what he wants to give formal expression to, is how we act, but also, crucially, how in acting we depend and bear on others. There is all the difference in the world, then, between the way a post-structuralist theorist such as Roland Barthes figures the freedom of the reader, and the way Olson, in 'The Kingfishers', articulates the inter-relatedness that frames human potential and responsibility. What makes it a great poem, in other words, is the way in which, in its postwar moment, it simultaneously invigorates agency and discerns its limits.

Such a negotiation of agency and its limits, an ultimately epic balancing that echoes Karl Marx's lifelong inquiry into the way people make history but not in the circumstances of their own choosing, can be said, as Stephen Fredman has suggested, to be Olson's abiding theme.[9] Subsequently, in *The Special View of History*, Olson took the term *'istorin* from Herodotus to articulate the necessity, as he saw it, for individuals to engage directly with the sources and materials that make up their worlds.[10] Similarly, *The Maximus Poems* is, among other things, an extraordinarily rich poetic history of the forces that shape but also bear the impression of human action, telling the story not just of

Introduction: Contemporary Olson

Gloucester, Massachusetts, but also more generally, in presenting that story, documenting the drives and narratives that result in the emergence of place. It is in 'The Kingfishers', however, that such a balancing first comes into view, Olson's animation of agency in that poem intersecting directly with his shaping of the work in terms of the field.

The clearest sense of the poem as field in 'The Kingfishers' lies, as is well documented, in its use of the space of the page itself. In the simplest sense, by the way Olson indents, centres, left and right aligns, by the way he uses the typewriter to open the poetic page up to the kind of dynamics one associates with painting, he disrupts the tendency to simply read the poem straight through. The natural consequence of such visual prompting is that the reader goes back and forth, actively setting and re-setting encyclopaedic accounts of the physiology of the kingfisher alongside records of Aztec burial rituals alongside fragments from the pre-revolutionary speeches of Chairman Mao. Such reading back and forth, the reading of one thing back into another, was fundamental to Olson. In 'The Kingfishers' he called it 'feedback' but later, in *The Special View of History* in particular, he would give the process its classical rhetorical name of 'chiasmus' (*CP*, 89).[11] Like readerly agency, chiasmus (indicating an inversion in a second phrase or clause of the word order of the first, but meaning more fundamentally 'crosswise arrangement') was hardly new to poetry. But no poet before Olson had rendered it quite so central to expression. The ongoing reciprocity and interference that the process implies was critical to the way he articulated the complexity of human relations.

The way Olson uses the page to produce a field of inter-related elements, thereby calling for a reading that cuts back and forth across space and time, is undoubtedly fundamental to his poetic practice. It should also be understood, however, to be of the order of a visual clue. What we are asked to understand is the way that visuality figures relations, especially human relations, how the reciprocity and interference of feedback inform both human agency and historical change. One can read Olson's understanding and expression of change into any line, or set of corresponding lines, in the poem. Consider, for instance, the way a phrase collaged from Mao gains meaning through displacement; the phrase's first appearance in Section I, Part 2 ('nous devons nous lever et agir') referring the reader to its original rhetorical context; the phrase's second appearance, in translation in Section II, aiming to invigorate the social and political context of the poem's own moment ('And we must rise, act. Yet / in the west') (*CP*, 87, 91). Or take the beautiful variation with which the poem ends:

> It works out this way, despite the disadvantage.
> I offer, in explanation, a quote:
> si j'ai du goût, ce n'est guères
> que pour la terre et les pierres
>
> Despite the discrepancy (an ocean courage age)
> this is also true: if I have any taste
> it is only because I have interested myself
> in what was slain in the sun
>
> (CP, 92–3)

Immediately one reads this passage one has to go back, to a line in the fourth part of section I of the poem: 'Around an appearance, one common model, we grow up many' (*CP*, 89). It is this variation through common-ness, through the shared field of human relations, that 'The Kingfishers', in all its collisions and historical correspondences, seeks to give form.[12] It is precisely in this spirit that the poem's closing lines record the way Olson, as poet, grows through his engagement with Rimbaud. The lines in French are the opening of Rimbaud's poem 'Hunger', part of the section 'Alchemy of the Word', from *A Season in Hell*. As with his later variation on Rimbaud's 'Ô saisons, ô chateaux' in 'Variations Done for Gerald Van De Wiele', Olson's version of the couplet from 'Hunger' is in no sense readable simply as translation, except in the sense that Olson preserves the definition of translation that means moving from one place to another. Where a literal translation of the couplet reads, 'If I have any taste, it is / For earth and stones – not much besides', in Olson's hands Rimbaud's lines give rise to a whole new statement: 'if I have any taste / it is only because I have interested myself / in what was slain in the sun'.[13] What matters in these lines, though, is not just the degree of variation Olson explicitly presents between his version and Rimbaud's original, but the human relation that variation proposes, a relation the poem catches in the explanatory phrase 'Despite the discrepancy'. It is a crucial phrase. The discrepancy, or difference (of time, geography, social context and personality) is not overcome. It is, nonetheless, the basis for dynamic and interconnected human activity, Olson formulating his version of human agency through, with, and in relation to Rimbaud. It is this image of agency that composition by field allows Olson to articulate, where the field of relations both conditions and enables human actions, and where the object of his poetry's expression is, as Robert Creeley put it, 'that variousness on which our humanity must finally depend' (*SW*, xii).

As his friend, collaborator, correspondent and editor, it is entirely appropriate that, in his introduction to the *Selected Poems*, Creeley should have set Olson's practice in its most respectful light. There is no question, however, that in aspects of his practice, as he set out to build a poetics grounded on the shared field of discrepancies, he sometimes failed (sometimes very badly) to execute the measure of tension and balance he could elsewhere so beautifully inscribe. As Rachel Blau DuPlessis rightly states in her essay in this volume, one such area of failure, a blindness in Olson's field of vision, was the difference of gender. More specifically, as DuPlessis also discusses, Olson's willingness to cross over into other fields and disciplines could result in a lack of appropriate professional decorum, as when for instance he mishandled artefacts (and therefore cultural difference more broadly) in Mayan archaeological sites. Such criticisms will be returned to, both in this introduction and in the volume as a whole, the clear expression of them being crucial to any contemporary account of Olson.

Before getting to those larger debates, however, it is worth sketching the ways in which Olson's sense of the poetic field evolved as his work developed. One signal expression of the idea was his 1965 'Reading at Berkeley', the transcript of which Ralph Maud presents in his volume of lectures and interviews, *Muthologos*. The interest of the 'Reading at Berkeley' in this context is partly, as Lytle Shaw has recently discussed, that Olson used the occasion to present something like a real-time performance (it might now be called an installation) of composition by field, but partly also that, as the performance played out late into the night of 23 July 1965, it showed the poetic persona and the poetic method to be at odds with one another in significant ways.[14] In a polite note by way of preface to the transcript of the reading, Maud observes that 'Some people present dissented' (*MUTH*, 137). What they dissented against was the scale but also the vigour of the performance. The reading at the Berkeley conference came two years after the conference at Vancouver, at which Olson had confirmed his prominence among the generation of poets Donald Allen had gathered in *The New American Poetry*, an anthology that had been instrumental in establishing Olson's authority. By the time of the Berkeley reading, then, Olson was at the height of his reputation and also, as Maud suggests, at the height of his powers. As a demonstration in speech of his intellectual method it is unquestionably a bravura performance, a live construction (in time rather than space) of argument, as Shaw points out, through 'independent clauses'.[15] The problem was that in commanding the room the way he did (and so often could) Olson allowed his view too readily to prevail, such that the ideal society he imagines himself to be addressing at Berkeley comes too easily to seem centred around Olson himself. One consequence of such performances was that Olson's attention to 'discrepancy' was obscured, the scope and manner of some of his pronouncements over-riding the manifold elements out of which they were generated.

It is possible to read the poems like this, *The Maximus Poems* in particular, as if Olson, in his address, were delivering a lecture, either to the reader or the inhabitants of Gloucester with whom his poem would partly speak. The opening of the first poem, 'Letter 1', 'I, Maximus of Gloucester, to You' would seem to encourage such a reading:

> Off-shore, by islands hidden in the blood
> jewels & miracles, I, Maximus
> a metal hot from boiling water, tell you
> what is a lance, who obeys the figures of
> the present dance.
>
> (MP, 5)

The lines are difficult in their array of materials, but one thing seems clear, that they are governed by a central figure, 'I, Maximus', whose function is to tell people things; things like, for instance, 'who obeys the figures of / the present dance'. In its spoken setting, then, this opening poem seems to cast forward to such occasions as the 'Reading at Berkeley', to a time when, with his authority established, Olson would command the room.

To read the poem like this, even the opening of the poem, is, however, to overlook a number of its defining factors. One such factor, straightforwardly, is that Maximus is a persona based on the actual historical personage of Maximus of Tyre, a peripatetic Greek philosopher of the second century AD. There is not a great deal known about Maximus, and therefore Olson's poem does not rest much on his original context. The crucial point, however, is that Maximus is not Olson, but rather a way Olson has of mobilizing his poem. Against which it could be contested that the difference between poet and persona (perhaps only ever slight) drops away quite quickly, as Olson plainly enters his own poem, not least when in conversation with contemporaries such as Paul Blackburn and Amiri Baraka (as Simon Smith and Michael Kindellan discuss here). Even so, even if one collapses the difference between Olson and Maximus, to read the poem as Olson's address neglects determining elements of its framework.

A first such element is the view. In Olson's thought, the view was a significant category, dealt with at length in the series of seminars delivered at Black Mountain College in 1956 (the transcriptions of which were subsequently published as *The Special View of History*). This text is treated in a number of essays in this collection, so it is sufficient to say here that the purpose of Olson's seminars was to gain an understanding of the concept of a human view, to grasp the historical and geographical forces that combine to shape it. Crucially, though, the view is *a* view, its definition and limitation being precisely what makes it one among many. When, at the beginning of his poem, Olson presents Maximus, 'Off-shore, by islands', what he is precisely presenting is a view, a strictly limited perspective. One could contrast the opening of *The Cantos*, which gives us no view. In Olson, authority is questioned from the outset.

A second element of the framework of *The Maximus Poems* too easily obscured by a reading of the work as Olson's address, is the field, to which the view, as the dictionary reminds us, is intimately related: 'the space or range within which objects are visible from a viewpoint or through a particular apparatus'. In the terms of this definition, Maximus is the viewpoint, or even, perhaps, the apparatus through which the world of Gloucester, Massachusetts – its politics, industry and environment – become visible. To re-introduce the field at this point (Olson's contemplation of which term, as the visual form of the opening poems reminds us, coincided with the writing of the earliest Maximus Poems) is to recall the emphasis on the range of the field's participants. Olson's epic, this is to say, unlike *The Cantos* and much more fundamentally than William Carlos Williams' *Paterson*, is founded in dialogue: actual dialogues between actual people, as well as the multiple exchanges and intersections that emerge from Olson's collaging of the poem's documents.

Finally, what a reading of *The Maximus Poems* as Olson's address overlooks is that, as much as the beginning of the poem looks like speech, it is in fact writing; subject, or rather, alive to, all the differences and ambiguities that writing makes available and that oratory, however deftly attended to, can so easily close down. Such discrepancies are felt from poem to poem, as when the second poem, 'Letter 2', 'Maximus to Gloucester', repudiates 'Letter 1':

> ... tell you? ha! who
> can tell another how
> to manage the swimming?
>
> (*MP*, 9)

It is not only between poems, however, that such differences and discrepancies are registered, but critically (and throughout) at the level of the line. To whom, for instance, does the 'who' of the final clause of the opening stanza of *The Maximus Poems* refer? Is it, as it most immediately seems, the 'you' who is being 'told', or is it, as the syntax does not rule out, the 'I' who is doing the telling? And so Olson's exploration of human agency in all its complexity and multiplicity, opens up, his poem embarking on an epic inquiry into the labour of a community, the conditions and prospects for collective action.

Critical views

Few twentieth-century poets have been as fortunate in the editorial commitment and calibre of scholarship they have attracted as Olson. This, it should be understood, was part of the project. In so far as it was Olson's intention to develop a poetic that, after the catastrophe of the Second World War, might be able to think through the limitations of Western culture, to think outside 'the western box', he needed collaborators.[16] Charismatic aesthetic and pedagogical leader that he was, Olson understood himself to be engaged in a shared intellectual project, one that depended substantially on the energies and abilities of others. Edward Dahlberg, and more so Robert Creeley, are credited as crucial voices in the development of 'Projective Verse', although Frances Boldereff's important contribution (as Robert Hampson observes in this volume) was kept from view.[17] Creeley remained a collaborator throughout and his editorial engagement with Olson's work was crucial to its reception, giving shape to a body of work (in *Selected Writings* and *Selected Poems*) that defies easy bibliographic presentation.

From an early point, though, the editorial presentation of Olson was itself an ongoing collective project. Among others, Cid Corman at *Origin*, Jonathan Williams at *Black Mountain Review*, LeRoi Jones at *Yugen*, Don Allen at *Evergreen Review* and in *The New American Poetry*, strategically ensured the transmission of Olson's work and ideas. Similarly in the UK (where Olson's work was crucial to a generation of writers seeking new intellectual bearings after the war) Elaine Feinstein then Jeremy Prynne at *Prospect*, Andrew Crozier and Tom Clark at *The Wivenhoe Park Review*, John James at *The Resuscitator*, Gael Turnbull and Michael Shayer at *Migrant*, and Barry Hall and Tom Raworth at *The Goliard Press*, all circulated his work.[18] Prynne's role, in particular, must be emphasized, his work for Olson in the archive not only feeding directly into the form of the poem itself, but enabling him to communicate the importance of *The Maximus Poems* at a very early stage in its reception. Prynne's unequalled grasp of the poem's scale was subsequently set out in the lectures he gave at Simon Fraser University in 1971, a statement that remains one of the most important critical articulations of the scope of Olson's aesthetic.[19] Subsequently the editorial work has largely taken the form of a number of sustained scholarly projects: George Butterick's editions of *The Maximus Poems*, *The Collected Poems of Charles Olson (excluding the Maximus Poems)*, of Olson and Creeley's *Complete Correspondence*, and his *Guide to the Maximus Poems*; Ralph Maud's *Charles Olson's Reading: A Biography*, his edition of *Selected Letters*, and of *Muthologos: Lectures and Interviews*; and Ben Friedlander and Don Allen's edition of *Collected Prose*.

The degree to which, as a consequence of such sustained scholarship, we know how to read Olson remains a moot point. Invaluable as the scholarship has been to the understanding of his work, one side-effect of its comprehensiveness has been that a fundamentally collaborative aesthetic project has come to appear as a somewhat self-enclosed poetic world, with the effect that Olson can too easily seem a separate, albeit rich and rewarding, field of study. In his recent study *Fieldworks: From Place to Site in Postwar Poetics*, Lytle Shaw coins the term 'Olsoniana' to describe the critical manifestations of this self-enclosed world. Recognizing, as he does, precisely how the Olson project gave rise to such attentions, he is nonetheless clear about the limitations that have resulted:

> Even within the pantheon of cosmological masters ... Olson's is an extreme position. This is because the legibility of his cosmology depends – even more so than most examples – not merely on understanding the texts of which it is comprised but on mastering Olson's highly eccentric takes on them. Coupled, then, with Olson's drive to 'find out for oneself' is the contradictory drive, within Olsoniana, to find out what a particular text meant for Olson. This latter drive become necessity works to contain much Olson criticism within his own idiosyncratic terms (as Charles Altieri noted as long ago as 1973).[20]

Shaw is one of a number of important new writers and critics, including Steve Collis and Miriam Nichols, for whom it now seems necessary to re-visit Olson's project. In doing so, Shaw's response to the idiosyncratic critical language that Olson has given rise to is, as he says, to read Olson 'against the grain'.[21] The reading of Olson's site-work that results is rich and highly stimulating. One can, however, query the passing implication that in Olson the grain goes one way. As one of its legacies, Olson's work can and should lead to an investigation of sources. Equally, however, as Creeley pointed out, the point of the source in Olson is not that one remains faithful to it. As Creeley observes, with respect to Olson's reading of Rimbaud in 'Variations Done for Gerald Van De Wiele':

> To call such a poem either translation or adaptation is to mistake how Olson uses the initiating work as material, not as a static accomplishment to be related by presumptive report or description.
> There is another accuracy which Olson far more valued, a reading competent to hear all that the source might provoke.
>
> (*SP*, xv)

This is only to observe that in Olson the grain goes different ways, and that if one route through his oeuvre is towards an investigation of the poetry's sources, another is to put his writing to the kind of creative re-use ('USE USE USE' as 'Projective Verse' has it) that characterized his dialogue with others (*CPr*, 240).

Shaw is certainly right to observe that the idiosyncratic critical language that developed around Olson is one reason his writing was gradually marginalized in the decades following his death in 1970. Miriam Nichols gives another account of that process of marginalization in *Radical Affections: Essays on the Poetics of Outside*. Nichols' argument is historical, relating Olson's posthumous reception to the emergence in the 1960s first, of the politics of identity and second, of the sceptical reading of phenomenology that found expression in deconstruction.[22] This argument relates back to Olson's intellectual development in the immediate aftermath of the Second World War, the crimes of which made it necessary for philosophers, writers and policy-makers alike to develop a vocabulary of shared humanity; witness Hannah Arendt's *Human Condition*, Olson's own essay *Human Universe*, as well as the issuing in 1948 of the Universal Declaration of Human Rights. By the mid-1960s two shifts had occurred. First, as Nichols observes, the vocabulary of shared humanity had itself come under severe but necessary scrutiny, both from the activists of different identity politics and from deconstruction. The changing political environment does not go un-registered in Olson's writing, as in the important Maximus poem 'I have been an ability – a machine' in which, as Michael Kindellan discusses here, Olson takes stock of an American national discourse that so excludes his friend, the poet LeRoi Jones (*MP*, 495–9). Equally, by the 1960s the balance of Olson's pre-occupations had tipped, becoming less political (less to do with the history of labour in Gloucester and the development of social organization he termed the 'polis'), and more to do with an expression of shared humanity at the level of myth. For this mix of reasons Olson's poetry, as Nichols puts it, became 'unreadable for a time'.[23] Undoubtedly true as this account is of the North American context, it is less so for the UK, where, as Gavin Selerie's essay documents, a number of important poetic projects of the 1970s and 80s, notably those of Allen Fisher, Jeremy Prynne and Iain Sinclair (as well as Selerie's own) continued to take Olson as an 'initiating work'. Even so, the combined effect of changing political and theoretical priorities along with the tendency of Olson criticism to emphasize the eccentricity of the work, had the consequence that in the decades following his death, albeit with some notable exceptions, his writing seemed to stand at a remove from the shaping currents of intellectual exchange.

The situation has changed. If, from the mid-1960s onwards, it seemed possible to characterize the postwar period in terms of the dissolution of the humanist subject and the commodification of culture, for the last decade such an account of postmodernity has seemed increasingly obsolete. With wars in Afghanistan and Iraq, the re-shaping of geo-politics through continued migration, and now the renewal of collectivist action in the form of the Arab Spring and the Occupy movement, the questions of shared vocabularies, of the definition and re-definition of political space, and of individual and collective human agency, are firmly back with us. The priorities of intellectual discourse have altered accordingly, such that Arendt's language of the *Human Condition* and her assessment of the failings of what she (like Olson) termed the polis, have been re-framed by Giorgio Agamben in his ongoing study of the exclusions of national sovereignty and bio-politics.[24] One consequence of these historical shifts is not just that Olson, with his emphasis on ethical agency and political relations, is readable again, but that his thought seems once more a necessary intellectual resource.

This is not, of course, Olson's historical moment. It is, though, as the Canadian poet Steve Collis suggests, at the beginning of his recent history of the Vancouver occupation, a moment for which Olson's terms can be of use – a moment in which it is timely to revisit the intellectual resources Olson's poetic inquiries set in place.[25] To do so requires that he be read critically, and also that we understand clearly the degree to which he was caught in his own contemporary nets of thought. What the essays of this book necessarily contemplate, therefore, is where Olson criticism should be looking next.

Contemporary Olson

Conceived as both a re-assessment of Olson's place in recent poetic history, and also as a way into his work for those not already familiar with his writing, this book invited three kinds of contribution. First, there are contextualising chapters, discussions that situate Olson's thought and work (by Robert Hampson, David Herd, Dan Katz, Anthony Mellors, Peter Middleton, Will Montgomery, Miriam Nichols, Reitha Pattison, Karlien Van Den Beukel). Second, there are chapters that have as their focus individual Olson poems, whether from *Maximus* or shorter lyrics (by Stephen Fredman, Michael Grant and Ian Brinton, Ben Hickman, Michael Kindellan, Ralph Maud, Sarah Posman, Simon Smith). Finally, there are essays by writers for whom Olson has proved a crucial interlocutor (Charles Bernstein, Rachel Blau DuPlessis, Elaine Feinstein, Gavin Selerie, Iain Sinclair).

Across these permeable formal divisions, and in aiming to explore what a contemporary Olson criticism can look like, the book has the question of dialogue at its heart. Broadly speaking that dialogue itself takes three forms. In the first place, a number of essays renew our sense of Olson's contemporary moment by recalling his exchanges with writers outside his immediate circle and with figures and ideas from other disciplines. The overarching purpose of this kind of contribution (for instance Smith's discussion of Olson's intermittent conversation with Paul Blackburn, or Middleton's investigation of his inquiry into contemporary science) is to break up the formations of Olson's reception and so to re-insert him in his own period. The second kind of dialogue involves contesting certain spoken and unspoken positions in Olson, positions for which contemporary criticism must hold him to account. In developing this kind of dialogue (witness Blau DuPlessis' discussion of the absence of women's labour in Olson's polis, or Mellors' critique of his partial engagement with ancient sources), the volume speaks to one of the points Benjamin Friedlander placed on the Olson agenda in 2006, that 'scholars should take Olson, as he took himself, as an object lesson, and examine his ideas, assumptions, and experience with a critical eye. He is not, God help us, a hero to be defended against all combatants.'[26] Finally, several essays consider ways in which Olson's body of work helps us to think through issues and questions that are pressing in our own moment (for instance, Minter's reading of recent aboriginal representations of 'country' through Olson's projective poetic, Hickman's account of Olson's understanding of historical agency, and my own consideration of the way Olson frames questions of human movement and polis). Such essays read Olson in dialogue with current discourses and so help to recover the collaborative impulse at the centre of his inquiry.

These different kinds of engagement with Olson are grouped according to key themes and preoccupations within his work. The essays of the first section probe Olson's relation to Knowledge, dwelling in particular on the way he looked to make poetry answerable to other ways of knowing. Miriam Nichols' essay is pivotal in this regard, exploring the defining tension in Olson that arises from his commitment to both myth and document as forms of knowledge. Showing how the two terms sustain one another in the knowledge production of *Maximus*, Nichols' essay considers how we can read Olson's investment in myth in an anti-mythological moment, suggesting in particular that myth in *Maximus* should be understood to function not like a body of belief but as a disposition towards the non-human universe. For Peter Middleton, the form of knowledge in question is science, Olson's interest in which has been much observed but less discussed. Tracking that interest back to the elemental thinking of 'Projective Verse' and also to Olson's construction of the curriculum at Black Mountain, Middleton shows precisely how procedures of observation and reflection in Olson's poetry demonstrate his willingness to absorb the implications of the

Introduction: Contemporary Olson

dominant intellectual discourse of his moment. If poetry was to have a place on the curriculum, as Middleton shows, then for Olson it had to understand its relation to contemporary forms of knowledge. Reitha Pattison's consideration of 'cosmology' pursues that Olsonian requirement. One task that a contemporary Olson criticism must undertake, as Pattison rightly observes, is to scrutinize and re-assess key elements of his lexicon. Working through source and etymology, Pattison relates Olson's articulation of 'cosmology' in his poetry to the matter first of 'space', then of 'breath', thus clarifying the function that all three terms ('cosmology', 'space', 'breath') have in his prosody, demonstrating, as she acutely puts it, how 'Olson's insistence upon the concrete and literal condition of all cosmic forms in his prose permits a more accurate sense of the textual space the writer heralded in Projective Verse'. Finally, in this section, in Michael Grant and Ian Brinton's essay the same preoccupation in Olson with space and breath is translated into a consideration of void and voice, as the poet's emphasis on the implied physicality of voice is placed under scrutiny. Providing a scrupulous account of 'In Cold Hell, in Thicket', Grant and Brinton read Olson's postwar image of hell in relation to Eliot's Dantean exploration of voice, 'The Love Song of J. Alfred Prufrock', thus testing Olson's understanding of the physically projected voice against the absence that for Eliot constituted the real knowledge of vocalisation.

The essays in the section on Knowledge underscore the degree to which Olson's work was founded in dialogue: with myth, with science, with poetic antecedents. The second section, on Poetics, brings the matter of dialogue to the fore. In his essay on Olson and Jack Spicer, Daniel Katz provides a reading of the poets' often fraught relationship that shows clearly how questions of poetics crossed lines of affiliation. Katz's essay is important not only as a reading of these significantly different poets but also as it requires us to reassess Olson's position in poetic arguments of the 1950s and 60s, reframing his standing and influence by recovering his dialogue with an often antagonistic contemporary. For Michael Kindellan, the question of dialogue itself is under scrutiny. Focusing on the Maximus poem 'I have been an ability – a machine', and in particular on the relation between the manuscript and George Butterick's published version, Kindellan considers Olson's insistence on the typewriter as a means of determining reading. Crucially, as Kindellan observes, the reader is not invited to participate in the making of an Olson poem, a stance which does not (as his reading of the poem shows) preclude exchange, but which indicates that for Olson such exchange was dependent on the clear enunciation of a given view. In 'Reading Blackburn reading Olson', Simon Smith documents the evolution of the Olsonian view through his intermittent but decisive correspondence with Paul Blackburn. As Smith observes, with particular reference to 'Maximus, to Gloucester: Letter 15', what the Olson-Blackburn correspondence confirms is not just the centrality of the form of the letter itself to Olson's poetic practice, but the degree to which, for both poets, aesthetic development depended on frank and urgent readings of others' work. Olson's didacticism, in other words (to take Kindellan's term), is founded on his exchanges with leading contemporaries. For Gavin Selerie, Olson's value can be understood not least through his influence on subsequent writers, and his essay documents the exchanges that enabled his work to speak in the British context. His reflection on his own engagement with Olson is an important case study in trans-Atlantic reading, showing how distance itself can facilitate the distillation of a writer's principal ideas. Finally, Elaine Feinstein's essay recalls the moment when Olson's poetics first intersected publicly with British poetry. Catching Olson in full flow, Feinstein's letter to Olson prompted a reply that became one of the most important statements of his stance. Reflecting on what it meant to receive such a communication, Feinstein confirms Smith's sense that Olson's was fundamentally an epistolary aesthetic. He wrote to and for the interlocutor.

This is to paraphrase a point made by Rachel Blau DuPlessis, in the first of the essays under the heading Gender. As DuPlessis observes, a 'root genre of Maximus is the epistle, a genre playing to Olson's strengths by transposing an informal, casual, intense rhetoric into a public intervention'. The question arising is what kind of public, or polis, Olson considered himself to be intervening on. As a consideration of, among other things, the long poem as genre, DuPlessis's essay contributes compellingly to this book's discussions on poetics. It is important, though, if we are to have a contemporary account of Olson, that the issue of gender – which can be framed as a preoccupation with masculinity – should be addressed directly. As DuPlessis observes, in its detailed attention to the world of work, Olson's poem of process is defined, among other things, by its singular lack of attention to women's labour. Such inattention is compounded by the fact that, as Robert Hampson documents, Olson's advances in poetics were made possible just as much by his intellectual relationship with Frances Boldereff as by his extended correspondence with such prominent male writers as Robert Creeley. The recovery of Boldereff's contribution to his thought is important as acknowledgement, not least as she directed him to such key sites of interest as Sumerian culture. As Hampson suggests, it also helps explain the fact that, as he cites Kathleen Fraser as observing, for all the focus on masculine agency in his writing, his formal inventions have proved crucial to the work of subsequent women poets. Like Fraser, Susan Howe has been clear in her acknowledgement of Olson's influence. As Will Montgomery shows, the third party of Herman Melville, whose marginalia have been crucial to both poets, mediates that influence. Following his discussion of Howe with a consideration of the British poet Redell Olsen, Montgomery explores differing ways in which the formal and procedural legacy of Olson has given rise to bodies of poetry sharply different from his own. None of this redeems Olson's gendered view of culture. It does indicate, however, as Howe (cited by Montgomery) has said, that:

> [T]he feminine is very much in his poems in another way, a way similar to Melville. It's voice ... It has to do with the presence of absence. With articulation of sound forms. The fractured syntax, the gaps, the silences are equal to the sounds in Maximus. That's what Butterick saw so clearly. He printed Olson's Space.[27]

If the feminine emerges in Olson as a discernible absence, his concern with History is plain. Like Pound, he took the epic to be a poem containing history, a position he modified by the exploration of historical agency he characterized as *'istorin*. In the context of this volume, the question of history surfaces in various ways. In Stephen Fredman's reading of 'The Lordly and Isolate Satyrs', the focus is on Olson's relation to his own moment. As scholarship has directed critical attention to Olson's sources, his relation to the fabric of his own historical context has been obscured in a way not true of, say, Ginsberg or O'Hara. Setting Olson's poem alongside the Robert Frank photograph that Donald Allen printed on the cover of the *Evergreen Review* in which the poem first appeared, Fredman argues for a contextual reading of Olson's poetry, one that clearly locates his cultural claims in the limits of his own historical moment. How those limits are negotiated is the subject of the next two essays. For Anthony Mellors, it is necessary to question Olson's own partial reading of history, not least his reading of Sumerian culture. For Mellors, Olson's project should cause us to interrogate the implied relation between poetry and scholarship, both as scholarship mediates the work (notably in the form of Butterick's *Guide to the Maximus Poems*) but also as Olson's own scholarship continually returns us to the problem of authority. In this respect, as Mellors argues, Olson's break from modernism is incomplete. In Ben Hickman's essay, the question of authority is related to the issue of historical agency. In a reading of 'As the Dead Prey Upon Us', Olson's elegy to his mother, Hickman explores the terminological pressure that builds as the poet considers how it is possible to articulate the 'will to change'. If Olson's poetry contains history, what it also contains, as Hickman observes, are individuals and groups struggling and managing to effect change. It is not least in such sustained attention to questions of agency, as Hickman suggests, that Olson's poetry speaks to our moment of developing crisis. For Sarah Posman, considering Olson's dialogue with European historiography, the image of change Olson became able to express poetically can be closely related to the articulation of duration and fictiveness found in the work of Henri Bergson. Exploring that affinity through a reading of Olson's poem-letter to Rainer Gerhardt, Posman again presses Olson into productive dialogue with an intellectual tradition not obviously his own. Tim Woods' essay is similarly concerned with Olson's historiography, although as he tracks Olson's understanding of history to his enactment of subjectivity, Woods speaks equally instructively to questions of ethics and perception. Starting with an account of the experience of reading Olson's ambiguous grammar, in all its restless mobility, Woods presents a compelling reading of the poetry's refusal to settle for linear historical narrative. Discussing him in relation to Benjamin and, more particularly, Adorno, Woods presents a poetic sensibility founded on the fact of difference. Olson's achievement, as Woods emphatically shows (underlining this book's emphasis on dialogue) lies in his ongoing animation of the subject's dependency on others. Finally, in this section, Charles Bernstein returns Olson's major early poem 'The Kingfishers' to the postwar scene of its composition. The war, as Bernstein vividly reminds us, was the background to Olson's radical formal experiment, the historical circumstance, as this Introduction has observed, to which his poetic inquiry was a considered intellectual response.

Critical to that response, as Bernstein observes, and as this volume concludes by considering, was the matter of relations within and across space. Like Bernstein, the Australian poet Peter Minter takes 'The Kingfishers' to be axiomatic, showing how the forms of cognition Olson arrives at in that poem help understand the spatial imagination at work in Aboriginal, especially contemporary Aboriginal, art. Taking Clifford Possum Tjapaltjarri's *Warlugulong* as an example, Minter reads the painting and Olson's poem through one another to arrive at a consummate sense of the way Olson re-imagined the relation between people and their environment. Here, as much as anywhere in the volume, open field composition is presented as a resource for contemporary use, as a way of picturing our relation to the world grounded in reciprocity and limit. In my own essay, the space in question is not environmental but that of political geography. Linking Olson's presentation of the space of the poem in 'Projective Verse' to the politics of *The Maximus Poems*, the essay shows how Olson makes movement, and in particular the figure of the crossing, central to his articulation of the polis. As with Minter's essay, what this discussion proposes is that the enduring value of Olson's writing rests deeply on the degree to which it re-negotiates space. What that renegotiation itself partly depends on, as Karlien van den Beukel records, is Olson's life-long interest in dance, especially ballet. Central to the Black Mountain curriculum, dance was also pivotal to the way Olson construed artistic inquiry, affording him a basis, in the period after the war, for re-imagining the limits and possibilities of human physiology. The last essay of this section, Iain Sinclair's recollection of the effect of reading and encountering Olson, returns us to 'the geography of it' and to Olson's position in Gloucester, at the sea's edge. What Sinclair catches above all is the arc and sweep of Olson's thought in *The Maximus Poems* – his determination to reacquaint us with the ground on which we stand.

In conclusion, Ralph Maud returns us to that ground, to the Cape Ann coastline that was the vantage point for much of his major writing but also the setting, as Maud observes, for Olson's first poem. The point of Maud's short commentary is to re-assess Butterick's interpretation of the archive and to wonder if the draft of 'Purgatory Blind' is not a better candidate for Olson's first poem than the revision. What Maud underlines is that Olson should and must be re-read, but also that it is precisely in the principle of the draft, of the ongoing work-in-process, that Olson found a poetic which could speak both to and beyond its moment of composition. As Melville put it before him, 'This whole book is but a draft–nay, but the draft of a draft.'[28] Melville's insight, offered via Ishmael, was that the consciously incomplete work, the work that understands itself to be in process, is the work that continues to stimulate and enable thought. Or as Olson put it:

> It is undone business
> I speak of, this morning,
> with the sea
> stretching out
> from my feet
>
> (*MP*, 57)

This is 'Maximus, to himself', arriving at an understanding, where 'undone' means ongoing, the necessity of engaging once more. In the entirely affirmative way Olson means it here, reading his body of work is an ongoing process. The essays of this volume help make him contemporary again.

Notes

1. Charles Olson, *Y & X* (Washington DC: Black Sun Press, 1949).
2. For a detailed account of Olson's life see: Tom Clark, *Charles Olson: The Allegory of a Poet's Life* (Berkeley: North Atlantic Books, 2000).
3. Charles Olson, *Call Me Ishmael* (New York: Reynal and Hitchcock, 1947).
4. For a full account of Olson's exchanges with Pound during this period see Catherine Seelye (ed.), *Charles Olson and Ezra Pound: An Encounter at St Elizabeths* (New York: Grossman/Viking, 1975).
5. Allen refers to Olson's letter in his 'Afterword' to the 1999 edition of the anthology: Donald Allen (ed.), *The New American Poetry, 1945–1960* (Berkeley & London: University of California Press, 1999).
6. Olson first used the term, referring to the 'post-modern world', in a letter to Creeley dated 9 August 1951.
7. All definitions given here are from the *Concise Oxford English Dictionary*.
8. As Olson writes, 'I take SPACE to be the central fact to man born in America, from Folsom cave to now' (*CPr*, 17).
9. 'Men make their own history, but they do not make it as they please; they do not make it under self-selected circumstances, but under circumstances existing already, given and transmitted from the past.' Karl Marx, 'The Eighteenth Brumaire of Louis Bonaparte' in Karl Marx and Frederick Engels, *Selected Works in One Volume* (London: Lawrence and Wishart, 1980), 96. For Stephen Fredman's excellent discussion of the theme of 'containment' in Olson see Stephen Fredman, *The Grounding of American Poetry: Charles Olson and the Emersonian Tradition* (Cambridge: Cambridge University Press, 1993).
10. For Olson's extended treatment of the term *'istorin*, which he paraphrases as the act of finding out for yourself, see Charles Olson, *The Special View of History*, ed. Ann Charters (Berkeley: Oyez, 1970).
11. Olson's reference to 'feedback' is a prime example of his willingness to explore other disciplines in his construction of the language of the poem. As Ralph Maud observes, the term is taken from Norbert Wiener's pioneering work, *Cybernetics: Or Control and Communication in the Animal and the Machine* (Cambridge, MA: MIT Press, 1948). See Ralph Maud, *What Does Not Change: The Significance of Charles Olson's 'The Kingfishers'* (London: Associated University Presses, 1998), 179.
12. As Maud notes, the line is from Heraclitus, cited by Plutarch in 'On the E at Delphi'. See Maud, *What Does Not Change*, 73–4.
13. The translation is from Jeremy Denbow's *Season in Hell: An English Translation from the French* (Lincoln, NE: iUniverse, Inc., 2004), 59.
14. Lytle Shaw, *Fieldworks: From Place to Site in Postwar Poetics* (Tuscaloosa, AL: The University of Alabama Press, 2013), 65–6.
15. Shaw, *Fieldworks*, 49.
16. As Maud notes, Olson first uses the phrase 'Western Box' in *Mayan Letters*, with reference to Pound's Guide to Kulchur in the context of an annotated bibliography (*SW*, 129).

17 The credits to Creeley and Dahlberg are explicit: 'Or so it got phrased by one, R. Creeley, and it makes absolute sense to me .... First pounded into my head by Edward Dahlberg' (*CPr*, 240).
18 I am very grateful to Ian Brinton for sharing his detailed understanding of Olson's early circulation and reception in the UK.
19 J. H. Prynne, 'On *Maximus IV, V, VI*', *Minutes of the Charles Olson Society* 28 (April 1999).
20 Shaw, *Fieldworks*, 53.
21 Ibid.
22 Miriam Nichols, *Radical Affections: Essays on the Poetics of Outside* (Tuscaloosa, AL: The University of Alabama Press, 2010), 2–4.
23 Nichols, *Radical Affections*, 1.
24 See in particular Agamben's trilogy: *Homo Sacer* (Stanford, CA: The University of Stanford Press, 1995); *State of Exception* (Chicago and London: The University of Chicago Press, 2005); *The Kingdom and the Glory: For a Theological Genealogy of Economy and Government* (Stanford, CA: The University of Stanford Press, 2011).
25 'In September 2011 I sat down to write a book about change. The words of the poet Charles Olson were at the forefront of my mind: "What does not change / is the will to change"', Steve Collis, *Dispatches from the Occupation: A History of Change* (Vancouver: Talonbooks, 2012), xiii.
26 Benjamin Friedlander, *Olson Now*, posted 27 May 2006, accessed 23 July 2013, http://olsonnow.blogspot.com/2006/05/benjamin-friedlandercharles-olson-now.html
27 Howe, and Edward Foster, 'Talisman interview,' in *The Birth-mark: Unsettling the Wilderness in American Literary History* (Hanover: Wesleyan University Press, 1993), 180.
28 Herman Melville, *Moby-Dick*, with an introduction and notes by David Herd (Ware: Wordsworth, 2001), 120.

Section I

Knowledge

1

Myth and document in Charles Olson's *Maximus Poems*

Miriam Nichols

Large in person, sprawling on the page, and epic in ambition, Charles Olson stands in mid-twentieth century American poetry like the diorite stone on Main Street to which he once compared himself (*MP*, 221). Such bigness and energy have both attracted and repelled readers. Since his death in 1970, Olson has received a number of extended readings from distinguished scholars, and he continues to engage more recent critics. Jeff Wild, for example, opens an essay titled 'Charles Olson's *Maximus*: A Polis of Attention and Dialogue' by remarking that 'every page of Maximus seems to open new angles on Olson, on the world, on reality and on myself'.[1] Not all of Olson's readers have been so enchanted, however,[2] and I think Robert Von Hallberg's remarks in one of the first book-length responses to Olson say why. Von Hallberg's *Charles Olson: The Scholar's Art* is an important early instance of a resistant reading, and for reasons that underlie subsequent critiques.[3] According to Von Hallberg, Olson arbitrarily arranges the historical and mythical narratives that make up the *Maximus Poems* and passes off the result as a public poem, more authentic, authoritative, and objective than it really is. The 'EGO AS BEAK' (personal preference) which Olson accused Pound of using as his principle of selection in the *Cantos* is a fault in his own work (*SW*, 83).[4] To further confound readerly expectations, the records and stories of Gloucester that Olson collages into volume one of *The Maximus Poems* are interwoven with myth and increasingly give way to it in volumes two and three. Again, Von Hallberg states the issue: 'In the second and third volumes of the sequence [*Maximus Poems*] Olson has abandoned faith in the possibility of deriving political understanding from an investigation of history. History and mythology are ransacked for analogues – which lead not to precepts, nor to anything properly called knowledge, but to a construct dependent upon a tradition of poetic license'.[5] Without precept or 'anything properly called knowledge', the *Maximus Poems* devolve from a would-be saga of Gloucester to 'little else than a show'.[6]

In my view, what Olson's resisting readers find problematic follows from the poetic principles that remain most radical and alive in his work. Olson does not offer precepts, particularly in the later volumes, nor does he offer much that counts for knowledge by logical or empirical measurement. He also undeniably ransacks myth and history for analogues, as Von Hallberg claims, and worse, these sources often reference human aggression: the explorer-heroes of the *Maximus Poems* were imperialists, whatever else their virtues, and the Mayan culture he championed was violently tribal. I want to suggest that these elements of Olson's poetry follow from: 1) an early rejection of subject-object dualism and consequent turn away from epistemological questions; and 2) an emphasis on stance and method over specific moral precept as the province of the poet. Olson displaces objectivity with shareable cultural paradigms and geohistories; he displaces lyric subjectivism with a personal response to public matters. Olson's rejection of dualism has far-reaching consequences that extend to his treatment of myth and document and motivate his search for a fresh means of ordering the perceptual field. In reaching for ways to articulate common ground *and* honour individual agency, Olson remains our contemporary.

As many readers have acknowledged, Alfred North Whitehead is key to Olson's poetics. In *Process and Reality*, Whitehead accounts for the things of the world as aggregates of 'actual entities' (atom-like 'drops of experience') that positively or negatively 'prehend' each other to form themselves accretively by selection.[7] Since every actual entity prehends every other, either positively or negatively, subject and object represent points of view rather than ontological differences: a thing that is subject for itself is object or datum for everything else. In an essay on Olson and Whitehead, Robin Blaser records Olson's response to this proposition in the margins of *Process and Reality*: '"The end of the subject-object thing-Wow"'.[8] 'The end of the subject-object thing' is behind Olson's major poetics essays. In 'Human Universe': 'What I do see is that each man does make his own special selection from the phenomenal field and it is true that we begin to speak of personality, however I remain unaware that this particular act of individuation is peculiar to man, observable as it is in individuals of other species of nature's making' (*CPr*, 161). Again, in 'Projective Verse', Olson writes: 'For a man is himself an object, whatever he may take to be his advantages' (*CPr*, 247).

Selection, then, accounts for the unique and particular; the common and continuous comes in with 'eternal objects' or 'forms of definiteness', Whitehead's term for those elements of creation that are essentially conservative (slow evolving) and that transmit the morphology of planetary life forms.[9] From Olson's angle, the two Carls, Jung and Sauer, complement this component of Whitehead's ontology in psychology and geography. From Jung, Olson takes up a quest for archetypes; from Sauer, the morphology of landscape.[10] For these companionable thinkers, the conservative components of life function like DNA; they constitute an enduring code that is differently expressed in each individual entity. Myth is thus significant for Olson as a kind of social-psychic DNA, discernible in master narratives and common patterns of human behaviour. This line of thinking leads him to a provisional, dynamic form of structuralism that allows for analogy between different orders of reality. Olson says in *The Special View of History* that the truth is 'that which holds up'; forms of the real remain valid until something happens to change the way we see them.[11] Myths, because they narrate inherited desires and attitudes, and because the affective charge they carry is transhistorical and widely shareable, are conservative forms of the psychic landscape.

One of the most immediate consequences of Olson's researches is his dismantling of the temporal partition between myth and history and his reach for a unified field theory through the concept of a human universe. In traditional cosmogonies, mythic events take place in a time sealed off from history, but archaic wonder at the *before* hardens into the dualism of *there* and *here* in Western religion and philosophy. This dualism lingers on in the conventions of languaged representation, past the liveness of the tradition.[12] In 'Human Universe' Olson attacks the 'UNIVERSE of discourse' – simile in particular – as consequent to his polemic against Platonism (*CPr*, 156). We have to 'find ways to stay in the human universe, and not be led to partition reality at any point, in any way,' he writes (*CPr*, 157). And in the same essay, 'a thing, any thing, impinges on us by ... its self-existence, without reference to any other thing' (*CPr*, 157–8). Maximus is not the *representative* of his tribe in the manner of archaic heros, or reducible to the *exemplum* of a precept; nor, as a member of the *human* universe, is he an oracle of unmediated perception. He is, rather, an allegory of the ontogenetic process. It is the process that is public, common, and repeatable, not the entities that come out of it and which are not, says Olson, *like* anything else. In *The Special View*, he credits Keats with the idea that 'a man's life ... is an allegory' and he returns to this thought later when he says that 'man is no trope of himself as a synechdoche of his species, but is, as actual determinant, each one of us, a conceivable creator'.[13] Olson clearly admires some of his characters and despises others, but the point of retelling their stories is to reveal them as allegories of self-fashioning and hence also of world becoming; in Whiteheadian ontology, self and world are mutually constitutive because each is an inflection of the other. Complexity, I take it, is a primary value of the philosophy of organism and of Olson's poetics as well; the best world is the one that best realises the potential of all at any given moment to come into form. Olson famously opens the *Maximus Poems* with the statement that 'love is form', 'born of yourself, born / of hay and cotton struts' (*MP*, 5, 7). So defined, form is a unique assemblage and inflection of what is. It is not solipsistic, as a fantasy might be, because the act toward form is a selection of things that lie in the common way; it is not objective either because it is an affective response to these things.

The poet, then, picks 'a private way / among debris / of common / wealths' (*MP*, 136). His view is unavoidably situated. The *view*, in fact, is one of Olson's most repeated tropes. '"Where'd you get those glasses?"' he records a fishing mate as asking him, 'after, like a greenhorn / I'd picked three swordfish out of the sun-blaze' (*MP*, 30). This poem, 'Letter 6', begins with 'polis / is eyes', and what the eyes of Maximus see varies dramatically with his position (*MP*, 30). Sometimes he is bobbing on the sea like the ship-wrecked Ishmael ('I set out now / in a box upon the sea'), at other moments, he is up high 'overlooking / creation' (*MP*, 373, 383). What gets into the poem is always the view-from-here. Like Melville's Ishmael, the poet is a character in his own narrative, bound to the truth, but equally bound to tell it slant. There is a strong distinction to be made here between the view as Olson constructs it and egocentrism: the former places the self in the world, the latter makes the world an extension of the self. Awareness of oneself as figure on an unmasterable ground begins the recovery of what Olson called the 'familiar': situatedness in space and time.[14]

As Olson moulds his researches into a poetics (a 'stance'), he proposes a number of terms that replace subject and object, muthos and logos, as organisers of the phenomenal field. In the 'Letter to Elaine Feinstein', he offers topos, typos and tropos (*CPr*, 252). In 'Maximus, from Dogtown II,' he writes that the genetic is 'Ma' and the morphological is 'Pa'; the Child is then the 'MONOGENE', the minim promising new form (*MP*, 179, 180). In the 'Bibliography of America for Ed Dorn', the triad is 'fact-act-datum' (*CPr*, 304). The famous Olson-Creeley proposition that 'FORM IS NEVER MORE THAN AN EXTENSION OF CONTENT' situates form in a given time-space field (*CPr*, 240). But as Olson develops the concept through the triads, the field comes to include 'all those antecedent predecessions, the precessions / of me', from family history to ice-age geology (*MP*, 184). This folding in of the various layers of history and place creates a very thick time-space field that displaces objectivity with a shareable human universe, and

Myth and document in The Maximus Poems   29

subjectivity with singular troping on this field. *The Maximus Poems* articulate typos as the enduring, mythical component of psychic and cultural morphology; topos as complex geo-social history; and tropos as the response of the individual to these existential givens.[15]

I turn to 'The Record', '14 MEN STAGE HEAD WINTER 1624/25', and 'Some Good News' from volume one of *Maximus* to demonstrate Olson's weaving of document and myth into stance through the triad typos-topos-tropos. According to George Butterick's information, 'The Record' comes from a Weymouth Port Book as cited in Frances Rose-Troup's history, *John White, the Patriarch of Dorchester [Dorset] and the Founder of Massachusetts, 1575–1648* (*GMP*, 174). The poem identifies the cargo of the *Amytie* and *Fellowship* as fish, furs and oil. It names the Captains of the ships and the companies receiving the goods in Weymouth. It footnotes the terms 'dry fish', 'corfish' and 'train oil' from information in Harold Innis's *The Cod Fisheries: The History of An International Economy* (*GMP*, 175). As uncommented document, 'The Record', simply shows that a shipment of fish and fur left Cape Ann bound for Weymouth in 1626, although in the names of the ships there is already a glimmer of the Puritan saga. The next poem takes a further step: '14 MEN' lists the equipment required for the establishment of a fishing station under the command of Captain Richard Whitbourne (*GMP*, 175). In a brief comment at the end of the list, Olson compares the cost of the Whitbourne venture in Newfoundland to that of the Dorchester settlement on Cape Ann in 1624, speculating that '[t]he difference may be the measure of a mere / station versus a plantation such as the / Dorchester Company was embarked on' (*MP*, 123). With this comment, document moves into historical narrative. In fact, 'The Record' and '14 MEN' suggest a skeletal history of the colonial enterprise in New England. Document says that the Cape Ann settlement began with venture capital, lured by fish and fur. To further this commercial venture, company-financed fishers were tasked with setting up a permanent settlement. They did this with '2 good axes, 4 hand hatchets, 4 / short wood hooks, 2 drawing irons, 2 adzes / 4 arm saws, 4 hand saws, 4 thwart saws, 3 augers, 2 crowes of iron, 2 sledges, / 4 iron shovels, 2 pick axes, 4 mattocks, / 4 cloe hammers [and] / heading and splitting knives' as well as provisions of food, cooking utensils, and candles (*MP*, 122). Fact implies act ('fact-act-datum'), in this case the hard labour of sailing, fishing, cooking, clearing, and building. To borrow a phrase from *Call Me Ishmael*, 'what lies under' history is document; what lies under document, however, is myth (*CPr*, 21).

'Some Good News' begins where '14 MEN' leaves off, not with act but datum:

> how small the news was
> a permanent change had come
> by 14 men setting down
> on Cape Ann, on the westerly side
> of the harbor
>
> (*MP*, 124)

Just as it says, the poem begins with a historical scrap – the small news of fourteen fishers wintering over on Cape Ann. From there, however, the story quickly expands into a history of the United States. Before the beginnings of European immigration, the region was well known to French, Spanish, and Portuguese fishers as well as the English. Olson slips this information in with an allusion to 'the old // North Atlantic (of Biskay, / and Breton, of Cabot's nosing into' and in speculating on the source of the name 'Georges', a fishing bank called Saint Georges Shoal: 'who gave her their / patron saint-England? / Aragon? or Portyngales?)' (*MP*, 124). In an apparent aside, he then repeats a comment from Christopher Levett's *Voyage into New England* (1628) to the effect that New England has perhaps been overrated as a settlement site ('"too faire a gloss" / is placed on her') (*MP*, 124). The 'faire gloss' resonates against the title of the poem, originally 'Good News! fr Canaan' (*GMP*, 176). 'Some Good News' still carries the biblical reference to Canaan in the Christian message of 'good news' and what that meant for the Puritan settlers to come: a new world in which to act out the reformation and establish a 'city on a hill'. So history is shot through with desire, the motivating muthos behind human action. In thirty-five lines, Olson condenses through the barest of allusions and in an apparently offhand manner the core of New England settler history: its economic beginnings in the fish and fur trade, its ideological beginnings in old world dreams of adventure and utopia, filtered through the Puritan imagination. The new world, Olson says, was 'Europe's / first West', its 'Westward motion', its utopian quest *and* its imperial venture (*MP*, 128, 125).

The voyage of discovery, redemption, or conquest is a master trope of many archaic cultures, including the Mediterranean, Mesopotamian, and Nordic civilizations that often appear in *Maximus*. In the third volume, Olson calls it the 'rose of the world':

> Migration in fact (which is probably
> as constant in history as any <u>one</u> thing: migration
>
> is the pursuit by animals, plants & men of a suitable
> — and gods as well–& preferable
>
> environment; and leads always to a new center.
>
> (*MP*, 565)

Historical journey segues into myth; myth leads back to history. Speaking of myth in the *Special View*, Olson says that 'It is at once commemorative, magical, and prospective', 'myths are only large pictures of pictures, enlargements'.[16] They re-enact 'what men have selected from what their ancestors did which seemed to them useful. It's what we call tradition. They call it rites'.[17] Master tropes like the journey narrative are cultural commonplaces that have lost historical specificity and human scale through repetition and enlargement. As Olson uses them in *The Maximus Poems*, they are data that reveal chronic human behaviours, not necessarily virtues. Typhon, for example, is a chthonic energy from Hesiod's *Theogony* who appears repeatedly in Olson's New England and has a counterpart in the indigenous serpent king of the pond (*MP*, 264, 265, 291, 312); He-with-the-House-on-his-Head is the protagonist of an Algonquin story about migration in search of plenty (*MP*, 179, 201, 311); Enyalion, the beautiful, is a Cretan war god that Olson syncretises with the Bulgar, wandering Indo-European horsemen (*MP*, 405–7). The myths hold onto the deeds of these outriders as they seek their own flourishing on a planet that is equally alive with its business. As a picture of historical pictures, myth records the desirousness of human enterprise, its affective engagements with nature, and its common imaginaries.

If typos is the well-beaten path, then topos is the 'wilderness' on either side of it, a dense geohistory there to be adapted to. John Smith is a recurrent figure of *The Maximus Poems* because he was an early recogniser of the possibilities specific to the Atlantic coast. Olson praises him in 'Some Good News' as 'the stater of / quantity and / precision', and in his essay, 'Captain John Smith', he says that he values Smith because 'the *geographic*, the sudden *land* of the place, is in there' (*MP*, 126; *CPr*, 319, original emphasis). Smith is the one who 'pointed / out / Cape Ann' and 'named her / so it's stuck' (*MP*, 128). New England was initially about fish, furs and timber, not 'old agricultural ... / Neolithic, sickles' as in the Mediterranean basin, and not 'gold, and murder' as these dominated the Spanish conquest of Mexico and South America (*MP*, 128–9, 129). In America, Olson writes,

> We kill
> as a fisherman's
> knife nicks
> abundance.
>
> Which we take
> for granted,
> we don't even earn
> our labor ...

> we do it all
> by quantity and
> machine.
>
> (*MP*, 129)

Olson takes space – 'quantity' – as the primary fact of the North American continent in *Call Me Ishmael*. For European settlers, the largeness of the continent was both a utopian abundance and a terrifying task. Consider the list of *hand* tools with which the settlers of '14 MEN' were equipped and the backbreaking labour these imply. The rapid advance of American technology – 'quantity and / machine' – was a response to the exigencies of place. As 'Some Good News' moves outward from the fourteen men, Olson suggests that the machine prepared the way for the Civil War of 1863. Again, he condenses: Grant 'did finally hammer out / a victory over // Clotho Lee, the spinner / the stocking frame / undid' (*MP*, 129). The stocking frame was a knitting machine invented by William Lee of Calverton in 1589 and an important first step in the industrialization of the textile industry. Olson layers this Lee with Robert E. Lee, the Confederate General and Clotho (cloth), the youngest of the three Fates and the one responsible for spinning the thread of life. Inventions like the stocking frame and the cotton gin (1793), the latter attributed to the American Eli Whitney, increased the potential for textile production and hence the dependence of the American economy on cotton and slave labour, an instance of 'quantity and / machine' that literally spun out the lives of African Americans, 'fated' to drudgery by Clotho. The growth of slavery then contributed to the Civil War. Hence,

> South
> and North—the world,
>
> tomorrow, and all
> without fate
> tomorrow,
> if we,
> who come from a housekeeping
>
> which old mother Smith
> started,
> don't find out the inert
> is as gleaming as,
> and as fat as,
>
> fish
>
> (*MP*, 130)

In this dense passage, Olson suggests that the military and industrial might of the United States ('the world, / tomorrow') was made possible by a certain kind of response to the divine inert.[18] America became a world power through cheap labour, an abundance of exploitable resources, and technological ingenuity. As Olson brings the poem home to his own historical moment in Gloucester, the long-term effect of the machine reveals itself in the harbour in front of him. The 'cornucopia' of the sea yields 'industrial fish' for the 'De-Hy' (dehydrating machine) that turns 'anything / nature puts in the sea' into cat food and fertiliser for overworked inland fields (*MP*, 131).[19]

The machine and the will to power constitute one response to the challenge of the continent. Olson offers Smith's 'quantity and / precision' as an alternative. Contrasting Smith with Miles Standish, he completes his triad in tropos, an individual response to a shared context. As a keen observer and map-maker, Smith compares favourably with Standish, the latter hired for 'corporative / murder', Olson says (*MP*, 129). Standish was a military advisor elected as commander of the Plymouth settlers in 1621. In his *History of Plymouth Plantation*, William Bradford records a letter of 1623 from the clergyman, John Robinson, who writes of Standish that 'ther is cause to fear that by occasion, espetially of provacation, ther may be wanting that tendernes of the life of man (made after Gods image) which is meete. It is also a thing more glorious in mens eyes, then pleasing in Gods, or conveniente for Christians, to be a terrour to poore barbarous people; and indeed I am afraid least, by these occasions, others should be drawne to affecte a kind of rufling course in the world'.[20] Short of temper and quick to strike, Standish was a 'terrour' to the indigenous population and an early example of the imperial tendency to respond to obstacles by rolling over them, just as the mechanised fishery of Olson's day indiscriminately scooped out the contents of Gloucester Harbor for the De-Hy. Smith was also an imperial adventurer, but he differed from Standish in the 'precision' of his approach to the new place: he mapped the Chesapeake Bay region, recorded the Algonquin place names and, in Olson's view, 'pegged the difference between the Maine coast and Mass Bay so rightly (1616) that you read it as you know that difference to this day' (*GMP*, 79). The effect of precision is to situate the actor in a territory that is still alive and gleaming with generative potential, that has not simply been sucked into the De-Hy of a commercial enterprise or whatever discourse – ideology, public policy – is current at the time.

Olson's triads represent a major push to restate human agency in a way befitting the position of the species as one of many on the planet. Topos and typos are counter tensions to tropos; they impose limits on agency that can be ignored only at the long term expense of reducing the potential of the whole to flourish. In a letter to Cid Corman (5 October

1951), Olson calls for the 'MORAL ACT' which he says 'is the / honest – "sincere" – motion in the direction of FORM'.[21] The heroes of *Maximus* – map-makers, fishers, craftsmen, historians – engage with the world in ways that embrace and record its complexities; the villains of the poem – capitalists, careless public servants, insurance men, or military types like Standish – dramatise the detached mind, locked into a will to power and careless of the creative energy it witlessly destroys. Myth is a significant element in Olson's restatement of the human universe not only because it reveals patterns in human behaviour and therefore says something about the species, but because it gives the living planet weight and agency in a way that history alone does not when nature is recorded as a standing resource and cultural others are obstacles to be overcome. In proposing that the 'MORAL IS FORM', Olson urges *mitsein* as a precondition for eudaemonia: 'felicity / resulting from life of activity in accordance with' (*MP*, 42). The preposition dangles because the 'what' of it is always just what is to be composed.

Much has been made of the diminishment or disappearance of the view or voice in the twists and turns of the poetry scenes that have followed Olson's death in 1970. The postmodern/poststructuralist position, anticipated by Von Hallberg, is that no discourse is more authentic than another and therefore Olson's intervention at the level of discourse, rather than language, seems to be a failure to recognise the mediated nature of the view. I do not think this epistemological argument holds up well to careful examination of Olson's poetics and it may in fact distract from other ways to frame differences between generations and poetic practices. It is always possible to argue that a point of view is a troping on various mediating systems (Olson's oeuvre is an extended demonstration of this point); it is equally possible to argue that the poet cannot actually remove herself from the work because any method of selecting text will bear the trace of a distinctive view. But if not by such arguments, how might Olson be distinguished and, more importantly, what might his work offer readers and writers now?

I propose that Olson gets into trouble with readers not so much for deep poetics but for his poetic performance. The only view in *The Maximus Poems* is that of Maximus. Indeed no other view is possible if we follow Olson's logic. But the point is that Olson does not perform the multiplicity of 'eyes' that make up a polis and so it is easy to see dogma rather than allegory in his work. Instead of being inspired to develop a special view, the reader is drawn into Olson's view. Secondly, there is the question of experience. The view-from-here includes a strong, experiential dimension, the credibility of which, in an era of ever-thickening technology, was famously challenged by Walter Benjamin in 'The

Storyteller' well before poststructuralism, language writing, or new conceptualism gained currency.[22] In addition to the powerful theoretical arguments deriving from such scenes of writing, poets now deal with a speeded-up digital world in which there are too many views-from-here, too many voices with too little agency, and too much commodification of narrative. The public audibility of the singular voice thus remains under question.

I am not going to argue these issues away, but thinking with Olson now brings forward a few propositions that might usefully be rolled into the conversation. With the triads, Olson reaches beyond the dichotomy of muthos and logos and his work here speaks to the on-going challenge, in poetry and theory too, of getting away from the either-or of relativism or positivism. The presentation of document usually implies a demand that others see what the presenter sees; document suggests empirical proof. On the other hand, myth, even as Olson redefines it, is about affective engagements that are as immeasurable as they are ineluctable. How might these engagements be figured in to the conversation without yielding to sentiment? Olson makes muthos respond to document and document vulnerable to the desirousness of muthos, thus grounding the singular imagination in a shareable world. Like a map, the resulting picture of the human universe is not infallible, but it can be judged by how well it stands up and how much it includes of what everyone else can also see and feel.

Another proposition: Olson emphasises creative imagination over critical detachment. There is a duck-rabbit ambiguity between these two modes of seeing the world: are all positions to be deconstructed, ironised, or announced in advance as failed form, or might they be treated as data for the making of relationships and hence new forms?[23] The difference between the negation of form and the imagination of provisional forms is a difference in affect rather than logic. Provisional forms, if they are dynamic, as Olson says they have to be, include their own negating movement toward self-transcendence, but unlike critique, they invite affective attachments. Do we love the world and care for it or do we simply wish to be right about it? The experience of being in the world does not disappear because of epistemological arguments, media racket, or the reduced agency of individuals in a global era, rather it goes to ground as intellectual obfuscation of emotionally necessary relationships to nature's things or expresses itself in the mind critically detached from every saying of world and self. 'Love the World – and stay inside it,' Olson says (*MP*, 582). I began by saying that Olson is our contemporary in his reach for a way to say the common without destroying the singular and vice versa. This is really a matter of moving past the negation of what is to a restatement of creative agency. Olson's method says that agency begins with a dialogue between the singular self and those other agents that press in against it. Where postmodern epistemology often seems to offer a monologue – no discourse more authentic than another, no nature that is not also culture – Olson holds the poiesis at the level of affective response rather than that of epistemology, the better that we might tell ourselves to ourselves in our habitudes and responsibilities as a species being here, among others, on the mother rock.

Notes

1 Jeff Wild, 'Charles Olson's Maximus: A Polis of Attention and Dialogue', *Olson Now*, Michael Kelleher and Ammiel Alcalay (eds), available at http://epc.buffalo.edu/authors/olson/blog/wild.pdf
2 For example, in a 2001 *Contemporary Poetry Review* essay, James Rother draws attention to the uneven reception of Olson's work: 'David Lehman, editor of the *Best American Poetry* annuals, recently asked the 12 guest editors of volumes in his series since 1988 – themselves celebrated poets – to name the 15 best poems of the century just ended. The results were for the most part predictable, occasionally wry and quirky – John Ashbery put *The Waste Land* at the head of his list of runner-ups …. But the truly surprising thing to emerge from the poll was that not one of the 12 respondents cited Olson as a major American poet of the 20th Century', James Rother, 'Charles Olson's *The Distances* (1960): A Retrospective Essay', *Contemporary Poetry Review* 2001, posted 10 July 2012, www.cprw.com/Rother/Olson.htm
3 Andrew Ross offers a more specifically poststructuralist version of Von Hallberg's critique: 'For Olson's objectism is a subjectivism turned on its head once more, and therefore every bit as essentialist as the position it sets out to attack …. It is …Olson's belief that objectism, as an antidote to subjectivism, can be brought about by changing the codes of discourse …. Purged of the "lyrical interference of the individual as ego", language would then be a more natural expression of man's relations with the object world, because it would no longer mediate these relations, it would dis-close them,' Andrew Ross, *The Failure of Modernism: Symptoms of American Poetry* (New York: Columbia University Press, 1986), 112. I disagree with Ross's conclusion, that Olson's reach beyond subject and object necessarily means a lunge for a more authentic mode of expression; it means a *human* universe, always already mediated.
4 Robert Von Hallberg, *Charles Olson: The Scholar's Art* (Cambridge, Mass., London: Harvard University Press, 1978), 215.
5 Ibid., 212–13.
6 Ibid., 213.
7 Alfred North Whitehead, *Process and Reality: An Essay in Cosmology*, Corrected Edition, eds David Ray Griffin and Donald W. Sherburne (eds), (New York: Free Press/Macmillan, 1978), 18.

8. Robin Blaser, 'The Violets', in *The Fire: Collected Essays of Robin Blaser*, ed. Miriam Nichols (Berkeley: University of California Press, 2006), 218.
9. Whitehead, *Process and Reality*, 22.
10. For a detailed reading of Olson and Jung, see Charles Stein's *The Secret of the Black Chrysanthemum*; see Sauer's essay on *The Morphology of Landscape* for a structuralist reading of landscape as a set of relations.
11. Charles Olson, *The Special View of History*, ed. Ann Charters (Berkeley: Oyez, 1970), 27.
12. This is where Olson differs from the language writers who followed him: he takes issue with the philosophical tradition as expressed in discourses of the humanities; language writers take up the argument at the level of language, not discourse. The difference presents as epistemological (no discourse is more authentic than another) and is anticipated by Von Hallberg's comments quoted above. I hope to show that this is not the best reading of Olson.
13. Olson, *The Special View*, 17, 49.
14. Ibid., 25.
15. For a path-breaking treatment of Olson's triads as linked to Whiteheadian process, see Don Byrd, *Charles Olson's Maximus* (Urbana: University of Illinois Press, 1980).
16. Olson, *The Special View*, 22, 57.
17. Ibid., 57.
18. Olson takes the 'divine inert' from Melville's *Moby-Dick*. In the essay 'Equal, That is, to the Real Itself,' he describes it as '*the inertial structure of the world*' (*CPr*, 125, original emphasis).
19. Paul Jaussen makes this connection in his essay 'Charles Olson Keeps House: Rewriting John Smith for Contemporary America', *Journal of Modern Literature* 34:1 (Fall 2010), 107–124, muse.jhu.edu/journals/journal_of_modern_literature/summary/v034/34.1.jaussen.html
20. William Bradford, *Bradford's History of Plymouth Plantation 1606–1646*, ed. William T. David, 1946 (New York: Barnes & Noble, Inc., 1964), 173.
21. Charles Olson, *Charles Olson & Cid Corman: Complete Correspondence 1950–1964*, Vol. 1, ed. George Evans (Orono, ME: National Poetry Foundation, 1987), 209.
22. Walter Benjamin, *Illuminations*, ed. Hannah Arendt (New York: Schocken Books, 1969), 84.
23. For example, in *Notes on Conceptualism*, Robert Fitterman and Vanessa Place, describing contemporary conceptual poetry, write that 'Failure is the goal of conceptual writing', Robert Fitterman and Vanessa Place, 'From *Notes on Conceptualisms*', www.uglyducklingpresse.org/wp-content/uploads/2013/07/Notes_free.pdf

2

Discoverable unknowns: Olson's lifelong preoccupation with the sciences

Peter Middleton

From start to finish of his career as a poet, Charles Olson believed that poets must reckon with the sciences of their time. One of his first publications after leaving his job with the Democratic National Committee in Washington took Ezra Pound to task for scientific illiteracy. In 'This is Yeats Speaking' Olson calls for the reassessment of Ezra Pound, then about to go on trial for treason. Awkwardly wearing the mask of the W. B. Yeats of *A Vision*, Olson criticises Pound for his 'obsession to draw all things up into the pattern of art' which led him to defer to the authority of elite figures, 'brawlers and poets' of the past and present (presumably the contemporary brawlers are fascist leaders like Mussolini whom Pound so admired).[1] If only Pound had recognised the importance of other knowledges, especially the sciences: 'He was ignorant of science and he will be surprised, as Goethe will not be, to find a physicist come on as Stage Manager of the tragedy'. Olson was determined not to make the same mistake, and would continue throughout his life to be fascinated by the sciences and scientists, not least by this Stage Manager, the leader of the Manhattan project, J. Robert Oppenheimer. Poets, Olson argued in 'Projective Verse', should be 'aware of some several forces just now beginning to be examined', and aim to make each poem a 'high-energy construct' (*CPr*, 240). He was no doubt thinking of such physicists as Oppenheimer when he wrote this. They understood what was entailed in the creation of a 'high-energy construct', whether a bomb that released the enormous energies governed by the equation $E=MC^2$, or a theoretical model that explained how those energies were squeezed into the atom. High-energy constructs were research tools, and by inviting poets to create them Olson was saying that he thought poets too could be researchers. In another early key essay, 'Human Universe', he tells poets: 'There are laws, that is to say, the human universe is as discoverable as that other [the physical universe]' (*CPr*, 155). Poets, at least those who are not ignorant of science, can help make discoveries about the inner universe as significant as those of the scientists who study the outer one.

Olson and the sciences

We can see what Olson thought it meant for a poet to be researcher by looking at a draft memorandum written at Black Mountain in March 1952. In this rough draft of a letter to the faculty, Olson is as explicit as he ever was about his affinities with the sciences. 'I am, then,' he says, 'concerned as any scientist is, with penetrating the unknown'.[2] Since late 1951 he had been leading the sceptical and often reluctant faculty at Black Mountain College in debates about the direction their educational policy should take. Olson favoured the idea of offering 'institutes' rather than conventional courses. After a meeting in March 1952, he drafted a statement for the faculty in which he tried to explain his vision of short, intensive sessions. The letter is nothing if not ambitious. The college was struggling, had little income, few students, and its campus was badly in need of repair, yet Olson proposes in this draft letter to the faculty that they take as their model the most prestigious research centre in America, the Institute of Advanced Studies at Princeton, and adopt the guiding principles of its famous director, physicist and chief architect of the atomic bomb, Oppenheimer, whom Olson quotes at length. At his elbow Olson had a copy of an article by Lincoln Barnett profiling the physicist at the height of his fame in an old *Life* magazine from October 1949.[3] Barnett's hagiographical portrait of Oppenheimer as a public intellectual proficient in both the sciences *and* the arts clearly inspired Olson. Barnett describes a scientific genius who can keep up with all the brains at Princeton, not just the scientists, because he himself 'has a Da Vincian range of interests and knowledge, encompassing the arts and humanities, the social sciences, current affairs and oriental philosophy', knows several languages including Sanskrit, and has an impressive literary style: 'his own rhetoric, both written and ad lib, is rich and exquisite'.[4] Did Olson wonder whether the same could be said of a modern poet?

Olson's letter to his colleagues begins with a question that presupposes a connection between art and knowledge: 'What is the present state of the field of knowledge? and who are the men who in the present are pushing knowledge forward at the edge of the unknown'?[5] After discussing the implications of this question, Olson realises that his argument needs more than exhortations and the appealing example of a famous physicist. What is needed is a strongly personal affirmation by Olson himself to demonstrate how strongly he, the lead poet on the faculty, personally believes that inquiry leading to knowledge is at least as important for the arts as it is for the sciences. So Olson starts by saying, 'because I am a poet', then digresses into a long looping parenthesis about how much he mistrusts such self-description – 'I should make clear that I abhor the word' – before he finally stops himself and begins again, this time becoming absorbed in a close identification with the physicists of his time:

> because I am, then, concerned as any scientist is, with penetrating the unknown (the difference is what unknown, the distinction above between *physis* & *psyche*, between nature as outside & of experimentable substance, and nature as man is inside & only experimental by *image*) I submit that the same conditions of simplicity and modesty are the actual functioning characteristics of the non-scientist. In fact, simply because they are confronted by the same reality today (allowing the difference of the emphasis) any of us have the common front, the common intent, the common necessities.[6]

The weight falls on the affirmation of Olson's own authenticating experience here (I know about these things, 'because I am a poet') and on the sincerity of his conviction that as a poet he is necessarily concerned with trying to understand what is unknown, a project that aligns him with the scientists.

We don't know for sure that the memorandum was ever sent, and it doesn't count as a publication in the usual sense, but as an unguarded statement of Olson's beliefs it carries considerable authority because it was written for a crucial task; to help save Black Mountain college. Here Olson is frank about the need for poetry and the arts to align themselves with scientific research. This was a belief he never abandoned. Although he wrote less explicitly about the sciences later in his career, his essays, letters and poems continue to intermittently invoke mathematics, astronomy, genetics, the new archaeology, and make brief allusions to other sciences, right up to the end of his life.

Yet despite this overt and sustained engagement, Olson himself never explains directly why the sciences matter so much to him as a poet. It is no accident that 'Projective Verse' does not use the words 'science', 'scientific', or 'scientist', though it repeatedly alludes to these concepts. Olson's stance towards science eludes description because there are both too many historical explanations to hand (mostly stemming from the growing hegemony of the sciences in American public culture), and too few literary critical means for representing how his varied interrelations with science actually shape the poems. Is he really emulating the Oppenheimers of the world of science and carrying out his own researches in poems, or is he pushing back against scientistic encroachments of the social sciences into the 'human universe', or is he attempting to develop a new science altogether?

In the remainder of this essay I shall first consider explanations which look to the cultural status of science at the time Olson was writing. I will then argue that there is another type of explanation based on his chosen poetic form, the open field poem. I shall argue that the new poetic form Olson developed requires a poetic address to the reader, requiring the reader to make inferences about the commitments made by the poem to its own assertions, and about the representations that result from them. Making these inferences requires the reader to make explicit the interrelations between the author's commitments and existing knowledges, especially scientific ones.[7] Penetrating the unknown may be a timely preoccupation for the poet; it also turns out to have poetic consequences once scientific knowledges and methods are inscribed in the field of the poem.

Olson's interest in science was widely shared by intellectuals of his generation and the next. He made the decision to write poetry at an unusual moment in modern American history. Physics was not only believed to have won the war, but its nuclear models dominated scientific theories of the cosmos. Physics claimed that it alone was able to provide complete nomological explanations of what all matter, and by easy extension, the entire universe and everything in it, was made of. Physics was philosophy, ontology and epistemology rolled into one. What more did you need? As a result, physics, or more precisely, nuclear physics, became the paradigm science of public esteem from the late 1940s to the early 70s, constantly held up as a prime instance of the scientific ideal of inquiry that is the best route to reliable knowledge. The preoccupations of nuclear physics were on the surface remote from most of the concerns of poetry, even though the threat of a mushroom cloud of extinction hung over American life. Every public building was plastered in signs to the nearest fallout shelter. No one was proposing a physics of poetry, the way that researchers are now offering neuroscientific and neo-Darwinist theories of literature, but a poet who wanted to claim truthfulness, make a contribution to knowledge, and find some cultural authority for poetry, had to reckon with this forbidding ideal of what constituted knowledge and the means to produce it. Science was everywhere. Over the next decade an impressive series of highly scientific achievements mounted up, including antibiotics, the conquest of polio, transistors, atomic power, the decipherment of the genetic code, and the launch of astronauts into space. Science's ubiquity and its influence on public life and policy also had political consequences for what Olson called the 'polis'. President Eisenhower's President's Advisory Committee insisted that 'a democratic citizenry today must understand science in order to have a wide and intelligent democratic participation in many national decisions'.[8]

Olson took physics very seriously as we can see in the many tacit allusions to energy, fields, and forces in 'Projective Verse', and in his conviction that poetic inquiry should also study its own forces and particles. Taking physics seriously meant listening to what the physicists were saying. Fortunately the physicists were sometimes willing to talk, both then and later. 'What does a physicist have to say to a poet?' is the arresting question that opens Robert H. March's textbook, *Physics for Poets*, whose title alludes to the many American university courses since the 1950s that have been called both formally and informally, 'Physics for Poets', aiming to introduce physics to liberal arts majors.[9] The adverb 'have' is significantly ambiguous: what *information* about the theories and discoveries of recent physics is there that can be told, what sort of *defence* or *justification* of the science can physicists offer, and what is it that *must* be told or is *necessary* for poets to hear at this historical juncture? Physics for poets turns out to be a method of inquiry based on the reduction of the blooming buzzing confusion of the world to models or constructs of its most basic constituents. If we look at a typical essay about nuclear physics published in 1960 in *Scientific American*, we see that these models turn out to have 'poetic' features.

In an essay about 'The Nuclear Force', Robert Marshak first glances back at Hans Bethe's striking observation back in 1953 that this mysterious force internal to the atom has absorbed 'more man-hours than have been given to any other scientific question in the history of mankind'. Marshak summarises the results of all this labour, a physical system composed of a very few types of particle that can be pictured as having spins, trajectories, and forces of mutual attraction and repulsion.[10] An attentive reader soon realises that this picture reveals a world very different to our everyday bulky reality, for we are in what he calls 'the quantum world' where ordinary expectations of solid objects often do not apply. Particles can pass directly through one another for instance, and physicists sometimes treat particles as energy waves. Marshak is scrupulous about the epistemological problems for the experimenter:

> Now throughout this detailed description of the dynamics of nucleon-nucleon interactions we have been speaking as if the actual particles were visible to us, and we could see them spinning, curving, diffracting and so on. It should be remembered, however, that all we can really see are the recording devices of a particle-counter, or the dark spots on a photographic emulsion, representing relative intensities of a particle beam scattered in various directions. From these data the experimenter draws a curve, which he then presents to the theoretical physicist and asks: What kind of force produced such a graph?[11]

Poets might well ask themselves what kind of imagination produced such a force. Was it not a scientific version of poetic imagination?

Firstly, and most obviously, such discourse presents scientific inquiry as proceeding by the reduction of complexity to the interaction of invisible minute constituents that, despite their unimaginable abundance, come in only a relatively small number of types, distinguishable primarily by their different energies. There is no individuality to particles, and they compose a world of energies in transformation. Secondly, this scientific inquiry proceeds by provisional pictures, theoretical models or constructs, using what Marshak openly describes as a *'semifictional particle language'* [my emphasis].[12] Marshak's ontological unease was widely shared. Michael Moravcsik's report on the Rochester Conference on high energy physics in 1959 uses a slightly more sophisticated term to make the same point when reporting that 'a complete (although not necessarily unique) *semiphenomenological* description of the proton-proton interaction has been given up to 400Mev in terms of phase shifts and the one-pion exchange contribution' [my emphasis].[13] Because of such hints that these theories are as much creative constructions as hard observations, Marshak stresses the importance of 'the empirical approach': 'we cannot even be sure that the equations themselves are right' although 'we are still confident that some day we shall be able to write down the correct equations and find a way of solving them'.[14]

A poet might conclude from reading such articles as Marshak's (and Moravcsik's if they were to make the effort to read the technical journals) that if poetry is going to be capable of its own form of valid inquiry then it too might best concentrate on the reduction of complexity to the interactions of a few basic particles, which, as in the case of physics, might variously be constituents of language, or self, or society. A poet might also conclude that the physicists were inviting other researchers to likewise acknowledge their own uncertainties. *Not knowing* need not be a sign of error or failure. Perhaps the composition of the poem could also be a self-reflexive process capable of making as explicit as possible its own 'semifictionality' or 'semiphenomenologicality'. This need not be a license for surreal flights of imagination. Simulating the rigour of physics might similarly require an empirical approach, observation and action that precede or are at least coeval with the writing. These are the lessons that Olson learns from the sciences, and from physics in particular, although his own poetic strategy also relies on an assumption about the nexus of self, language, and world which is his own.

To see what this assumption is, it will help at this point to ask ourselves what Olson doesn't do with science. He doesn't employ specific scientific ideas in their proper form, as Gary Snyder uses the ecological theory of a climax community for poems about human impact on the American wilderness, or as Allen Fisher takes the quantum theory of decoherence to talk about the interconnectedness of different domains of experience. Nor does Olson respond directly to specific scientific texts. He is not writing through scientific essays as Jackson Mac Low does in *Stanzas for Iris Lezak*. Nor does Olson play the sort of poetic games that Alice Fulton or Edward Dorn do with scientific metaphors, and nor does he do what Rae Armantrout does and test the resilience of scientific metaphors by subtly juxtaposing their scientific usages with their articulation in irreducibly everyday human situations. Olson's main use of science is instead as authorisation for the methodology of his own researches in and through his poems. He wants his poems to 'penetrate the unknown', that is, he wants his poems to be part of the intellectual gold rush to the frontiers of knowledge, and so he treats his own poetic statements as sites of what is 'discoverable', just as he treats such documents from the archives as John Smith's poem 'The Sea-Marke' or Port Book information on trade between Weymouth and Cape Anne in 1624 to 1625.[15] Both personal affirmations and documentary chunks have the empirical actuality of Gloucester's coastal position, or the existence of tansy on the city's hillsides in the early part of the century. In treating all this material, whether expressive or documentary, as a site of investigation, he frames it with an expectation that the result will be reliable enough to stand alongside scientific communications.

Consider, for example, the curious poem, 'Maximus to Gloucester, Letter 27 [withheld]', which was excluded from the first volume of *Maximus*. Ralph Maud suggests that the likely reason for withholding this poem from the location in the first volume of *Maximus* where its numbering would place it, was that the poem relied too openly on the authority of a single thinker, Alfred North Whitehead, despite Olson's many strictures on epistemological self-reliance, on *'istorin*, or finding out the truth for oneself.[16] Once Whitehead became a regular guest authority in the second volume of *The Maximus Poems* there was no reason to withhold this earlier and obviously significant poem, so Maud's theory is surely right. However, there may be another reason for Olson's initial hesitation about the status of this poem, that its striking reflexivity risks undermining the very claim the poem makes to be demonstrating a new form of thought that synthesises poetry and science.

The poem opens with two charming stanzas in which the poet recalls the joys of a family in which even his father can play inventive games. Its opening line, 'I come back to the geography of it', characteristically uses a phrase whose significance depends on an interplay of literal and rhetorical meanings; that his thoughts revert to memories of summer play on the parklands of Gloucester, and that he is recapitulating an argument he has made before, that geography is fundamental. Keeping these two meanings in play is crucial for the poem, whose logic I want to explore in more detail.

Having recalled childhood memories of summer life in Gloucester, seemingly typical nostalgia which anyone might have, Olson then sketches in poignant and idiosyncratic detail that marks this memory as his and his alone, before abruptly switching to a metapoetic register with the deictic 'this'. Now he will treat these poetic lines as examples of a new form of American thought:

> This, is no bare incoming
> of novel abstract form, this
>
> is no welter or the forms
> of those events, this,
>
> Greeks, is the stopping
> of the battle
>
> It is the imposing
> of all those antecedent predecessions, the precessions
>
> of me, the generation of those facts
> which are my words, it is coming
>
> from all that I no longer am, yet am,
> the slow westward motion of
>
> more than I am
>
> There is no strict personal order
>
> for my inheritance.
>
> (*MP*, 184)

This poet is stopping the battle between Platonists and materialists, just as ancient bards, according to Robert Graves, could use their poetic skills to halt a battle and even resolve the conflict.[17] One risk is immediately obvious. Such an abrupt shift is exactly what T. S. Eliot practised in *Four Quartets* where he offers a compacted, heavily troped lyric followed by a disavowal: 'That was a way of putting it—not very satisfactory: / A periphrastic study in a worn-out poetical fashion'.[18] Olson may be much more confident that he is offering a fresh poetical style waiting to be worn, but the rhetorical move is so similar as to risk seeming worn-out.

The most striking feature of these lines is the claim that 'those facts are my words', that the memories are equivalent to 'facts', and not just any facts but ones that have been generated 'from all that I no longer am', from his own history in the world. Yet this is not to be taken as we are likely to take it, as a personal confession, this inheritance is not, as we might say, 'strictly personal', the opening lines of memory are something else. If it is not personal then what is it? What Olson believes makes this opening to the poem factual is that these facts stem from empirical history, from 'antecedent predecessions, the precessions // of me'. Predecessions are, according to the OED, states or conditions of being a predecessor, and therefore adding the adjective 'antecedent' merely intensifies the point that his memories of his parents and the city refer to a series of progenitive events and peoples receding far into the past. But whereas 'predecessions' refers to familial and social inheritances, 'precessions' has a different semantic range. This largely scientific term (it does have obsolete meanings which include 'procession', 'preceding', and the process whereby a vowel sound shifts to a more closed form, but these are so rare as to leave only the most distant semantic echoes here) is used in astronomy to describe the shifting of the axis of the earth's rotation over long periods of time, a process that results in changing views of the heavens. 'Precessions of me' implies that the poet's self is as solid a point of reference, despite its slow cyclical changes, as the earth itself.

Olson's poetry repeatedly faces its readers head on. The logic in this poem is that what appears in the opening to be a mere personal recollection is revealed to be a new kind of poetic strategy in which what is said becomes fact for both writer and reader to treat as the object of scientific study. When the poet later affirms that 'I have this sense, / that I am one / with my skin' the important point is not so much that there is no mysterious soul temporarily inhabiting a body, rather that the 'I' that is speaking in the poem is no more nor less than Olson the flesh and bone man, living in a specific time and space. What is said in the poem is not voiced from behind a mask, or attributed to language, nor are we invited to explain a statement made by the poet in terms of inner mood or unconscious drive. The poem faces the reader head on and asks for a cogitated response to its affects and claims. This is key to Olson's negotiation with the sciences. His poetry expects the reader to listen to how the poet affirms the truthfulness *for him* of every line, phrase, word that is written (and often made to simulate utterance), whether those words are his expression, or he has taken them from an archive. When they are someone else's words and authority, Olson nevertheless adds his own backing, and the poem works with this warrant. He is telling the truth as surely as he can, as he sees it. The fundamental assumption is that every proposition, every statement that the poem makes, is fully warranted by the poet, and faces us with its demand that we weigh up its demands. The poet asks the reader: are you yourself prepared to ascribe any truth to the myriad assertions and moods in this poem?

There are two problems with this. One is the problem that bedevils the logic of reflexive statements. Do they also justifiably refer to themselves? Eliot was careful to say 'that was a study' to avoid reflexively referring to this very statement itself. When Olson says that 'this ... is the stopping of the battle' he could be referring to the previous section of the poem, or to the entire poem, including the statement 'this ... is the stopping of the battle'. He could even be referring to the whole Maximus project. Olson evidently does not want exemptions, so he uses 'this' repeatedly and his insistence on the reflexive cue invites us to wonder if the very passage that makes such a claim is itself an example of what it is claiming. Is it?

At the very least a reader is likely to find this implicit claim only half persuasive, especially as Olson is alluding to a passage in *Adventures of Ideas* in which Whitehead criticises both Plato and Aristotle for their mistaken ideas both about the 'generation' of new experience and the way in which the stability of identity is maintained in the face of the new. The philosopher claims to have formulated a new ontology based around a relativistic geometry of space-time events. Whitehead writes: 'it was the defect of the Greek analysis of generation that it conceived it in terms of the bare incoming of novel abstract form. This ancient analysis failed to grasp the real operation of the antecedent particulars imposing themselves on the novel particular in process of creation'.[19] Here is the second problem with the poem, a problem even more obvious later on when Olson unequivocally says that:

> An American
> is a complex of occasions,
> themselves a geometry
> of spatial nature.
>
> (MP, 185)

This passage, as with elements of the earlier passage quoting Whitehead on the origins of novelty, relies entirely on second hand knowledge derived from Whitehead and in so doing commits the sin that Olson repeatedly criticises others for. But Olson is drawn to take these risks because behind the opaque language Whitehead uses is a simple emboldening claim for first-hand experience; that its ontogeny is not merely personal, but draws on a multitude of contributory historical forces.

By the late 1950s Whitehead had become Olson's main source of understanding of the nature of science and the possibilities for poets to engage with it. As Miriam Nichols says, 'from Whitehead he took the basic contours of transcendental empiricism'.[20] Joshua Hoeynck, who has made the most extensive study yet of Olson's debts to Whitehead, argues that Olson's position is 'a mode of ecological and cosmological measurement that complements scientific measurement'.[21] In support of this interpretation of Olson he cites two statements by Whitehead in *Process and Reality*: 'all *exact* observation is made by perception in the mode of presentational immediacy', and, 'if such perception merely concerns a private psychological field, science is the daydream of an individual without any public import'.[22] Olson would be very interested in his own dreams, but always insistent on their 'public import'.

Some of the clearest examples of Olson's treatment of his own perceptions as material for research are his dream poems, and a brief discussion of these can help us see why Olson was willing to risk Whitehead undermining the poet's commitment to first-hand inquiry. Many of his best known poems are presented to the reader as authentic accounts of actual dreams and are interwoven with a thoughtful self-analysis that guides the reader towards at least provisional interpretations of their meaning and seriousness. 'As the Dead Prey Upon Us', 'The Twist', 'Letter 22', and 'The Librarian' are all constructed around one or more recorded dreams. These poems keep to the dominant format of an Olson poem: start with the account of an actual moment of disorientation, subject it to extended analysis which draws in historical analysis, then offer a provisional interpretation. In recording and sometimes interpreting actual dreams he was far from unusual amongst such contemporaries as Allen Ginsberg, Jack Kerouac and Robert Duncan, who all recorded their dreams in notebooks. Yet of all of these writers, Olson, the scholar most dedicated to exact historical knowledge of America and its early settlements, is one of the most thorough examiners of dreams, despite being apparently uninterested in travelling down the royal road to any sort of unconscious. As we can see in the four poems just mentioned, the landscapes of a dream were as important as the details of Gloucester's geography and history for the construction of *The Maximus Poems*. The unknown turns out not to be knowledge of the past waiting to be uncovered, nor hidden or not yet understood patterns of historical action. The unknown is a realm requiring special cognitive powers, and dreams can sometimes tap into these as well as, or better than, other more consciously directed efforts.

In 'The Twist' Olson tries to penetrate the unknown as he mingles elements from several dreams from 1953 in which his unconscious mind pictures Gloucester variously as a place where his wife has had a baby in a house at the end of the trolley line, where he takes a journey with his father during which they watch other people diverge from them, where his wife leaves him to live in a house like a cake, and where that one part of the city he calls 'the whole Cut' becomes a village made of paper. It is crucial to the workings of the poem that Olson actually dreamed these dreams; they are not invented nor even pimped a little. 'The Twist' is a poem about the distorting nostalgias of absence as well as his growing preoccupation with the history of Gloucester (he is writing the poem while living at Black Mountain). What especially interests the poet are his glimpses of the law-like workings of the human universe, the manner in which a series of thoughts, both daylight and dream thoughts, can twist themselves into a complex point: 'this pin-point / to turn // in this day's sun, // in this veracity // there, the waters the several of them the roads // here, a blackberry blossom' (*MP*, 89–90). The poem suggests that in daylight dreams become mere toys, and also that too much consciousness, like urban planning, can mistakenly 'tear down' their seemingly out of date construction.

In poems such as 'The Twist', Olson treats his dream material as if it were the best possible evidence of who he is, of what his inner world is all about. For him, this dream material has greater authenticity, truthfulness and sincerity than any waking affirmation or consciously argued logic he could bring to the poem. And though he certainly endorsed Jungian ideas, his dreams are not fountaining up from a personal unconscious to invite appropriate decoding. In Olson's eyes, they are more like dreams of the populace, dreams of history, or part of the incoming perceptual data that demands the rigorous attention of the unified science that he hoped Whitehead's ideas would enable him to create.

Robin Blaser overstates the case when he says that Olson's main project was 'the translation of science into poetry', yet he captures a central feature of that poetry.[23] Almost everyone who has written about Olson is struck by his omnivorous desire to know more and more about his world, as well as by the paradox that he was also seemingly willing to entertain all sorts of speculation, mythological narratives, and even dreams alongside scholarship. Paul Stephens astutely argues that Olson's writings reveal 'a thirst for knowledge so great that it threatened to undermine the very collectivities – his family, Gloucester, Black Mountain – that meant so much to him', and he charts the damage this thirst caused.[24] Stephens defends Olson by arguing that his quest was not for knowledge so much as 'information' or 'data' because he did not want to 'sequester knowledge from an engagement with the immediacy of perception'.[25]

In this essay I have shown that placing Olson's thirst for knowledge in relation to the enormous hunger for knowledge of contemporary scientists makes such thirst look less excessive and more coherent. The struggle for coherence which Olson mentions several times in his early writings was a very real struggle for him, and it is at the borders between coherence and incoherence that he did his best work, inspired by the way physicists were also struggling with the strange incoherences of quantum theory and its 'semiphenomenological' observations.

Notes

1. Catherine Seelye (ed.), *Charles Olson and Ezra Pound: An Encounter at St Elizabeths* (New York: Viking Press, 1975), 28–9.
2. Charles Olson, 'A Letter to the Faculty of Black Mountain College', *Olson* 8 (Fall 1977), 31.
3. Lincoln Barnett, 'J. Robert Oppenheimer', *Life* (10 October 1949), 120–38.
4. Ibid., 121.
5. Olson, 'A Letter', 26.
6. Ibid., 31.
7. My underlying poetic theory relies on a historicist reading of the work of the new pragmatists, notably Robert Brandom. His major work of philosophy is entitled *Making it Explicit*. See for instance Robert Brandom, *Articulating Reasons: An Introduction to Inferentialism* (Cambridge, Mass.: Harvard University Press, 2000). Some of the issues are explored in my essay 'Open Oppen: Linguistic fragmentation and the poetic proposition', *Textual Practice* 24:4 (2010), 623–48.
8. John Troan, 'Science Reporting – Today and Tomorrow', *Science* 131:3408 (22 April 1960), 1193.
9. Robert H. March, *Physics for Poets* (New York: McGraw Hill, 1970).
10. Robert E. Marshak, 'The Nuclear Force', *Scientific American* 202 (March 1960), 98–114, 99.
11. Ibid., 107–8.
12. Ibid., 101.
13. Michael J. Moravcsik, 'High Energy Physics: An informal report of the Rochester Conference', *Physics Today* 12:10 (October 1959), 20–5, 21.
14. Marshak, 'The Nuclear Force', 114.
15. Referring respectively to 'Maximus, to Gloucester: Letter 15', and 'The Record' (*MP*, 71, 121).
16. Ralph Maud (ed.), *A Charles Olson Reader* (Manchester: Carcanet Press, 2005), 67.
17. The battle is also mentioned in 'Letter 22'. George Butterick provides detailed information on the allusions to Graves and Whitehead (*GMP*, 140, 262–4). I think it is worth noting that according to Graves, the poets stop the battle because they admire the 'valour' of the combatants, and want to commemorate the battle. Olson is not dismissing either those who have argued for the soul, or those who have insisted on a severe, reductive materialism. Robert Graves, *The White Goddess: A Historic Grammar of Poetic Myth*, enlarged edn (New York: Farrar, Straus and Giroux, 1966), 22.
18. T. S. Eliot, *Collected Poems 1909–1962* (London: Faber and Faber, 1983), 198.
19. Alfred North Whitehead, *Adventures of Ideas* (Cambridge: Cambridge University Press, 1933), 242.
20. Miriam Nichols, *Radical Affections: Essays on the Poetics of Outside* (Tuscaloosa, AL: University of Alabama Press, 2010), 30.

21 Joshua S. Hoeynck, *Poetic Cosmologies: Black Mountain Poetry and Process Philosophy* (Ann Arbor: Proquest, 2008), 110.
22 Alfred North Whitehead, *Process and Reality: An Essay in Cosmology*, Corrected Edition, eds David Ray Griffin and Donald W. Sherburne (New York: Free Press, 1978), 333. Cited in Hoeynck, *Poetic Cosmologies*, 191.
23 Robin Blaser, *The Fire: Collected Essays*, ed. Miriam Nichols (Berkeley: University of California Press, 2006), 204.
24 Paul Stephens, 'Human University: Charles Olson and the Embodiment of Information', *Paideuma* 39 (2012), 200.
25 Ibid.

3

'Empty Air': Charles Olson's cosmology

Reitha Pattison

What did Charles Olson understand by the term cosmology? He supplied a succinct answer to this question while giving his course of lectures, *The Special View of History*, at Black Mountain College in 1956: 'I stress that, at the moment, simply that a cosmology [...] would seem to be the most obvious inclusiveness – in fact the classic example, I should suppose, of same: the attempt of man to see order throughout creation and to define it.'[1] In his indispensable study, *Charles Olson's Reading*, Ralph Maud sees in the composition of *The Special View* the writer's development of a 'new cosmology', and several accounts have been given of the novel character of Olson's cosmological stance in various theoretical and philosophical contexts.[2] Olson's is a self-announced phenomenological pursuit of 'a new cosmology, issuing from the order of man and his inquiry'.[3] Although there are instances in his authorship that speak of an exterior condition as that 'other' universe, he largely cedes to the primacy of a 'human universe' as the one worth definition,[4] and more vehemently so in his later writings.

In his early essay entitled 'Human Universe', Olson claims that 'the only two universes which count, the two phenomenal ones', are 'that of himself, as organism, and that of his environment, the earth and planets' (*CPr*, 56). Developing this cosmological discrimination via his more schematic essayistic mode in *Proprioception*, published ten years later, he locates the phenomenally exterior universe within the 'human universe', the human body being the site of the same. Experience, or the 'kosmos inside a human being', as Olson calls it in *The Special View*, can then be fully claimed and defined, not left in an ambivalent epistemological state as partially our 'interior' physiological, perceptive and unconscious processes and partially 'wallowing around sort of outside, in the universe' as non-human stimuli; this 'universe flowing-in, inside' would achieve the recognition of a cosmic condition of 'inclusiveness'.[5]

Two prominent sources for Olson's cosmological thinking are clearly identifiable: his organicist approach was profoundly informed by Alfred North Whitehead's 'philosophy of organism', and he found a rich source in modern relativistic physics, quantum physics, and non-Euclidean geometry, and their philosophical implications. What is distinctive about his cosmology and what it owes to preceding cosmologies have nevertheless proved to be highly contested questions. Yet in spite of the relative wealth of critical responses, the majority of readings ignore or inaccurately articulate the frictions and disparities between the central ideas and terminology of modern relativistic physics, on which Olson appears to draw so heavily, and his own cosmological premises, which exhibit a reversion to older cosmological paradigms. Characterising this reversion provides a powerful optic for clarifying Olson's cosmological thinking: the draw of older cosmological paradigms for the writer is deeply connected with his search for a primal authenticity via the cosmogonies of earlier civilizations through a literal or euhemeristic treatment of the content of their mythic cosmoramas. This pivotal aspect of his work has been the greatest source of contestation, and some commentators argue that Olson retreats into a reliance on a mythic order, and that his grand mythopoeic gestures in *The Maximus Poems* recruit the essentialist structure upon which myth is predicated. He has been criticized for plying a cosmicity that lauds objectivity while its attitude is subjective, to the extent that his apparently 'new cosmology' does not look past the 'human universe', thereby re-inscribing the terms of the humanist project that he arrogated. Andrew Ross argues that Olson's language is new, but his stance is only a newer version of an old, dubious outlook: he manages, Ross surmises, to 'successfully produce a new cultural humanism out of novel and radical mutations in language, idiom, form, and subjectivity.'[6]

The relation between Olson's 'idiom' and his cosmology is my broad concern in this chapter, as I believe that his work stands in need of an attentive re-assessment of its cosmological language. The writer uses a distinctive vocabulary which he calls his 'private nomenclature of knowledge', to articulate his own cosmorama.[7] Olson's use of a masterset of cosmological terms – space, time, place, history, myth, the actual, the local – have caused critics, including those well-disposed toward his work, to admit to a difficulty in fixing definitive meanings, regardless of whether such a mode of meaning is explicitly sought or not. Don Byrd explains that Olson's 'vision' is 'so removed from common Western assumptions that words no longer mean quite what they have traditionally meant', and he describes the 'unusual rigour of language' required to 'speak meaningfully' of Olson's work, especially of his *Maximus Poems*.[8] Judith Halden-Sullivan praises Olson for what she perceives as a Heideggerian concern for restoring ourselves to the recognition of a liberating 'human mode of being', but nevertheless she is compelled to admit that, 'His canon presents persistent movement toward something whose totality remains ineffable.'[9]

The traditionally assumed meanings of Olson's cosmological master-set may seem to have been abandoned by the writer, as each term is variously and sometimes contradictorily submerged, complicated and equated with every other in the set. This embedded intricacy and equity is not necessarily systematically articulated, but it is the outcome of Olson's belief in the continuum at a meta-level: it is an inclusive cosmological principle, which necessarily includes the linguistic. Olson's articulation of universal 'inclusiveness' through such lexical and discursive fusion served in part to dissolve a universe abstracted from the 'two phenomenal ones' he prioritized in 'Human Universe', that order of linguistic categorization he saw as the petrified taxonomies of discourse that belong to the '"UNIVERSE of discourse"' (*CPr*, 156). Inherited from the 'Greeks', brought to perfection by Plato's 'world of Ideas, of forms as extricable from content', and blithely maintained as the 'refuge of all metaphysicians since', this ideal discursive universe is a system Olson saw as the defining feature of a swingeing western philosophical tradition, marked by the compartmentalization of knowledge (*CPr*, 156). Olson's practice as philologist or etymologist was actuated by his wish to identify and reconstruct an originary language, chronologically untainted by such discursive insulation. He sought to revive older meanings of words whose roots and accompanying historical contexts could assert his cosmology, his most heavily-cited example being the recovery of history through its Herodotean root of the verb *'istorin*. In this verbal act, rather than hypostatized noun, the writer wished to re-signify history as 'story' in order to recover the legitimacy of personal witness and evidence, to equalize knowledge with the processive act and experience of 'finding out for oneself'.[10] This personal experience would then constitute one individual human cosmos (the 'kosmos inside' any one of us) among all other human cosmoi.

Although Olson claims that, cosmologically, 'a period has closed in which any known previous vocabulary applies', he continues to apply extant cosmological vocabulary, and I find that it is not useful to see his meanings as 'removed' from 'common western assumptions' as Byrd suggests, and that the 'novel and radical mutations' of the writer's language that Ross asserts, although *ad hominem*, are in fact not so 'radical'.[11] These 'mutations' can be more productively explored as recalibrated throwbacks to a multifaceted and prior cosmology that the writer delineates in his prose, and enacts through his poetics. The particular focus here is one item in Olson's master-set: space. While most studies of Olson contain some comment, if not an extended analysis, on this prominent subject in his authorship, the sense in which there are no 'common western assumptions' in his understanding of this cosmic term has become a severe limitation when trying to account for its complex nexus of meanings. My purpose is to consider the novelty of the writer's 'nomenclature' of space by attending to the interplay between his cosmological and figurative usages of the word, and how he partially and contradictorily interpolates cosmological theories, especially those of modern relativistic cosmology. What emerges from this consideration is a fresh view of the relation between space as a fundamental term in his prose, and its attendant identity in his verse practice.

Ann Charters's consideration of Olson's excessive use of the word 'space' in his early writings on Herman Melville will help to exemplify my argument. Charters suggests that although Olson 'avoids any definition' of 'space', he uses it constantly with the hope that by 'the dogmatic weight of the word itself, the reader will find it meaningful.'[12] She then cites several extracts from *Call Me Ishmael*, and concludes that:

> gaps in Olson's interpretation are exposed with these sentences about "space". The word is used in such varied contexts that any precise meaning evaporates, leaving the reader holding onto... empty space.[13]

Charters's reading, likewise, does not explicitly offer a definition of space to compare with Olson's multiple renditions, and does not venture to query what it is about either commonplace or specialized uses of the word that might permit or invite him to use it so promiscuously. This is certainly an extreme example of critical disengagement, and I will refer to more vigorous readings below. Nevertheless, there is an explanatory power in her mode of expression: it discloses a definition by proxy implicitly with its elliptical aporia, its reflexive exposure of 'gaps', and its metaphors of emptiness and evaporation. We have a malleable concept of space, with commonplace and intuitive associations, informed by philosophical and scientific discourses, which may, for instance, allow it the status of an abstract or purely mental idea, an absolute solidity or substrate, a material presence and continence, as well as the signification of physical emptiness and epistemological or metaphorical vacancy. It is not hard to see where Charters may have encountered the particular pliancies of Olson's usage that her aborted description involuntarily captures. As a postscript to her book, *Olson/Melville: A Study in Affinity*, she reproduces one of Olson's own recollections of his formative confrontation with the word:

> *space*, as a factor of experience I took as of such depth, width, and intensity that, unwittingly, I insisted upon it as fact (actually tried, there, to

bring it down out of the abstraction of the word of it and away from the descriptive error of the illustrations of it I was then capable of [...] to give space, by that noun [...] the mass and motion I take it to have, the air that it is and the lungs we are to live in it as our element.[14]

Olson's insistence upon space as 'fact' is articulated throughout his early work on *Moby-Dick* in *Call Me Ishmael*, and his other prose about Melville, particularly his essay, 'Equal, That Is, to the Real Itself', in which he mounts a reading of the 'spaces' of *Moby-Dick* via the topological geometry of nineteenth-century mathematician, Georg Riemann (*CPr*, 123). Olson sees space in *Moby-Dick* as the same 'central fact' that confronted European colonizers of America: its geographic vastness, its plenitude of freedom, and its accompanying merciless lack of the familiar, enforced this.[15] Yet the writer is also exacting about the character of this 'fact': space is a concrete entity, capable of 'mass and motion', like any other object or particle, an invisible but nonetheless concrete 'element', the substance of life as breath, and physical containment.

To repose these observations in the cosmological context of Olson's later prose, the several related arguments about the condition of space as concrete or abstract, as absolute or relative, as plenum or void, appear in *The Special View* under the auspices of what he calls the 'old' cosmology.[16] This 'old' cosmology constitutes for the writer not only the cosmogonies of ancient civilizations, but their concepts which have perseverated in a compromised condition – because divested of their mythic resonances – into the character of thought in the twentieth century. Olson relates that:

> Hanging over into the present from the old cosmology are three drags, each of them the offsets of the principle desire of man for Kosmos during the two millennia and a half preceding us. And the three hang about people's necks like dead birds. They are Void, Chaos, and the trope Man. Or, to put them in the order of their occurrence, Chaos, Man, Void; that is Chaos was the imagined unformed on which the order Kosmos set form. Man was the later child of the same act – a teleology of form as progressive was the hidden assumption of the old cosmology, and Void is what's left when the Kosmos breaks down as the interesting evidence of order, Man falls when the purpose falls, and so Void is the only assumption left; that is, Kosmos infers Chaos as precedent to itself and Man as succeeding, and when it goes as a controlling factor, only Void becomes a premise of measure. Man is simply filling empty space.[17]

According to Olson, these cosmological dead-weights have hung around for too long, and the idea of vacuous, 'hollow' space is the heaviest 'drag' that he would like to jettison from his cosmology.[18] However, I want to put a little pressure on Olson's assumption about the relation between 'Chaos', 'Void' and 'empty space' and observe, in this regard, that the Greek and Indo-European etymologies of 'Chaos' have an important double aspect. On the one hand, as in the deified 'Χάος' in Hesiod's *Theogony*, which provides so much mythic material for *The Maximus Poems*, it had the meaning of the primordial unformed matter, the origin of all forms, all gods and men. On the other hand, 'Chaos' also signified a 'vast chasm' or 'void' and – with a highly suggestive qualifier that I shall consider further below – 'a gaping void' or 'yawning gulf'.[19] Rather than being separate cosmological principles, which in Olson's reading of the 'old' cosmology are set in distinct order of cosmogonic appearance before and after 'Man', we may register 'Chaos' as a binary of material potential and 'Void'.

The import of the presence and absence of matter in empty space as an unreconciled cosmological condition for Olson can be apprehended by comparing his pronouncements of space as an elemental and solid reality, a 'fact' we live and breathe in, with his integration of aspects of relativistic physics. There is certainly a high frequency of references in Olson's work to Albert Einstein's relativistic space-time continuum. Einstein explains how, 'In the pre-relativity physics space and time were separate entities. [...] One spoke of points of space, as of instants of time, as if they were absolute realities', but this is no longer the case for the space and time of relativity, which has unified the notional four dimensions of space and the one dimension of time.[20] In *Process and Reality*, Whitehead gives a long exposition of Isaac Newton's influential cosmology, in which he similarly describes the 'receptacle' theory whereby 'bits of space and time were conceived as being as actual as anything else, and as being 'occupied' by other actualities which were the bits of matter.'[21] Whitehead announces at the outset of *Process and Reality* that he exclusively engages in 'philosophical thought upon the most concrete elements in our experience', and later confesses that there is 'great merit' in Newton's absolute and immovable '"receptacles"' for the philosophy of organism because they have a concrete, absolute presence as cosmic substrate for his philosophy to maintain its own tenet.[22] The dichotomous character of space as ponderable void comes into play when Whitehead compares the ontological certainty of the godhead of the cosmos with its barest form of existence: 'There is no going behind actual entities to find anything more real. They differ among themselves: God is an actual entity, and so is the most trivial puff of existence in far-off empty space.'[23] This is no rhetorical gesture. Whitehead insists upon space as 'concrete' and full of 'actual entities' to suit his philosophy of organism, but the cosmos of his philosophy must retain the notion of 'empty space' as the receptacle and site of all actuality, including itself.

We get an inkling of why this is also the case for Olson in *The Special View*. In spite of the many references to the facets of the space-time continuum that he recruits as evidential to his stance, he concludes: 'the world hasn't been the most interesting image of order since 1904, when Einstein showed the beauty of the Kosmos and one then does pass on, looking for more – then *order is man*.'[24] By 1968 his mild but erratic disinterest has turned to disbelief: 'I honestly think,' he confides, 'that the whole great creators of our minds in this nineteenth century are all fallacious, including Einstein, and all this testing of the universe which is proving him right.'[25] And by the time he wrote his short sketch, 'The Animate versus the Mechanical, and Thought' in 1969, a year before his death, the writer is firmly 'anti-Newton, and anti-Einstein' (*CPr*, 369). Olson considers Newtonian space and time to be as abstract and 'Mechanical' as Einstein's space-time, even though, for relativistic physics, Newtonian space and time are the abstractions, abjected from and unaffected by the matter that supposedly exists within them. For Olson, space-time is an equally 'powerful abstraction': he protests that it, too, divorces space from the human, whom he does not accept as merely matter, or even that more humanistic term of the physical sciences, bodies.[26] The writer has no interest in materialism, scientific, historical or otherwise: 'Man is matter is now so dated,' he writes, and its removal as a maxim provides the 'more interesting mentext: man is, and is in, void.'[27] In this instance, man as 'Void in, void out' is, after all, the more compelling context for Olson's cosmology, and not only because of the perceived inorganic nature of Einstein's provable theories.[28] What Olson implicitly rejects, because he does not explicitly acknowledge the dichotomy, Einstein captures with great concision in his own description of the basic position of relativity: 'space-time is not necessarily something to which one can ascribe a separate existence, independently of the actual objects of physical reality. Physical objects are not *in space*, but these objects are *spatially extended*. In this way the concept of "empty space" loses its meaning.'[29] Relativistic space and time are not separate absolutes or solid realities; instead, the relation between objects is spatio-temporal. Absolute space and absolute time considered as universal inertial frames of reference are redundant. Instead, frames of reference are relative: all bodies move relative to one another. Olson's work, like Whitehead's, exhibits some doubt about whether the concept of 'empty space' has lost its meaning for the 'human universe' because 'empty space' underpins the concept of space as imminence for the writer. It is an actual 'element', a solid fact, which is both cosmic container and potent substrate, itself generative of physical being.

This spatial complication is not confined to Olson's prose: we also encounter it in the poetics of projective verse and in his own projective poetry. The method of composition that he sets out in 'Projective Verse' is 'BY FIELD', and the scientific field theory provides the *'kinetic'* framework for his manifesto (*CPr*, 240). A projective poem is a 'high-energy construct' of 'elements', and these 'elements' are the 'objects of reality' that constitute the poem: 'the syllable, the line, as well as the image, the sound, the sense' (*CPr*, 240, 243). Einstein relates how, in the nineteenth century, with the advances that Michael Farraday made in his study of electromagnetism:

> A new concept appears in physics, the most important invention since Newton's time: the field. It needed great scientific imagination to realize that it is not the charge nor the particles but the field in the space between the charges and particles which is essential for the description of physical phenomena.[30]

However, field theory still retained the Newtonian notion of the 'space between the charges' and 'particles' as empty and absolute, and so a theory of 'Aether' was advanced to take the place of the interstitial emptiness. Taking its name from the primal god of Hesiod's *Theogony*, 'aether' also meant for the early Greeks 'the bright, untainted upper atmosphere, as distinguished from Aër, the lower atmosphere of the earth', and was the name Aristotle used for the indestructible and unchanging fifth element, or quintessence, of the quaternary system of elements.[31] The aether under discussion, however, was an imperceptible medium which filled the otherwise empty space, and it was finally dispensed with as the intermediate filler in field theory when Einstein established the cosmological constancy of the speed of light, the fundamental equivalence of mass and energy, and relativity as the principle of all motion. Shahar Bram explains that when physicists perceived that 'light, magnetism, and electricity are aspects of a single force, there was no longer a need for a medium such as aether to transfer waves of light in space; changes in the field spread in it like waves.'[32] To relate this cosmological paradigm shift to Olson's practice as poet, in his poetic field, as 'Projective Verse' proposes it, the 'king and pin' is the syllable, and the poem is a 'construct' of syllables which signal their semantic relations spatially (*CPr*, 241). For a projective poem to be successful, Olson warns, the poet must register 'the acquisitions of his ear *and* the pressures of his breath' (*CPr*, 241). Recalling the writer's formative perception of space as a concrete 'element' in which we live and breathe, something like the aether medium and its accompanying requisite of 'empty space' emerges in the manifesto: 'If a contemporary poet leaves a space as long as the phrase before it, he means that space to be held, by the breath, an equal length of time' (*CPr*, 245). Since this visually blank, empty space on the page is a metric of breath, it is tempting to equate it to the burden of 'empty space' carried over from the 'old' cosmology referred to above. Thereby, 'only Void becomes a premise of measure', and in spite of Olson's claims to the contrary, we are not strictly dealing with a poetics informed by relativistic physics at all.

A pertinent spatial complex, which resonates with the etymological 'gaping void' or 'yawning gulf' of 'Chaos' and its buccal or oral aspect, is further clarified when we look at an unpublished prose piece Olson wrote in 1946, entitled 'Mouths Biting Empty Air', a phrase he lifted from Ezra Pound's *Hugh Selwyn Mauberley*.[33] It is certainly the overture to 'Projective Verse' and parts and phrases from it are reproduced in the manifesto; in this early articulation, a poem is the sum of 'any and all the conditions atoms and breath can create'.[34] Olson also adapted the title of this prose piece for incorporation in a poem, 'ABCs (3—for Rimbaud)', written in the same year:

> To have what back? Is it any more than
> a matter of
> syllables?
>
>   Yes, mouths bit
>   empty air
>
>   They bit. What
>   do they bite,
>   now? [...][35]

(*CP*, 175)

Taking this as a projective poem which enacts the real through the 'solidity' of 'speech', in which everything 'can now be treated as solids, objects, things', and reading off the space around the words as the tangible lack of speech, is this, spatially, the instantiation of a mouth 'biting empty air', the 'gaping', non-vocalic void (*CPr*, 244)? Olson's question about what the mouth bites now that the 'syllable' is 'matter' remains rhetorical in the poem, but his prose supplies the answer: the poetic mouth bites space as typographic blankness, as 'empty air', which stands for the poet's resting breath. Although it is mute or empty of words, the printed page remains a space substantively poised to actuate objects and their energies that exist within it, the same elemental plenipotentiary in Olson's prosaic cosmology. This compromised relativity is echoed, but not made unequivocally explicit, in extant criticism. Joseph Riddel describes how in projective verse, 'the line, in its turn, is a unit marked by the inevitable next "breath," it signifies its own disruptive, discontinuous play, like a path cut through space, like a geo-graph or a map.'[36] In this reading, space is 'cut through' by the lines as if it were a textual substrate. Bram gives a very clear explanation of the development of relativistic field theory, and registers that words in a projective poem should not be considered as 'connected to one another across the empty space (the page)', but concludes and contradicts his analysis by asserting 'Space itself' as the sum of 'the processes, the active forces, the potentially actualized energy', as an entity capable of self-actualization and cosmogeny for Olson.[37]

Miriam Nichols describes Olson's humanizing use of the plural pronoun 'we' in the utterance of Merry's mythic struggle with the bull in 'MAXIMUS, FROM DOGTOWN—I' from *The Maximus Poems VI, V, VI*. She argues that this operative 'we' draws the reader into the recognition of a similar site of actualization akin to Olson's airy space, which she terms the 'common, elemental space between heaven and earth where living things manifest'.[38] This is the mythically charged mortal air that Hesiod differentiated from divine air, or Aether, in the *Theogony*, both of which Olson refers to in the double-entry poetic list of perquisites, actions, and prophecies, 'MAXIMUS, FROM DOGTOWN—II'. We read of:

> Air a e r the Ta of
> Dogtown (the Ta metarsia
>
>> is the Angel Matter
>> not to come until (rill!
>> 3000 [...]
>
> (MP, 179)

Dogtown's 'a e r' has extra interstitial typographic *signes*, little empty breaths, to signify a superabundance of earthly air, which Olson also obliquely refers to with 'Ta metarsia', the Greek for the earthy winds and mists, or weather more generally. This air is wilfully equated to the absent but desired 'Angel Matter', which may be the divine *pneuma*, meaning both spirit as breath and air. This spirit seems not to have properly materialized by volume three of *Maximus*, where we find the universal man of letters looking at Gloucester and still 'wishing' for 'the air | of heaven' (*MP*, 384). This aspiration is for divine inspiration, and the hoped-for descent of the winged heavenly breath from its ethereal heights, from spiritual abstraction to solid spatial 'element', in order to mix with and regenerate the Dogtown air, is still to come.

In spite of this disappointment in *Maximus*, Olson's prosaic etymological search for origins of the cosmological 'terms' he reckoned had 'so overlayed [sic] our natures', and his urge to recondition them with his findings, lead him back to the origin of the word myth to the ancient Greek word, *mu*, or mouth.[39] Myth was the cosmology that was spoken, not a rite of referral but an instantiation in the act of speaking, its enactment. Space, like myth, had to be as actual, solid, and factual as everything else in Olson's 'Kosmos', written and spoken. The cosmology that actuated his versification is partially disclosed in the writer's various pronouncements upon the 'drags' of the 'old' cosmology which he tried and failed to abandon, and in his dismissal of relativistic physics, which did abandon the dominant conceptual drag of 'empty space'. Apprehending the extent of Olson's insistence upon the concrete and literal condition of all cosmic forms in his prose permits a more accurate sense of the textual space the writer heralded in 'Projective Verse'.

Notes

1 Charles Olson, *The Special View of History*, ed. Ann Charters (Berkeley: Oyez, 1970), 53.
2 Ralph Maud, *Charles Olson's Reading: A Biography* (Carbondale, Edwardsville: Southern Illinois University Press, 1996), 104.
3 Olson, *The Special View*, 48.
4 Olson, 'Human Universe' (*CPr*, 155).
5 Olson, *The Special View*, 53; Olson, 'Proprioception' (*CPr*, 183).
6 Andrew Ross, *The Failure of Modernism: Symptoms of American Poetry* (New York: Columbia University Press, 1986), 97.
7 Charles Olson, lecture given as part of the 'Institute of the New Sciences of Man' at Black Mountain College in 1953, reprinted in Ann Charters, *Olson/Melville: A Study in Affinity* (Berkeley: Oyez, 1968), 87.
8 Don Byrd, *Charles Olson's Maximus* (Urbana, Chicago and London: University of Illinois Press, 1980), 93.
9 Judith Halden-Sullivan, *The Topology of Being: The Poetics of Charles Olson* (New York: Peter Lang, 1991), 2, 6.
10 Olson, *The Special View*, 20.
11 Ibid., 48.
12 Charters, *Olson/Melville*, 49.
13 Ibid.
14 Olson, lecture for 'Institute of the New Sciences of Man', in Charters, *Olson/Melville*, 83.
15 Olson, *Call Me Ishmael* (*CPr*, 17).
16 Olson, *The Special View*, 47
17 Ibid., 47–8.
18 Ibid., 27.
19 Lesley Brown (ed.), *The New Shorter Oxford English Dictionary*, 2 Vols (Oxford: Clarendon Press, 1993), Vol. I, 372.

20 Albert Einstein, *The Meaning of Relativity*, trans. Edwin Plimpton Adams (London: Methuen, 1922), 33.
21 Alfred North Whitehead, *Process and Reality: An Essay in Cosmology* (London: Cambridge University Press, 1929), 97.
22 Whitehead, *Process and Reality*, 24, 113.
23 Ibid., 24.
24 Olson, *The Special View*, 47.
25 Olson, *Poetry and Truth* in George Butterick (ed.), *Muthologos: The Collected Lectures and Interviews*, 2 Vols (Bolinas: Four Seasons Foundation, 1979), Vol. II, 36.
26 Olson, 'The Resistance' (*CPr*, 174).
27 Olson, *The Special View*, 48.
28 Ibid.
29 Albert Einstein, *Relativity: The Special and the General Theory: A Popular Exposition*, trans. Robert W. Lawson (London: Routledge, 1993), vi.
30 Albert Einstein and Leopold Infeld, *The Evolution of Physics* (Cambridge: Cambridge University Press, 1947), 258–9.
31 See Hesiod, *Theogony* in *The Homeric Hymns and Homerica*, trans. Hugh G. Evelyn-White (London: William Heinneman; Cambridge: Harvard University Press, 1950), 87. Hermann Weyl gives a brief history of different theories of aether in a book from which Olson drew much cosmological grist. See Weyl, *Principles of Mathematics and Natural Sciences*, trans. Olaf Helmer (Princeton: Princeton University Press, 1949), 175– 7.
32 Shahar Bram, *Charles Olson and Alfred North Whitehead*, trans. Batya Stein (Lewisburg: Bucknell University Press, 2004), 21.
33 Ezra Pound, 'Mauberley 1920' from *Hugh Selwyn Mauberley (Contacts and Life)* in Lea Baechler and A. Walton Litz (eds), *Personæ: The Shorter Poems of Ezra Pound* (London: Faber and Faber, 2001), 198.
34 Original typewritten manuscript, 'Mouths Biting Empty Air', by Charles Olson, 27 October 1946, Box 32, Charles Olson Research Collection, Archives and Special Collections at the Thomas J. Dodd Research Center, University of Connecticut, Storrs.
35 Olson, 'ABCs (3—for Rimbaud)' (*CP*, 175).
36 Joseph Riddel, 'Decentering the Image: The "Project" of "American" Poetics?', in Josué V. Harari (ed.), *Textual Strategies: Perspectives in Post-Structuralist Criticism* (Ithaca: Cornell University Press, 1979), 353–4.
37 Bram, *Charles Olson and Alfred North Whitehead*, 22.
38 Miriam Nichols, *Radical Affections: Essays on the Poetics of Outside* (Tuscaloosa, AL: The University of Alabama Press, 2010), 61.
39 Olson, *The Special View*, 24.

4

A reading of 'In Cold Hell, in Thicket'

Ian Brinton and Michael Grant

The first draft of 'In Cold Hell, in Thicket' was sent as a letter to Frances Boldereff in May 1950 and its immediate context was the entangled dilemma facing a man who was torn between the love offered to him by two very different women: his partner Constance and this new admirer who could write in an early letter that she is 'so sure that the circle of our lives will bring us face to face some day'.[1] However, the complexity of the poem is also compounded by Olson's awareness of the Nazi concentration camps and his recent visits to the battle sites of the Civil War which he undertook early that month. Olson's awareness of the horrors of the camps had been underlined by the publication of his first chapbook of poems, *Y & X*, with its drawings of Buchenwald by a camp survivor, Corrado Cagli, and the enduring echo of this history was further enmeshed by his visits to Ezra Pound in St Elizabeth's Hospital between 1946 and 1948. In 'A Lustrum for You, E.P.' there is an association between the 'smell of flesh in a furnace' and the poet-father-figure's racist pronouncements during these visits.[2]

The questioning and self-doubt which faced Olson throughout his dilemma concerning his adulterous attraction to Frances Boldereff was highlighted in a 1986 interview with Olson's biographer, Tom Clark, in which Boldereff emphasised Olson's inability to make a clear decision. She claimed, 'He had the kind of personality that simply could not clarify and decide', a statement which echoed his letter to her from June 1950 in which he asserted his preference for staying 'in a sense, fluid, as though the SUM was not to be of my doing (as, in truth, of course, it is not) but to be taken care of, by others (as, in truth, it will, of course).'[3] Soon after receiving the first letter from Boldereff in November 1947 Olson had written in his journal, 'Faust Buch', 'The broken step continues …Unable to work or figure out what to do with myself' and it is this questioning anguish that is woven into the fabric of 'In Cold Hell, in Thicket', a love song centred on a protagonist trapped in an eternity of pain.[4]

A reading of 'In Cold Hell, in Thicket'

The questions, reiterated in Part I, section 2 – 'How can he change?', 'How can he make?', 'How can he make out?' – lead to the overwhelming question in section 3, 'Who / am I?', and any attempt at resolution of these questions comes in Part II, section 2 with the imperative gesture, 'He shall step, he / will shape, he / is already also / moving off' (CP, 156, 157, 159). The aim of the projective is to identify both poetry *and* action in the world with each other, an identification whose achievement is inseparable from any moral rebirth the poet/speaker can lay claim to, and it is precisely this claim to which the poet is giving expression in the more assertive and self-convincing note on which the poem ends: 'He will do what he now does, as she will, do / carefully, do / without wavering' (CP, 160). This concluding 'wavering', repudiated earlier in the poem, now returns associated with nature ('as even the snow-flakes waver in the light's eye'):

> as even forever wavers (gutters
> in the wind of loss)
>
> even as he will forever waver
>
> precise as hell is, precise
> as any words, or wagon,
> can be made
>
> (CP, 160)

This assertive note here is nonetheless inseparable from contradiction inasmuch as 'waver' and 'precise' are presented as terms appropriate to what 'can be made' and echo the epigraph to T. S. Eliot's 'The Love Song of J. Alfred Prufrock' in which Dante's Guido da Montefeltro endures in the wavering flame for having given false counsel to Pope Boniface VIII. Similar to Eliot, Olson wishes to find in the fire-consumed sinner a figure with whom the poetic activity may be identified. In Eliot's case, however, the sinner is a figure for the poem as such, whereas Olson's concern is psychological engagement with what the poet makes: the precision and worth of what he makes and does.

The 1950 essay, 'Projective Verse', places particular emphasis on the central importance of syllables, the particles of sound, as Olson registers at once 'the acquisitions of his ear *and* the pressures of his breath' (*CPr*, 241). This concentration upon the centrality of breath is reinforced by the etymological derivation of the word 'is' from the Sanskrit root, *as*, to breathe, whilst 'be' derives from *bhu*, to grow, and negation, as in 'not', from *na*. The purpose behind such pointed derivation is to establish the identification of the form of the poem with the pulsing form of natural energy to make, in Olson's terms, two unified elements of the poetic act:

>   the HEAD, by way of the EAR, to the SYLLABLE
>   the HEART, by way of the BREATH, to the LINE
>
>   (*CPr*, 242)

Rejecting rhetorical figures, such as similes, which may tend towards 'slackness', the shape of the poem is formed on 'the threshing floor' of the line where the dance of the intellect may take place amongst the syllables. The totality of poetic elements participates in the kinetics of the poem as do objects of reality in the kinetics of the actual world: 'these elements are to be seen as creating the tensions of a poem just as totally as do those other objects create what we call the world' (*CPr*, 243). It is breath that allows the poem its full kinetic force, a force that is not merely comparable *to* but participant *in* the energy of relation between objects in the world. In contrast to Eliot's very different mode of working, Olson insists that 'a projective poet will [go], down through the workings of his own throat to that place where breath comes from, where breath has its beginnings, where drama has to come from, where, the coincidence is, all act springs' (*CPr*, 249). Reaching down into himself to achieve expressive unity of mind and body, voice and syllable, the poet accomplishes a return to origins, the redemptive energies which Olson also sought in myth and archetype. When man 'chooses to speak from these roots' he 'works in that area where nature has given him size, projective size' and Maximus becomes a mythic embodiment of the projective poet (*CPr*, 248).

Slavoj Žižek proposes an alternative view of the inseparability of voice and breath, one which challenges Olson's position:

> An unbridgeable gap separates forever a human body from 'its' voice. The voice displays a special autonomy, it never quite belongs to the body we see, so that even when we see a living person talking, there is always a minimum of ventriloquism at work: it is as if the speaker's own voice hollows him out and in a sense speaks 'by itself', through him.[5]

Every manifestation of the voice is, in effect, ventriloquism since the voice's source can never be seen and, as noted by Mladen Dolar, '[the voice] stems from an undisclosed and structurally concealed interior' and 'it cannot possibly match what we see'.[6] To insist upon the word ventriloquism is to clarify that the voice comes from within the body and that this is not simply compatible with the activities of the mouth. The voice is not demystified because we can see the aperture of the mouth ('the voice doesn't stick to the body, it is an excrescence which doesn't match the body') and we can often recognise in everyday experience that there is something incongruous between a person's appearance, or aspect, and that same person's voice before we adapt to it.[7] Freeing itself from the body, the voice points to an interior that cannot

A reading of 'In Cold Hell, in Thicket'

be disclosed: appearing in the void and arising from what it does not fit. Dolar questions the idea that etymology provides any justification for the unity of souls and body in the breath:

> The voice, by being so ephemeral, transient, incorporeal, ethereal, presents for that very reason the body at its quintessential, the hidden bodily treasure beyond the visible envelope, the interior 'real' body, unique and intimate, and at the same time it seems to present more than the mere body – in many languages there is an etymological link between spirit and breath (breath being the 'voiceless voice', the zero point of vocal emission); the voice carried by breath points to the soul irreducible to the body.[8]

Far from vindicating the union of breath, body and soul, etymology points to their rupture. It is desire that transforms the voice into the signifier, into meaning, which, by definition, is addressed to the 'other' whilst (being the driving force of meaning) it can never be exhausted by a limit or set boundary. As a by-product of this operation, the voice connects language to the body whilst not belonging to either and Dolar emphasises that:

> the voice stands at a paradoxical and ambiguous topological spot, at the intersection of language and the body, but this intersection belongs to neither. *What language and the body have in common is the voice, but the voice is part neither of language nor the body.*[9]

The voice stems from the body without being part *of* it and, at the same time, it supports language without belonging *to* it. Nonetheless, the voice is the only point body and language have in common, and as such the voice is an object that does not coincide with any existing thing: it is a void evoked by the actual objects, words, sounds, gestures –utterances – associated with it. This is to emphasise the split between diacritical signifier and the singular condition of utterance as an inescapable and, as it were, 'transcendent' condition of discourse.

The significance of Olson's title, 'In Cold Hell, in Thicket', becomes apparent: whatever the discursive thrust of the poem, the insistent repetitions, constituting one crucial mode of its unfolding, effect a shift from representation to a vision of the surface of language as such leading to an utterance whose internal structure is one of self-cancelling:

> In cold hell, in thicket, how
> abstract (as high mind, as not lust, as love is) how
> strong (as strut or wing, as polytope, as things are
> constellated) how
> strung, how cold
> can a man stay (can men) confronted
> thus?
>
> (CP, 155)

'Cold hell' and 'thicket' constitute a gap or void around which the text, endeavouring to represent just that very gap, circulates. A similar pattern of displaced insistence is evident elsewhere, as, for example, in the indented section of Part 2 which begins 'How can he change, his question is' (*CP*, 156). Robert von Hallberg quotes Olson to the effect that he saw the lines of his poetry as characterised by 'a progressing of both the meaning and the breathing forward, and then a backing up, without a progress or any kind of movement outside the unit of time local to the idea.'[10] The writing pushes forward only to curl back on its own progress whilst doing so, folding over upon its own passing beyond itself. Inscribing a Möbius loop in which the movement forward twists round on itself, Olson's poetry in 'In Cold Hell, in Thicket' discloses within itself its own point of enunciation: it stands beyond and behind itself. Consider, for instance, the line: 'How shall he who is not happy, who has been so made unclear' (*CP*, 156). In a movement of anaphora (or anamorphosis) the second clause turns back on the first and the torsion constructs neither a conclusion nor a climax but a sense of partial movement, first this, then that. Or as the poem subsequently observes:

Who am I but by a fix, and another,
a particle, and the congery of particles carefully picked one by another
(*CP*, 157)

Tenses set in the passive and active submit to something akin to a reflexive middle voice: 'that they are, in hell or in happiness, merely / something to be wrought, to be shaped, to be carved, for use, for / others' (*CP*, 159). The result is a partially realised montage of self and other and the poem wavers and gutters to a concluding statement: 'precise as hell is, precise / as any words, or wagon, / can be made' (*CP*, 160).

Dante's Guido is imprisoned in a flame and his words only become audible as the flame's tip vibrates in response to his tongue's movement giving us the palpability of separation between voice and body. The voice of Guido belongs to neither language nor his body and the flame's tip intersects at this meeting of nothing with nothing. By placing the lines from Dante at the opening of his poem Eliot suggests that Prufrock also is speaking from Hell and this licenses the reader to trace the echo of 'ti rispondo' through its reworking as 'you and I'. The flames enveloping Guido are not those of a refining fire for this is fire that is endured by one who is neither alive nor dead, one who is caught between two deaths. For Prufrock death will only come when 'human voices wake us, and we drown' echoing the Dante line 'Ma per ciò che giammai di questo fondo / non tornò vivo alcun' ('But since no one ever came back alive / From this deep place').[11] This 'deep place' is the place of poetry, and Prufrock's being, conferred by a poem formed of such a place, is that of neither life nor death but is that of the un-dead. Guido da Montefeltro is thus the persona of the poem. It would seem right to ask, in this context, who are 'we'? Is death possible only when the 'I' of the poem has been passed beyond? Or is it that the poem achieves a point that is supernumerary, where that which persists does so beyond parts and wholes? Eliot's writing engages with a non-rational excess that is out of kilter with any system of either classification or predication and Prufrock's 'Love Song' leaves the reader suspended in a space opening onto the singular.

Despite the overt references to *Inferno*, the negativity of Olson's hell is not that of Dante but is psychological and he is trapped not by eternal fire but by a guilt which emerges from adulterous sex. In Part 1, section 3, 'the same each act' carries an aural suggestion of ejaculation, whilst 'fix' carries a sense that is both colloquial and navigational; the former being 'look what a fix I'm in!' It is this shifting and uncertain 'fix' that leaves the poet 'pinned and wriggling on the wall' (as 'Prufrock' has it): 'Who am I but by a fix', Olson's speaker asks; a notion that is immediately run together with the fixing of 'particles' which become waves once they are observed.

Immediately following this, Olson's indented lines begin with 'as in this thicket'. These lines play, crucially, upon a dependence between body and thicket where 'roots lie, on the surface, as nerves are laid open' and they include a sudden inserted, bracketed, reference to 'her': '(the bitterness of the taste of her)' (*CP*, 157). This phrase evokes possibilities which the poem takes no further although one might note in this connection that 'pincer', two lines further on, seems to carry an allusion to a *vagina dentate*, to be identified it seems with the displaced and isolated 'this' of:

>   this
> is the abstract, this
> is the cold doing, this
> is the almost impossible
>
>   (*CP*, 157)

The phrase 'cold doing' is as insistent in its repudiation of enjoyment as is the pattern of repeated assertion. Repetition and assertion, a highly self-conscious mode in their presentation, constitute what Olson terms 'traceries' in the penultimate line of this section whilst also hinting that the poem's style can be seen as a series of 'fixes', the remnants of ritual acts performed by a shaman. The political implications of being 'a fixer', 'in a fix' or 'fixing' inevitably merge with the drug-use connotation of 'a fix' as well as the further sense of remedial action although, in this context, one can hardly remain unaware of Prufrock's helplessness as he is pinned by 'eyes that fix you in a formulated phrase'.[12]

It is in Part II of the poem, however, that the psychological thrust of the poem is made explicit, notably in the first section, where hell becomes identified with the inner self (what Olson terms 'your core') and the poet's entrapment within it. Hell, for the poet, is described as 'the coat of your own self, the beasts / emblazoned on you', a description which establishes metaphor as the reigning rhetorical figure of the text around which the poem is organised and to which it continues to return (CP,158). In this context the sexual act, where 'the beasts are met' and where 'she / who is separate from you, is not separate' is equated with 'the making of one hell' (CP, 158). The lines that effect the equation constitute, in the metaphoric conjuncture they set up, a commentary on just those figures they are in the process of employing. Again, one finds underpinning the lengthy final paragraph of this section a metre, / the iambic feet of which work to reinforce, punningly, 'why / his feet are held' (CP, 158). Olson prepares for this with a reference to his formal structure: '(this is why he of whom we speak does not move, why / he stands so awkward where he is', where the promise implicit in the use of an open bracket appears to conflict with the iambic ordering of the subsequent phrases (CP, 158). Olson undertakes a foregrounding of formal structure that leaves little doubt that, for him, palpable enactment is the essential condition of poetic meaning. Thus metrical and syntactic repletion work together on this occasion to create an almost physical sense of being fixed, as if Olson, like Prufrock, remains 'formulated, sprawling on a pin'.[13] The following lines are also pertinent to this line of argument:

> And who
> can turn this total thing, invert
> and let the ragged sleeves be seen
> by any bitch or common character?
>
> (CP, 158)

The phrasing here can hardly fail to evoke certain well-known images in 'Prufrock': 'lonely men in shirt-sleeves, leaning out of windows? .... I should have been a pair of ragged claws / Scuttling across the floors of silent seas'.[14] It is difficult to resist the conclusion, then, that 'In Cold Hell, in Thicket' should be seen as a self-conscious response to, even re-writing of, 'Prufrock'. Positing this relation should not, however, obscure the significant differences between the modes of these two poems and we must recognise that Prufrock, as subject, is *in* and *of* the poem, an effect of a certain procedure of writing, whereas Olson is present *in propria persona*. His poem is confessional in a way that Eliot's is not and he aims to align the reader with the predicament of the poet himself, beset with 'fixes'. The anguish and violence consuming Olson in the flames are stated directly: 'that men killed, do kill, that woman kills / is part, too, of his question' (CP, 158). Part II, section 2, of his overwhelming question follows immediately although it appears, retrospectively, to partake less of a question and more of an extended assertion:

> That it is simple, what the difference is—
> that a man, men, are now their own wood
> and thus their own hell and paradise
> that they are, in hell or in happiness, merely
> something to be wrought, to be shaped, to be carved, for use, for others
>
> does not in the least lessen his, this unhappy man's
> obscurities, his
> confrontations
>
> (CP, 158–9)

Men, or at least 'this unhappy man', will escape the fix by what they or he can make, by what comes from the hand being so shaped or carved that, in its truth to the material of its being, it can acquire redemptive force by virtue of that truth of being 'equal to the real itself.' If this is the redemptive promise of projective verse, it is one which appears very uncertain in this poem.

Olson's reflections on breath subordinate the voice to the signifier. Spacing on the typewriter is used to indicate the poet's breath (his voice) and gives the signifier, the differential structures of the symbolic, dominance over the sonorous, the voiced. This way of proceeding exhibits a common sense or pragmatic idea of word and expression. However, by contrast Eliot's procedure attends to words not merely as signifiers but as sound objects and what comes to the fore is the sonorous substance of words, echoes, resemblances, homonyms, and rhymes, elements that are purely contingent and unpredictable in relation to the differential 'logic' of the signifier. Poetic expression in 'Prufrock' is not language taken in the register of the signifier because Eliot's language depends for its understanding on a response to the difference between two 'logics': on the one hand the necessary difference internal to the concept of the signifier, which exists only in relation to a certain notion of logic, and on the other the contingencies and unpredictabilities of word sound which constitutes a 'logic' that is far from logical. Signifier and sound do not stand outside each other but nor do they coincide.

The result of such writing is uncanny as it resonates in a void of alterity, otherness, the locus of which is the page. The poem resonates in otherness and is returned to us by that otherness as a voice, but one created out of nothing, as an inaudible echo of resonance. Prufrock puts his questions in the hope of response but all that both he and the reader gets is the voice, the becoming other of what is said: we hear what is said but we hear it in its otherness. The language of the poem returns to us as an uncanny presence of absence, undecidable difference in which the speech is our own (we have 'said' the poem's words) but the voice pertains to otherness, created *ex nihilo* in the loop of alterity itself. It is as though the words come back to us out of a loop they have themselves engendered but altered in the precise sense of being other. It is this loop that Prufrock invites us into with his 'Let us go then, you and I'. At the poem's end there is a drowning brought about on being wakened by 'human voices'; ordinary language in a context of significant use plunging us back into itself, the 'white and black' water of the text. In this way 'Prufrock' accomplishes a double estrangement which both retains the thing and is estranged from it. It is an estrangement that brings about, in effect, a suspension of speech, during the course of which one may, perhaps, come to hear a singular voice internal to language, and also separate from it. The essential point is that what it recounts is what, in the act of becoming a poem, it wrenches itself away from. The resulting space, or rupture, an opening ceaselessly induced by the poem itself, is where the poem has what being – what being of un-being – it has.

Olson's aesthetic is crucially different: central to his work is the poetic experience, the 'lived moment', the poetic 'state'. 'In Cold Hell, in Thicket' engages with the physical and psychological presence of Olson himself, a presence the poem seeks to transform into that of the very writing whose projective thrust constitutes the poem as the poem it is: writing, Olson would insist, that is equal to the real itself. What has been argued here, however, is that, in the event, writing, as Olson conceives of it, whether in his manifestoes or in his practice, turns out to be, no less than Eliot's, a function of the lack engendered by it.

Notes

1 Charles Olson and Frances Boldereff, *A Modern Correspondence*, ed. Ralph Maud and Sharon Thesen (Hanover: Wesleyan University Press, 1999), 6.
2 Catherine Seelye (ed.), *Charles Olson and Ezra Pound: An Encounter at St Elizabeths* (New York: Grossman, 1975), xv–xvi.
3 Tom Clark, *Charles Olson: The Allegory of a Poet's Life* (New York: Norton & Company, 1991) 172; Maud and Thesen, *A Modern Correspondence*, 387.

4 Clark, *Allegory*, 138.
5 Slavoj Žižek, *On Belief* (London: Routledge, 2001), 58.
6 Mladen Dolar, *A Voice and Nothing More* (Cambridge, MA: MIT, 2006), 70.
7 Ibid., 61.
8 Ibid., 71.
9 Ibid., 73.
10 Robert von Hallberg, *Charles Olson: The Scholar's Art* (Cambridge, MA: Harvard University Press, 1978), 145.
11 T. S. Eliot, *Collected Poems* (London, Faber and Faber, 1963), 13
12 Ibid., 15.
13 Ibid.
14 Ibid.

Section II

Poetics

5

From Olson's breath to Spicer's gait: spacing, pacing, phonemes

Daniel Katz

'If nothing happens it is possible / To make things happen,' wrote Jack Spicer in 'A Postscript for Charles Olson,' the final poem in his posthumously published book *Admonitions*, of 1957. And these lines, already, make something happen – as a 'postscript' in a book in which almost every poem is dedicated to a member of Spicer's artistic entourage, Spicer is allocating to Olson a clear position with regard to it: just beyond its margins, but still inside its cover. Demarcated as external yet held inside, Olson here occupies a position not unlike the 'cyst' that Spicer had deemed integral to poetry in *After Lorca*. 'The poet encysts the intruder' in his life, Spicer writes, which allows the poet to go back to being the ghostly 'dead man' who writes poetry, having recovered from the moment where 'he loses his balance for a moment, slips into being who he is.'[1] Rhyming with this model is the pearl and the oyster to which Spicer refers in the Vancouver lectures, as he explains that where he allows the 'personal' to 'interfere' in the dictated poem, the poem comes back like an oyster to a grain of sand, 'encasing' it in its transformative secretions.[2]

Certainly, Spicer received Olson as an 'intruder' into his circle. Spicer had befriended Robert Duncan well before Olson met him, and as both Spicer's and Duncan's biographers make clear, Spicer was consistently jealous of Olson's growing importance to Duncan, which left his relationship to him and his work never entirely free from ambivalence, along with various forms of acting out.[3] In fact, Lewis Ellingham and Kevin Killian explain that the lines from the 'Postscript' cited above allude to a nasty exchange between the two poets during Olson's visit to San Francisco in February 1957, when the latter derisively accused Spicer of trying too hard to 'make something happen' in a botched Tarot reading which Spicer had staged, hoping to impress the distinguished guest.[4] Less trivially, around this time Spicer expresses reticence towards Olson's work in several places, for example writing to Robin Blaser, probably in 1957, 'you know how unable I am to understand most of Olson.'⁵ Yet whatever reticence Spicer might have had about Olson for personal and poetic reasons, the power of the latter's work did not fail to impose itself upon him, and the story hardly ends with Spicer's frustrations of 1957. As opposed to professions of incomprehension, by the time of his last public appearance – at the Berkeley Poetry Conference in July 1965, only a few weeks before his final collapse – Spicer was content to assert, 'Olson is probably the best poet that we have in the country.'⁶

Such a divergence in views represents not only a progression in Spicer's thinking about Olson, but also a fundamentally discordant position that Spicer seems to have maintained towards Olson's work, which he takes in without fully assimilating, perhaps leaving it suspended between grit and pearl – a foreign body, like the poem itself in Spicer's theory of dictation. This is all the more suggestive, as it is precisely around the question of the body as space and ground that Spicer and Olson will most significantly differ. As encysted intruder, however, Olson – or at least, a popular understanding of the projective position – can be seen as both the target and the foundation of Spicer's late thinking on poetry as 'dictation', occupying a doubled and contradictory position which in and of itself is typical of Spicer's poetics. On the one hand, 'dictation' in its validation of the poet as 'receiver' of alien signals can very easily be read as a near total inversion of Olson's pro-jective project, advocating on the contrary something one might well wish to call 'receptive' verse. For if one reads 'Projective Verse' as demanding that the poet begin with the most proximate form of his own interiority – the natural rhythm of his breathing – and then project that outward towards the reader in an 'energy-discharge' implicitly likened to a 'projectile,' 'dictation' can be seen as just the opposite (*CPr*, 239–40). In 'dictation' the poet is not an Olsonian launching pad but 'something which is being transmitted into' from what Spicer calls the 'Outside', a space of radical otherness he associates with 'Martians' or, following the precedent of Georgie and W. B. Yeats' experiments in automatic writing, 'ghosts' or 'spooks'.⁷ Above all, however, working out of Jean Cocteau's film *Orpheus*, in which poetry is received from the underworld through a car radio, Spicer posits the radio receiver as his privileged model for the poet. As he put it in his late poem 'Sporting Life':

> The trouble with comparing a poet with a radio is that radios don't develop scar tissue. The tubes burn out, or with a transistor, which most souls are, the battery or diagram burns out replaceable or not replaceable, but not like that punchdrunk fighter in the bar. The poet
> Takes too many messages. The right to the ear that floored him in New Jersey. The right to say that he stood six rounds with a champion.⁸

Aggressive interpellation and provocation are explicit elements of Spicer's poetics, and it is hard to believe that he was indifferent to the potential of 'dictation' to be read as an assault on Olson's 'projection', reversing that term's directionality and replacing the natural human body as figure for the ground of poetry with the inhuman technological apparatus of the radio set. On the other hand, however, by the time of the famous 'Vancouver lectures' of June 1965, Spicer turns this possibility on its head; indeed, he is at pains to place Olson squarely *within* the tradition of dictated poetics that he is delineating. 'Olson's idea of energy and projective verse is something that comes from the Outside,' Spicer affirms, and his only quarrel with Olson is that the latter doesn't present energy as sufficiently distant from the poet, or adequately unsettling in its mode of arrival.[9] According to Spicer, Olson's energy 'is not something from a great galactic distance out there but something you plug in the wall, and it's really the machine which is the converter of the electricity .... And I don't agree with that either, but I go nearer to that.'[10] As Peter Gizzi's excellent notes to the lecture indicate, and I would like to stress, Spicer doesn't need to look far to find what might seem a counter-intuitive Olson who corresponds well with the general economy of poetic transfer and exchange which Spicer calls 'dictation'. Near the beginning of 'Projective Verse' Olson writes of 'the *kinetics* of the thing. A poem is energy transferred from where the poet got it ... by way of the poem itself to, all the way over to, the reader' (*CPr*, 240). Later, Olson again sounds like Spicer, writing 'Objectism is the getting rid of the lyrical interference of the individual as ego .... For a man is himself an object' (*CPr*, 247). When Spicer evokes dictation, it is often in terms of making one's own language available as objects – or, following Spicer's figure, 'furniture' – put at the disposal of the 'guests' from the Outside whom one hosts. In this rhetoric, the task of the poet is simply to become a hospitable dwelling: 'Language is part of the furniture in the room. Language isn't anything of itself. It's something which is in the mind of the host that the parasite (the poem) is invading.'[11] Or as Spicer concludes, 'Then the language is one of the pieces of furniture, or maybe just the way the walls are built .... But the first thing, if you're going to build a house and furnish it and set a table and all of that – the first thing to do is make sure that you have a guest.'[12]

Surprisingly, then, as much as Spicer's 'dictation' is a rejection of 'projectivism', it is also to largely the same extent no more than a hyperbolic extrapolation of some of its principles – he finds hidden in plain sight complexities of Olson's kinetics which go too often overlooked. Not untypically, Spicer at once posits a clear opposition between Olson's poetics and his own but also deconstructs it, pointing to Olson's frequent

Poundian stressing of the poet as node, transmitter, and object thrown into the 'field' of composition. That said, Spicer's reading of Olson is also tendentious. Indeed, Spicer seems to follow only half of Olson's projective equation, as Olson himself programmatically proposed it:

Let me put it baldly. The two halves are:

> the HEAD, by way of the EAR, to the SYLLABLE
> the HEART, by way of the BREATH, to the LINE
>
> (*CPr*, 242)

To put it no less baldly, Spicer will work carefully through Olson's head, ear and syllable, while rejecting his heart, breath and line almost entirely. At stake here is the place of the body and its relation to language, as well as the latter's negotiation of the page, and intersubjective space. Ultimately, the issue for Spicer here is the local, both as geographical space and as virtual loci for companionship, and it is in this context that Spicer's telecommunicational model of the 'broadcast' opens him up to a sense of distance – in contrast to Olson's SPACE ('I spell it large because it comes large here') – which breaks decisively with the breath-based dicta of 'Projective Verse', while pointing to an extension of Olson's emphasis on the syllable (*CPr*, 17). These issues come to the fore in the question and answer session of the third Vancouver lecture, when it is suggested to Spicer that his Vancouver poems seem to use a 'different line' than his other work. Spicer responds, 'I know what you mean. The whole rhythm of Vancouver is different from the rhythm of San Francisco and I do think that there is something to that. I hate the word "measure" – I've always despised it – but there is some kind of natural measure to a city that does change things.'[13] Asked to elaborate, Spicer tellingly explains, 'say, you are walking with your grandmother who is seventy-five years old. You walk different. You have to get a different pace to your legs, and that's what Williams and everybody has meant by "measure", if they meant anything. It's the kind of pace of walking .... It's the way you use your legs. And in a way, it has nothing whatsoever, so far as I can see as a linguist, to do with the metrics of poetry. It's a kind of thing that does happen differently in different cities, and the difference in the city undoubtedly has made a difference in the metric.... you walk different in Vancouver.'[14] At this point, in a series of linked questions, the poet Dorothy Livesay attempts to ground walking, and by extension, measure and the line, in breath: 'surely the gait is a part of the whole body's rhythm which comes from breath, and the way you breathe.' Spicer answers: 'Yeah, but the gait also comes from where you're walking. If you're walking on a catwalk, twenty storeys high, you walk different than you do when you're walking down a street, you know, or through the Broadway tunnel …. You just walk with a different gait. And you also walk with a different gait with a different person that you're walking with.'[15] In the end, Spicer discounts the importance of gait to some extent, grouping it with all the other essentially indifferent elements or 'furniture' that the 'Martians' make use of when they dictate into a particular poet-receiver: 'What I'm trying to say is that I think that the difference that a town makes in poetry is this kind of way of walking …. and I think it's rather accidental …. What matters is getting from place A to place B, and you do that whatever gait you use.' When Livesay goes on to insist that, 'surely there is a basic rhythm that comes from the way you actually speak, and is "you", which isn't the furniture. It's your only possible voice,' Spicer emphatically denies that his 'only possible voice' is built into the poem, just as he consistently denies that 'his' poems are really his: 'I really honestly don't feel that I own my poems,' he had declared in the first lecture.[16]

Clearly, at issue in this exchange is Spicer's resistance to a certain reading of projective verse: one that anchors the poetic fact in breath, itself grounding both the integrity of the line and the singularity of the voice, and views proprioception as closeness to the primal given of the body as presence. In such a framework, if the space of the page is crucial, it is through its ability to receive the imprint of processes and elements which are essentially aural, temporal and above all, cyclical, and also rooted in the internal workings of the body. Olson stresses this at length when discussing the ability of the typewriter to 'indicate exactly the breath' and provide a 'script' for the 'vocalization' of the poem (*CPr*, 245). When Spicer rejects breath for gait, however, he bequeaths to space an entirely different dimension – movement through space *is* the poem, and moreover, it is this space which defines the poem's shape – rather than seeing shape as bestowed by the elementary unity of the body. Consonant with this, of course, is Spicer's stressing of the companions who walk with the poet, which casts poetry as a constitutively collaborative act, not only a contingently communal one. Singular bodily interiority and proprioception are no longer the starting point from which the poet and poem reach out, extend, 'project' into SPACE, but rather for Spicer the traversing of space itself and the heteroglossic exchanges constitutive of such traversing are defined as primary. Finally, although the phrase 'what matters is getting from place A to place B' can be read as a teleologically utilitarian notion of poetics, Spicer's emphasis on accidental circumstance throughout this discussion makes the poetic gambol feel much more like a situationist *dérive* than a plotted trajectory.

Both breathing and walking are rhythmic and repetitive acts of the body, but a breath implies cyclic completion and wholeness of process in a manner that a step does not. And of course, breath implies an entire metaphorics of inspiration which, if implicitly acknowledging an 'outside', would probably for Spicer too strongly suggest an untroubled appropriation of this outside through an easily functioning natural process – one quite different from uncannily penetrative radio waves, or the stubbornly inassimilable yet inexpugnable cyst of *After Lorca*. On the other hand, Spicer's emphasis on gait can be tied both to his sense of the serial poem, and to Olson's own hints on 'composition by field' (*CPr*, 239). Olson writes, 'From the moment he ventures into FIELD COMPOSITION – puts himself in the open – he can go by no track other than the one the poem under hand declares, for itself' (*CPr*, 240). This sounds like many of Spicer's own comments on the serial poem, but even more, echoes the way for Spicer the line is something other than an emanation from the body, but rather a vector of movement, directionality and adjustment on several levels. Spicer questions the line as holistic, essentially bodily unit in many places in his work: 'My house is Aquarius. I don't believe / The water-bearer / Has equal weight on his shoulders. / The lines never do.' [17]

But even more than this, Spicer's location of measure in walking rather than breathing and speaking leads logically to the path-breaking argument put forward over 25 years ago by Ron Silliman, that Spicer is 'the first truly sentence-centered poet in the American language,' for whom 'The sentence became the unit of composition, and the line … a means for locating stress within the sentence.' [18] As Silliman puts it, 'Spicer's use of the line break is semantic, as distinct from prosodic or projective. Spicer, unlike many of his generation, demonstrates little concern with the use of the text to construct a credible facsimile of speech.'[19] This insight seems echoed in Spicer in lines which also use a rhetoric of walking: 'It is not for the ears. Hearing / Merely prevents progress. Take a step back and view the sentence.'[20] Meanwhile, as Silliman notes, 'Spicer's sharpest assault on the indulgences of "Projective verse"'[21] is probably found in his poem 'For Harvey' from *Admonitions*, the same book that ended with the 'Post-Script for Charles Olson'. Here, beyond enjambment, we see that the line is important, not for what it can capture as whole, but for what it can break, down to the poem itself:

> When you break a line nothing
> Becomes better.
> There is no new (unless you are humming
> Old Uncle Tom's Cabin) there is no new
> Measure.
> You breathe the same and Rimbaud

Spacing, pacing, phonemes

> Would never even look at you.
> Break
> Your poem
> Like you would cut a grapefruit
> Make
> It go to sleep for you
> And each line (There is no Pacific Ocean) And make each line
> Cut itself. Like seaweed thrown
> Against the pier.[22]

The disagreement with a certain projectivism could not be clearer, given not only the references to 'measure' and breathing, but also the use of a line that stutters, interrupts, and interferes. As Spicer himself indicates, the lines not only 'locate stress' within the sentence but slice it open, do violence to it. They subject the sentence to a dismemberment which is not compensated by the building blocks of coherent and integral lines.[23] Spicer's opening lines, in their double meaning (itself conveyed by way of line breaks) demonstrate well Spicer's double position: that the shape of a line has no essential meaning or value of the order that projectivism might imply, but that lineation can also be a means to enhance the negativity, the Nothing, that underlies so much of Spicer's poetics. Of course, this doesn't necessarily clarify Spicer's relationship to Olson's own practice. For example, 'The Kingfishers' – whose first line Olson himself cites as an example of projective practice – hardly seems an example of the kind of thing 'For Harvey' might be opposing. The poem begins like this:

> What does not change / is the will to change
>
> He woke, fully clothed, in his bed. He
> remembered only one thing, the birds, how
> when he came in, he had gone around the rooms
> and got them back in their cage, the green one first,
> she with the bad leg, and then the blue,
> the one they had hoped was a male
>
> (*CP*, 86)

If line follows breath, and breath-group follows syntactic unit, as it tends to do in speech, then line should follow syntax, as those above most pointedly do not. Olson affirms that 'breath allows *all* the speech-force of language back in' and that in this way a poem has 'by speech, solidity' yet the breaks in lines two and three above, like so many of Spicer's, militate *against* the sort of solidity that one might imagine Olson to be invoking here (*CPr*, 244). Meanwhile, if Olson cites the first line of the poem as an example of how the typewriter comes to the poet's aid if 'he wishes a pause so light it hardly separates the words, yet does not want a comma – which is an interruption of the meaning rather than the sounding of the line', the effect (willed or not) seems very close to an internal version of the 'semantic line break' Silliman identified with Spicer (*CPr*, 246). Based on acoustic evidence, Michael Davidson reaches conclusions which are already suggested by Olson's handling of the line on the page: 'Readings given by Olson, however, reveal that he by no means intends a one-to-one correspondence between breath and line. Instead, the printed line appears to indicate a general emotional thrust, one to which the written line refers but does not precisely score. The shape and configuration of lines on the page "map", to use Olson's favourite term for notation, the pervasive mood of the poem.'[24] Spicer's refusal to handle the line according to 'heart' and 'breath' emerges then as a possibility which 'Projective Verse' also embeds, despite itself. [25] Heart and breath, for Spicer, themselves derive from where the body walks and who its companions are, as his quarrel with Dorothy Livesay in Vancouver makes clear.

Where Olson is perhaps a more crucial companion for Spicer, however, is in his far less frequently discussed account of the syllable in 'Projective Verse.' In some of the essay's strangest rhetoric, he describes how intensely 'close' the ear is to mind in the following terms:

> it is close, another way: the mind is brother to this sister [the ear] and is, because it is so close, is the drying force, the incest, the sharpener ...
> it is from the union of the mind and the ear that the syllable is born.
> (*CPr*, 242)

What Olson seems to describe here is the uncanny intimacy of sound and thought, which is of course the basis of language. Strikingly, Olson describes this intimacy not in terms of the semantic unit of the word but rather by way of the more fundamental building block that is the syllable. As the mechanics of poetry, specifically rhyme and meter, tend to break words down into their constituent syllables, one might suggest that part of the project of 'Projective Verse' is to lay bare the originary incest at the core of meaning, leaving it in dialectical tension with the line, composed of the molar conglomerates which are words and phrases.[26] Though Olson speaks of the syllable and the line as two halves, much of 'Projective Verse' implies that they are less constituent parts of a coherent whole, but conflicting, contradictory energies. For Olson, the 'joker' is that in composing, one 'lets-it-rip' when it comes to the syllable, while the line requires 'the attention, the control' (*CPr*, 242).

To think of Olson as a poet of the syllable would give us a very different poet from the one we usually receive under his name, yet in 'Projective Verse' he proclaims, 'I am dogmatic, that the head shows in the syllable. The dance of the intellect is there, among them, prose or verse. Consider the best minds you know in this here business: where does the head show, is it not, precise, here, in the swift currents of the syllable?'(*CPr*, 242–3) Olson alludes to Pound here, for whom 'the dance of the intellect among words' defined logopoeia, a kind of poetry which 'employs words not only for their direct meaning, but it takes count in a special way of habits of usage, of the context we *expect* to find with the word, its usual concomitants, of its known acceptances, and of ironical play.'[27] There is much to say about a poetics that would displace this 'dance' onto the level of the syllable itself, not least, that it might imply a poetry closer to Zukofsky's than to what critics tend to look for in Olson. Indeed, a different Olson emerges should one listen carefully to the stakes of such lines from 'The Kingfishers' as, 'with what violence benevolence is bought / what cost in gesture justice brings' or 'what pudor pejorocracy affronts' (*CP*, 92). For our purposes, however, let us note that Spicer is one of the first theoreticians of this sort of poetry, and it leads directly to his last book, *Language*.[28]

As a trained linguist, Spicer was well placed to rigorously theorise what Olson called 'the smallest particle of all, the syllable ... king and pin of versification' (*CPr*, 241). Modern linguistics offers two concepts for categorising what Olson refers to: phoneme and morpheme. If the phoneme names a unit of sound within a particular language (always phenomenally perceptible only within the larger phonetic system of differences underpinning the language in question) and thus corresponds in some ways to Olson's 'smallest particle', the morpheme comes closer to the incestuous union of head and ear. Morphemes, generally understood as the smallest units of meaning in language, can be single words, but also smaller meaning-bearing elements. For example, prefixes and suffixes, which cannot stand alone as individual words (and thus are referred to as 'bound morphemes') are nevertheless not simply syllables or phonemes; they are forms which carry with them distinct properties within a language. So, –ly and –ness, for example, are not simply syllables or sounds, but in English, syllables which imply distinct grammatical forms (hence the name, morpheme). At the same time, as Spicer pointed out in detailed notes on linguistics he kept towards the end of his life, the 'er' in father, for example, is not the same as the 'er' in bigger (the latter, of course, being a morpheme which transforms an adjective into a comparative).[29] Yet a poetry which would pressure these two morphologically distinct instantiations of the same phoneme against each other might very well approximate the Poundian logopoeia, or 'dance of the intellect' that Olson saw as possible on the level of the 'syllable'. And such a poetry is one that Spicer begins to establish in his last book,

Language, of which two of the sections are named 'Morphemics' and 'Phonemics'. The second poem in 'Morphemics' explicitly discusses these sorts of questions: after mentioning the 'loss of innocence' the poem goes on to specify that in that word 'The [inn-] / With its geminated consonant / Is not the inn in which the Christ Child was born' for the very good reason, which Spicer doesn't explicitly mention, that [inn-] is a bound morpheme, and 'inn' is not.[30] Similar interrogations are pursued in 'Phonemics,' while there Spicer emphasises above all a sense of 'voice' not as breath or presence, but as construct or system, that can only convey meaning through the codings or 'routings' that linguistics describes: 'Your voice / consisted of sounds that I had / To route to phonemes, then to bound and free morphemes, then to syntactic structures.'[31] This poem, about the telephone or 'distant sound'[32] as Spicer etymologises, is about language as distinct from breath and timbre in its capacity to produce meaning. Indeed, taken as a whole the section 'Phonemics' thematises distance: 'The unstable / Universe has distance but not much else,'[33] and if the telephonics of language can traverse such distance, it is only because language is separable from the breath of whoever utters it, inscribing distance at the heart of all speech, and therefore of all intimacy: 'Telekinesis / Would not have been possible even if we were sitting at the same table. Long / Distance calls your father, your mother, your friend, your lover. The lips / Are never quite as far away as when you kiss.'[34] This is the well-known deconstructive Spicer (*avant la lettre*), dismantling a projective poetics of presence many derive from Olson. Yet for Spicer, distance is not simply a condition of interpersonal relationships or the field within which language operates; it also comes to name the structuring principles of language itself for him, occupying a role traditionally given to the term 'difference' in Saussurean linguistics: 'Being a [poet] a disyllable in a world of monosyllables. Awakened by the distance between the [o] and the [e].'[35] Olson's 'union of the mind and ear' is at the heart of Spicer's last poetics, only rather than figure this union as the incestuous proximate, this relationship itself becomes the ground for Spicer's inscription of Olsonian SPACE, in a logopoetical play on projective verse. In this exchange – and not without companions – the intellects of Spicer and Olson dance together. It's not coincidental that 'Phonemics' also contains a bitter and winsome elegy for the most logopoetical of jazz musicians, immortalised in a Dantean, Poundian, paradise of phonemes:

> None of you bastards
> Knows how Charlie Parker died. And dances now in some brief
> kingdom (Oz) two phonemes
> That were never paired before in the language.[36]

Notes

1 Jack Spicer, *My Vocabulary Did This To Me: The Collected Poetry of Jack Spicer*, ed. Peter Gizzi and Kevin Killian (Middletown: Wesleyan University Press, 2008), 168, 150.
2 Jack Spicer, *The House that Jack Built: The Collected Lectures of Jack Spicer*, ed. with an Afterword by Peter Gizzi (Hanover: Wesleyan University Press, 1998), 71.
3 Spicer's resentment of Olson's influence is a recurrent element of his biography. For example Lewis Ellingham and Kevin Killian, *Poet, Be Like God: Jack Spicer and the San Francisco Renaissance* (Hanover: Wesleyan University Press, 1998), 66.
4 Ibid., 88.
5 Jack Spicer, 'Letters to Robin Blaser', *Line* 9 (1987), 50.
6 Spicer, *House*, 161.
7 Ibid., 7.
8 Spicer, *Collected Poetry*, 373.
9 Spicer, *House*, 5.
10 Ibid., 9.
11 Ibid.
12 Ibid., 85.
13 Ibid., 111.
14 Ibid., 112.
15 Ibid., 113.
16 Ibid., 113, 115.
17 Spicer, *Collected Poetry*, 379.
18 Ron Silliman, *The New Sentence* (New York: Roof Books, 1987), 164–5.
19 Ibid., 157.
20 Spicer, *Collected Poetry*, 384.
21 Silliman, *The New Sentence*, 150.
22 Spicer, *Collected Poetry*, 160.
23 In this respect Spicer reveals himself as the student of a poet whose relation to his work has been insufficiently studied, Marianne Moore.
24 Michael Davidson, '"By ear, he sd": Audio-Tapes and Contemporary Criticism', *Credences* 1:1 (1981), 105–20, accessed at: http://www.audibleword.org/poetics/Davidson-By_Ear_He_Sd.htm.
25 See Michael Kindellan's 'Poetic Instruction' in this volume for an insightful account of the contradictions and difficulties of the claim in 'Projective Verse' that the typewriter allows the line (and page) to become a 'score' for the human voice.
26 Interestingly, 'In Cold Hell, in Thicket' – a poem written about the same time as 'Projective Verse' – portrays the relationship between the individual and space as brother-sister incest: 'arched, as she is, the sister, / awkward stars drawn for teats to pleasure him, the brother / who lies in stasis under her, at ease as any monarch or / a happy man' (*CP*, 155). These figures can be read as an ambivalent counter-movement to everything in Olson which

aligns with a Spicerian emphasis on the removal of the ego and availability to the Outside, here enclosing forms of exteriority, including erotic, within the space of a narcissistic projection. The conflation of the sexual with primal nourishing as brother-sister glides into son-mother, only reinforces this impression.

27 Ezra Pound, *Literary Essays of Ezra Pound*, ed. T. S. Eliot (New York: New Directions, 1968), 25.

28 It is also worth noting that Robert Duncan stresses Olson's work on the syllable in several important passages in *The H. D. Book*, ed. Michael Boughn and Victor Coleman (Berkeley: University of California Press, 2011), 272–4, 330–2. Duncan at once recognises how Olson's 'incest' can lead to readings where syllabic punning and over-determination open the way to psychoanalytic readings of displacement on a micro-level. Also, in a manner not out of keeping with structuralist analysis, he argues that Olson suggests that the poem's essential energy derives from that part of language which is 'back of the word or phrase' (332). In this way, too, he ties Olson's work on the syllable to a psychoanalytic reading of the poetic impulse that locates it beyond conscious semantic meaning.

29 For an extended analysis of these notes, taken for Spicer's work on a children's literacy project at Stanford and held at the Bancroft Library, University of California, Berkeley, see Daniel Katz, *The Poetry of Jack Spicer* (Edinburgh: Edinburgh University Press, 2013), 142–7.

30 Spicer, *Collected Poetry*, 392.
31 Ibid., 394.
32 Ibid., 395.
33 Ibid., 393.
34 Ibid., 394.
35 Ibid., 402.
36 Ibid., 395.

6

Poetic instruction

Michael Kindellan

Charles Olson is a didactic poet, a 'poet-teacher'.[1] Though, for instance, he wrote several conspicuously 'didactic poems', such as 'Ballad for Americans', the 'ABC' poems, 'Letter for Melville 1951' and 'The Collected Poems Of' to name but a few, the *Maximus* poems undoubtedly constitute the core texts. Not only are these poems intentionally and explicitly didactic – the very first poem presents the eponymous creature Maximus coming to 'tell you' what is what – but they are used by Olson *as* pedagogical texts (*MP*, 5). 'Causal Mythology', a lecture delivered at the University of California (Berkeley) poetry conference in July 1965, amounts mostly to a reading, and sometimes a re-reading for purposes of clarification and explanation, of poems interposed by authorial commentary 'almost like an exegesis of text'.[2] Olson's other recorded talks – such as at Goddard College in April 1962, the Vancouver Poetry Festival in August 1963 and Beloit College in March 1968 – follow similarly constructed programmes. At Goddard, Olson begins by saying:

> that's that problem of reading [...] it's become a performing art and you feel as though you have an audience and you're supposed to do a concert [...] I don't think I believe in verse in this respect at all. In fact, I know I don't.[3]

Olson does not say in which respect he does believe in verse, but the answer is implied evidently enough by the manner in which his talks invariably proceed: readings are a species of lecture wherein the main purpose is not to delight but to instruct. To read a poem, as Olson makes clear at the outset of his Beloit lectures, is to *tell* a kind of truth (communicate information).[4]

In a related manner, the theories defining and defending composition by field Olson presents in 'Projective Verse' (1950) are basically pedagogical allegories. The three central tenets of his poetics outlined near the beginning of that essay – 'a poem is energy transferred'; 'form is never more than an extension of content'; and 'one perception must immediately and directly lead to a further perception' – Olson calls 'dogma', openly and without hesitation (*CPr*, 240). 'Projective verse teaches' a poet 'to register both the acquisitions of his ear *and* the pressures of his breath'; these aspects of methodology are part of Olson's 'lesson' (*CPr*, 241). Pedagogical designs are legible at even the most abstract levels of poetic endeavour. Not that Olson can be said to have *a* poetics *per se*, but looking for something resembling a basic principle underlying substantial portions of his written work, we could do worse than turning to an early definition of *methodology*, 'the word to cover the necessities that the execution of form involves':

> The science of method or arrangement; hence:
> (a) A branch of logic dealing with the principles of procedure
> (b) *Educ.* The science which describes and evaluates arrangements of materials of instruction.[5]

Procedurally, methodology impinges upon the arrangement of material that is ourselves; educationally, Olson contends, method pertains to the arrangement of materials for others. Put otherwise, the description and evaluation of the poet's arrangements – let us call this *prosody* – is for Olson educational. He makes an associated point most emphatically, as far as I know hitherto overlooked in a familiar passage:

> The irony is, from the machine has come one gain not yet sufficiently observed or used, but which leads directly on toward projective verse and its consequences. It is the advantage of the typewriter that, due to its rigidity and its space precisions, it can, for a poet, indicate exactly the breath, the pauses, the suspensions even of syllables, the juxtapositions even of parts of phrases, which he intends. For the first time the poet has the stave and the bar a musician has had. For the first time he can, without the convention of rime and meter, record the listening he has done to his own speech and by that one act indicate how he would want any reader, silently or otherwise, to voice his work.
>
> (*CPr*, 245)

The last sentence identifies two distinct benefits derived from 'the machine' which map fairly neatly onto this dual notion of 'methodology'. Firstly, the typewriter functions as a recorder; secondly, it facilitates an exertion of control over the event of reading. Though Olson does later call the typewriter 'the personal and instantaneous recorder of the poet's work', its real value lies in its ability to guarantee that a reader's voicing of a poem presented to him or her in the projective mode will re-enact perforce the author's formal intentions (readers will, in other words, necessarily follow the same principles of procedure as the poet) (*CPr*, 246). In this sense, the typewriter's capacity for precision is more important to the secondary act of (quasi-supervised) reading than the primary event of drafting a poem in the first instance. It is worth noting, however counterintuitive it sounds, that such precision is not also of a piece with, say, clarity of meaning. Indeed, taken at his word in 'Projective Verse', Olson means such precisions exist to reify the 'speech-force of language' so that it becomes 'the "solid" of verse'; a poem, well-composed in this manner, allows 'these elements' to keep 'their proper *confusions*' (*CPr*, 244). By 'confusions' I think Olson has in mind both *perplexities* or *uncertainties* (the foregoing passage from which I quote discusses the '*secret* of a poem's energy'), and (through an apparent etymology) a *con* + *fusion* of elements, a principle of writing best expressed in the untitled 1962 poem 'tesserae / commissure' (*MP*, 269). Either way, projective verse controls its confusions.

It is widely known that Olson frequently wrote poems on whatever writing surface happened to be at hand, but it is perhaps less widely considered how such conditions actually exerted palpable restrictions upon Olson's professed purpose to write free from pre-established formal constraint, really preferring, as he put in in 'Human Universe', the 'language as the act of the instant' to 'language as the act of thought about the instant' (*CPr*, 155). The reader might decide for themselves whether the back of a chequebook imposes fewer limitations on the possibilities of breath than does a sonnet. In my experience of looking at Olson's manuscripts, the idea that projective verse is somehow more germane to the primary event of writing, which in Olson's case usually consists of holographic inscription, rather than to the secondary event of writing (its instructive arrangement on the typed page) is the exception rather than the rule. Manuscript evidence for 'I have been an ability—a machine', a poem from *The Maximus Poems: Volume Three* written in February 1963, shows that the iconic curl on the penultimate page of the poem is in fact caused by a lack of space rather than its over-plus (*MP*, 498). What looks like an autonomous gesture of formal originality results instead from its opposite. In the universe of managed reception that is projective verse, the intention behind the design of this curl is probably arbitrary and therefore ambiguous. The same cannot be said for the poem's final page whose phallic aspect Rachel Blau DuPlessis notices is a 'generally accepted interpretation'.[6] Not only does the holograph original – incidentally, the *sole* version of the poem Olson produced – make such a reading seem entirely far-fetched because it bears so little in common with its typeset approximation (see Fig. 1), but to construe Olson's prosodic 'arrangement' as iconic in the first place is to misunderstand the purpose of his poetry's visuality: the 'look' of Olson's poems assists their mental and physical re-presentation determined in advance by the exclusive authority of the poet himself (the iconic mapping of 'Letter, 2 May, 1959' is not, I would contend, intended to be 'voiced' at all) (*MP*, 150–6). To write a concrete poem would be to open up a space between what the poem says and what the poem is. That said, 'I have been an ability—a machine' exposes a tension between the flexibility of holograph and the rigidity of typescript. This tension itself indicates an important contradiction at the heart of projective verse theory, pitting what Butterick calls 'the actual condition of a manuscript, what might be called a phenomenology of text' against the circumspect didacticism of carefully mechanised spacing and line breaks. Explaining the editorial methodology behind *Volume Three*, Butterick says 'the important thing was a manuscript had to be retrievable; it had to be legible'. If a document considered for inclusion was handwritten, 'it had to be able to be transcribed with certainty, not only as far as individual words were concerned, but also the poet's intended order of lines and sections'.[7] The poem shortly under inspection defies this certainty.

Furthermore, the pedagogical aspect of Olson's projective poetics, in particular the emphasis upon stringent, self-determined control over the arrangement of his lines, is legible as a kind of prolepsis insofar as it closes down certain forms of critical examination in advance. Put another way, Olson's prosody minimises, albeit subtly, the range of possible 'interpretation' since it already provides the reader with specifications for *how* to read. Olson's proscriptions aim to collapse the difference between acts of reading and the possibly more self-reflective processes of study. In this sense Olson's poems are more like lessons to be learned than artefacts to be queried. A poem, for Olson (as he puts it in 'Human Universe'), is kinetic, and 'there is only one thing you can do about kinetic, re-enact it' (*CPr*, 162). Such an insistence upon compliant reading is expressive of what might be considered Olson's consistent antipathy towards criticism. In a particularly bad-tempered note to Cid Corman he wrote:

> Forget criticism. It's a phoney [...] Good god, merely read what's sd. And don't so fucking much worry abt what you are going to say abt what you have read. it ain't written to be criticized. It is written to be read, that's all. (Doesn't that occur to you? [...] writing critiques, for "Poetry"! Shit. Just shit.[8]

The way Olson wants – and as a consequence does *not* want – to be read is directly connected to the way he sought to work. In an unpublished 1949 prose fragment called 'Credo', Olson outlines 'THE VIA' of his developing poetics: 'to get it all down as it is, with avoidance of (avert avert) all interpretation, explanation, evaluation'.[9] Olson's instructive control over his poems intends beyond readerly voicing. His latent resistance to critical analysis has encouraged critics to read paratextual statements *about* his poetics before reading his poems. (The irony is not lost on me that in identifying this tendency I also *enact* it).

Robert von Hallberg's *The Scholar's Art* is perhaps the best and most important example of a consenting approach to Olson's work; he argues on the first page that 'a study of his poetics should logically precede an examination of his poetry' because Olson's 'poems cannot be adequately appreciated within the terms of recent poetic theory'. He continues: Olson's 'poetry raises questions of poetic theory with unusual directness, and these questions, rather than the poems themselves, are my subject'.[10] Hallberg's point is that Olson's 'expository poems' resist close reading for the relatively simple reason that he rarely goes in for irony or imagery or anything else 'modern critics have argued is essentially poetic'.[11] That Hallberg is right might be proved insofar as something akin to paraphrase has become a critical orthodoxy, routinely manifest as an exposition of what Olson tells us he thinks his poems do, followed by a demonstration thereof. That this is actually the right way to read Olson's work is implied by the poetry itself. Refusing any connection to shared, historically determined 'practice of verse as it has been' by emphasising a new base in personal physiology constitutes a refusal of existing tastes, beliefs and critical assumptions – by 'existing' I mean existing *for Olson*; *his* tastes, beliefs and critical assumptions still radically precede *ours* (CPr, 248). But to take just one relevant example of how Olson's eschewal might appear in practice, Don Byrd has suggested that:

> judged by conventional standards [...] Olson does not have a good ear. The necessities to which he is party seldom allow the resonance and regularity of rhythm [...] The revolution for which Olson claims responsibility does not allow a poet to appropriate a public ideal to shape his own private musings.[12]

As I understand it, Olson's 'bad ear' is a willed form of artistic disinheritance, a rejection of all manner of received forms. The term 'appropriate' is particularly useful because it evokes questions of ownership and permission (read: authority, authorship), perennial issues at stake in Olson's verse both implicitly and overtly.[13] To a certain extent it would be possible to believe Olson actually understood rhythm as a form of *property*: 'there is no way of knowing any rhythym [sic] OTHER THAN YOUR OWN'.[14] Rhythm purely one's own is a disinheritance from tradition full stop. But Olson's maverick 'bad ear' expresses more than a forceful attack on 'convention'; it also agitates against an 'audience' construed as having precisely nothing in common with the poet, neither

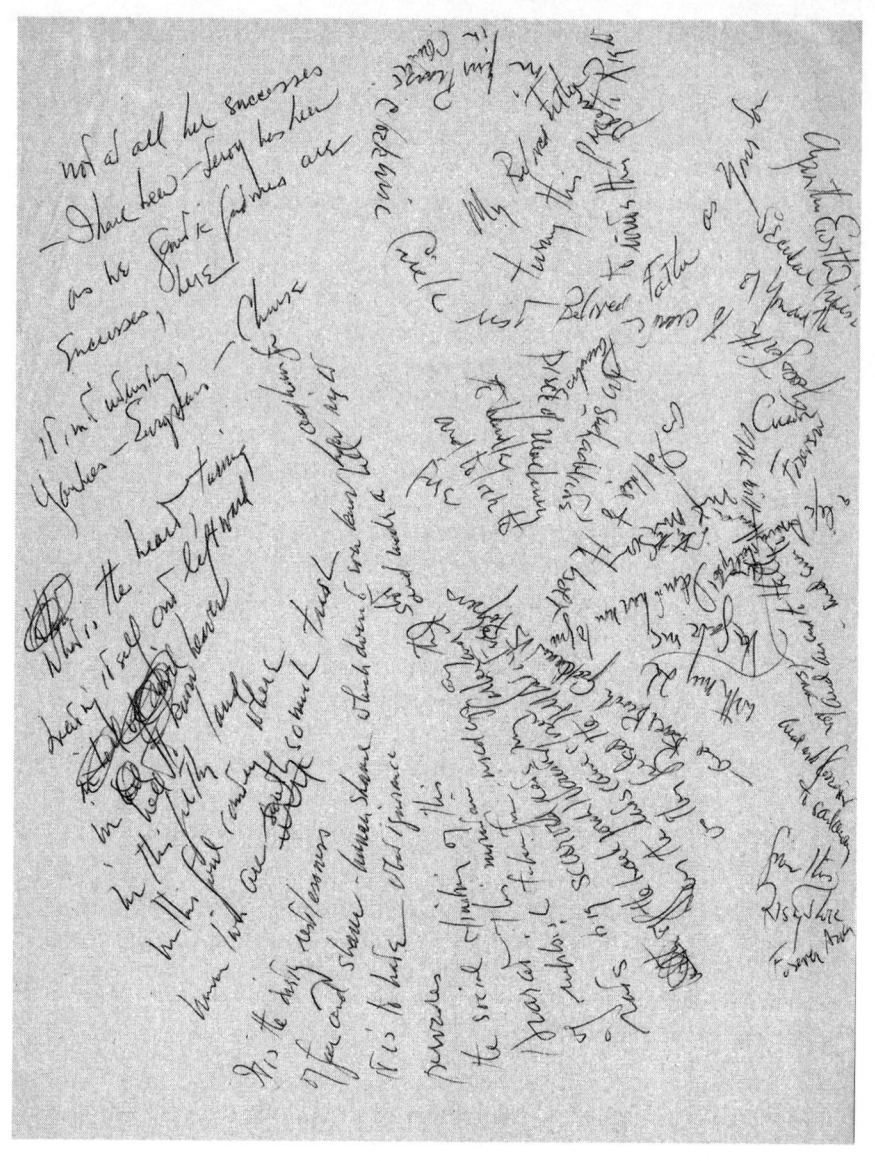

1 Charles Olson, 'I have been an ability 11' (1966).

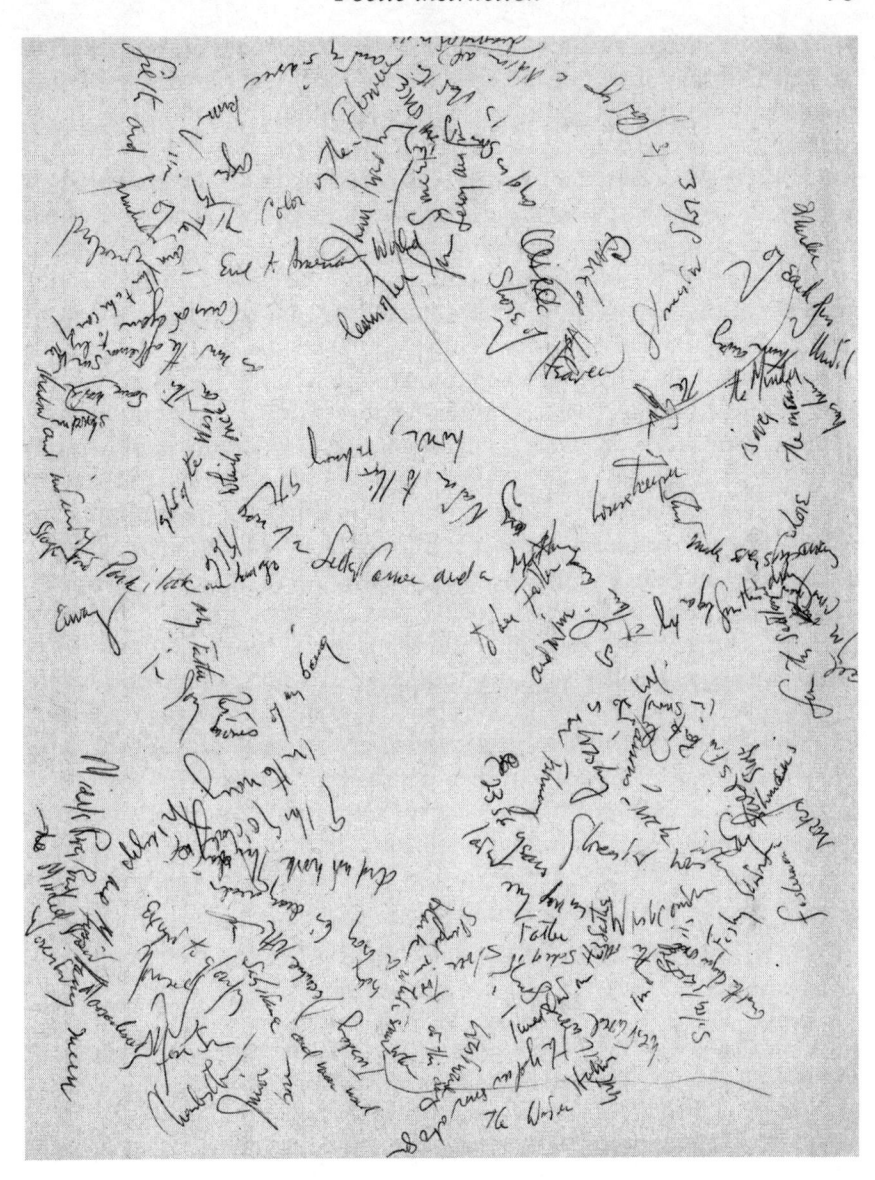

2 Charles Olson, 'I have been an ability 12' (1966).

rhythm nor image, neither knowledge nor construct.[15] Olson said at Goddard he cannot believe in verse as a 'concert', but he knows it needs agreement and anticipates its amenable reception.

Thinking of form as exclusively caused by the poet's own perceptive body making only its 'own special selection from the phenomenal field' (*CPr*, 161) guarantees that, 'to take it at its best, the poem as his most lucid thought (the poem is his thought)'.[16] At some point, arguing for this kind of physiological determination will have to take account of wider biological factors. This intersection, along with, I want to suggest, everything else I have been trying to articulate, comes to a kind of culmination in 'I have been an ability—a machine'. What is particularly awkward about speaking of either this poem or pretty much any other in *Volume Three* is that, because Olson wrote it only in holograph and died before overseeing its type-scripted layout, we as readers are put, entirely inadvertently, right where Olson wants us: we cannot begin to query the instructions latent in the 'prosody of the page space'[17] because Olson didn't authorise them in the usual way, which usually entailed meticulous attention 'to the very spacings and placement on the page', often at the proof and always at the typescript stage.[18] That projective verse reaches such an apotheosis of control precisely where it fails gives us a sense of how robust (plastic? compliant?) a theory it really is. We cannot question this poem's spatial prosody because it is only a first manuscript draft not subjected to the revisions Olson regularly made; this poem is not technically projective verse since it is a manuscript reflecting original intentions that could perforce exclude final decisions.[19] And yet, strangely, the poem seems to know something in advance about its peculiar condition. It begins:

> I have been an ability—a machine—up to
> now. An act of "history", my own, and my father's,
> together, a queer [Gloucester-sense] combination
> of completing something both visionary—or illusions (projection? literally
> lantern-slides, on the sheet, in the front-room Worcester,
> on the wall, and the lantern always getting too hot
> and I burning my fingers—& burning my
> nerves   as in fact John says or Vincent Ferrini they too
> had to deal with their father's existence.   My own
> was so loaded in his favour as in fact so patently
> against my mother that I have been like his stained shingle
> ever since   Or once   or forever   It doesn't matter   The love I learned
> from my father has stood me in good stead
> —home stead—I maintained this "strand" to
> this very day. My father's   And now my own
>
> (*MP*, 495)

The poem's first lines identify and intermix various kinds of authority: literary and parental/biological (it will later speak also of social and administrative authority in terms of betrayals of postal workers' attempts to organise and jingoistic federal immigration policies). Under immediate advisement, however, is a concern that Olson, who has consistently billed himself as an originator of unique forms, might not be very original at all. The poem implies from its beginning a 'self-referentiality': 'it is always in part "about" its own creation, whatever else its content'.[20]

'Machine' stands out in this respect, not least because it is the word Olson uses to refer to the typewriter in the oft-quoted passage from 'Projective Verse', given above. Olson's favoured *Webster's Dictionary* defines 'machine' as an 'assemblage of parts that transmits forces, motion and energy one to another in a predetermined manner', a definition which chimes nicely with the language Olson used in the 'kinetics' section of 'Projective Verse': a machine, like a poet, is a mechanism that transfers energy from A to B, but one that is, importantly, given the questions of hereditary genetics the poem raises, predetermined. Does the holograph inscription point a way beyond the projective? The grammar of the first line implies a kind of synonymy between 'ability' and 'machine', indicating that projective directions of energy are kinds of competence, skill or proficiency; but does 'up to now' connote a sea-change of some order? Certainly the dynamics of projection are of urgent concern. The end of the fourth line – 'illusions (projection? literally' – might in a way constitute doubt or uncertainty over the process as such.

Another term important to Olson's theoretical and didactic speculations is not far to seek: 'history' in line two cannot go unnoticed here, flagged up for our attention by scare quotes. (It will strike the reader that the way I have decided to avoid discussing the form of Olson's language is instead to talk about his language of form). Olson's special understanding of the word 'history' at that time of writing can be traced to a 1961 letter he received from Robert Duncan, in which Duncan splits the word into 'a) histology & b) story'.[21] The consideration of 'histology' could explain why Olson admits in lines nine and ten that his own existence is 'loaded in his [father's] favour' so that he [Olson] is like a 'stained shingle'. A shingle is at once cell-like – insofar as it denotes a small piece of building material – but also denotes rounded detritus or alluvial matter found especially in coastal regions, so that taken together, a sort of horizon of concern begins to emerge. Is Olson, too much like his father, a 'projection? literally', whose genes furnish his person with a real but necessarily abstract kind of definition, an inner design expressed outwardly; or does one's own place and the process of finding it out for one's self articulate an equally real and quite immediate formative pressure upon his development, an exteriority inwardly impressed?

Continuing an inquiry along morphological lines, through a sort of genetic association of its own (etymological cognates within a single line), 'stead' in line fourteen' was originally complemented by the word 'stand'. Olson revised the holograph so that 'stand' became 'strand':

> —home stead—I maintained this ~~"stand"~~ "strand" to
> this very day. My father's   And now my own.[22]

For Olson 'stance' bears a near totemic value, especially in its relation to writing and his 'special view of history'. His 1956 lecture series of that same title is an 'attempt to state a view of reality which yields a stance nexal to the practice of verse, narrative and theatre now',[23] it is the form through which 'space finds its realization as fact'.[24] The second part of 'Projective Verse' is also an attempt define a new 'stance toward reality' (*CPr*, 239). But does swapping 'stand' for 'strand' indicate a significant qualification thereof? It is hard to say. To maintain a strand is to keep lines of historical communication open and active; to maintain a stand is a posture of decided individuation. Archaically, 'strand' means 'beach' or 'seashore' (as it still does in German, of which Olson had a smattering), so in a sense replacing 'stand' with 'strand' emphasises the littoral particulars of his lived experience, while, at the same time, not disqualifying the secondary meaning of inheritance (i.e., genetic line of descent) *per se*. Though 'strand' leaves a sense of lineage and connectedness intact, overwriting 'stand' with 'strand' nevertheless counts as a small but significant act of *dis*inheritance as well: 'strand' comes from a different etymological root than do 'stead' and 'stand'. The former stems from the proto Indo-European root *ster-*, to stretch out; the latter both come from the PIE root *sta-*, to stand. Furthermore, strictly speaking 'strand' refers to that part of the shore lying between tide marks, so that Olson's revision can be understood as significantly widening his poem's scope: suddenly a whole cosmological aspect bursts into view.

Such a cosmological aspect is something that J. H. Prynne has evocatively described, in relation to the first two volumes of *Maximus*, as participating in 'the condition of coast', a 'going out and a coming in', a circular, 'curving rhythm'.[25] It is tempting to think Olson might have known this about his own discovery, and to read the iconic curl on the penultimate page of the poem as an indication thereof. But 'I have been an ability—a machine' in fact threatens to break out of this cycle once and for all – 'to sail away / from this / Rising Shore / Forever Amen' – as well as to break out of the closed hermeneutic circuitry that is projective verse (*MP*, 499). In this poem the real extensions of promising beginnings – the righteous plans of a father seeking to unionise a labour force, or the colonisation of America's first shore – have come to nothing noble. In the case of the former, '"Americans" failed him in his fight and he had to turn to Swedish-American societies for aid'.[26] Regarding the latter, new shore is quickly exposed as cultural violence:

>   my father a Swedish
> wave of
> migration after
> Irish? like Negroes
> now like Leroy and Malcolm
> X the final wave
> of wash upon this
> desperate
> ugly
> cruel
> Land this Nation
> which never
> lets anyone
> come to
> shore
>
> (*MP*, 496–7)

The condition of coast is now a degradation:

>   how many waves
> of hell and death and
> dirt and shit
> meaningless waves of hurt and punished lives shall America
> be nothing but the story of
> not at all her successes
> —I have been—Leroy has been
> as we genetic failures are
> successes, here
>
> (*MP*, 498)

What Prynne very beautifully describes as 'home' is for Olson in this poem at least, itself corrupted, a failure to heed originally proscribed intentions.[27] At the reiteration of 'I have been' on the poem's fourth page the poem moves increasingly towards a state of indeterminacy.

As Butterick describes it in the introduction to his *Guide*, the holograph manuscript runs for several pages in a fairly clear manner only to suddenly enter 'a series of unreproducible and increasingly illegible spirals' (see Fig. 2). The configuration on the final page of the poem – beginning 'My beloved Father' – is only 'an approximation', after which point 'the helixes become increasingly personal and confused—hopeless snarls on the page' (*GMP*, liii). These confusions, however, are not the 'proper' – read: genuine, authorised – confusions of projective verse. As such, these holograph drafts show that during the process of their inscription, Olson's poem transitions from publicly-intended poetic artefact to another kind of writing. The point at which this transition is complete comes at the very juncture where the editors could no longer ascertain *how* to read the poem because they were left to make the most basic decisions for themselves: which way is up; where to begin. In this sense, the open field of projective verse totally excludes a 'rejection of closure', to borrow Lyn Hejinian's phrase. Olson may have objected to the poet's performing his poems, but projective verse continues to presuppose that a reading audience cannot have similar objections, with the proviso that such performance is not a fulfilment or completion of the work but its re-presentation. When presenting his poems in public – giving either lectures indistinguishable from readings or readings indistinguishable from lectures – the audience is construed as witness to something akin to Mill's notion of 'eloquence'.[28] Olson's poems are indeed, in this sense, not lyric. They want to be *listened* to: 'No, I wanna talk. I mean, you want to listen to a poet? I mean, you know, a poet, when he's alive, whether he talks or reads you his poems is the same thing. Dig that! [APPLAUSE]' (*MUTH*, 150). By extension, projective verse is not meant to be *overheard*. The peculiarity of his poetry, like Mill's sense of eloquence, lacks 'the poet's utter unconsciousness of a listener'; rather, it actively 'court[s] their sympathy', their consensus.[29] To read the indeterminately arranged verses that exist beyond the ellipses that conclude the published version of 'I have been an ability—a machine' would be to read without the permission and authorisation latent in the strict formal arrangement that is projective verse. Put otherwise, it would be to act without Olson's instructions. This would be tantamount to making poetry *with* Olson, for whom 'no poet wants any hearer to write a poem'.[30] Reading Olson's work like this, Butterick knew, is a privilege we may not have. It is hard not to read this poem as somehow dramatizing, if not the breakdown of projective verse, then at least the failures of its rigid prohibitions.

Notes

1 Ryan Dobran, 'Introduction', *Glossator* 2 (2010), 5.
2 Charles Olson, *Causal Mythology*, ed. Donald Allen (San Francisco: Four Seasons, 1969), 4. 'Almost' is a generous modifier if Olson means something other than his poems are inherently self-explanatory.

3 Charles Olson, 'At Goddard College', http://writing.upenn.edu/pennsound/x/Olson.php, accessed 16 September 2012. See also Charles Olson, 'At Goddard College' in *Muthologos: Lectures and Interviews*, ed. Ralph Maud (*MUTH*, 14). My transcription disputes that of this edition. I think Olson says 'problem of reading' whereas it prints 'problem of being'.
4 Charles Olson, 'At Beloit College', http://writing.upenn.edu/pennsound/x/Olson.php, accessed 17 September 2012. See also: Charles Olson, 'Poetry and Truth' (*MUTH*, 240).
5 Charles Olson, '13 June 1952', *Letters for Origin*, ed. Albert Glover (London: Cape Goliard, 1969), 105.
6 Rachel Blau DuPlessis, *Purple Passages: Pound, Eliot, Zukofsky, Olson, Creeley, and the Ends of Patriarchal Poetry* (Iowa City: University of Iowa Press, 2012), 129.
7 George F. Butterick, *Editing The Maximus Poems: Supplementary Notes* (Storrs: University of Connecticut Library, 1983), ix.
8 Olson, '23 November 1953', *Letters for Origin*, 130–1.
9 Charles Olson, 'Credo', typewritten manuscripts, c. May–December 1949, Box 29, Folder 1519, Charles Olson Research Collection. Archives and Special Collections at the Thomas J. Dodd Research Center, University of Connecticut Libraries. I am grateful to the Estate of Charles Olson and the University of Connecticut Libraries for their kind permission to reproduce archival material herein.
10 Robert von Hallberg, *Charles Olson: The Scholar's Art* (Cambridge: Harvard University Press, 1978), 1, 2.
11 Ibid., 2.
12 Don Byrd, 'The Possibility of Measure in *Maximus*', *boundary 2* 2:1/2 (Autumn 1973–Winter 1974), 40.
13 For a fascinating and rather more patient reading of 'ownership' see Stephen Thomson, 'Craft: Boats and Making in Olson's *Maximus Poems*', *Edinburgh Review* 114 (2004).
14 Olson, '5 October 1951', *Letters for Origin*, 83.
15 See Olson, '* Added to' (*MP*, 584) and 'ABCs (2)' (*CP*, 173).
16 Charles Olson, 'As Aimed As His poem Is', typewritten manuscript, 1956, Box 29, Folder 1492, Charles Olson Research Collection. Archives and Special Collections at the Thomas J. Dodd Research Center, University of Connecticut Libraries. There is no way to make Olson's grammar normative here without rewriting the sentence. Olson reiterates this claim at the beginning of his first Beloit lecture.
17 Eleanor Berry, 'The Emergence of Charles Olson Prosody of the Page Space', *Journal of English Linguistics* 31:1 (March 2002).
18 Butterick, *Editing The Maximus Poems*, vii.
19 Ibid.
20 Charles Stein, *The Secret of the Black Chrysanthemum* (Barrytown: Station Hill, 1979), 30.
21 Charles Olson, 'On "History"', *Olson* 4 (Fall 1975), 41.
22 Butterick, *Editing The Maximus Poems*, 55.

23 Charles Olson, *The Special View of History*, ed. Ann Charters (Berkeley: Oyez, 1970), 13.
24 Don Byrd, *Charles Olson's Maximus* (Urbana: University of Illinois Press, 1980), 22.
25 J. H. Prynne, 'On *Maximus IV, V, VI*', *Minutes of the Charles Olson Society* 28 (April 1999), 7.
26 Charles Olson, 'The Post Office' (*CPr*, 220). With the lines beginning 'to sail away' Olson probably has in mind a childhood trip with his father Karl to Plymouth, where they toured a replica Mayflower. This trip also marked the beginning of Olson's father's protracted fight against union authorities, which eventually killed him (he suffered a stroke).
27 Prynne, 'On *Maximus*', 13.
28 John Stuart Mill, 'Thoughts on Poetry and its Varieties', *Dissertations and Discussions*, Vol. 1 (London: Longmans, 1867), 71.
29 Ibid.
30 Olson, *Letters for Origin*, 103.

7

Reading Blackburn reading Olson: Paul Blackburn reads Olson's 'Maximus, to Gloucester: Letter 15'

Simon Smith

On 2 January 1953 Paul Blackburn dispatched a letter to Charles Olson inviting a contribution from the poet to a recording for an LP Blackburn was editing for Caedmon records at the end of the year: '[I] want you to have 15 minutes or better on it .... Will you send me – quickly – something new you would like to read aloud'.[1] It appears to be a New Year's resolution: the letter is zippy, unusually for Blackburn it's handwritten, and full of suggestions, 'one or two longish things would be best'.[2] There is other news: Blackburn has been asked to teach creative writing at Black Mountain College by Robert Creeley; Blackburn can get the people at Caedmon to come to Olson to do the recording; he's trying to complete a review for the *New Mexico Review*. Details crowd in in the order of the moment, on the fly, there is a sense of urgency, of the necessity to get things done – 'do answer this soon – need all assistance I can get to finish things up with any show of adequacy'.[3]

What follows through 1953 is an exchange of letters and poems between Olson and Blackburn, and a (minor) literary spat, which reveals how Blackburn reads Olson, and Olson reads Blackburn. There are other revealing details among the artefacts (archived at the Special Collections Department at University of Connecticut, Storrs and the Mandeville Special Collections Library at the University of California, San Diego), which weren't exchanged, and which in some cases remained unpublished, showing how both poets were engaged with the challenges set, right through the 1950s.

The archaeology of the surviving materials is this:

September 1950: Blackburn's first reading of 'In Cold Hell, in Thicket';

8 December 1950: Blackburn requests Olson might want to contribute to a 'junket' of poetry manuscripts and correspondence he is planning to circulate amongst like-minded poets, and mentions his first (critical) reading of 'In Cold Hell, in Thicket'.

2 January 1953: Blackburn requests a contribution from Olson to the Caedmon LP.

9 January 1953: Blackburn expresses reservations about 'The Kingfishers' from an earlier reading of the poem, and requests typed copies of that piece and 'In Cold Hell, in Thicket'.

17 January 1953: Olson sends the manuscript of 'The Kingfishers' and 'In Cold Hell, in Thicket'.

15 February 1953: Blackburn rejects 'In Cold Hell, in Thicket' and sends 'The Kingfishers' on to Caedmon. He offers to mail back the manuscript of 'In Cold Hell, in Thicket' but would like to keep it if possible.

4 May 1953: Olson writes to Blackburn on Blackburn's remarks that Olson is 'sounding' like Pound.

8 May 1953: Olson writes 'Maximus, to Gloucester: Letter 15' – not sent to Blackburn. The same day Olson writes a letter to Blackburn regarding Blackburn's poetry, and informs him he has written a new Maximus poem.

19 May 1953: Blackburn sends a letter to say that he now 'gets' 'In Cold Hell, in Thicket,' and mails him the poem 'Letter to O'.[4]

[Undated, and later sent at an unspecified date]: Olson's 'Maximus Letter #27'.

28 December 1958: Olson returns to his correspondence with Blackburn, and their discussions of 1953.

15 January 1962: Olson writes 'A Later Note on / Letter #15' (*MP*, 249).

What emerges from looking over the correspondence as a whole, and placing the dates of composition and publication of the essays and poems beside these unpublished letters, is not only how the correspondence interweaves with the poems, essays and publications by both writers – not simply in chronological ordering, or the housekeeping practices of the two poets – but what emerges through the interchanges is how the correspondence starts to shape, inform and then articulate itself into the poems and essays. In short, what is revealed is how the exchange comes to challenge and figure in both poets' literary practice. What Blackburn and Olson seem to want from their letters is far more than straightforward communication, the exchange of mundane facts, or the usual fare of literary back-biting. There is a necessity to the engagements that these two poets are asking of one another, in a kind of honesty and openness, alongside some hard-headed questioning. The tone of the correspondence is straight-talking and earnest, not sycophantic or one-sided – it's not a case of Olson, the older poet, talking down to the younger one. Both poets want to air ideas of poetry and poetics on an equal footing with a view to forging a method of getting new poems done. There is a sense in which Olson and Blackburn need answers from one another, and an excitement and expectation at the prospect of taking poetry into the future, almost in a kind of choreography.

Edith Jarolim's note to 'Letter to O' is understandably confined to the immediate circumstances of context for that poem's composition.[5] What it therefore misses is the overview of the engagement which Blackburn and Olson are already absorbed in. Blackburn has been working with Olson's poems and essays since at least 1950. The whole point of the letter of 8 December 1950 is to involve Olson in a 'circulation of ideas'. Blackburn had most likely come across the 'Projective Verse' essay, and is viewing Olson as a new and important poet to include in the conversation:

> Dear Olson: –
>
> There's a scheme afoot we would like you to come in on.
>
> A circular packet of mss. oddments by young writers, experiments which editors might dodge, poems with tough technical problems etc. Anything with new ideas or methods which might not otherwise have circulation, will have circulation, readers, critics.
>
> Circulation of ideas without help from the mags.
>
> Independent.[6]

Note the sense of urgency; the whole tone of the project is subversive, like some kind of secret, dangerous mission to upend poetry out of its present, comfortable order. Changes are afoot.

Blackburn then goes on to say this about 'In Cold Hell, in Thicket,' and situate his own poetry practice in relation to it:

> RE: your Cold Hell &ct, my critical notings, if you are collecting them, went like this:
>
>> real dearth of concrete imagery; main techniques rhetorical, carrying the weight of the ideas and the length; possibly too long for these techniques.
>
> This is aside from the good things, esp. your handling of rhythms, your strong point, I think.
>
> I have a conditioned taste ... working at present on Provencal translations ... Keeps my stuff, my own stuff short. For the last year scrounging around for technical ability to carry a long poem; i.e. a narrative style which will move ... Hence I think all long poems should be essentially narrative in material if not in style. An extended series of lyrics with a central idea, theme, or system carrying the weight can work. Only I think a plot or even a simple story line does it better.[7]

Aside from the last sentence of that paragraph, Blackburn could be describing the method of the Maximus poems, in his kind of breathy shorthand. Blackburn wants Olson 'in' on the project but doesn't want one of Olson's strongest poems, not because it's not good enough, but because it doesn't fit his purpose or projection into the field of energy ahead. It's as though he is raising the bar further: he sees Olson's work to date as potential, more than achievement. This is the trajectory of the correspondence, to challenge and question rather than accept; to *push*, to *project* the poetry into another place or field, so that we find ourselves standing, startled, in a place we weren't expecting, not allowed to pause, but to press on, restless, without a moment to reflect. Blackburn rejects 'In Cold Hell, in Thicket' because of his own interests in finding a method for the new long poem. The problem is that this poem of Olson's is not the answer. The question becomes for Blackburn how to 'extend' the short poem into the breath or field of the long poem. Basically, he has no *use* for 'In Cold Hell, in Thicket'; at least only in so far as he positions the poem to pitch against and find purchase for his own poetry, and in the projection of a new poetics. As Olson opens the 'Projective Verse' essay: 'Verse now, 1950, if it is to go ahead, if it is to be of *essential* use, must, I take it, catch up and put into itself certain laws and possibilities of the breath, of breathing of the man who writes as well as of his listenings' (CPr, 239). More fundamentally, however, the act of letter writing becomes an act, a form of writing with an '*essential* use', a way of forming a new poetic, as an activity in itself, through the dialogue of criticism, a form of the projective through practice in a process akin to the poem. Letter and poem become different paths to the same place, and in this exchange of correspondence between Olson and Blackburn what Olson applies to the poem applies to the letter also: 'A poem is energy transferred from where the poet got it (he will have several causations), by way of the poem itself to, all the way over to, the reader' (CPr, 240). The key is in the parenthesis: 'he will have several causations'. Letter writing, for Olson and Blackburn, is a projective act in the Olsonian sense; letter writing is one of those causations.

The 'junket' scheme is obviously one which fails, or is short-lived, and Blackburn's later approach to involve Olson in the Caedmon recordings is a fresh attempt to keep the conversation with Olson going. What Blackburn wants (it seems), as does Olson, is to keep in dialogue, to continue the engagement in order to shape and progress the writing of poems and the thinking out loud of a new poetic. Blackburn is quick to follow up his handwritten, hasty letter of 2 January 1953 with a dense missive on 9 January.[8] After some preliminaries on his possible trip to Black Mountain, and after lamenting the state of the electricity supply to his apartment, he gets down to business. What Blackburn requests seems odd at first: a typescript of 'The Kingfishers' and 'In Cold Hell, in Thicket'. It is likely he would have seen at least a published version of 'The Kingfishers' already. In this letter Blackburn reports Robert

Creeley as saying that Olson reads these two poems best, and Blackburn makes clear his view of the earlier poem:

> I read the former long long time ago, still half-educated etc. 1st I saw of yours, didn't like it, thot it too fragmented etc. Can't for the life of me remember it all now, which makes me think the reading too peremptory that first time. So w o u l d l i k e you to
>
> type
>
> copies of both Kingfishers and In Cold Hell. To see. D o y o u k n o w t h e r e a d i n g t i m e o f b o t h o f t h e s e? [9]

This section of the letter is composed by field, with a deliberate layout and spacing for the typography. Blackburn has to see (and more importantly hear) how the poems are laid out and sounded out for performance, scored; this will determine how he will decide whether to include them in the project or not. The emphasis is on length and duration; Blackburn sees Olson as one of the contemporary poets who is most interesting and most able to create work which will succeed in these terms: 'why I want something from you: (1) to give your voice as total range as is possible on such a reading'.[10] The emphasis is on the process of reading aloud. Blackburn needs to see how these poems work as notation for the projective 'act,' so he can clarify to himself how the visual 'field' of the page 'translates' or transposes the text into the aural performance.

By the letter of 15 February Blackburn has made his decision: 'well, I've turned in the Kingfishers to Caedmon. Shall I send you back I C Hell? If you don't need it, I'd like to have it around'.[11] The rest of the letter contains news of Black Mountain (he won't be going, after all), some talk of Jung, and then Blackburn returns to 'In Cold Hell, in Thicket': 'Still, years after that first reading, I dig ICHell as too fragmented a piece, tho it reads more of a piece than the first time certainly. Have made some progress myself in that time'.[12] The important thing here is that Blackburn wants to continue his engagement with Olson's work, even after rejecting it, and there will be a continuing need for Blackburn to revisit and re-read 'In Cold Hell, in Thicket'. His own reading of this poem will enable him to make 'some progress myself,' in his own writing.[13] It appears Blackburn's own poetry and poetic, at this stage, progress through their relationship to reading Olson's work, in a kind of dialogue – a form of attempting to answer Olson's challenges. Through this, the process of his own reading of 'In Cold Hell, in Thicket,' Blackburn recognises this will be a shifting process over time, and across the field of space.

A spat is in full swing by the time of Olson's 4 May letter, in which he writes: 'I just don't know abt this biz of "sounding" like EP. And it strikes me funny, just when I have sent off (last week) the mss of 1–10

108 Section II: Poetics

of the Max Poems' (SL, 190–1). Despite all of Olson's rationalisations it does seem as though Blackburn has hit a nerve:

> Any present signs of derivation (such as I seem charged with) only look so, because the present is such a narrow eye view.
> (I say it that way, not out of any pinch, simply, that how it comes out, seems to me so much the way i am (((yr own analysis of how i do it))) ... that I'm no longer bugged by coincidental resemblance
>
> (SL, 191)

This exchange seems to be a major point of interest in the correspondence, but taken in full context there are other features just as important. The apparent closeness of Olson to Pound is only one topographical outcrop, sharpening Olson's sense of the place of his own work in the literary landscape. What follows, however, reveals how the correspondence starts to infiltrate and shape both writers' poetry and poetics.

The letter of 8 May, rather than showing distance between Olson and Blackburn in the light of Blackburn's accusations about the possible influence of Pound on Olson, actually reveals Olson trying to engage with Blackburn more closely. He identifies Blackburn's mother, Frances Frost, as someone he knew (though Olson is actually thinking of Robert Frost's daughter, and no relation); and talks through some of Blackburn's poems, which have just appeared in the magazine *Artisan* 2, with sensitivity and approval: 'But it is a pleasure to say them to you – (woke up fr a nightmare last night, with you on my mind ... a pleasure I promised myself I'd have today, and am having, in stead of playing, as I might be, baseball'.[14] Towards the end of the letter Olson gets to what he really wants to say:

> ((Maybe I wanted to write to you simply that i suppressed to you (instead, made another Max Letter out of it) a 2nd PS to that letter to you, in which i went for a ride on how Pullman cars are the winners, fr my point of view of the practice of "poetry" – that how you had it, "digest, first", is, to me, like their celebration of, goods, things already done offered, with words, for buyers.[15]

What Blackburn has said comes to weigh on Olson's mind – he seems almost haunted by Blackburn's take on his poetry and poetics. Olson is so fully engaged with the aesthetic consequences of Blackburn's remarks, rather than any personal quarrel, that he writes, 'Maximus, to Gloucester: Letter 15', a poem which appears to be in dialogue with their exchange of letters (MP, 71–5). The level of discourse in the personal letter starts to lap at and tip over into the poetry of the Maximus sequence. The shaping of their correspondence actually infiltrates the poem, with their argument or disagreement just beyond its frame:

He sd, "You go all around the subject." And I sd, "I didn't know it was a subject." He sd, "You twist" and I sd, "I do." He said other things. And I didn't say anything.

> Nor do I know
> that this is a rail
> on which all (or any)
> will ride (as, by Pullman
> > that sense the ads are right abt, that you are
> > taken care of, you do
> > not sleep, you are
> > jolted
>
> > And if you take a compartment,
> > the whole damned family . . .
>
> I sd, "Rhapsodia . . .

(MP, 72)

At this very point the correspondence presses in directly, so the poem itself becomes a kind of second 'PS', taking a secondary position to the letter, as these lines are a re-versioning of lines from the 'PS' to the 4 May letter:

> Not ... that i think i have proved ... that one can take language ... and make it a rail on which anyone else will ride (as in a Pullman, with that sense the advertisements are right about, that, you are being taken care of, in fact, if you take a compartment, your whole damn family, especially, the kids!)

(SL, 193)

And, tellingly:

> Why you are right it all is meant to be heard ... language is sound, not eyes, ears are what it is
> > rhapsodia: to bang on the ears of sd listener

(SL, 194)

These lines point to material (in the letters) beyond the poem, which might counter or at least threaten the very existence of that aesthetic category of 'the poem'. The 'PS' to this letter begins to demand more a status of equivalence than afterthought; and this appendix becomes a further manifestation of the projective.

Equally important and pressing is the fact that their correspondence starts to undermine Olson's grounding of the sequence in documentation too. The poem begins with corrections to the eyewitness account of the Eppie Sawyer:

> It goes to show you. It was not the "Eppie Sawyer." It was the ship "Putnam." It wasn't Christmas morning, it was Christmas night .... In

other words it was the beacon at Gloucester, not the light on Baker's Island – there was no light on Eastern Point until 1831.

(*MP*, 71)

The immediacy of their correspondence is beginning to alter the aesthetic of the Maximus sequence itself; indeed, their interchange vies for authoritative equivalence with the historical documentation that Olson is accumulating for the Maximus poems. This seems a crucial point, that beyond the obvious documentary method Olson is building through the sequence in general, as evidenced in particular in 'Letter 15', documentary as a form of immediate interaction with other poets is also taking place. In this sense, Olson is building an archive upon an archive, and, more fundamentally, he appears to be recording polis itself, the conversation among equals which the whole project of Maximus celebrates, yearns for, and in this particular instance has achieved, through textual enactments and interactions between poems and letters. Not only is the course of Maximus altered by the factual data Olson is accumulating in the opening prose section of 'Letter 15,' but also in his immediate interaction with Blackburn, documented here as dialogue in the text, to transform the course and aesthetic field of *The Maximus Poems*.

On 19 May 1953 Blackburn dispatches another densely textured letter ontaining some good news: 'quarrel's done, at lunch today ... I turned to IN COLD HELL .... Caught. Absolutely in it all the way'.[16] Here, Blackburn is attempting to connect with Olson at a personal level and engage with the Maximus project as a whole: 'Gloucester I do not know, tho years back, a great or great-great grandfather on my father's side whaled out there'.[17] Which prompts a direct response from Olson in the shape of 'Maximus Letter #27,' not included in the main Maximus sequence (and not to be confused with 'Maximus to Gloucester, Letter 27 [withheld]'). This poem was only published later, in the *Olson* journal in the 1970s, well after both poets' death, and yet is very revealing about the shaping of the relationship between Blackburn and Olson, and how Olson starts to integrate events from Blackburn's family history into his own project and documentation process: 'Blackburn / able to talk about a great grandfather / whaled out of Gloucester'. This is a poem written with some affection, with a pencilled note in the manuscript: 'PB: thanx! And tho you don't have the context (26 preceding, + some after), I am under the illusion this one stands by itself'.[18] This poem is more than just an affectionate squib; it is, as it were, a further footnote, with Olson not quite nesting this text in the context of the main Maximus sequence, though pointing an alternative possible route for Maximus.

Much later, in 1958, Blackburn is poetry editor at *The Nation* and contacts Olson again. Here, in the opening gambit of his reply of 28

December 1958, Olson tellingly recalls their conversations. Again, the most important information appears after the opening of parenthesis, as an aside to the main point:

> I am always plagued by that statement of yrs so many years ago, that I don't "think" ... not plagued so much as, then, bugged, and since, moved by it every time so many times.
>
> Did you know, e.g., that one of the Maxies (the one abt Smith previously, & Pullman cars ... turned all on you? Probably you do, for one section includes direct quotes from you?
>
> Anyway, yr thought there, that I didn't, was about the other valuable 'thought' ... TO which I answered, and still have no answer to yr conundrum!, each poem etc.[19]

This is a most revealing passage. Blackburn is still on Olson's mind (note the use of that word 'bugged,' imported from the letter of the 4 May 1953) (*SL*, 191). If anything the effects of Blackburn's comments are even more important to Olson than any 'advice' he might be offering Blackburn. The way the verbs shift – 'plagued' to 'bugged' and then the emphatic 'moved' – show him declaring the importance of Blackburn's feedback to the shaping and development of his thinking and poetic practice over the past five years. He is 'moved' – the writing of Maximus has changed fundamentally, its aesthetic DNA altered: 'not plagued so much as, then, bugged, and *since, moved by it every time so many times*' (my italics). So new poems and a further developed and developing poetics emerge from this dynamic of the correspondence.

Much later, in 1968, Paul Blackburn replied to an enquiry from George Butterick confirming much of the factual information mapped out above, and characterised the exchanges between the two poets:

> On first coming to Charles' work, of course I found it difficult and wanted to question the basis of his constructions, my own work being in a much more formative stage at that point, so that what comes out as crit/ in the conversational form, and a lovely redaction it is, was more a probe imbedded in whole paragraphs of talk about the texts themselves, or the ways to come at a poem. The following lines re: the poem as sleeping car which wraps you in cellophane and takes you there, i.e., you do not TRAVEL that way, came also out of that correspondence.[20]

In the end, however, it is Olson who traces how far he has shifted his practice and poetics in 'A Later Note on Letter #15' of 1962. As important as Whitehead's philosophy in this poem, or Olson's own reflections on Herodotus, are his exchanges with other contemporary poets, such as Creeley and Duncan, of course, but also Paul Blackburn; exchanges which sit in the margins of the poems, modifying Olson's poetics and

112 Section II: Poetics

The Maximus Poems themselves, helping him reach the point where the poem faces forward into the provisional, into contingency and fluidity, the fundamental state of poetry, where, 'the poetics of such a situation / are yet to be found out' (*MP*, 249).

Notes

1 Paul Blackburn, Letter to Charles Olson, 2 January 1953, Charles Olson Research Collection, Archives and Special Collections at the Thomas J. Dodd Research Center, University of Connecticut, Storrs.
2 Ibid.
3 Ibid.
4 According to Edith Jarolim's note to the poem in Paul Blackburn, *The Parallel Voyages*, intro. Clayton Eshleman, ed. Edith Jarolim, illus. Ellen McMahon (Tucson, Arizona: SUN-gemini Press, 1987), 116–17.
5 Blackburn, *The Parallel Voyages*, 116–17.
6 Paul Blackburn, Letter to Charles Olson, 8 December 1950. Charles Olson Research Collection, Archives and Special Collections at the Thomas J. Dodd Research Center, University of Connecticut, Storrs.
7 Ibid.
8 Paul Blackburn, Letter to Charles Olson, 9 January 1953. Charles Olson Research Collection, Archives and Special Collections at the Thomas J. Dodd Research Center, University of Connecticut, Storrs.
9 Ibid.
10 Ibid.
11 Paul Blackburn, Letter to Charles Olson, 15 February 1953. Charles Olson Research Collection, Archives and Special Collections at the Thomas J. Dodd Research Center, University of Connecticut, Storrs.
12 Ibid.
13 Ibid.
14 Charles Olson, Letter to Paul Blackburn, 8 May 1953 [?]. Paul Blackburn Papers. MSS 4. Mandeville Special Collections, University of California San Diego Library.
15 Ibid.
16 Paul Blackburn, Letter to Charles Olson, 19 May 1953. Charles Olson Research Collection, Archives and Special Collections at the Thomas J. Dodd Research Center, University of Connecticut, Storrs.
17 Ibid.
18 Charles Olson, 'Poem to Paul Blackburn', 1953? Paul Blackburn Papers, MSS 4, Mandeville Special Collections, UC San Diego Library.
19 Charles Olson, Letter to Paul Blackburn, 28 December 1958. Paul Blackburn Papers, MSS 4, Mandeville Special Collections, UC San Diego Library.
20 Paul Blackburn, Letter to George Butterick, 12 February 1968. Charles Olson Research Collection, Archives and Special Collections at the Thomas J. Dodd Research Center, University of Connecticut, Storrs.

8

From Weymouth back: Olson's British contacts, travels and legacy

Gavin Selerie

Given his roots on the eastern seaboard it was natural that Olson should reach over the Atlantic, as effected in the central part of *Call Me Ishmael*, where the Elizabethan dimension of *Moby-Dick* is traced via annotations to Melville's copy of Shakespeare, loaned by the author's granddaughter in 1933–4.[1] In the essay 'Projective Verse', Olson says, 'I return you now to London, to beginnings, to the syllable', before quoting Orsino's tribute to the power of music (and related poetic breath) from *Twelfth Night* (CPr, 245). Olson wrote an unpublished book on Shakespeare and he shared with Melville a fascination with the rhythms of early modern English and the literature that bears upon the European settlement of North America.[2]

In 1953 Olson was contacted by the English scholar Ronald Mason, who had appreciated Olson's piece 'The Materials and Weights of Herman Melville' in the *New Republic*.[3] A lively correspondence followed, in which Olson set out his quarrel with traditional syntax and emphasised the need to retain the pressure of the instant in poetry.[4] He recalled his visit to England as a student in 1928 and regretted that he could not take up an invitation to visit Mason's seventeenth-century house at present.

A more crucial acquaintance was Gael Turnbull of Migrant Books, who distributed Jargon Society publications in the UK from late 1956 onwards. These included two early sections of *Maximus*. Turnbull wrote to Olson in January 1956, wanting to publish the 'O'Ryan' sequence as a broadside.[5] The link here was Robert Duncan. In a second letter Turnbull describes how he 'read MAXIMUS to the assembled faithful at G. S. Fraser's place [in Chelsea], and also the Mexico one, THIS.' He had assumed 'that no one listens anyway', but later two people said that they had not understood what Olson was writing until they heard Turnbull read the work. This leads Turnbull to remark: 'Your poems DO lend themselves to be listened to as few poems can be heard.'[6] The encounter left its mark. While Turnbull's work does not, on the whole, leap around the page, it has considerable oral force, with a measure reflective of the event or occasion rather than any absolute scheme.

Procedures associated with Black Mountain poets were beginning to filter through elsewhere in Britain. Elaine Feinstein founded the Cambridge magazine *Prospect* in order to introduce the work of Olson and others to British readers.[7] J. H. Prynne, the third editor of *Prospect*, contacted Olson in November 1961, reporting the sense of release he had found in the latter's work and informing him about a new dictionary of roots – a resource proposed in the 'Letter to Elaine Feinstein' (*CPr*, 250).[8] Prynne contrasts 'the expansiveness, the new air' which he experienced the year before at Harvard with English 'provincial squeamishness' and 'the malicious blindness of ... Bloomsbury'. Reading Olson's 'various things', he says, 'was like reading for the first time the back of my own hand.' A poem such as 'In Cold Hell, in Thicket' shows how features of perception and imagination turn to 'fill out their necessary & musical spaces'. He speaks of learning 'the reach of one's own limbs and eyes, the outward pressure of real concern' and of 'the revelation of others [which] can ... further the whole endeavour, by setting its own fierce limits.' He goes on:

> Pokorny's [dictionary] sits on my shelf like a bomb, ready to explode at a touch with the most intricately powerful forces caged up inside, a storehouse of vectors.[9]

Presumably the context here is his own work but Prynne soon played a vital role in supplying source material for *Maximus*, volumes two and three. This involved, particularly, the records of shipping activity at Weymouth, the port from which the settlers of Cape Ann, Massachusetts, sailed in 1623.[10] Other matter concerned ancient history, a mutual interest. Olson was impressed with Prynne's speed and thoroughness, referring to him as 'my *Mercury*'.[11] In 1964 the Cambridge don prepared a typescript of *Maximus*, volume two, assembled from manuscript with the writer's ongoing corrections (*GMP*, xliii). Prynne published one of these poems in *Prospect* 6 (1964).

The Cambridge/Black Mountain axis was reinforced when Prynne's colleague and fellow poet, Andrew Crozier, studied under Olson at SUNY, Buffalo in 1964–5. In this capacity he helped foster the Norse strand in *Maximus*.[12] This link continued with the publication of Olson texts in *The Wivenhoe Park Review* from 1965 on. In his 1969 review published in *The Park*, Prynne registers the 'exilic' publishing context of *The Maximus Poems* (London, and before that Stuttgart), while stressing an American counter-practice:

That notion of age as incremental is European and Wordsworthian, and not at all the relevant structure here. Olson's poem is growing back into itself and its historic matrix, not outwards and upwards from it. The mythography ... can [now] touch with true levity upon its base.[13]

Another strand here involves Tom Raworth and Barry Hall, of Goliard Press, who published Olson's *West* in 1966.[14] Presumably this came about via Raworth's friendship with Ed Dorn at Essex University, Dorn having been there since the autumn of 1965. Olson appreciated Hall's skills as designer and typesetter, and this relationship continued after Goliard was absorbed by Cape. Getting the second volume of *The Maximus Poems* into an appropriate printed form stretched these resources to the utmost.[15] Cape Goliard also published *Letters for Origin* and *Archaeologist of Morning*, while Cape Editions, under the editorship of Nathaniel Tarn, reissued *Call Me Ishmael*.

Olson finally got to England in early November, 1966, his first visit since 1928. Arriving, like Melville, in Liverpool, he celebrated the 'wild speech' that he heard.[16] Much of his remaining time was spent in London, at the house of his ex-lover Panna Grady in Hanover Terrace. Pitched into the counter-culture scene of that time, Olson made an immediate impact, attracting the attention of Mick Jagger and donating money to help fund *International Times*.[17] As Ginsberg recalls:

> [H]is non-stop conversation made him the centre of attention.... He would ... stay up late ... at night talking; he would still be reading and making little notes long after everybody else had gone to bed. I remember him in his huge bulk sitting at the table, leaning on his elbow – that moonlike face with big round eyes looking right down into yours; it was like being a tiny rocket ship looking up at the moon.[18]

That summer (1967) Olson spent five weeks in Dorchester, examining the Weymouth port records.[19] This was the enterprise he had 'always wanted to be in England for'.[20] He worked mainly in the County Museum. It is not known whether he visited Weymouth itself, but he did go to a Celtic hill fort – presumably Maiden Castle – with the Director of the museum. Speaking to Charles Boer in 1969, Olson remarked on the similarity between the Dorset/Devon landscape and that around the University of Connecticut: the houses pitched on land 'like the seaward exposure' in England, with 'the hills continually shift[ing]'.[21]

On 12 July Olson read at Queen Elizabeth Hall, alongside Ginsberg, Ungaretti and Patrick Kavanagh.[22] Iain Sinclair brings this vividly alive in *The Kodak Mantra Diaries*, describing the contrast between the earlier poets' 'spidery musk of deadness' and Olson's effort-ridden but sonically charged performance – or projection – of 'An Ode on Nativity':

> He worked it, the long gushes of breath, the runs: letting each line have its pull. It was an excitement, heart in mouth, to listen. He beat time with the ball of his fist. The other hand rubbing at his throat.[23]

Clearly, Olson represented something equivalent to Pound in terms of exploration but his cultural position seemed less elitist and dogmatic. Restating the modernist case for a fragmented lyricism, he was part of a breakthrough which, in the late 1960s, might at last claim a broader audience.

Among those who experienced an awakening of poetic possibility were Chris Torrance and Barry MacSweeney. Torrance speaks of finding 'a structure to back my own impulse to express myself freely and spontaneously'.[24] MacSweeney had difficulty writing about Newcastle until he discovered Olson's approach to the local: that is, 'taking a language outside of the ego, the self' to engage with the 'land out there'.[25] Perhaps this involved an appreciation of Olson's middle voice, intermediate between active and passive, a means of expression aware of itself. Significantly, Olson's comments on this element of grammar slide into notions of performance, as where he recalls learning from David Tudor (via Stefan Wolpe) how to make poetry work.[26] Getting into language is something beyond self expression. You 'take the meanest little possibility / rather than / the grandest'.[27] You 'let the illiteracy stand'. It is a matter of 'Declaring a behaviour, for, the word, as though <u>sometimes</u>, they better be shown as performing animals!'[28] The business is 'how to dance / sitting down' (*MP*, 39).[29]

Exposure to Olson's work helped MacSweeney to move away from closed syntax and 'little lyrical stuff'. This set him against editors such as Jon Silkin and mainstream publishers. Something other than narrow literary poetics was needed.[30] In Alasdair Clayre's 1968 interview for a BBC broadcast, Olson acknowledges the power of a Charles Tomlinson poem written in 'sharp, stark couplets' but says he himself 'never let[s] the thing stay that set':

> I'm going to move on or break it the moment it happens because I don't want it to sit down that long; and I can't 'finish the song'.... You know ... somehow or other I don't make poems.[31]

The effect of Olson's ideas upon sympathetic British readers is well indicated by these extracts from the *Riverside* interview with Tom McGrath:

> Olson talks ... about the close use of things; he's putting in his poems the fathoms, depths in the bay..... [Y]ou turn over a page of *The Maximus Poems* and you just get a list of people ... that he has dug out of some old record. That's where history is.... Olson [also] ... led me straight to Keats['s] ... idea that we must live in the contradictions.

[When Olson reads] one of his poems ... it cuts into the air; the sound ... is like sculpture.... [A]lthough he seems terribly mannered, in fact he's got into average speech or something. There's no kind of poetic tongue to it; he just puts it down. Plus the fact that he's totally rejected any kind of conceptual overlay, that he's only perceiving ... within that particular moment.

Olson, for all [his waywardness] was insisting on a very direct accuracy: the way he scrabbled among stones, picking up the objects which remain. [...]

If you don't see truth as a noun, then you don't see it in a nominative way ... Olson saw everything in a verbal, very active way. Then truth becomes like a proliferation of rivulets and rivers, and there is no totalization of it.... He showed me how to follow my thought as it actually was, as opposed to how syntax had made me think it was.[32]

McGrath, who spent time with Olson via his friendship with Alexander Trocchi and his role as editor of *IT*, ended up forming a jazz group called Proprioception[33] and it is clear from McGrath's comments in the book that Olson continued to influence his subsequent career as playwright.[34] The play *Animal*, for instance, stresses the physiological aspects of speech and has a strong kinetic dimension.[35]

Eric Mottram, a key figure in the London poetry scene, recognised how such 'technics' could offer 'accurate articulations of the actual complexities of our lives' and was enthusiastic about Olson's 'Whiteheadian event-interaction-process'.[36] Bob Cobbing – at Better Books, the Poetry Society and Writers Forum – also knew the value of Olson, although the association may appear tenuous. No direct influence is discernible in Cobbing's work, but as a workshop convener and publisher he encouraged a kinetic treatment of word and line, with habits of visual performance on the page. Younger poets experimented with spatial layout and worked on projects that combined deep research with aleatory procedures. Allen Fisher's *Place*, Robert Hampson's *Seaport*, and my own *Azimuth* are examples of this span of operation.[37] If the subsequent reaction against dominant 'voice' and referential apparatus seemed to displace Olson as a model for experiment, the resources and techniques which he made evident remain useful, as Susan Howe has argued. As a woman she feels 'thrown into a confrontational relationship' with the poet's 'idea of power'. Yet Olson gave her 'a vocabulary for going forward into a past which is part of the living present.' Thus '*Call Me Ishmael* gave birth to *My Emily Dickinson*.' Crucially, in Olson's best writing, 'frontiers are in constant flux.'[38]

Although it might be a mistake to see Prynne as representative of a British renegotiation with Olsonian practice, the progress of his work is revealing. The relationship between the two writers' poetics is complex, consisting of mutual exchange and radical reaction or redefinition by the younger poet. Prynne's letter of 22 February 1981 to Edward Dorn, which the latter incorporated in his Charles Olson Memorial Lectures at Buffalo, is a key document for charting these shifts. After challenging Tom Clark's assumption that Black Mountain College avoided 'the inner light and leading star format', Prynne remarks:

> Olson is the prime instance of a man who saw Pound's mistake and then pushed right on and made it. When I belatedly did meet him you know how shocked I was at the vulgar bullying deafness to reality he blandished, and his hook into what he wanted.[39]

Earlier Prynne had been inspired by Olson's investigative urge and his enactment of discovery on the page. The combination of registers in a single text or linked series (with ideas colliding or accordant), the engagement with scientific data, the imperative 'assumed' voice, all offered ways of making a vital art beyond the simply self-expressive. But Prynne's sense of the poem as energy construct is different, even in the period of notable influence (1965–1970), and from *Brass* (1971) onwards he shows a more severely analytical approach to the use of information, with inwardly directed contexture. As Veronica Forrest-Thomson says in relation to 'Of Sanguine Fire', 'no amount of arcane knowledge will help [the reader] produce an interpretation'; rather, despite reference to the world outside, the construction of meaning has 'to take place within the levels of the poem'.[40] Increasingly Prynne, while retaining his own conceptual drive, disrupts the sweep and generalizing gesture of Olson's poetics.

A similar distrust of totalisation is evident in work by younger poets such as Drew Milne, Sean Bonney and Jeff Hilson. The influence of Language Poetry has resulted in greater playfulness, for instance in the texts of Caroline Bergvall. Behind these manoeuvres there is also the other modernist experimental tradition of Gertrude Stein. The risk with linguistic self-consciousness is that it can appear to be an end in itself and this limits the power of some new practitioners. The time seems ripe for a reassessment of what a content-specific and/or field-scoped poetry can offer.

Olson's stress on the interconnectedness of things, and on their equality of being, fed into landscape or topographical texts which can, on one level, be seen as an emerging ecopoetics in Britain. The ability to present a range of perspectives at once and to reshape forms of expression made him a more radical influence than, say, Gary Snyder. This line may be hard to trace but an early example is Maggie O'Sullivan's

A Natural History in 3 Incomplete Parts, which resists any label in its charting of phenomena. Olson's layered sense of history can also be seen as an influence upon the urban texts of Allen Fisher and Iain Sinclair. In the case of these three writers it is over-restrictive to use any term such as 'ecopoetics', but at a general cultural level it is fair to suggest some link with what, for instance, Harriet Tarlo has gone on to write.[41] Sinclair's analysis of the Olympic site development, cutting through a distorted civic-speak, might recall salvos that Olson sent to the *Gloucester Times* ('A Scream to the Editor' and 'Rocking meter over desolation'), although the former's prose has a different weight and angularity.[42] An example of pastoral with typographic play is Frances Presley's 'The Landscape Room', which uses grids and splays to critique a digital simulation of parkland and enclosed space itself.[43]

In accounts of American poetry critics tend to concentrate on the impact of Olson's prosody. But equally important is the marshalling and deployment of information – the grappling with ideas. Of course the two are intertwined, the local business of the word and the line being part of a larger mental process. Yet it may be useful to concentrate on structures of thought in order to appreciate how Olson's practice has continued to resonate in the UK. I would argue that Olson's 'prosody of the Page space'[44] has informed the work of British poets without on the whole being a literal model. One can see equivalents of Olson's 'spatialized concept of language'[45] in Fisher, MacSweeney and O'Sullivan. Naturally, any voice influenced by another retains or develops its own particular characteristics. But it is striking how, for those indebted to the theory of projective verse, Olson's curiosity, habits of research and mixed stock of information spawn something closer to the English lyric tradition. In other words the open field is mediated through forms to which it was originally opposed, and this often sets up a useful tension. It may be, in Keston Sutherland's phrase, 'a negative lyricism'[46] yet it carries its complexity by a native cellular drift. Examples here would include Prynne's *The White Stones* and more recent books such as Wendy Mulford's *East Anglia Sequence* and Peter Riley's *Excavations*.[47] Chris McCabe's 'Kingfisher' openly acknowledges a debt to Olson's processes of discovery, while situating itself in a condensed temporal frame.[48]

There has, perhaps, been a less dramatic reaction against Olson in the UK than in North America. Certainly there have been parallel anxieties concerning self-assertion, magic, and gender stereotypes, but there were other, more threatening elders to counter or shrug off. Many younger poets simply evaded the strategies of another era, arcane or grandiose. An exception is Redell Olsen's sequence 'The Minimaus Poems', which challenges the bardic ego and its assumptions about audience through playful undercutting of Maximus modes and motifs.[49] Even here, however, the critique implies depth of regard.

Olson's procedures still represent an important measure of possibility: to soak oneself totally in a situation, to shift from dream and myth to mundane circumstance, to make sense of things while leaving some mystery, to chart moments of perception or experience in a page medium that retains an oral charge. There are many poems, such as 'The Librarian' and 'Maximus Letter #whatever', which hold my fascination (*CP*, 412–14; *MP*, 201). But, in terms of what a poem does or can do, I value particularly 'The Twist' (*MP*, 86–90) and 'Maximus, to Gloucester: Letter 15', which embody or act out the process of discovery:

> He sd, 'You go all around the subject.' And I sd, 'I didn't know it was a subject.'
> He sd, 'You twist,' and I sd, 'I do.'
>
> (*MP*, 72) [50]

Coda: discovering Olson

We sometimes forget the extent to which poetry is a social art: that is, although writing tends to be a solitary occupation, it emerges from and continues through a network of contacts. Much of what I have said above involves this conjunction between personality and poetics. By this I don't mean ego or the public jostling which Olson himself dismissed as 'dull and *social*', although clearly this is an issue when any marginalised voice struggles to be heard.[51] My stress is, rather, on the interaction by which writers shape and disseminate texts.

Having got interested in the Beat poets in the mid-1960s, I became curious to discover other contemporary work. I came across Denise Levertov in Penguin Modern Poets and Edward Dorn in a Studio Vista volume.[52] Then, in March 1968 I picked up Donald Allen's *The New American Poetry* in Chicago, where I was living at that point.[53] Olson is given pride of place in this anthology, the first poem being 'The Kingfishers'. Back in England in November 1968 I acquired the first two *Maximus* volumes, which offered a dynamic model for inquiry and the treatment of information. Subsequently, in the mid-1970s, I borrowed reel-to-reel tapes of Olson's Vancouver readings, with additional material, which I transferred to cassette and listened to on headphones over and over again.[54] Even though I knew the texts quite well, the timbre and pace of Olson's voice made the material more vibrant and exact. Later I obtained a copy of the Folkways record and got to know Barry Miles, who explained the background to this recording.[55]

In August 1978 I made my first visit to Gloucester, Massachusetts, where I saw Olson's house and many of the features explored in *Maximus*. I had long been interested in this part of America, but – to borrow Ed Dorn's distinction – it is not the landscape as such which counts so much as its activation in a poetic context. So the journey was undertaken to inhabit some of this process. In 1980 I published an anniversary tribute, *To Let Words Swim into the Soul*.[56] Around this time I met George Butterick, who helped me gain access to the archive at University of Connecticut. Among other items, I read Olson's projected book on Shakespeare, of which the published essay 'Quantity in Verse' seems to have formed part (*CPr*, 270–82). I also had fruitful discussions with Ann and Sam Charters, and subsequently with Ralph Maud. The Riverside Interviews that I conducted with various poets in the early 1980s include much commentary on Olson's procedures. These include discussions with Robert Creeley, Cid Corman and Amiri Baraka, which have yet to be published.

Between 1972 and 1984 I wrote *Azimuth* which, in its combination of the personal with the mythical or universal, particularly reflects the influence of *Maximus Poems, Volume Three*. I sought to preserve the looseness and randomness of discovery alongside textured patterns of repetition and variation. A decade is laid upon a longer cultural history but both narratives are displaced through alteration of perspective and tone. Such interference patterns involve an integrity to the moment as well as a distrust of the organised whole. I learned, partly from Olson, how to create a mini-sequence within a larger unit: that is, a series of poems that operate locally in relation to one another and in spaces beyond. This practice continued in my subsequent books. A striking example from Olson is the sequence running from 'Maximus Letter #whatever' to 'A Maximus Song' (*MP*, 201–5).[57] An equivalent device I have used, from Renaissance and modernist epic, is the placing of parallel pieces at some distance from one another. For Olson, as for me, these patterns emerge by a mixture of deliberation and coincidence – a feature which also applies to the sources I drew upon for *Azimuth* and an academic thesis on Renaissance drama. Any worthwhile programme is incremental, whatever parts are later ignored or jettisoned. The preliminary report of Olson's reading published by Butterick in 1974–7 included historical, literary and anthropological material that was familiar to me; other, unknown texts demanded attention[58] but the essential stimulus was that of method.

With *Roxy*,[59] written 1985 to 1996, my procedures shifted towards a less eclectic surface texture, although the range of sources and reference remained wide. The book, in fifty-two sections, is left-margin aligned, which gives it a very different feel from *Azimuth*, where the text moves around on the page. By this point I was also eschewing the more eccentric features of Olson's practice, for example the unclosed parenthesis. The time demanded a language that was, in one sense, more fiercely formal. A residual faith in the oral was retained but the highly polished or refined was allowed its place, with an inbuilt critique of stylistic precision. *Roxy*, through its subject contexts, is inherently dramatic and the use of the line, syntax and diction reflects this. What appears to be tightly controlled is founded on flexible process. Within sculpturally arranged blocks of text there is a juxtaposition of voices that clash or mesh. The play of multiple elements in a single frame, for example in section 46, may be compared with Olson's mode of simultaneous apprehension.[60]

Le Fanu's Ghost,[61] written 2001–6, is my most extended exercise in layered perception. Combining documentary and imaginative matter, it tracks the history of a family and a city (Dublin), using a looped chronology. Both individual pieces and the work as a whole resemble Celtic tracery, particularly that found in illuminated manuscripts. At one level it is a continuous reading at the margin, with dissolving and re-apparent focus. Despite recurrence of reference and context, no form is repeated exactly. There is much playful conversion of text into other forms, as in the piece 'Liquid Syntax'.[62] Olson's stress on deep investigation and kinetic language remain an influence in what may not immediately be perceived as 'projective' or grammatically 'open'. This is also the case with *Days of '49*, the book I wrote with Alan Halsey.[63]

My current project *Hariot Double* engages with voyage literature and the New World. A childhood enthusiasm, this interest was intensified through noting what Olson does with such texts. He sometimes radically reshapes material and at other times leaves it 'found' or lightly tweaked. I am still impressed with the way he layers these historical fragments with contemporary experience. An example is his first real voyage into the North Atlantic 'under the mast', which feeds into several poems about the schooner *Doris M. Hawes* (MP, 30–1, 42–4, 95, 603).[64] Often where my own work seems most reliant on external sources it is based on direct experience, and I am now making use of early sea memories. The book also focuses on English encounters with American Indians, particularly on a linguistic level, and (mainly in the Old World) on scientific and mathematical thought. The other half of the project involves jazz innovation. Both parts are rooted in London, with juxtapositions across the centuries. In utilising such technical and historical information, I have to bear in mind Olson's tenet that 'poetry is a process, *not a memoir*'.[65]

After circulating Olson tapes to various people in the 1970s, I discussed his work at length with Allen Fisher, Clive Meacham, John Temple and others. Recently I took part in a discussion where Maurice Scully spoke of his engagement with 'Variations Done for Gerald Van De Wiele', one of my favourite pieces from that Vancouver reading.[66] Scully's own 'Variations' form part of the Postlude in *livelihood* (2004).[67] We have all moved on from any literal imitation. What remains for me is an approach to writing that could be described as splayed rigour. Olson is noted for breadth of field but it should be remembered that, both within the *Maximus* series and elsewhere (as in 'The Ring of'), he is capable of economy (*CP*, 243). By 'splayed' I do not necessarily mean expansive in line or word length; rather, a spread of energy through remade language. Although this shaping of words includes the social, it is not simply an expression of personality. Rigour may demand a renegotiation of pronouns, especially 'I', a grappling with things beyond reducible 'content', and music active as a signalling circuit.

Notes

1 Charles Olson, *Call Me Ishmael: A Study of Melville* (London: Jonathan Cape, 1967), Part Two: Shakespeare; Olson, letter to Ann Charters, 10 January 1968, quoted in Charters, *Olson/Melville: A Study in Affinity* (Berkeley, CA: Oyez, 1968), 6–7.
2 Shakespeare Chapters and Parts, unpublished typescripts by Charles Olson, 1954 (Box 35, Charles Olson Research Collection, Archives and Special Collections at the Thomas J. Dodd Research Center, University of Connecticut, Storrs).
3 Ronald Mason, letter to Olson, 21 April 1953 (Box 174, Charles Olson Research Collection, University of Connecticut); *New Republic* 128, 8 and 15 September 1952.
4 The correspondence was published in *PN Review* 149, February 2003. See also *SL*, 197–202.
5 Gael Turnbull, letter to Olson, 24 January 1956 (Box 217, Charles Olson Research Collection, University of Connecticut).
6 Gael Turnbull, letter to Olson, 21 October 1956 (Box 217, Charles Olson Research Collection, University of Connecticut). An account of the G. S. Fraser evenings is included in 'Alan Brownjohn Remembers Peter Porter', *TLS*, 22 February 2012.
7 See Feinstein's discussion with Michael Schmidt in *PN Review* 118, Nov–Dec 1987.
8 Julius Pokorny, *Indogermanisches etymologisches Wörterbuch* [*Indo-European Etymological Dictionary*] (Francke Verlarg, 1959).
9 J. H. Prynne, letter to Olson, 4 November 1961 (Box 206, Charles Olson Research Collection, University of Connecticut).
10 'Reading at Berkeley: The Day After' (*MUTH*, 193–4); Ralph Maud, *Charles Olson's Reading: A Biography* (Carbondale, Il.: Southern Illinois

University Press, 1996), 153, 305–6; *GMP*, 513–14. Although Olson states he was overwhelmed with the mass of material, there is evidence that he made some use of it.
11 Olson, letter to Ralph Maud, 25 November 1965 (*SL*, 130).
12 Maud, *Charles Olson's Reading*, 169–70.
13 'Charles Olson, Maximus Poems IV, V, VI' in *The Park* 4 and 5 (Summer 1969), 64–5.
14 See 'Tom Raworth: An Interview' in *Vort* 1 (1972), 32, and *SL*, 364–5.
15 Ibid., 404–7.
16 Letter to Kate Olson, 4 November 1966 (Ralph Maud archive), *SL*, 381.
17 *The Riverside Interviews 1: Allen Ginsberg*, ed. Gavin Selerie (London: Binnacle Press, 1980), 31; *The Riverside Interviews 6: Tom McGrath*, ed. Gavin Selerie (London: Binnacle Press, 1983), 86–7.
18 Selerie, *The Riverside Interviews 1: Allen Ginsberg*, 30.
19 Maud, *Charles Olson's Reading*, 184–5.
20 Olson, letter to Suzanne Mowatt, 23 May 1967 (Box 194, Charles Olson Research Collection, University of Connecticut).
21 Charles Boer, *Charles Olson in Connecticut* (Chicago: Swallow Press, 1975), 109.
22 Tom Clark, *Charles Olson: The Allegory of a Poet's Life* (New York: Norton, 1991), 336.
23 Iain Sinclair, 'Reading at the Queen Elizabeth Hall' in *The Kodak Mantra Diaries* (London: Albion Village Press, 1971), [10].
24 'Chris Torrance interviewed by Peter Hodgkiss', *Poetry Information* 18 (Winter/Spring 1977–8), 4.
25 'Poets from North East England interviewed by Eric Mottram' in ibid., 30.
26 'Reading at Berkeley' (*MUTH*, 173); see also 'Tyrian Businesses', Section 5 (*MP*, 40).
27 Clark Coolidge, 'Notes Taken in Classes Conducted by Charles Olson at Vancouver, August 1963' in *OLSON: The Journal of the Charles Olson Archives*, 4 (Fall 1975), 51.
28 Boer, *Olson in Connecticut*, 63; this comment is from the back of the envelope containing an explanation of how Tudor taught Olson to read his work aloud, ibid., 62.
29 'Tyrian Businesses', Section 2 (*MP*, 39).
30 'Poets from North East England interviewed by Eric Mottram', *Poetry Information* 18 (Winter/Spring 1977–8), 31.
31 'BBC Interview' (*MUTH*, 291).
32 Selerie, *The Riverside Interviews 6: Tom McGrath*, 86–9, 97.
33 Ibid., 85–8.
34 Ibid., 104–5, 109, 120, 124, 142; see also editorial comments, 28–30.
35 The play had two major productions: Edinburgh Festival (1979) and Scottish Theatre Company tour (1981). The text, still unpublished, exists in a number of different versions. A full account of the play may be found in Selerie, *The Riverside Interviews 6: Tom McGrath*, 60–6 and *passim*.
36 Peterjon Skelt (ed.), *Prospect into Breath: Interviews with North and South*

Writers (Twickenham & Wakefield: North and South, 1991), 35; Amy Evans and Shamoon Zamir eds, *The Unruly Garden: Robert Duncan and Eric Mottram: Letters and Essays* (Oxford: Peter Lang, 2007), 75.
37 Allen Fisher, *Place* (Hastings: Reality Street, 2005); Robert Hampson, *Seaport* (Exeter: Shearsman Books, 2008); Gavin Selerie, *Azimuth* (London: Binnacle Press, 1984). See also Selerie's subsequent projects, discussed below.
38 'Since A Dialogue We Are', in *Acts* 10 (1989), 166–73; Susan Howe, *My Emily Dickinson* (Berkeley, CA: North Atlantic Books, 1985).
39 Lindsey M. Freer (ed.), *Edward Dorn: Charles Olson Memorial Lectures* (New York: CUNY: Lost and Found series, 2012), 29. The context for these remarks is the interview with Tom Clark conducted by Edward Dorn in *Little Caesar* 11 (1981). Prynne also responds to Dorn's summary of events presented by Clark in *The Great Naropa Poetry Wars* (Santa Barbara, CA: Cadmus Editions, 1980), which includes the comment: 'Ginsberg happens to subscribe to the star system [whereby the genius of] heroes of art and thought ... ought to be religiously revered' (21).
40 Veronica Forrest-Thomson, *Poetic Artifice: A Theory of Twentieth-Century Poetry* (Manchester: Manchester University Press, 1978), 48.
41 See, for instance, *The Nab* (Buckfastleigh, Devon: Etruscan Books, 2004) and Tarlo's comments in 'Radical Landscapes: Experiment and environment in contemporary poetry', *Jacket* 32 (April 2007).
42 Iain Sinclair, *Ghost Milk: Calling Time on the Grand Project* (London: Hamish Hamilton, 2011); Olson, *CP* 634–7 and *Archaeologist of Morning* (London: Cape Goliard Press, 1970), [232–4]. The poems date, respectively, from 1965 and 1968.
43 Frances Presley, *Paravane: New and Selected Poems 1996–2003* (Cambridge: Salt Publishing), 39–41; see also Frances Presley, 'Common pink metaphor: from The Landscape Room to Somerset Letters', in *How* 2, 3:2 (2008).
44 Eleanor Berry, 'The Emergence of Charles Olson's Prosody of the Page space', in *Journal of English Linguistics* 30:1 (March 2002), 51–72.
45 Joanna Drucker, *Figuring the Word: Essays on Books, Writing, and Visual Poetics* (New York: Granary Books, 1998), 125.
46 Talk on Prynne's poetry, English Department, Birkbeck, University of London, 14 December 2006.
47 Wendy Mulford, *The East Anglia Sequence* (Peterborough: Spectacular Diseases, 1998); Peter Riley, *Excavations* (Hastings: Reality Street, 2004).
48 *The Restructure* (Cambridge: Salt Publishing, 2012), 74.
49 Redell Olsen, *Secure Portable Space* (Hastings: Reality Street, 2004), 75–109.
50 The 'He' quoted in Letter 15 is Paul Blackburn (*GMP*, 101).
51 Olson, letter to Cid Corman, 2 January 1958; George Evans ed., *Charles Olson and Cid Corman: Complete Correspondence, 1950–1964*, Vol. 2 (Orono, ME: National Poetry Foundation, 1991), 155.
52 *Penguin Modern Poets 9* (Penguin Books, 1967); *The Beat Poets* selected by Gene Baro (London: Studio Vista, 1965).

53 Donald M. Allen (ed.), *The New American Poetry, 1945–1960* (New York: Grove Press, 1960).
54 My contact here (*c.* 1975) was Tony Ward who had obtained the tapes from the University of Essex. A digital version of the Vancouver Poetry Conference reading (1963) is now held at SUNY, Buffalo.
55 *Charles Olson reads from Maximus Poems IV, V, VI* (Folkways, 1975). The title is slightly misleading since Olson also reads from *Mayan Letters* and from the projected third *Maximus* volume.
56 Gavin Selerie, *To Let Words Swim into the Soul: An Anniversary Tribute to the Art of Charles Olson* (London: Binnacle Press, 1980).
57 See my analysis in *To Let Words Swim into the Soul*, 8–13; reprinted (revised) in Clive Bloom and Brian Docherty eds, *American Poetry: The Modernist Ideal* (Basingstoke: Macmillan, 1995), 179–86.
58 'Olson's Reading: A Preliminary Report' in *OLSON: The Journal of the Charles Olson Archives*, 1 (Spring 1974) through to 7 (Spring 1977).
59 Gavin Selerie, *Roxy* (Hay-on-Wye: West House Books, 1996).
60 Ibid., 105–8.
61 Gavin Selerie, *Le Fanu's Ghost* (Hereford: Five Seasons Press, 2006).
62 Ibid., 246–50.
63 Alan Halsey and Gavin Selerie, *Days of '49* (Sheffield: West House Books, 1999).
64 'Journal of Swordfishing Cruise on the *Doris M. Hawes*' [1936] in *OLSON: The Journal of the Charles Olson Archives*, 7 (Spring 1977), 3–42.
65 Jonathan Williams, *The Loco Logodaedalist in Situ* (London: Cape Goliard, 1971), 32.
66 'Maurice Scully Roundtable', Contemporary Poetics Research Centre, Birkbeck University of London, 17 October 2012.
67 Maurice Scully, *livelihood* (Bray, County Wicklow: Wild Honey Press, 2004), 311–19.

Acknowledgements: thanks to Melissa Watterworth at the Thomas J. Dodd Research Center, University of Connecticut, and to the late George Butterick, for access to material from the Olson archive.

9

A fresh look at Olson

Elaine Feinstein

Looking now at the letter I received from Charles Olson in May 1959, it no longer seems to me particularly obscure, though it is certainly *mannered* in the way it shifts between hammering spontaneity, abbreviations and mathematical formulations. It was an important letter however; no less than his latest take on poetics, the first since 'Projective Verse' many years earlier. Reading it now I make out something I missed half a century ago. Olson had a sense of humour which he could employ against himself. He begins to explain, for instance:

> I am talking from a new 'double axis': the replacement of the Classical-representational by the *primitive-abstract* ((if this all sounds bloody German, excuse the weather, it's from the east today, and wet)).... Ok. I'm running out of appetite, Let this swirl—a bit like the Crab Nebula—do for now. And please come back on me if you are interested. *Yrs.*
> (*CPr*, 251, 2)

Of course, I regret not replying to his letter as he encouraged me to do. (Jeremy Prynne exchanged more than one hundred letters with him, beginning a year or two after he took over *Prospect*.) I have other regrets too. In the absence of any photocopier, my response to the Grove Press editor who requested a copy of Olson's letter for publication in the same year, was to post the original air-letter back to New York rather than typing it out carefully as he must have expected. This was not because I had failed to understand Olson's significance. Indeed I used the two Maximus poems he sent with the letter to define the direction I was hoping to find in new English poetry; I used them alongside Donald Davie's witty essay 'Remembering the Movement' to set out my stall.

In my own poems, it is easier to make out what Olson liberated me from than exactly what I learned from him. His attention to syllables I might have drawn from Pound or even the Elizabethans, but his emphasis on *breath* was new and helped me to listen to the shape of my own lines. Those early lyrics from *The Maximus Poems* which I published in *Prospect* in 1959 shaped the sound of all the lyrics which went into my first book *In a Green Eye*. And the sound of a powerful voice running across the stanzas, along with his use of typography to notate the natural pauses in a spoken voice, were invaluable to me as I came to translate the poems of the great Russian poet Marina Tsvetaeva and to look for a rhythm which could run down a whole page.

Olson had begun *The Maximus Poems* in 1950: a sequence of verse letters to his friend Vincent Ferrini and modelled on Pound's *Cantos*. Maximus is named after an itinerant Greek philosopher of the second century. Dismayed by the culture of contemporary Gloucester, Olson examines its origins in the European settlement of America, the long cultural extension to Europe itself and reaching back as far as Mesopotamia. Though I have always liked Jeremy Prynne's phrase 'fertile obscurity', the first Olson poems I published in *Prospect* were entirely comprehensible.[1] I have always liked poetry which is bony and direct. Olson made me imagine the rocky coast, the ocean and the men from Dorset who first saw the shore of Massachusetts, even though I knew nothing of Gloucester, the fishing village where Olson had grown up, or of John White, a local clergyman who had written the history of Gloucester:

>   And the snow flew
> where gulls now paper
> the skies
>
> where fishing continues
> and my heart lies
>
> (*MP*, 112)

Looking at the poem now, that last line seems less than perfect, but the second poem from the same sequence was sharp as an etching. The scene is the same, but the narrative moves confidently from John White's days into Olson's own. I now know that he was able to do so with such energy because his own house was built on the very place those first explorers landed. 'a Plantation, a beginning' records that fact:

> I sit here on a Sunday
> with grey water, the winter
> staring me in the face.
>
> (*MP*, 106)

The winds and drama of fishermen's lives were part of his ancestral heritage and must have taken him to *Moby-Dick*, and his first book, *Call Me Ishmael*. He certainly introduced Melville to me, a novelist from a completely alien world who has continued to fascinate me.

Mexico, especially Yukatan, was a more exotic adventure for Olson, a man who had not been outside the United States for more than 20 years. He was given a grant to follow up his passionate interest in Pre-Columbian hieroglyphs and once he found himself able to learn their language – he was a good linguist and for a time held a post in the foreign language section of the Office of War information under the Roosevelt administration – he set about translating the hieroglyphs with dedication. It was a release for him, from that ocean-battered landscape of Massachusetts. His letters to Creeley (subsequently published as *Mayan Letters*) convince us of Olson's delight in his escape, from an American comfort he found dull into a wonderfully new world of strange creatures, especially birds he had never seen before:

> God, it was wonderful, black, wonderful long feathers, and the wing spread, overall, what, five to six feet. Never got such a sense of a bird's strength, inside strength, as this one gave, like I say, more animal, seemingly, and sure, none of that small beating heart. That's why its victory, over these mean little pricks, was so fine.
>
> (Its silhouette, anyway, above us each day, is a lovely thing, the fore part of the wing not a curve as in a gull, but angled like a bat's a third out from the body. And this strange double tail splitting in flight like the steepest sort of an arrow).
>
> (SW, 70–1)

It was not only the natural world he wanted to explore but the ancient way of relating to it which specifically belonged to the Americas. And that enjoyment brought from him a memorable long poem.

'The Kingfishers' was written over a few months in 1949, and brought out in 1953 as the longest poem of *In Cold Hell, in Thicket*, a book I still treasure. It is closer to 'Prufrock' in manner than the *Cantos*. It stirs the same instant recognition as some of Eliot's poem, especially in the first section where Olson is describing the aftermath of a drunken house party. It is a poem which has over the years attracted much praise from unlikely quarters, such as Ian Hamilton, who preferred the directness of it to the obliquity of Richard Wilbur and James Merrill. However, he found little feeling in it. (Since Olson himself disapproved of poems which depend on subjective feelings, he might have been pleased.)

I admired 'The Kingfishers' on first reading. The poem opens with a sonorous proposition:

> What does not change / is the will to change
>
> (CP, 86)

But almost at once that declaration is undercut by the image of a man waking fully dressed on his bed, with memories of the preceding night's party returning haphazardly, and coalescing into a vision, at once funny and sad, of a couple attempting drunkenly to get two recalcitrant birds back into their cage. The house is not described in detail but it must be large enough to allow those kingfishers out of their cage – it surprises me they can survive in one – to let them loose in a room. The birds are not metaphorical creatures but seemingly kept as we might keep budgerigars, and for all the beauty of their feathers – once valued as currency – they are shabby creatures in this household. One of them has a bad leg. Hamilton was probably mistaken in thinking that 'the will to change' had no domestic resonance. Olson's partnership with Connie was already under strain, and they separated a couple of years later. Certainly, however, the main thrust of the poem is an impersonal valuation of two visions of civilisation. Reading it with hindsight I am less sympathetic. I distrust his insistence on the natural wisdom of the primitive world. It seems to me sentimental to believe that earlier ages were any happier or more spiritually healthy than our own. I suspect he may be as wrong about that as he certainly was in quoting Mao, *'L'aurore est devant nous'*; a political hope almost as mistaken (in the light of later crimes) as Pound's belief in fascism (though Mao's atrocities were not yet committed). But the beauty of 'The Kingfishers' is redolent of a more ancient East. Olson looks to it as civilisation indigenous to the Americas which night replace Pound's vision of a European heritage going back to Greece. Olson knew his debts to Pound, but had quarrelled with his political vision on a visit to St Elizabeth's and was eager to define a vision of his own, or rather one he had uncovered.

In the third section of the poem, after reflecting on ancient rites for the burial of a dead child, Olson muses:

> with what violence benevolence is bought
> what cost in gesture justice brings
> what wrongs domestic rights involve
> what stalks
> this silence

(CP, 92)

The music is persuasive. The prose of *The Mayan Letters* spell out the anthropology underpinning it. As Professor M. L. Rosenthal once suggested to me in conversation, Olson's dogmatic voice resembled Lawrence. He must have had *The Plumed Serpent* in mind. Certainly both writers had their own way of appropriating the Mexican past. Olson found in Aztec and Mayan art the idea that human beings are no more important than the creatures around them, and disliked the Judaeo-Christian notion that other creatures only exist for human benefit. He wrote as though there were essentially two cultures in Mexico, the fierce Aztec and the gentle Mayan, which could be made out to this day. Is this so? I don't know. But when I went round the magnificent museum in

Mexico City and looked dubiously at images of their gods, I was equally struck by the ferocity of both.

The poetry was not all that excited me about finding Olson. Through him, and later through his protégé Ed Dorn, I found a place in an underground network of poets who could write for one another without taking much account of metropolitan publishers. It seemed immensely seductive to write poems, share them with talented friends and become part of a counter-culture which had strong voices like Roy Fisher in Birmingham, Tom Pickard in Newcastle and lyric poets like Andrew Crozier in Cambridge. What held us together were pamphlets like Gael Turnbull's *Migrant* and, most importantly for me, *The English Intelligencer*, for which Olson was a vital figure and Jeremy Prynne the presiding spirit.

Many of those who began to write for those mimeographed sheets, which came out from the Roneo machine of Jeremy Prynne's office at Caius College, had been to Buffalo and all were one way or another aware of Olson and Black Mountain. I was the only woman among the first mailing of twenty-eight, though later the women attached to the group included Wendy Mulford, Denise Riley and Veronica Forrest-Thomson.

Many of the young men featured in its pages came to sit on my Trumpington floor in the late sixties. Political views were very disparate. John James I remember as a Communist. Others were committed to exploring *Englishness*, its local history and geology, in search of their own roots. Some unease about this particular strand can be found in my first letter to the Intelligencer:

> Surely the language of the island belongs to whoever lives there and uses it? ... let's not have any fictional Englishness. What could be nastier?[2]

The measured tone of this letter hardly covers my unease. Wasn't I joining a group of fellow outsiders? Perhaps not. My roots in this country only went back to 1890. Both sets of grandfathers came from Odessa.

Among the many poets Olson influenced who are part of my own story, Donald Davie might seem the most surprising. However that brilliant essay written for the first issue of *Prospect*, 'Remembering the Movement', offers a clue to the attraction.[3] He was already working on Ezra Pound, and eager to repudiate the cautious tones of the new Movement poets and to open himself up to a transatlantic world. By then, Olson and Lowell represented opposing extremes of possible American influence. No surprise that the academic English poets were more attracted to the patrician Lowell. When Davie became Professor of the new Department of Comparative Literature at the University of Essex, however, he invited Dorn to join the Essex Faculty, and was intellectually excited by Olson himself, whose texts he introduced into postgraduate seminars. What Davie found in Olson was complex: but it certainly included an invitation to experience being alive more fully. Dorn, slim and cool in jeans looked like a handsome westerner from a movie and the students adored him.

At eighty three, I sense a change in my own work after taking a fresh look at Olson. I am glad to return to the poetry I once admired so intensely and begin to experience again an urge to sprawl rather than tidy up; to shrug off constraints and boundaries and once again risk listening to the sound of my own voice, so that the lines can take their own musical shape.

Notes

1 J. H. Prynne, 'On *Maximus IV, V, VI*', *Minutes of the Charles Olson Society* 28 (April 1999), 2.
2 Elaine Feinstein, Letter to *The English Intelligencer*, Series 1, Issue 2; reprinted in Neil Pattison, Reitha Pattison, Luke Roberts (eds), *Certain Prose of The English Intelligencer* (Cambridge: Mountain Press, 2012), 3.
3 Donald Davie's essay 'Remembering the Movement' was subsequently published in *The Poet in the Imaginary Museum*, ed. Barry Alpert (Manchester: Carcanet Press, 1977), 72–5.

Section III

Gender

10

Olson and his *Maximus Poems*

Rachel Blau DuPlessis

'The advantages of a long poem, is like pot au feu, it creates its own juice [...] Or put it formally: the long poem creates its own situation.' (Olson, 'From Notebook "I ... Sept. 15, 1957"')[1]

Here they are. *The Maximus Poems*. An 'Alps' – that other, American Alps.[2] A masterpiece of poesis, particularly for people curious about the workings of a very long poem. For many readers, it exists not in the mode of monument but in the related, equally pertinent mode of midden or ruin. At the end of the book, all the pages fall out. This work may be bound, but it is not bounded. Ben Friedlander has proposed that the totality of Olson's work – published and unpublished, books and notes – should be taken as a borderless 'archive'.[3] This honours the remarkably suggestive findings list of the Olson Archive at University of Connecticut, Storrs, and it also honours the poignant complexities of the 'ending' of *Maximus*, the rush to organize materials in Olson's last months and the painstaking chronological sequencing of some of Part III made after Olson's death by George Butterick and Charles Boer.[4] However, one must also honour the critique of the book and of the merely literary that Olson made by his long poem.

So the rubric 'archive' can be borrowed back to describe the impact of *The Maximus Poems* as codex and bibliographic site, particularly as accompanied and compounded by its 'evil twin' – the documentary manifesto in *Collected Prose* called 'A Bibliography on America for Ed Dorn' (written 1955, published 1964). *The Maximus Poems*, like many long poems, is itself a culture – both an idiosyncratic simulacrum of a geo-political culture and an actual institutional culture devoted to exfoliating the work. The latter propels the claims of the former.[5] Both 'archive' and 'culture' are grand rubrics that challenge conventions of intellectual closure and aesthetic finality. While many literary genres tend toward specific modes of closure, the very long poem, in its drastic and allusive genre hybridity, in its scale, and sometimes in its temporal irregularity of production avoids conventions of closure deliberately – and/or accidentally – or does something peculiar in closing.[6]

Olson's willy-nilly critiques of professionalism, completion, and modulated form – for instance, his principled resistance to the repetitive (and hegemonic) architectonics of *Four Quartets* – contribute to his poem's open-ended recklessness. Olson gambles on the very long poem as an adequate instrument for investigative poesis and historical-syncretic suggestiveness, while making the work intentionally absorptive, processual, post-literary and post-'literature'. He is particularly interested in the sweep of millennia and their particular instantiation in the local and now – wanting to find synoptic, overarching themes and tendencies particularized at any given 'crossroads', whose outline is the two-line crossed poem, one of many self-elegies in Part III (*MP*, 438). His goals for this work were to present fact 'continuous, and not as history but as data as essence' along with intermittent upsurges of Poundean 'repeats', or 'archetypal memory' emerging not only within biographical 'persons' but in them as talismanic historical will.[7]

The Maximus Poems as a whole – poem after poem cast like sorts between 1950 and 1969 – becomes a compendium of Olson's associative thought and activities in words. Acts of working in language become the work; the notes toward the poem are so similar to the poem that one might almost claim they are the same. It is not representation but enactment he is after, the Pound/Fenollosa passion for word-act without the barrier or obliterations of conceptual generalization, abstraction or exposition. A personal favourite on the cusp of conceptual and expressivist acts is '3rd letter on Georges, unwritten' beginning '[In this place is a poem which I have not been able to write...', a poem – all in square brackets – of circuitous but palpable narrative energy in which the impossibility of writing 'a poem' generates a writing from thinking (*MP*, 277). *The Maximus Poems* are as much a 'record of struggle' as Pound, in a pensive/defensive mode, claimed *The Cantos* were.[8] A tremendous splay of material assimilated? – or actually not assimilated? – by someone passionately aroused, electrically flashing ideas and feelings, writing so fast that he is almost not writing at all, but making lists, abbreviating ideas, clustering half-completed associations, sketching, combining, and lumping materials. The work is impulsive, unsettled. It is not even a '*record* of struggle'; the reader sees the struggle in real time. With 'the defects inherent', *The Maximus Poems* and Olson are disorderly, determined, aroused, orbsessive.[9] That's it: ORBsessive. Taking the whole world, the whole earth, even the whole universe in and correlating it, co-real-relating it. Olson is, as he said late in the work, 'hungry for every thing' (*MP*, 604).

His goal was an investigative poem – a meditative poem including/ citing documents, where one small corner of Massachusetts (the fishing port, Gloucester) holographically summarized the promises and failures of the United States. The westward spatial thrust (from Phoenicians – the 'Semitic origin' of the Odyssey, into Gloucester and across the continent), the potential uniqueness of America, and the force of individual male will are central assumptions of the work (*CPr*, 301). Olson proposes that a great experiment in pragmatism and community work was made in Gloucester but it fell under siege by theocratic and neo-aristocratic forces of Puritanism, by developing capitalist economies and now neo-liberalism, and by the failure of the men themselves to grasp their existential newness (*MP*, 138–9). This utopian moment of thinking into 'American space' was thus compromised (*MP*, 133).

Olson devoted at least five years before 1950 to making various plans for his long poem (including the self-debate: why a *poem* and not prose?) and to analysing the implications of these plans. The work took off only intermittently between 1950 and 1953, with Olson's slow recognition that Maximus and his epistles were indeed the portal through which this long poem became possible (*GMP*, xxix-xxxiii). Among the prior proposals are WEST – a study of world heroes in their historical moments from the Stone Age and Bronze Age until now and culminating in US and Meso-American heroes – an epic mixture of ancient archaeology and cultural studies infused with dramatis personae from Williams' *In the American Grain*. The plan focused on labour and culture/image-making as similarly crucial work. A second plan was a research-based documentary poem provisionally titled 'Operation Red, White & Black': 'I see in the Indian, white and Negro life here on this continent a series of FACTS which, if properly selected, juxtaposed and coldly told, will together make a FABLE mostly now unknown' concerning 'THREE RACES and THE LAND'.[10] Plans for both poems were more historically chronological than *Maximus* is. And most of the characters were already known within historical record and mythic narratives (Lincoln, Boone, LaSalle, Quetzalcoatl, Cabeza de Vaca); in contrast, *Maximus* features unknown working men.[11]

It has often been remarked – or perhaps it has simply been remarked a good deal by me – that there are hardly any female figures in all of *The Maximus Poems*, certainly not ones active in the work of community or nation-building. Yet gender is central to Olson; he focuses on the gendered relations among men. The activities celebrated in this poem are boat-work, navigation, fishing, salting and preserving fish, trading, shipbuilding. There is some claim to understanding this set of work relations among relative equals as the economic basis of 'polis' – fundamentally Olson's idea of a working and well-integrated community. Yet other economic forces were at work in the later seventeenth century, undermining the 'quasi-independent' status of fishermen.[12] And vital women's work does not appear in Olson – work at home, sustenance farming, gardening, poultry and swine raising, preserving, making things like bread, soap, candles, clothes, possibly taking in income-supplementing boarders, as well as running some family businesses when their husbands were at sea.[13] The net effect of his selective socio-economic vision is to lose women, erasing them as workers and members of the polis. Although Olson is trying seriously to grasp the authenticity of the past, to perceive its quotidian life and its economic-political crises, he gives no concerted attention to the work of actual women in his poem, making his loosely historical picture of polis partial and incomplete.

The long poems of modernity (*The Cantos*, '*A*', *Paterson*, *Trilogy*, *Four Quartets*) often commence within ruin or disaster – this is not unknown to the classic epic, either – and elaborate the terms of that ruin, sometimes war, sometimes economic and ecological devastation, sometimes civic or spiritual frustration. These works differ in the degree to which hope is generated, the 'timing' and 'mechanism' of hope's appearance within the poem, and the rationale for that hope.[14] In Olson's *Maximus Poems* this 'Gloucester' promise is only *almost* lost, and thus might be redeemed. 'Polis' is Olson's term for the evanescent, idealized political possibility. Polis begins as a vanguard formation of people who have a kind of collective will to know, to synthesize, to act. It is also, ideally, a site where the individual body, the geography of the place, the world, and both US and world history are continuous and inter-involved; there are no impediments to their continuity and (this is a curiosity) no contradictions among them. This is an ideal affirmed even in the triple rhyme: 'Polis is this' and in the remarkable, inclusive gesture that Olson makes during a reading of this work (video clip available on YouTube) (*MP*, 185). In that reading, one cannot tell exactly whether 'this' refers to the poem in which history is condensed into one incident from Olson's childhood and the meditations he generates (in 'Letter #27 [withheld]'); whether 'this' gestures outward, including the audience as community; or whether 'this' is Olson's charming and happy performance of his embodied, totalizing presence facing that audience (*MP*, 184–5).

Olson builds this polis (or identifies its workings in the poem) by calling out to men who are alive in their own time.[15] One climax of the whole poem? 'It is a pleasure to report, / to a city which is now so moribund, / that there are men still, / in some of these houses, of evenings, / who are of this make' (*MP*, 476). Olson is the angel of male annunciation – the power of men to generate more men, announced to men. The poem itself substitutes for the ocean and the continent as sites through which a community of worker-visionaries is authenticated. Therefore, by a logic whereby civic adhesion to, citizenship in the poem's simulacrum of culture becomes participation in the institutional study of the poem as a culture, the designated remnant, who might redeem the nation from the loss of possibility, often became Olsonites – the active community that formed around this poem and the knowledge it demanded. Polis, viewed in this way, is a utopian, investigative space created by the palpable claims of the poem on its readers.

As for the synoptic investigation whose shard-y evidence is this poem, it is not so much Grand Theory / Grand Form – the quondam modernist mode – as Grand Particularity / Grand Urgency – a rush across time to get this said. The poem is not a 'whole' but a mobile complex across time. While Olson himself was the first (or one of the first) to use the term 'post-modern', he himself was on the cusp between the totalizing claims of modernist thought and the disaggregating particularities of postwar thought. Indeed, his poem is perhaps the last Anglo-American long poem trying for the mytho-informational, encyclopaedic, 'hypertextual' mode, before the long poem shifts in the hands of Creeley, Oppen, Hughes, Ashbery, and perhaps Zukofsky, to a serial and secular proposal of calibrated psycho-social exploration. Indeed, this 'cusp' between epochal modes of the very long poem is arguably found inside *The Maximus Poems*, in the shift from Books I / II (as one unit) to Book III.

'person-as-continuation-of-millennia-by-acts-of-imagination-as-arising-directly-from-fierce-penetration-of-all-past-persons, places, things and actions-as-data' ('A Bibliography on America for Ed Dorn')

This hyphenated bolus articulates the anti-fictional poetics of this poem. The single person is a major crossing point of gigantic millennial forces of the past pivoting toward the present-future. The person is penetrating (mentally driving a thought through) but also penetrated by all the other 'persons ... and actions' taken as data, for he will contain or carry them. The interplay of penetration and reception, the generative claim of penetration with continuation is part of the erotic tension of the poem, but also its necessity for haste. One cannot possibly keep up with one's own acts of imagination whether being penetrated (fiercely) by the assembled, demanding, self-different forces of the past taken as data, or whether penetrating them (for there are always more to penetrate).

Maximus is an authoritative persona of Major Man, an ancient philosopher returned, a Big Man addressing a small city. The name Maximus is a gesture both of containing and of amplifying the penetrating/penetrated forces that Olson felt. As the name of a figure from the ancient Phoenician world, it is thesis-bearing about the sweep of exploration, risk, human progress, and heroic knowledge-seeking reborn in the US context. As a word, it is the masculine form of the Latin 'maximum', with such meanings as 'the greatest possible quantity, degree, or number', the 'highest point', greatest or largest. It is an onomastic indicator of an inclusive, powerful speaking subjectivity, for (as with Olson as a person) 'nature has given him size, projective size' (*CPr*, 248). A figure so named is a glyph for wholeness – without having to do more with the relation of parts to whole than use this name. In 'Projective Verse' (1950), an enabling statement of purpose, Olson foresees a poetics that gets 'rid of the lyrical interference of the individual as ego, of the "subject" and his soul', apparently obliterating the whole romantic/poetic tradition in one summary gesture (*CPr*, 247). Yet that tradition is not so easily dismissed. The name Maximus returns 'individual' and 'ego' (and later, in Book III, lyric-diary) to the poem by enveloping them with a vulnerable grandeur that absorbs the contradictions between part and whole and among alternative poetics – conceptual and expressive, documentary and lyric.

For the name Maximus allows this figure to serve the crucial double function of totality (whole community, spirit of incipient polis) and individual prophet/provoker of this polis. As in *Moby-Dick*, Olson has a double hero – collective protagonist and narrator-griot. Anything that the eponymous title figure writes or thinks is the poem, and the poem is the body of words, the archive of the historical construction of a Maximus-community via the work. The hero is reflective and contemplative, not active, but he turns contemplation to action via the gestural poetics of the page. In a sense – well illustrated by *Maximus* as well as by *The Cantos* – some very long poems tend to dissolve into notational jottings and fragments. For example, in 'A *Maximus*' the page is a sketch of proper nouns, rubrics ('marine / architecture'), and private (not exfoliated) associations, along with irritated self-questioning. The notes to the poem have become the poem, and the conceptual act of planning becomes the 'epic' action of the poem – the magnetic gesture of writing as heroic act (*MP*, 193). Olson is the epic griot of his own poesis.

'The trouble is, it is very difficult, to be both a poet and, an historian' (*Mayan Letters*, October 1953)

The first section of *Maximus* was written in May 1950 after a prehistory through the late 1940s. Olson's sense of the work's method gains propulsion during the six months he spent in Lerma, Campeche, Mexico as a self-anointed archaeologist. This key moment of consolidation of purpose for the poem and for Olson's intellectual authority leaves a problematic residue. There is often a striking split between Olson's energetic and polemical principles and his practices in putting (or attempting to put) these principles into texts and acts. To focus on this split is not to disparage Olson but rather to examine the lived intellectual and aesthetic meaning of his contradictions.

Olson went to the Yucatan in February 1951 on a self-generated expedition. There he began to make knowledge claims based on proprioceptive intuition. Yet as he notes in a letter to Creeley, to do a 'total reconnaissance of *all* [potential] sites [..] I need (1) Spanish; (2) the beginnings of a mastery of Maya; and (3) friends'.[16] This is difficult. He seems to think the contemporary Mexicans will know 'Mayan' – yet Spanish is generally current, and he is 'bitched' that 'Maya not in much use'.[17] Olson's non-knowledge of relevant languages, his personal isolation, his professional over-reaching and social difference were, in his own mind, trumped by the power of his dynamic presence.

Olson felt as if his whole body-mind, conceived as one functioning unit, became a dowsing rod for the truth of fact and for the freshness of the archaic. There was the truth of claiming he will find hidden water for a farmer, the truth of his intuition of the force of the glyphs on the Mayan stele, making surmises from a language that he did not yet know how to read.[18] He overrode social, national, and cultural difference with a claim of human presence: sheer Being authenticated his insight, fuelled by 'my abhorrence of modern academicism'.[19] It was phenomenology in reverse.

Olson's desires to reject (or to transcend) both the academic and the technocratic were intensified by this expedition. By disparaging those experts whom he assumed lacked feeling for place or situation, Olson resisted their expertise. By the primal authenticity of his anti-academicism, he sought a historical-cultural epiphany that would make up for 'some ignorance on this particular front, of, what shall I call it, archeology plus'.[20] He claimed that someone of passionate intensity and speculative finesse could, in a few weeks of study, make sense of what experts haven't seen and couldn't see. This expedition epitomizes Olson as the inventor of suggestive subject positions – critical anti-professional, cosmic investigator and intuitive scholar. The later 'Bibliography on America for Ed Dorn' (in circulation in 1955) reveals his continuing conflict about professionalism, his desire to transcend the plodding, the academic, the careful, the temperate – proposing an inspirational intuitive study via 'love' and not (solely or exclusively) via 'any study of the books about' (*CPr*, 297).

By gathering the shards of the Mayan pottery and ceramics that he found, eagerly removed from the field and examined, Olson felt direct and unmediated connection to ground that kept him in a state of intellectual arousal.[21] He did not know much about the politics of the country, nor about existing expeditions and their claims, nor even about archaeological protocols (of recording where materials are found and not taking them, his 'pockets ... bulging with potsherds').[22] Yet Olson felt that as an intelligent outsider, he could intuitively grasp materials and make efficacious knowledge claims. This is precisely because he is not trapped by minutiae of technical knowledge. These included professional socialization (into what he reviled as small-scale thinking and soulless pedantry), care with the 'normal' (and often impeding) procedures of permissions and local negotiations, and the politically sensitive rules or courtesies of dealing with another culture, even one whose features you don't particularly admire. Olson did not have connections to Mexican and United States archaeologists, and he already suspected their expertise and their limited vision.[23] This constellation of claims is pure essence of Olson: he was an individual, a free agent, a bold thinker beyond category, with an unquenchable energy for synoptic leaps of thought. Olson wanted world-historical insight; his method was juxtaposition, flashes of intuitive synthesis, serendipity, analogy and inspired correlations of material.

In this personal expedition to some Mayan sites and ruins, Olson began his dramatic enactment of method – the selection of specific shards zooming to sweeping generalization and overview – that also animated *The Maximus Poems*. Olson is strangely antiquarian in his intellectual motions, accumulating sets of wonderful details that are rarely contextualized or organized into data sets; as well, he is loosely New Historicist in his findings – that detail is exploded into a synoptic explanatory theory. The Yucatan months became viral for him. He was infected with inchoate possibility from them; they were one muse for his long poem.

'Books' are inadequate – too artful, too selective, and, crucially, too slow; one needs 'documents' and 'archives' – an instantaneous plethora of materials prior to argument, pre-interpretation, and – perhaps paradoxically (or inaccurately), quick to be understood because not yet systematized (*CPr*, 307). Taking a field back down to the ground and finding and studying the relevant documents are, of course, vital tasks, but Olson claims that he can forever keep interpretation/abstraction at bay by endless, continuous streams of document. The Herodotus-ian mantra – '*istorin*, to find out for oneself' – is a key axiom for him (*CPr*, 308). But this perspective does not preclude a person's making interpretive syntheses based on reasonably full analysis of data, in an informed dialectic between 'fact' and 'theory', and with an engagement with prior thinkers, both empirical and synoptic.

Still, positing a pure (direct, untainted) source of primal data was Olson's insistent but sometimes naïve test of authenticity. Herodotus is valued because the *Histories* (says Olson) are based upon a man confronting the historian with a story – the authentic presence is intimate, direct, touching, experiential, and thereby convincing. '[Herodotus] is always talking of men and things, not of societies and commodities' (*CPr*, 344; from 1955). In this sentence, Olson validates his claim rhetorically, by choosing Anglo-Saxon short words versus Latinate abstractions. Read another way: these sets are virtually the same, though one is made to seem specific and singular, the other grouped and generalized.[24] Olson's avoiding the word 'commodity' is also a nativist-pragmatic avoidance of a word linked to Marxist economic theory.

Despite Olson's hopes for *The Maximus Poems*, so similar to his hopes for what he could accomplish in Yucatan, it is not the work's content or findings or intellectual claims that remain pertinent.[25] That is, this poem has value only in the realm of literature and culture (hardly a bad thing, but less than he wanted). It is read by people interested in poetry, in literary genre, in the problems of the long poem, as well as in cultural poetics, as Michael Davidson uses the term. It is not read, as a work of foundational theory might be, by philosophers, historians, political theorists, or ethnographers.[26] Olson attempted to found a new field – cultural morphology? – in which his work has significant value. However, a new field is generally not propelled by the will of one singular figure but by social, cultural, political and intellectual forces in a multi-community upsurge motivated by various interests and desires. An exceptional individual thinker may magnetize these issues, but it is rare that such a person can initiate them without a social, cultural, or intellectual movement behind them. Even the intense originality of 'psychoanalysis' (with Freud) and 'Marxism' (with Marx) drew on and synthesized a range of prior empirical and analytic thinkers. One does suspect, however, that these precise thinkers were Olson's models, and his *bêtes noires*. What foundered was his attempt – in poems, essays, teaching, and the archive – to replace Jewish humanists (as he explicitly characterized them) and their 'deterministic' thought with post-humanist cultural theory of the active will, and to displace their intellectual authority with his own.[27] In contrast, this poem and Olson's essays construct a literary achievement, not a fundamental theory of culture nor a theoretically transformative reading of history. Rather than his methodology, his theorizing or his findings, Olson's meditative, documenting and epistolary activities as praxis, and the passionate, visually scintillating page as poesis are a heritage, precisely for literary culture.

'the generation of those facts / which are my words' (Olson, *The Maximus Poems* [ca. 1954])

As in many other long poems of the twentieth century, an epic trace is visible as one of the many genres at play in *The Maximus Poems*. The work mixes mythography and historical claims, and centres on the investigative quest of two related heroes – the griot-speaker and a community of men whose deeds are allusively recorded. An epic depicts men running things, making decisions (bad and good), deploying resources to an end, calculating cause and effect, calibrating 'cost-benefit analyses' in a world of war, fate, chance and god-systems. Contemporary long poem writers – Olson, Williams, Pound, even Zukofsky – were well aware of the gendered nature of the heroic subjectivity in epic and took up various attitudes to it.[28]

Maximus, itself a postwar poem, proposes the war of work itself, workplace struggles, male factive-ness, battles with the elements, and the struggle for the economic and political soul of America from its rebellious beginnings to its callow compromises in the contemporary period. Olson does not depict war in the sense of battle – but rather work as a political struggle, as well as an economic one with the forces of nature and society, a struggle to maintain both community and individual action. Olson insists on the epic acts of his men – saying, for example of an anti-monarchical English rebel come to Gloucester: 'he founded Troy / on this side of history' (*MP*, 398). The work celebrates the common entrepreneurs and workers, their male bonding and loyalty with the virtues of competency and will, the men with *techne*, and those who disappear into near-anonymity and sometimes into the sea (*MP*, 158). This is a profound 'common man' torque of epic motifs, articulating the popular front ethos that Olson overtly disavowed.

Another root genre of *Maximus* is the epistle, a genre playing to Olson's strengths by transposing an informal, casual, intense rhetoric into a public intervention.[29] This rhetorical realm becomes one of Olson's most charismatic sites. Epistles negotiate I/you relations, with an intimacy addressed simultaneously to an individual (to you alone) and to a collective (to all of you). Hence the poems perform a galvanic call into an incipient social space, engaging individuals by means of that community. As in the New Testament, an epistle both constructs and animates a community; it is hortatory and didactic.

In his epistles as Maximus, Olson addresses others and himself in the active mode of *tenzone*, so that one sees the propulsions and interior debates of argument enacted in the antiphonal rhetoric of exterior or interior dialogue. He involves the listener as an engaged observer of the alternating positions and of the scintillations of facts. Olson forcefully represents the twists and turns of his thought while achieving what often end up as his *obiter dicta*, but ones made unstable by the syntactic wobbling and even by the obscurity of reference that characterizes his writing. The energy generated by any self-debate in Olson – in poetic epistles, in his essays – was the 'projective'. It isn't simply that one thought follows upon another, but that these thoughts are often seen in fruitful collision. Even when his (intellectual, ideational) conclusions seem reductive or under-informed, the energies of argument in the alternating shifts of position remain dramatic and attractive.

I take SPACE/TIME to be the main element of this poem, and (as Ron Silliman has intimated) of any long poem. Olson's *Maximus* begins with a historical space but ends with time. 'Space' is both thematic and material – the question of pushing continental boundaries and the maximal length of this poem; the poem is both pushing at historical frontiers and pushing into the cosmological.[30] Suggestive and even touching sections concern the particular body as a site of time-space crossings, with the emphasis on time's processes in space. Thus a sense of extent, a space of cosmic, earth-shaping processes is continually brought to this moment. This is why the senses of haste, of now-time, the manifesto-like sound of many of Olson's communiqués, the apocalyptic urgency are so characteristic and compelling. The rhetorics of the poems are time-based, excited at the minute, suggestive, sparking thoughts, making incomplete arguments, manifesting an intense (projective) pulse of thinking aloud, right here, right now. The enormous sense of rush and pulse finally explodes into mourning mortality itself.

So the real utopia of this poem is neither polis nor its incorporative prophet (Maximus) but its projective sense of living in space/time – at coordinates, exactly tracking sunsets, notationally recording a certain thought happening at this time and place. Olson's dated meditations on particular conjunctions of mood, weather, winds, tides, days, nights, phases of the moon are catalogued in poem after poem of Part III. Olson delivers a sense of metamorphic time in political, economic, geologic space.

Like many modern works with a trace of the epic mode, this work engages seriously with its chthonic shadow – the nekuia moment – of testing, of prophecy, a seeking of the wisdom of the dead, or receiving messages from an uncanny space – which is simply the space/time in which we live.[31] The frightening trip of the hero to the underworld, and the fierce (even sexual) grip of the chthonic shimmers behind a number of Olson's sections – the bullfight and Merry being only one example. Several sections in Part III show Maximus dissolving into the land on which he lies or walks as if he has melted down into archaeological strata. The work is loosely elegiac therefore, and veers between an engorging, declaiming public man pointing toward manly work, and the overwhelmed private figure speaking about yearning and loss. Readers of this long poem often feel as if they have gone, with the writer, into this evocative chthonic underground.

Notes

1 Charles Olson, 'Notes and uncollected *Maximus* Materials', OLSON: *The Journal of the Olson Archive* 5 (Spring 1976), 61; hereafter referred to as OLSON 5.
2 Basil Bunting's near-curtal sonnet, 'On the Fly-Leaf of Pound's Cantos' begins: 'There are the Alps.' Basil Bunting, *The Complete Poems* (Oxford: Oxford University Press, 1977), 114.
3 Friedlander argues that 'Olson abandoned the book as ultimate horizon and worked instead to produce an archive' in the service of writing as 'knowledge production'. However because of my interest in the long poem, I disagree that the 'frame of the Maximus poems should be set aside altogether'. Benjamin Friedlander, *Olson Now*, posted 27 May 2006, http://olsonnow.blogspot.com/2006/05/benjamin-friedlandercharles-olson-now.html
4 The last poem, however, was declared 'last' by Olson – a word, I'd note, that does not mean final, but, as Butterick suggests, might have been motivated by his imminent fate of dying (*GMP*, xlvii).
5 Not incidentally, Olson had little use for the pettiness of the term 'culture', substituting such grander concepts as 'morphology', and 'historical geography'. (*CPr*, 301, 308 and Robert Creeley, *Jacket* 12, http://jacketmagazine.com/12/olson-p-cree.html)
6 Just thinking of Zukofsky's 'A' here.
7 Olson's notes from 1953. See *OLSON 5*, 55.
8 Ezra Pound, *Guide to Kulchur* (London: Peter Owen, 1966), 135.
9 Ibid.
10 Charles Olson, 'OPERATION RED, WHITE & BLACK (1947)', in *OLSON* 5, 27, 28.
11 At this point, the work was not gender-exclusive. In one planned iteration, female figures were to appear as Witches in Salem; while considering Gloucester as a port, Olson mentions 'witches and women' (possibly prostitutes?) to discuss; at a third moment the people in Gloucester listed include historical females. (*OLSON 5*, 42, 46, 48.) A few female figures, notably Anne Hutchinson, do briefly appear in the poem now (*MP*, 133).

12 Daniel Vickers, *Farmers and Fishermen: Two Centuries of Work in Essex County, Massachusetts, 1630–1850* (Chapel Hill: University of North Carolina Press, 1994), 167.
13 Ibid., 133, 175–6.
14 Hart Crane's *The Bridge* is an interesting exception, infused, as it is, with perpetual mythic promise.
15 One part of that call is, 'I mean if we can't make love right now as I do with Robert Creeley and Robert Duncan and Ed Dorn and and and and Ed Sanders and and a girl in the back of the room and Kenny Tallman–And I don't mean in any sloppy sense'. (Charles Olson, *Charles Olson Reading at Berkeley*, transcribed by Zoe Brown (San Francisco: Coyote Press, 1966), 10.) This is the eros of poesis, not *sexual* seduction. One sees how men are named; women are simply designated as that gender.
16 Olson to Creeley, 18 February 1951 in Charles Olson and Robert Creeley, *The Complete Correspondence*, George F. Butterick, ed., Vol. V (Santa Barbara: Black Sparrow Press, 1983) 25, 26.
17 Ibid., 14.
18 Ibid., 63–4.
19 Ibid., 26.
20 Ibid.
21 Ibid., 61, 63, 65.
22 Ibid., 26–7, 63. Granted that the protocols of archaeological ethics were under-developed at that time.
23 Ibid., 25
24 Commodities are things: specific things explicitly produced for sale in the market.
25 Michael Davidson's recent proposals about Olson's value seem to differ on this point, with his eloquent defense of Olson's inspiration to a 'cultural' importance as well as a 'literary' one. By 'cultural' Davidson first means inciting 'a cultural poetics that performs for poetry what narrative has served for cultural studies' (I certainly have no quarrel with that goal); then he means Olson's lesson of 'active engagement with the present moment, utilizing a language engaged with its social context' (and Olson was one path to that goal, among other poets). However, Davidson has more faith than I do in Olson's claims of a kinetic, embodied 'methodology' as offering a serious hermeneutic tool for understanding our culture, another culture, and their histories. See Michael Davidson, *On the Outskirts of Form: Practicing Cultural Poetics* (Middletown, CT.: Wesleyan University Press, 2011), 11, 141, 127–8.
26 But see Peter Middleton's argument that Olson's problems with time are an important finding consistent with modern science, in Peter Middleton, 'Charles Olson: A Short History', *Parataxis* 10 (2001), 62–3.
27 Rachel Blau DuPlessis, *Purple Passages: Pound, Eliot, Zukofsky, Olson, Creeley and the Ends of Patriarchal Poetry* (Iowa City: University of Iowa Press, 2012), 128–9.

28 Contemporary women writers who have looked into the epic poem as near analogues for their work are eloquently and critically aware of this hierarchy of gender in epic. I am thinking particularly of H. D., Anne Waldman and Alice Notley.
29 Here the 'muse' of the poem would be his collected correspondence, particularly the epistolary relationships with Frances Boldereff and with Robert Creeley, not forgetting the initiating epistle to Vincent Ferrini (*GMP*, xxx).
30 Ron Silliman, 'Un-seen, ur-new: The history of the long poem and "The Collage Poems of Drafts"', *Jacket* 2, 14 December 2011, http://jacket2.org/article/un-scene-ur-new.
31 The episode called Nekuia (the visit to the underworld) suffuses *The Waste Land* and *Helen in Egypt*, enters part of *The Cantos*, traces through Notley's *Descent of Alette* and Mackey's *Song of the Andoumboulou*, and pulses intermittently in my *Drafts*.

11

'When the attentions change': Charles Olson and Frances Boldereff

Robert Hampson

In her essay 'Translating the unspeakable', Kathleen Fraser addresses Charles Olson's 'freeing of the page as a graphic site for poetic composition' and how this has been taken up in 'current female writing practice'.[1] She begins by referencing three contemporary American poets (Norma Cole, Susan Gevirtz and Mary Margaret Sloan) and describing 'a longing to make visible one's own peculiar way of experiencing how the mind moves and how the senses take note'.[2] She argues that the desire to articulate 'formerly inarticulate states of being' has found a 'visual apparatus' by 'expanding onto the FULL PAGE – responding to its spatial invitation to play with typographic relations of words and alphabets'.[3] She further argues that this use of the page-space could not be 'adequately thought about without acknowledging the immense, permission-giving moment of Charles Olson's "PROJECTIVE VERSE" manifesto'.[4] Fraser then discusses several pages from *The Maximus Poems* to demonstrate Olson's 'graphic intervention in the field of the regularised page' before addressing the work of a number of women poets, including Susan Howe, whom she presents as the 'primary extender of Olson's pictographic use of type and syllable'.[5] Since she begins by mentioning the 'male imperatives' behind the 'excitement and insistence of Olson's spatial, historical and ethical margins', the essay's attention to women poets writing in this tradition implicitly suggests a female or feminist appropriation or deturning of a notoriously masculinist poetics.[6] In the essay that follows, I want to document how this deturning is, in fact, a returning to source: that there was a significant female input into projective verse and composition by field that the critical emphasis on Olson's relationship with Pound, on the one hand, and Creeley, on the other, has served to occlude.

My focus in this essay will be that part of Olson's correspondence with Frances Boldereff which has been edited by Ralph Maud and Sharon Thesen.[7] The correspondence between them began in November 1947, when Olson received a letter from Boldereff praising *Call Me Ishmael*, and ran on until Olson's death. The Maud/Thesen volume covers the period from November 1947 to August 1950, when their relationship was particularly intense and productive. It is also the period during which, for a time, Olson and Boldereff were lovers. The most important thing to state, at the outset, is that Boldereff, by profession, was a Pennsylvania State College book designer, but she was also pursuing her own serious intellectual quest.[8] This is manifested in the series of books on Joyce which she wrote later, which drew together a number of her earlier research interests: *Reading Finnegans Wake* (1959), *A Blakean Translation of Joyce's Circe* (1965), and *Hermes to His Son Thoth* (1968). The first of these insists on 'formal scholarly achievements' as part of the necessary make-up of the poet.[9] In support of this, Boldereff quotes from Joyce's 1902 essay on Ireland's 'national poet', James Clarence Mangan: 'it must be asked concerning every artist how he is in relation to the highest knowledge'.[10] She then offers a reading of *Finnegans Wake* as 'the most intensely national poem in existence', bringing together the symbolic structure of the universe (as explored by Blake and Yeats), the history of Ireland, and daily life.[11] In accordance with her own programme, she reads *Finnegans Wake* as freed from any 'allegiance to dead beliefs' and Joyce as aiming, instead, 'to bring into being for his country a symbol of her unattainable desires'.[12] The third of these volumes, *Hermes to His Son Thoth*, begins with a celebration of Joyce's publisher, Dora Marsden, and her book *The Definition of the Godhead*.[13] In this book, Boldereff claims, Marsden 'named the error which all civilizations since the Egyptians have gone wrong on' and was 'trying to bring before the physical senses of man the non-physically observable, but psychologically true mode of existence of man'.[14] In opposition to 'the European (Faustian) man's conviction of the superiority of the intellect over the intuitive as a method of understanding the universe', Boldereff asserts 'Hermetic truths', 'Egyptian religion', and the continuing validity of myth as an expression of relations between humanity and the cosmos.[15]

As Thesen suggests, Boldereff was important to Olson both through her training as a book designer, which encouraged Olson 'to consider the role of typographic spacing', and intellectually.[16] As Olson soon discovered in his early correspondence with her, Boldereff had a passionate interest in Egyptian and Sumerian cultures, and Boldereff's intellectual pursuits encouraged Olson's own interest in the archaic and in myth. It was Boldereff, for example, who introduced Olson to Samuel Noah Kramer's work on 'the Sumerian sources of the Gilgamesh myth'.[17] In addition, Boldereff objected to the Judeo-Christian tradition because of what she called its 'depraved sex morality': she wrote to Olson (26

November 1949) that she wanted to 'take the whole Sumerian-Semitic myth and cast it out'.[18] She also recommended to him Jozef Stryzgowski's *Origin of Christian Church Art* (1923) as a way to access a pre-Christian world-view and aesthetic. Stryzgowski dismissed the dominant naturalistic tradition in Western art derived from Greece and Rome in favour of a non-representational tradition from Egypt, Mesopotamia and Islamic Persia that came into Europe along the trade routes. As Boldereff puts it in a letter, instead of 'the boys who gave us representation', this book presents 'all passion and non-representational decoration – the rhythm to speak direct, no copy of nature'.[19] From Olson's perspective, Strzygowski's emphasis on cultural transmission along trade routes chimed with 'the economics my pal Brooks offers in "The New Empire"'.[20] Ten years later, in his letter to Elaine Feinstein (May 1959), Olson harks back to this reading when he observes that he is 'talking from a new "double axis": the replacement of the Classical-representational by the *primitive-abstract*' (CPr, 251). Having qualified this by explaining that 'primitive' is not meant in 'that stupid use of it as opposed to civilized', he goes on: 'Content, in other words, is also shifted – at least from humanism, as have had it since the Indo-Europeans got their fid in there (circum 1500 BC)' (CPr, 251).

As Thesen suggests, Boldereff helped Olson 'to form the notion of what he came to call the postmodern' through her emphasis on the necessity of what she called the 'unHebraic': her interest in Sumeria provided an alternative both to the box of 'western civilisation' derived from Greece and Rome and to the Hebraic tradition.[21] Their shared engagement with 'the archaic' led to his perception that the 'judeo-christian-european-american tradition' had been 'wrong from the start', which was an important element in his notion of the 'postmodern'.[22] Their correspondence also formed the context for the 'Projective Verse' essay and the early parts of *The Maximus Poems*. Thus, on 10 January 1950, Olson wrote to Boldereff about 'this uproar in me at "lyricism"': 'it is only now that it suddenly comes to me that the opposite, what I have for so long hammered away at with the word "object", is IMPERSONALITY'.[23] On the same day she wrote to him: 'keep it clean, direct, open, proud and detached ... no God business, just man enlarging the use of his senses, and not substituting mental images for real objects'.[24] Boldereff was picking up here on an earlier letter (5 January 1950), in which she had quoted from Trigant Burrow's *The Genesis of Man's Dissociation*: 'a whimsical numen or false image of authority had replaced the authority that resides in the consistent correspondence between man's senses and the external world'.[25] A further quotation from Burrow's book in the same letter clarified the implications of his concept of the 'false image': 'In the semiotic systematizations of pseudo-religion, philosophy and metaphysics, man could only employ further elaborations of the symbol in attempting to explain himself to himself'.[26] According to Burrow, 'With the interruption of man's organic fidelity to external stimuli... man sustained a biological trauma of incalculable severity', and this alienated state is further compounded by the 'false image of authority' invested in the religious and philosophical discourses produced in this alienated state.[27]

Later, on 16 January 1950, Olson responded to Boldereff's letters by sending her a poem (beginning 'nature/ does not have / hierarchies / They // are of man's making / She // flows') which explores the 'stance towards reality' when man is no longer conceived of as the dominating 'subject', but rather as an object 'in the larger field of objects' (*CPr*, 247). In the accompanying letter, he also comments on the act of composition: 'This is the struggle. And it is permanently difficult, is new each time, & defies any law other than the new one each new one creates. And the only clue is rhythm, which is only to be described as the force & use of, the discipline of, the individual who has listened, & wants, at the moment he or she writes draws hammers shapes, to speak'.[28] We can see developing in this correspondence both that 'stance towards reality' and that address to the process of composition that emerge again in the 'Projective Verse' essay.

The 'Projective Verse' essay is clearly written in dialogue with various essays by Pound, including 'A Retrospect' (1918), 'How to Read' (1928) and his edited version of Ernest Fenollosa's essay 'The Chinese Written Character as a Medium for Poetry'. This engagement is marked, for example, by the references to composition by 'the musical phrase' or 'the dance of intellect'.[29] Olson also clearly acknowledges his debts to Dahlberg and Creeley, but, for various reasons, the relation between the essay and his correspondence with Boldereff is not acknowledged. Yet his comment on lyricism and the object in his letter to Boldereff is clearly part of a line of thought that the essay picks up on:

> Objectism is the getting rid of the lyrical interference of the individual as ego, of the 'subject' and his soul, that peculiar presumption by which western man has interposed himself between what he is as a creature of nature (with certain instructions to carry out) and those other creations of nature which we may, with no derogation, call objects.
>
> (*CPr*, 247)

James E. Miller has argued that, with this concept of 'objectism', Olson attempts to situate himself 'somewhere between Pound's ego-dominance and Williams' ego-submission'.[30] However, the Boldereff correspondence suggests that the Scylla and Charybdis that Olson realises that he is attempting to negotiate are Poundian ego and Eliotic impersonality. That 10 January letter also made clear the path Olson would follow: 'The only path to the universe is through yourself'.[31] In a letter of 10 March 1950, he refers to 'the making of himself as the form of his own objectification' and links this with 'open verse': 'to stay in the struggle for open verse as against closed, in order to arrive at forms which come not from the outside, inherited or – the better – narrative, but from the inside, from the working along with the self and the stuff in the open until some form comes out of it which is fresh and implicit to the-thing-needed-done itself'.[32] More importantly, that 'peculiar presumption' mentioned in the essay can be read, like the poem in Olson's 16 January letter, as a gloss on Burrow's concept of the 'false image'. At the same time, Olson's account of the 'struggle' involved in the act of composition – the sense that each new poem creates its own 'law', the centrality of rhythm, and the relation of rhythm to listening and speaking – anticipates the essay's assertion that the poet involved in composition by field 'can go by no track other than the one the poem under hand declares, for itself' and that the poet has to 'register both the acquisitions of his ear *and* the pressures of his breath' (*CPr*, 241). However, in the essay, the notion of rhythm that has been present in the correspondence is now firmly linked with the body and breath of the poet.

On 6 February 1950, Olson began his letter to Boldereff by announcing the 'Projective / (projectile / (prospective' and then, on 11 February, he sent the first typed version of the 'Projective Verse' essay to her. In this version, Olson cited the opening lines of 'The Kingfishers' and the first three lines of 'The Advantage' – both poems with a particular meaning in their relationship – as examples of projective space notation. On 15 February he wrote to her about typography, saying that he had 'a whole series of things to take up with your knowledge abt the shifting of type face' and that he would 'want to talk abt this when we are together'.[33] He goes on: 'If I am right abt what the typewriter has offered the poet in composition, then it seems to me to follow that, in the printing of language which is projective, there ought to be another convention accepted by the reader – that type-face may change page to page'.[34] Clearly her professional knowledge of typography and graphic design was part of the attraction she had for him. In June 1950, when Olson wrote a letter to Robert Giroux at Harcourt Brace recommending Boldereff for work, he noted that 'her sense of printing is not type alone but a profound understanding of the space which a page is'.[35] Was this a knowledge that Olson himself owed to Boldereff?

With this letter of 15 February, Olson returned to Boldereff the typescript of her essay 'Walt Whitman and the Millennial Re-Union'.

Boldereff begins this essay by describing a situation where: 'an older alien Culture lies so massively over the land that a young Culture, born in this land, cannot get its breath and fails not only to achieve pure and specific expression forms, but even to develop fully its own self-consciousness'.[36] In his letter of 21 February, Olson seems to have taken this on board. He writes: 'the artist today must be a culture carrier'.[37] The suggestion of a shared campaign is developed in his letter of 2 March 1950, when he observes: 'What I mean is, the shift which makes possible new culture, new history, new life, is a shift of the point of vantage'.[38] On 14 March she responds: 'I want more than anything in the world to come off with a NEW – an unhebraic notion of life... and the angle I want is so very unGreek too'.[39] She goes on: 'I want to combine Melville's sense of the power of the out there – the immensity of what man does not and cannot know ... with Blake's fiery belief in energy'.[40] By 17 March, Olson is proposing 'to act, straight, clean, from the center' and to reject 'what was done to the sex of my being by Catholicism, new englandism, americanism'.[41] That sex is a key issue in this 'new culture' is clear from Olson's letter of 30 March, where he refers to 'a confusion at the very root of that miserable religion of 3000 years' and then affirms that 'sex is only the deepest part of a continuous system': 'sexual – SENSUAL – INTELLECTUAL'.[42] In short, sex is 'the kinetic of the human'.[43] This new 'point of vantage' was arrived at through his erotic relationship with Boldereff.

On 17 May 1950, Olson wrote to Boldereff about the practical problems of achieving a 'music-contained' poetry and observed that the 'Projective Verse' essay, which had not yet been published, was 'only scratching the skin of it':

> It is the craziest sort of feeling, this, of not being able to match the done! ... I suppose this plane is the sex of writing art, the underpart, the nervousness because love is not born. One loves only form, and form only comes into existence when the thing is born. And the thing may lie around the bend of the next second.[44]

Olson had sent poems to Boldereff and had written letter poems to her before. In this case, the letter both contains an early draft of the first of the *Maximus* poems ('I, Maximus') and provides the basis for the final version. The first four sections of the first *Maximus* poem start from phrases from this passage: 'the thing you are after / may lie around the bend'; 'love is form'; 'the underpart is, though stemmed, uncertain'; 'one loves only form / and form only comes / into existence when / the thing is born'. The letter marks an important stage in the genesis of the poem. Thus, for example, as Clark notes, in re-typing this passage as verse, Olson mis-typed 'next' as 'nest' and then, accepting the error in the spirit of the passage, generated from what was given 'under hand' the key image of 'the bird, the bird'.[45] (The mis-typing was, perhaps, influenced by the emphasis on the nest in the second part of 'The Kingfishers'.) In a similar way, 'the sex of writing art, the underpart,' produces the expanded account of 'the underpart' and the second line of section 3: 'is, as sex is, as moneys, are, facts!' The sexualised imagery of the opening to *The Maximus Poems*, the foregrounded concern with love and even perhaps the inclusion of the address to 'my lady of good voyage', the statue of the Virgin Mary which acts as 'the invoked muse of the poem', clearly derive from this original context of a letter between Olson and Boldereff (*GMP*, 11).[46]

The letter to Boldereff concludes:

> Anyhow, I give you the
> deepest sort of recognition, speak out from hidden islands
> in the blood which, like jewels and miracles, you invoke.
> And I, as hard-boiled instrument, as metal hot from boiling
> water, tell you, he recognizes what is lance, obeys,
> the dance [47]

An already difficult passage becomes even denser when turned into the opening lines of the first Maximus poem. The letter ends with this passage I have just quoted already turned into the compressed lines of verse that become the opening lines of the poem:

> Off-shore, by islands hidden in the blood
> jewels & miracles, I, Maximus
> a metal hot from boiling water, tell you
> what is a lance, who obeys the figures of
> the present dance
>
> (*MP*, 5)

Perhaps working backwards from 'islands', Olson adds 'Off-shore' to register the de-centred (and de-centring) position of Maximus of Tyre in relation to both the Greek world and the city of Gloucester which he addresses. The letter's reference to 'dance' is also reworked to draw in the phrasing of the 'Projective Verse' essay: Olson's insistence there on the scrupulous listening to the syllable is vividly enacted in these lines.[48] The reworked phrase thus anticipates the insistence 'By ear, he sd', which combines scrupulous listening with improvisation, and the contrast with the 'mu-sick, mu-sick, mu-sick' of pejorocracy. Butterick suggests that this first *Maximus* poem was 'probably written in May 1950' as 'a letter to Vincent Ferrini' (*GMP*, 5).[49] Olson revised the version of the text he had sent to Boldereff and sent a copy to Ferrini in response to Ferrini's request for a contribution for a new Gloucester-based magazine, *Voyager*. This request presumably influenced Olson's attention to the use of Gloucester material and the form of a public letter addressed to its people. However, the relationship with Boldereff is obviously a vitally important context for the start of *The Maximus Poems*. Olson clearly draws on letters to Boldereff – and, as I will suggest, even the practice of writing verse-letters – in setting up the project. This does not, of course, preclude a simultaneous address to Ferrini: as Clark suggests, Olson was practiced at producing a double address, 'one public and literary, one private and coded for translation only by his directive Muse'.[50] In this case, the word 'obeys' repays some attention as it plays across private and public spheres. In the original letter to Boldereff, it operates in the context of his avowal of 'the deepest sort of recognition' for her, which is qualified by that reference to the 'blood', a code word derived from their shared interest in D. H. Lawrence.[51] What in the private letter is an expression of a deep 'recognition' rooted in the body and its desires, turns, in the public address, in 'the *present* dance', into obedience to the 'several forces' and various 'participants in the kinetic' of the poem (*CPr*, 243). As with 'my lady of good voyage', private and public overlap and various parties are drawn into a subtly striated project.

As Clark suggests, Boldereff was an important influence on Olson's poetry from the beginning. Having praised *Call Me Ishmael* in her first letter to him, she was one of the few early readers of *Y & X* to respond positively to the work.[52] What Clark calls the 'confidence-building exchange' of letters between them encouraged Olson to plan a long poem, 'Proteus', early in 1949, while her challenge to him to provide evidence of the 'new America' that he claimed to detect resulted in him sending her 'The Kingfishers' as his 'answer' at the end of the year.[53] 'The Praises' is all that emerged from the 'Proteus' project: drawing on Plutarch's *Lives* and the history of geometry, it engages with mathematical patterns in nature, with the need 'to be clean / in a dirty time', and with the transmission of knowledge:

> that that which has been found out by work
>   may, by work be passed on
> (without due loss of force)
> for use
>   USE
>
> (*CP*, 100)[54]

Boldereff also had a more direct input into Olson's poetry. Her copies of Kramer's translations of Sumerian poetic and religious texts, which she sent to Olson, led directly to his poem 'La Chute', and metaphors in her letters (her references to herself as an uprooted Sequoia and her comparison of his role in the culture to releasing the spores of a puffball) were adopted by Olson in his poems 'These Days' and 'The Advantage'.[55] As Clark notes, Olson regarded his eventual meeting with Boldereff as a watershed in his life as a poet: Clark quotes a journal entry in which Olson records meeting Boldereff for the first time in November 1949 (a meeting which ended in their spending the following night together) and then marks Spring 1950 as when 'the writing starts'.[56] This bears comparison with Olson's 1964 note on Maximus: 'Maximus, hero, a metal hot from boiling water, born in the winter, 1949–50, age 38–39' (*GMP*, 5).[57]

May 1950 was certainly an immensely productive period for Olson: it began with 'I, Maximus of Gloucester, to You' and 'In Cold Hell, in Thicket', and included 'For Sappho, Back' and 'Help Me, Venus, You Who Led Me On', all addressed to Boldereff. She not only encouraged his writing, but also, as we have seen, provided material for the writing. (Indeed, as Clark suggests, she began to worry that this was her main role for Olson). In addition, some of Olson's letters to her became first drafts or try-outs for subsequent poems. Indeed, through his experience of this correspondence, he also perhaps came to see 'the letter' as the solution to a new formal problem he was addressing: 'the problem of larger content and of larger forms' (*CPr*, 248).[58] Thus, on 26 June 1950, he wrote to Boldereff: 'I am beginning to try to figure out an assault on form larger than what a man can get done in one go'.[59] The poetics of the 'Projective Verse' essay worked for a single poem – 'a poet stays in the open, and goes by breath, not by inherited form' – but this does not address the formal and structural problems of the long poem.[60] He goes on: 'What I need is some methodology to go on day after day on the same content as the day before, with the same steam up, inside the same amnion, until I can come out with a form which could be an extension of a larger kind of content'.[61] He perhaps also glimpses a solution, when he observes: 'you know, from their coming into being, most of them, in letters written of afternoons to you, about how much stamina a man can keep up, and keep inside one tone, one problem, one attack on a material'.[62] With his letter of 29 June 1950, he included a complete draft of 'I, Maximus of Gloucester, to You'.

I suggested at the start that Boldereff encouraged Olson's interest in the archaic. For all the earlier emphasis on the need for a new culture, the letters exchanged between Olson and Boldereff during the summer of 1950 repeatedly return to this topic. Thus, in Olson's letter of 6 July 1950, after offering a critique of Jung, Olson adds:

> For the presence in each of us of, such archaic figures as, dreams produce, is, whether it is phylogenetic or not, of absolute importance to a rebirth of

conduct and structure and force: simply because it was from these areas that, originally and now, men discovered ambiguity of experience which told energies they wot not of .[63]

As in his Mayan work, Olson turns to archaic cultures to discover energies and ways of being unknown or lost to modern, Western culture. At the same time, the archaic is also present within us – and accessible, for example, through dreams. As Olson wrote on 14 July 1950, 'the joker is, the archaic or chthonic is not, and never was, horizontal and history: it is always present perpendicularly in each of us'.[64] In a letter of 10 August, he develops this thought further: 'the archaic or primordial is not at all "past" ... we are a perpendicular axis of planes which are constantly being intersected by horizontal planes of experience, coming in from the past'.[65] These horizontal planes of experience include memories, visions and dreams, and Olson sees in them a way of contesting 'the so-called rational, egotistical, realistic'.[66] Olson's interest in these different planes and axes is part of their shared cultural project ('the absolute dynamiting of, the PATRIARCHY'), but also part of his inquiry into method: 'the images and events which I have found floating in myself are not merely images and events but are energies as legitimate for myself and for others as the "thoughts" or "reports" or mere "sense perceptions"'.[67]

At the same time, Olson's letters also address the question of dealing with a more recent past. As he wrote in his letter of 13 July: 'we are also children of that immediate past as well as children and projectors of that more chthonic, archaic thing which we, perhaps more than any two living beings, are living out, pushing the arc of, ahead'.[68] As well as seeking to draw on chthonic energies, Olson also had to devise a method to deal with 'that immediate past'. In his letter of 6 July, he had outlined the problem: 'to devise some other method to accomplish coverage of the whole field of knowledge'.[69] In his letter of 14 July, he introduced his 'new friend, Apollonius of Tyana' and the solution he embodied: 'get back to yr local hero-god, take yr power up here, don't buy the Olympians, Greek or Roman, stick to your own ground, and your old cults'.[70] However, as Butterick points out, Olson was not interested in the local, but rather the particular (*GMP*, 8–9).[71] Apollonius thus embodied another lesson, which Olson spelled out in his 5 August letter: 'a belief in particulars not as important in themselves but as CARRIERS, as notation: for the way they get themselves down is such a revelation of the senses'.[72] Through these letters to Boldereff, we can see Olson working out some of the basic principles of the method of the Maximus poems.

At the same time, as we have seen, the necessarily clandestine nature of their emotional and sexual relationship encouraged one of the more problematic aspects of Olson's work, the privately-coded allusions.[73] Private allusions designed to escape the attention of Olson's wife, Connie, also pose problems for later readers. To put it another way round, details from Olson's meetings with Boldereff and his correspondence with her, as we have seen, often provide the clue to opaque or difficult passages in his poetry. Thus, 'In Cold Hell, in Thicket', which one critic explained as 'the epistemological climate that the non-projective man finds himself suffering as he begins to feel the impact of the "return to space"', might also be read, as Clark does, as Olson's inability or refusal to choose between the two women in his life.[74] The Egyptian cosmology drawn on in the poem appears here (as elsewhere) as a covert tribute to Boldereff.

On 21 April 1950, a new figure entered Olson's life, Robert Creeley, and Olson's next major essay, 'The Gate and the Center', in which he called for a return to the cultural consciousness of Sumerian civilisation, began as a letter to him. In a letter of 17 March 1950, Olson had written to Boldereff recalling how *Call Me Ishmael* had introduced them to each other: 'you met me under that hebraic name i am now – because of *us*, I venture to think – rejecting'.[75] As I have noted, he rejects 'what was done to the sex of my being by catholicism, new englandism, americanism', and, instead, plans 'to act, straight, clean, from the center'.[76] The critique of 'American and Western education', the emphasis on 'primordial & phallic energies', which were the products of his relationship with Boldereff, were offered up to Creeley at the start of what was to become a massive correspondence between the two men. In the meantime, Olson's erotic relationship with Boldereff had come to an end. In September 1950, when he turned up at her apartment in Brooklyn 'after months of stalling', Boldereff turned him away with the news that there was a new man in her life.[77] Six months later, on 31 March 1951, Olson wrote to Creeley about the 'shift' that had taken place in his life in the previous year, 'with you coming in, and three others going out ... my mother, Ed [Dahlberg] ... and another, which, to my bewilderment, had to be gone by'.[78] It is, perhaps, understandable that the married Olson should be a little reticent about his relationship with Boldereff in his early correspondence with a new friend, but, though his correspondence with her continued alongside the correspondence with Creeley, he never mentions her again. The occlusion of her contribution to his thinking and to the early development of his poetry in this correspondence with Creeley sets the critical pattern that was to continue until Clark's biography and the editing (by Maud and Thesen) of the early correspondence between Olson and Boldereff. However, the obvious significance of this relationship for Olson's work not only adds to the picture of the major contribution of women to the visual poetics of the twentieth century but also, perhaps, complicates our sense of gender in relation to Olson's work.[79]

Notes

1 Kathleen Fraser, 'Translating the unspeakable: Visual poetics, as projected through Olson's "field" into current female writing practice', in *Translating the Unspeakable: Poetry and the Innovative Necessity* (Tuscaloosa, AL: University of Alabama Press, 2000), 174–200. This was originally given as a paper at the 'Assembling Alternatives' conference at the University of New Hampshire in 1996.
2 Ibid., 175.
3 Ibid.
4 Ibid.
5 Ibid., 178, 198. For a fuller discussion of Howe's debts to Olson, see Will Montgomery, *The Poetry of Susan Howe: History, Theology, Authority* (London: Palgrave, 2010), 90–4.
6 Ibid., 177.
7 Ralph Maud and Sharon Thesen (eds), *Charles Olson and Frances Boldereff: A Modern Correspondence* (Hanover: Wesleyan University Press, 1999).
8 Tom Clark, *Charles Olson: The Allegory of a Poet's Life* (New York: W. W. Norton, 1991), 136.
9 Frances Boldereff, *Reading Finnegans Wake* (Woodward, Penn.: Classic Non-Fiction, 1959), xi.
10 Ibid., and see 'James Clarence Mangan' (1902) in Kevin Barry (ed.), *James Joyce: Occasional, Critical, and Political Writing* (Oxford: Oxford World's Classics, 2000), 54. 'Ireland's national poet' is taken from the translation of Joyce's later lecture, 'James Clarence Mangan' (1907), 127.
11 Boldereff, *Reading*, xii.
12 Ibid., 59, 60.
13 Dora Marsden was the editor of the *Egoist*, which published Joyce's *A Portrait of the Artist as a Young Man* as a serial.
14 Frances M. Boldereff, *Hermes to His Son Thoth: Being Joyce's Use of Giordano Bruno in 'Finnegans Wake'* (Woodward, Penn.: Classic Non-Fiction Library, 1968), 16.
15 Boldereff, *Hermes*, 20.
16 Maud and Thesen, *A Modern Correspondence*, xv.
17 Ibid.
18 Ibid., 72.
19 Ibid., 136.
20 Ibid., 204.
21 Ibid., xv.
22 Ibid., 515.
23 Ibid., 111.

24 Ibid., 115.
25 Ibid., 106.
26 Ibid.
27 Ibid., 107.
28 Ibid., 124.
29 See Ezra Pound, 'A Retrospect' (1918) for the reference to composition by 'the musical phrase' rather than by the metronome, while 'the dance of the intellect among words' appeared as a definition of 'logopaeia' in Pound's 1928 essay, 'How to Read'. See T. S. Eliot (ed.), *Literary Essays of Ezra Pound* (New York: New Directions, 1968), 3, 25.
30 James E. Miller, Jr., *The American Quest for a Supreme Fiction* (Cambridge: Cambridge University Press, 1979), 205.
31 Maud and Thesen, *A Modern Correspondence*, 111.
32 Ibid., 230.
33 Ibid., 174.
34 Ibid., 175.
35 Ibid., 380.
36 Ibid., 176.
37 Ibid., 189.
38 Ibid., 204.
39 Ibid., 238.
40 Ibid., 239.
41 Ibid., 249–50.
42 Ibid., 282.
43 Ibid., 283.
44 Ibid., 335.
45 Clark, *Allegory*, 166.
46 It is worth noting that Olson signed off the letter 'a kylix, charles'. This re-appears in the poem's invocation 'o kylix, o / Antony of Padua' as a coded alignment of the bird and Antony of Padua with Olson.
47 Maud and Thesen, *A Modern Correspondence*, 337.
48 'For from the root out, from all over the place, the syllable comes, the figures of, the dance' (*CPr*, 242).
49 Butterick notes Ferrini's letter of 20 May 1950, which acknowledges his receipt of the poem.
50 Clark, *Allegory*, 167.
51 See Olson's 1950 essay, 'The Escaped Cock: Notes on Lawrence & the Real', published in *Origin* and collected in *Human Universe and Other Essays*, ed. Donald Allen (New York, Grove Press, 1967).
52 Clark, *Allegory*, 145.
53 Ibid., 146.
54 This anticipates the concern with energy transfer and use in the 'Projective Verse' essay. Consider how Creeley's apothegm, 'Form is never more than an extension of content' is handed on 'for USE' (*CPr*, 240) and Dahlberg's statement, 'One perception must immediately and directly lead to a further perception', is followed by the advice 'USE, USE, USE the process at all

points' (*CPr*, 240). There is, perhaps, a similar shift in these lines from noun to imperative.
55 Clark, *Allegory*, 158–9.
56 Ibid., 153.
57 This was part of a biographical note Olson wrote for the anthology, *New Writing in the USA*.
58 At the end of this essay, Olson turns to this problem and, in a comparison of Pound and Eliot, suggests that the *Cantos* do not solve the problem, but 'the methodology of the verse in them points a way by which the problem ... may be solved'.
59 Maud and Thesen, *A Modern Correspondence*, 387.
60 Ibid. One motive for Olson's turn towards the long poem is suggested by his letter of 29 May 1950, in which he expresses the urgent need to 'displace' Pound (Maud and Thesen, *A Modern Correspondence*, 356).
61 Ibid.
62 Ibid.
63 Ibid., 397.
64 Ibid., 419.
65 Ibid., 478.
66 Ibid.
67 Ibid., 413, 480.
68 Ibid., 412.
69 Ibid., 396.
70 Ibid., 419.
71 Butterick cites a later note (10 February 1960) left by Olson among his papers: 'The interest is not in the local at all as such – any local; and the choice of Gloucester is particular – that is the point of the interest, particularism itself: to reveal it, in all possible ways and force, against the "loss" of value of the universal'.
72 Maud and Thesen, *A Modern Correspondence*, 472.
73 Problematic in a different way is his response to her letter of 18 April 1950, where she describes her sense of vulnerability in their relationship by reference to a friend who 'undressed to nakedness' and 'in the greatest loneliness ... drowned herself in the Hudson River'. Olson's only response was to incorporate her words into a poem 'here i am, naked' (Clark, *Allegory*, 164).
74 Olson sent 'In Cold Hell, in Thicket' to Boldereff on 23 May 1950.
75 Maud and Thesen, *A Modern Correspondence*, 248.
76 Ibid., 250, 249.
77 Clark, *Allegory*, 185.
78 *Charles Olson & Robert Creeley: The Complete Correspondence*, Vol. 2 (ed. George Butterick), 137–8.
79 For more on women's contribution to twentieth-century visual poetics, see Robert Hampson and Will Montgomery, 'Innovations in Poetry' in Peter Brooker, Andrzej Gasiorek and Andrew Thacker (eds), *The Oxford Handbook of Modernisms* (Oxford: Oxford University Press, 2010), 66–8.

12

'The pictorial handwriting of his dreams': Charles Olson, Susan Howe, Redell Olsen

Will Montgomery

'I get tired of hearing that Charles Olson was six foot seven and towered over everyone,' writes Susan Howe in her 1989 essay 'Since a Dialogue we Are', one of two she wrote on Olson in the late 1980s. 'Bigmans I and II, the heft of his books in advance. The constant reminder of brute force crosses and confuses his influence. Maybe it is antipodal to his nature.'[1]

Susan Howe's early work is made in the bulky shadow of Olson. In her published remarks on Olson she remains strikingly ambivalent. She says that Maximus *IV, V, VI* was a 'crucial' model as she switched from the visual arts to poetry in the early 1970s.[2] *Call Me Ishmael* was similarly important to her criticism: 'For me, Olson gave birth to Melville, and *Call Me Ishmael* gave birth to *My Emily Dickinson*.'[3]

Yet, she objects: 'Had he been my teacher in real life, I know he would have stopped my voice.'[4] This alignment of Olson with patriarchal censure has been pervasively felt among postwar poets of the modernist line. As Howe writes:

> The tradition of dead fathers weighs heavily on writing that passes itself off as a liberated field. So much of it comes down to an idea of power, that while inflicting blows on literary and political authority only circles back to its own despotic centrality.[5]

This idea of an equivocal relation to authority returns in various guises in her writing on Olson. She rejects the misogyny in his writing, but repeatedly returns to the liberating formal possibilities available in the work. An asterisk beside the title of her 1987 essay 'Where Should the Commander Be' leads to the footnote: 'A preliminary exploration of the hidden feminine in Melville and Olson'.[6] Howe's responsibility as a critic to read against the grain of the text is made clear: 'A critic's dialogue with the thinking of writing should be a clarification and understanding that an author's major meanings are often unspoken.'[7] In an interview with Edward Foster conducted two years later she observes:

If there is Woman in Olson's writing (there aren't women there), she is either 'Cunt', 'Great Mother', 'Cow', or 'Whore'. But the feminine is very much in his poems in another way, a way similar to Melville. It's voice... It has to do with the presence of absence. With articulation of sound forms. The fractured syntax, the gaps, the silences are equal to the sounds in *Maximus*. That's what Butterick saw so clearly. He printed Olson's Space.[8]

In this period, when the politics of poetic form verged on the utopian for some avant-garde writers, it was not unusual for Howe to force energetic collisions of motifs from such distinct areas as poetic form, page space, gender or politics. Howe's own intractable texts, in which non-saying and resistance become motifs of revelatory opacity, embody an exploration of Olsonian space by other means; she goes on to tell Foster that she shares Olson's interest in the 'stutter in American literature'.[9] In the 1980s, Howe is inspired by the formal energy of Olson's writing. She leaves aside the capacious mythopoesis of *Maximus*, pursuing an oppositional historical poetics that draws on the dynamism of Olson's montage-like use of page-space. In 'Where Should the Commander Be' she writes:

> At his best, Olson lets words and groups of words, even letter arrangements and spelling accidentals shoot suggestions at each other, as if each page were a canvas and the motion of the words – reality across the surface.[10]

There are many ways of linking Howe to Olson. One might discuss, for example, the relationship in terms of visual poetics. Or the use of archival and documentary material in poetic montages that crush together wildly distant spaces and times in counter-historical constellations. Or the development of a form of literary criticism that, similarly, made montage a first principle. Or a revisionary American history: both Howe and Olson are concerned with events occurring during the settlement of the north-east coast of America in the middle of the seventeenth century, each suggesting that the Puritan leadership of the Bay Area Colony in this period established a model of social authority that was to have lasting and damaging consequences for American political life.

The line I'd initially like to follow, however, runs through the father. In 'Where Should the Commander Be' Howe notes that *Call Me Ishmael* was completed in August 1945. August was the month of Melville's birth and the month in which the whaling ship the *Essex*, real-life precursor of the *Pequod*, set sail from Nantucket. It is also, writes Olson in *Maximus*, 'my father's month'.[11] For Howe, Melville clearly assumes a paternal role for Olson, both inhibiting and enabling. What lies unstated is the struggle with Olson-the-father in her own writing.

In the second of Howe's Olson essays she writes, 'A phoenix soars from cinders of his father. An old fiction yields a new fiction.'[12] She also rhapsodises on the epigraph to *Call Me Ishmael*:

> O fahter, fahter
> gone amoong
>
> O eeys that loke
>
> Loke, fahter:
> your sone!
>
> (CPr, 5)

For Howe, whose poetry of the time often circulates around motifs of paternity and absence, this gesture was inspirational: 'Time and again I have wondered over these five lines and have been inspired by their oddity to take chances in my writing.'[13] In Stephen Collis's edition of Howe's letters to George Butterick, her first letter to Olson's editor, from February 1977, asks him for the source of this quote. The letter concludes 'It haunts me, – Susan Howe'.[14] The figure of the father is isolated as a central problem in Howe's account of Olson in her late 1980s essays, where she argues that he was engaged in an Oedipal struggle, a story of fathers and sons. The emphasis in each, however, is different. In her 'Commander' essay she argues that 'Through long study and great love for another, Olson reached his own Prime: "I am"'. She asserts that in *Call Me Ishmael* Olson: 'stood free of, and contemporary with, his Soul's cold fire-father, a Captain among hunters, an "original aboriginal" mediator-Moses'.[15] In support of this 'freeing' relationship to an earlier writer, she cites a moment of Oedipal enablement in *Call Me Ishmael*: 'immediately that Macbeth murders the king he strides hugely forward into the mystery.'[16] In the later 'Since a Dialogue We Are', however, Oedipus is not negotiated successfully. Rather, it prevents Olson from taking up the formal challenge offered in his own work:

> Instead of allowing the vertiginous multiplicity a fictitious name suggests, to create an open field, he fences it with a collective Oedipalism. In this economy of exchange – of FORCE – man's business; are we a Dialogue?[17]

Monologic patriarchy is set against an open field; the feminine, dialogic energies of which, according to Howe, Olson was only partly able to recognise. What is called for, she suggests, is a movement beyond patriarchy, a disavowal, not a sacrificial slaying of the father, as that can only perpetuate the agonistic cycle. In the two Olson essays, Howe is doing something comparable to her better known work on Dickinson: articulating her own poetics through her engagement with another writer. Her position on Olson – that he was not fully alert to the implications of his most important innovation, the open field – involves, ironically enough, a sacrificial slaying of its own, while the Dickinson work announces an unequivocal identification with a female forebear. In her gendered critique of Olson, Howe looks beyond the author of Maximus to Melville for a liberating orphanhood of the text:

> In 'Hawthorne and his Mosses' Melville writes: 'Would that all excellent books were foundlings, without father or mother, that so it might be, we could glorify them, without including their ostensible authors.'
> In the passionate dis-order of Olson's Master Foundation of America, I can find no other horizon than collapsing contradiction.[18]

In Howe's 'Commander' essay, through a process of displacement, Moses becomes Hawthorne's Mosses becomes Moby: 'Where was Moses when the lights went out? Moses Mosses Moby maybe'.[19] Olson, in Howe's elliptical account, extends Melville's 'drowned dreams, somnambulisms, reveries'.[20] 'I don't know of another American poet,' she writes, 'who shows the *pictorial handwriting* of his dreams to such a degree' [original emphasis].[21]

The foundation for Olson's montage-like critical work in *Call Me Ishmael* lies in his pioneering postgraduate textual scholarship, which uncovered several key items in Melville's library. Olson was particularly concerned with Melville's marginalia, especially Melville's annotations to his edition of Shakespeare. These he held to be the working notes to *Moby-Dick* and the key to its meaning: a primitive rebellion against the God of the Old Testament.[22]

A notion of marginalia so expanded that it collapses the materiality of the page with social and political themes is a sustaining element of Susan Howe's writing of the 1980s and early 1990s, notably her work *Melville's Marginalia*. She condenses, in short, a late-twentieth-century regard for the annotations and slips that destabilise the ostensible positioning of a text (hence, for example, the recovery of a 'feminine' opacity from a poetry suffused with male authority) with a concern for the silenced and marginalised voices in American culture.

Despite, or perhaps because of, the affinities with her own work, Howe does not dwell in her 'Commander' essay on the role that textual scholarship plays in Olson's Melville book. Her essay reflects on 'Dis-order'. But this principle of instability is not simply valorised as a catch-all sanctuary of inexpressibility. Building on Olson's 'ENERGY [...] SPEED [...] DIRECTION',[23] his invocation of Proteus and flux,[24] Howe advances a theory of reading that is both battered and enriched by the shocks of unconscious processes, alert both to 'content's conceptualisation' and the 'muffled strata of sensual Dis-order'.[25]

Call Me Ishmael makes explicit use of psychoanalysis as a critical tool. One means of explicating the repressed savagery in Melville lies, for Olson, in an adaptation of Freud's theory of the primal horde, as expressed in *Moses and Monotheism*, in which the founding moment of the institution of society is the murder of the father/leader by his sons. (Olson wrote *Call Me Ishmael* before he came under the sway of Jung.)[26]

Moby-Dick is for Olson a book of the 'old dispensation', predating the feminising influence that, he argued, Christianity would exert on Melville's later work. He writes that, 'The Melville who wrote *Moby-Dick* ... was not weakened by any New Testament world. He had reached back to where he belonged. He could face up to Moses: he knew the great deed and misdeed of primitive time. It was in himself' (*CPr*, 76).

Olson's reading of Melville is permeated with metaphors for a paternity in crisis: 'Melville was agonised over paternity. He suffered as a son. He had lost the source. He demanded to know the father.' But this leads him to 'Original Act [...] First Murder':

> Now he [Melville] counted his birthdays as the Hebrews did: a son's years gathered not from the son's birth but from the father's death. Another Moses, Melville wrote in *Moby-Dick* the Book of the Law of the Blood.
> (*CPr*, 73, 76)

Ahab's monumental conflict with the whale, Melville's 'god', is pitched at the level of an infernal struggle over paternity: 'The White Whale became the biggest single creature a man has been pitted against and Ahab's rage and hate is scaled like Satan's, the largest enemy of the Father man has imagined' (*CPr*, 75). Moses is doubly invaded by Melville's identification: he is both father and son, pitted against God the Father and (following *Moses and Monotheism*) murdered by his savage followers.

Moreover, it is possible to pursue this, following Freud, by drawing an analogy between individual and group psychology. The vicissitudes of the Jewish religion, in Freud's argument, recapitulate the passage of neurosis: 'Early trauma – defence – latency – outbreak of neurotic illness – partial return of the repressed.'[27] Freud theorises social identification as an affective bond occurring in the presence of the leader, while Melville, for all his scepticism about Ahab, celebrates 'that democratic dignity which on all hands, radiates without end from God; Himself! The great god absolute! The centre and circumference of all democracy! His omnipresence, our divine equality!'[28]

Ahab's quest is to the limits of knowledge. The paternal pacific, which, Olson argues, gave Melville 'the right of primogeniture', is the murky end-point of an intellectual quest: 'The Pacific is the end of the

UNKOWN which Homer's and Dante's Ulysses open men's eyes to. End of the individual responsible only to himself. Ahab is full stop.' The son of 'the father of Ocean', *Call Me Ishmael*'s final paragraph concludes, is instability raised to the status of a principle: the 'prophet Proteus' (*CPr*, 102, 105).

Philippe Lacoue-Labarthe and Jean-Luc Nancy's reading of *Moses and Monotheism*, however, shows us how Freud uses two powerful figures of dissimulation to undermine the figure of the father. These allow us to recontextualise the Oedipal lineage proposed by Olson by offering the inauthentic father as a supplement to the present-absent father in *Call Me Ishmael*. First, through the workings of the return of the repressed, the memory of the great God of Moses becomes associated with the figure of the small-time local god Yahweh. Moses was of another race, so the Moses of the Old Testament hands down the religion of the oppressor. Social identity, to broaden the argument into group psychology, is constituted 'from without'.[29] Second, with the slow passage of the return of the repressed in history, the 'father once more became the head of the family, but was not by any means so absolute as the father of the primal horde had been'.[30] The originating father is recognised only on his return. The figure of the father, a memento of a forgotten trauma or 'unforgivable crime', is, argue Lacoue-Labarthe and Nancy, eternally false and deferred:

> The Freudian re-elaboration of the origin is not a simple narrative or chronological reworking of the 'dawn of man' but actually touches on the logic of the origin itself, upsetting its schema and structure. [...] Freud's entire demonstration in *Moses and Monotheism* is always, from whatever direction one approaches it, the position or supposition of that which no logic (at least, no logic of the origin) is capable of mastering: namely, that the origin is second.[31]

In Olson's account of Melville, the Pacific Ocean itself was this enigmatic 'father', as well as a place of dreams. A watery grave offers the only route to this shadowy figure. Olson cites Melville's outburst, in the middle of a description of the Pacific:

> Where is the foundling's father hidden? Our souls are like those orphans whose unwedded mothers die in bearing them; the secret of our paternity lies in their grave, and we must there to learn it.

(*CPr*, 102)

Howe's essay on *Call Me Ishmael* repeats Freud's analogy between the psychic and the social, fanning out quickly into an indictment of an urge for mastery within American culture:

[Moses and Monotheism] was crucial to *Call Me Ishmael*, and to much of his later writing. Desire, demand, and primeval parricide articulate his methodology. Closer to home, in American history, the political and religious underpinning of Colonialism and Capitalism as exploitation of workers in a 'Book of the Law of the Blood'. Explorers, conquistadors, ministers, priests, pioneers, hunters and industrialists had, 'Like Ahab, American, one aim: lordship over nature.'[32]

Susan Howe's 'exploration of the hidden feminine' in Olson (or rather in *her* rather carefully positioned Olson) is a means of unsettling that claim to lordship. Her own poetry oscillates between the poles of mother and father, with the father, who died before Howe became a poet, taking precedence in the early work, up to 1993's *The Nonconformist's Memorial*. In this period, paternity is nearly always depicted as absent, false or deferred. This can be taken, at one level, as autobiographical: Howe's father was away at war for several years when she was a girl. It can also, at another level, be read into the work's frequent invocation in her poetry of the language of negative theology, in which no positive statement of the divine is feasible. Or it can be understood as a figure for the wide-ranging critique of the metaphysics of presence that was current in the academy at this time. And it can be read in concretely political terms, as a querying of a social authority that is gendered as male.

One example, among many, of Howe's attempts to unpick this 'Corruptible first figure'[33] is her 1989 work *A Bibliography of the King's Book, or Eikon Basilike*. The poem cites and develops Pierre Macherey's contention that the discourse of fiction is: 'sealed and interminably completed or endlessly beginning again, diffuse and dense, coiled about an absent center which it can neither conceal nor reveal'.[34] Howe's fundamental conceit in the poem is to re-imagine this 'absent center' as 'the ghost of a king'.[35] The poem builds on numerous documentary sources surrounding the execution of Charles I, stitching together a sequence of 'fragmentary narrative enclaves'.[36] Milton's role in denouncing the apocryphal pamphlet *Eikon Basilike*, popularly supposed to have been written by the king, is explored as the poem pursues an examination of the nature of authorship. The regicide melts into numerous Shakespearean motifs for paternal haunting: 'The real King's last word "Remember" recalls the fictive Ghost-king's admonition to his son. The ghost of a king certainly haunted the Puritans and the years of the Protectorate. Charles I became the ghost of Hamlet's father, Caesar's ghost, Banquo's ghost, the ghost of Richard II.'[37]

Commenting on 'Olson's wonderful sentence: "I take SPACE to be the central fact to man born in America,"' Howe has said: 'I am a woman born in America. I can't take central facts for granted.'[38] A similarly decentred notion of femininity enters *Eikon* in the form of a paraphrase in a forged pamphlet of a prayer taken from Sidney's *Arcadia*. The prayer is delivered by the shepherdess Pamela to a pagan deity. 'A captive Shepherdess has entered through a gap in ideology,' writes Howe. '[She] confronts the inauthentic literary work with its beginnings in a breach.'[39]

In Howe's version of Olson, this feminine third term is lacking:

> In the dream of murderous union between fathers and sons, pieces of a Past are broken and eaten. Pushed backward through time, Man's hierarchical position is a recent invention. *What lies under?* Is the human universe definable if you have left women out of the definition? Where is the mother then?[40]

Here she is clearly echoing Melville's 'Where is the foundling's father hidden?' She goes on to cite Melville:

> 'There she breaches! There she breaches!' was the cry, as in his immeasurable bravadoes the White Whale tossed himself salmon-like to Heaven.[41]

It is in this notion of a breach that Howe finds a gendered principle with which to challenge Olson. Not to reject the work, but to pursue its protean energies to the point at which Olson's restless enquiries begin to peter out, hesitate and stutter.

In Howe's work, dense and fragmentary interweavings of public and private history are presented as documentary montages that radiate multiple threads of meaning. She notes, in the 'Commander' essay, Olson's affinities to early Soviet montage, using Eisenstein's 'montage is conflict' as an epigraph. She writes:

> Acute visual sensitivity separates *The Maximus Poems* from *The Cantos* and *Paterson*. This is strange, because Olson built his idea of Projective Verse on the length of a line, and the poet's breath. Maximus is for viewing. Eisenstein's principle of visual counterpoint sets Olson's writing on edge.[42]

In montage, she continues, 'The alchemy of stimuli is a metrics of vision and sound. Collisions and combinations of images and rhythms, mysterious adjacencies and ambiguities are tied together in a common denominator.'[43]

In a later essay on Dziga Vertov and Chris Marker, she asserts that not only was Olson using montage in *Call Me Ishmael*, but that the form is evident in the innovations of Whitman, Melville, and Dickinson.[44] Her own poetry, which, as Peter Nicholls writes, 'constantly courts the non-cognitive in its preoccupation with graphic and phonic elements',[45] may ultimately depend on a combination of signifying and non-signifying elements held together in the conflictual movement of montage, as described in her essay:

> Short cuts, mixed credits, news items, archival material, nonfictitious science, science fiction, pulp fiction, travel narratives, epigraphs, ballads, and passages from the Bible represent the delayed beginning of Herman Melville's *Moby-Dick*. First the effusive dedication to Hawthorne, next the 'Etymology' and 'Extracts' sections. Aside from the dedications, and possibly even there, all of these scattered particles of fact and or fable meet in the word-event 'whale'.[46]

Olson reimagines Melville through the dislocating, mobile prism of montage. Howe applies a similar technique in her reimagining of Olson, locating its dynamism not in the body or in breath, but in the juxtapositions of its 'spatial expressiveness'.[47] Recent visual texts such as 'Fragment of the Wedding Dress of Sarah Pierpont Edwards' and 'Frolic Architecture' demonstrate Howe's continued commitment to presenting 'scattered particles' of documentary material that are inflected by a preoccupation with women's position in the historical record.[48] The writing's passionate ambivalence about figures of origin points the reader both to the energies of dispersal in a radical acceptance of modernism and the often hidden lines of association binding authors to one another.

I would now like to extend my discussion of Olson's shadow to the work of the contemporary UK poet, Redell Olsen.[49] Olsen is known for her engagement with diverse media: her work embraces video, installation, and performance as well as the writing of poetry. As a critic, she has written on Susan Howe and Hannah Weiner, as well as artists Grace Hartigan and Abigail Child. Her 2004 book *Secure Portable Space* (Reality Street, 2004) contains a series of poems, 'The Minimaus Poems', that engages in an active encounter with her near namesake.[50] With these poems, the British poet, whose mother was born in Gloucester and who has strong familial ties to Gloucestershire, writes through, with and against *Maximus*, using humour and a self-consciously 'minor' perspective to present a counter to the declarative ambitions of Olson's epic.

Several of the Minimaus poems do a version of *Maximus*, rewriting Olson's words, following his numbering and titling, but relocating the texts to the mercantile scramble of the provincial English high street. Commerce is felt as an all-embracing environment that suffuses both the private and public dimensions of everyday experience. The material and virtual are collapsed into one another in similar fashion. At the beginning of the Minimaus series, Olsen reproduces the map of Gloucester, Massachusetts used by Olson on the cover of the first volume of *Maximus*. However, she superimposes upon it a map of her Gloucester. The doubled image is a visual analogy of her methods in 'The Minimaus Poems'. Only one of the jokes here is that the British cathedral city becomes the unglamorous understudy to its American namesake; source and copy are inverted to reflect changing stocks of wealth and literary prestige.

So, for example, the opening poem of *Maximus* shifts from:

> Off-shore, by islands hidden in the blood
> jewels & miracles, I, Maximus
> a metal hot from boiling water, tell you
> what is a lance, who obeys the figures of
> the present dance
>
> (MP, 5)

to, in Olsen's version:

> Inland, by *Iceland* hidden by the blood of
> jewels and discounts, I, Minimaus
> sitting on hot metal, boiling in a vest
> ask you who speeds obediently
> are we past ENTRANCE [51]

Maximus becomes a cartoon figure (both Minnie Mouse and Maus); 'present dance' becomes 'ENTRANCE' (with both senses of the word active); and 'islands' become the discount frozen-food chain store Iceland. Some of the poems that follow diverge considerably from Olsonian precedent, and some remain close. A reference in Olson's Letter 7 to the carpenter William Stevens's arrival in Gloucester in 1642 becomes in Olsen's poem an allusion to a notorious urban myth about a local soldier who believed he had witnessed the 'angel of Mons' in 1914.[52] Olson's archival work on American origins is thus refracted in Olsen's poem into an early 2000s hoax that was reported in the *Sunday Times* and that drew a substantial offer from Hollywood.[53] In the same poem, Olson's '(Marsden Hartley's / eyes—as Stein's / eyes' (MP, 34) becomes 'Polke's / eyes – as Gloucester's / eyes'.[54] The reference to 'Capitalist Realism' on the following page confirms that Olsen has in mind the German artist Sigmar Polke. Marsden Hartley's pro-Dada modernism is replaced by the 1960s artistic tendency comprising Polke, Wolfgang Vostell, Gerhard Richter and Konrad Lueg. The Capitalist Realists, influenced by Pop Art, sought to explore and exploit the visual vocabulary of commerce and advertising. Comparable moves are discernible in Olsen's re-thinking of *Maximus*. While Olson condemned 'mu-sick' and 'pejoracracy' and sought the proprioceptive basis for a re-founding of polis, Olsen has no such hopes of finding herself on the outside of the representative modes of contemporary capitalism. Any archaeology is constrained by the present, as with '5th century burial / at the BMW site on Kingsholm Road'.[55] The encounter with the local past – the references to the poet Ivor Gurney, to slavery as recorded in the Domesday book, or to Roman ruins – are melancholic and bathetic, always marked by the compromised imperatives of the investigator. A piece of found text that seems to be a picture caption describing a local fire-fighting river-vessel in action in 1906 concludes 'The "flames" on the warehouse roof have been added later'.[56] The early-twentieth-century flames resonate with early-twentieth-century fears: towards the end of the book Olsen cuts Olson together with newspaper material relating the arrest of a local Muslim who had been planning a suicide bomb, his explosives stored above a shop named Pound Plus. The blacked-out text on the facing page, following the word 'devout', conjures both Olson and the redaction of official documents. Rather than discovering some restitutive energy in finding things out for oneself, Olsen's self-aware textual montages uncover knowledge that is highly questionable. Although Olson acknowledges the mediated quality of the materials he finds, that mediatedness teeters on the brink of chatter in Olsen, its corporate or commercial imperatives always close to the surface. Sceptical of the claims of both lyric and epic, the sequence can only 'Sing modemly! / Whine!'[57]

In her most recent book, 2012's *Punk Faun*, Olsen continues to address themes of genre, displacement and irony. The book, which includes open-field poetics among the array of poetic forms it embraces, is a baroque pastoral; though 'bar-rock pastel' is the only means available in the text of uttering that phrase. The book emerges from a consideration of the decorative, masquerade, masquing and the ephemeral. The contemporary artist Matthew Barney (associated with the contemporary baroque) and the Renaissance patron of the arts Isabella d'Este provide the book's epigraphs. Bambi, not Minnie Mouse, is the cartoon avatar of the book. The figure of the deer is both subject and object of a poetic move in which hunter and game interpenetrate: Olsen dramatises the power-play at work in the lyric mode since Wyatt. In 'the matter of cloven-poetics: or, even the title against itself', a short statement of position published in 2012 that forms an oblique commentary on some aspects of *Punk Faun*, Olsen describes the mobility of her methods: 'a transformation of sorts that is always on the move and toward a redrawing'.[58] She continues by describing the relationship of criticism to practice in her work:

> The critical matter of a cloven-poetics might not necessarily propose its conceptual other as elsewhere. That might not mean that it is without substance, or that a cloven-poetics is without matter. Or that criticism does not.

Out from and over the ha-ha.

A cloven-poetics might also refuse to stand alongside an object, to refuse what it is supposed to call 'its'.[59]

Both poetry and poetics show an unwillingness to address the world from a static vantage point. The writing does not seek, in the manner of *Maximus*, to place itself at the leading edge of human understanding, fusing history, myth and contemporary science into a new vision of human potential. Instead it proceeds from the position that there simply is no uncontaminated space available, either of critical objectivity or lyric subjectivity. While it announces itself as poetry, it does not erect barriers between itself and other modes of speech. Neither does it allow itself refuge of a settled poetics of pastiche, procedure, anti-lyric or appropriation. All of these modes may be deployed but the writing's dynamism stems from its desire to be 'always on the move and toward a redrawing'.

The poetry in *Punk Faun* frequently gestures beyond the page. The sequence 'as performed in our own person', for example, is a series of unperformable pseudo-scores that fuse spectacle, self-display and the pressure of commerce. The book is formally varied and highly visual, whether the poems are arranged in short two-line stanzas or in explorations of page-space. The sequence 'barriers at map' uses a diversity of verse forms to combine distinctly spatial emblems of democracy: material sourced from descriptions of a deer that still observes the now-absent physical barrier of the Iron Curtain (a central figure in the book as a whole) and a 1960s Max Neuhaus live radio-art project in which the artist processed audio material phoned in by listeners. This sequence also contains many references to sound – Neuhaus's project, sonic deer deterrents, headphones – as if forming an 'aural topiary' that addresses noise as a medium both of communication and control.[60]

Elsewhere in *Punk Faun* the elaborate artifice of the masque is invoked as a kind of gilded cage:

> besydes musycke and syngynge
> we commuters hum inside spaces
> blindly open to the world bars or
>
> little flexi paires of iron brackets
> to set up divers exquisite authors
> six or seven gallyards in mornynge[61]

In Olsen, the documentary resources of the past are not presented as a space of retreat or potential renovation. Space, indeed, is always subject to a 'redrawing'. In this respect her work might be seen as a development of the montage-based documentary poetics advanced, in different ways, by Olson and Howe. In this work, a thoroughgoing commitment to contingency and mobility directs the reader to an awareness of unrealised linguistic and conceptual potential; what, in 'cloven-poetics', Olsen presents as a 'shopped-in cavity that might be negotiated while dangling from the ceiling in a full-body harness with pencil and paper handy'.[62]

Notes

1. Susan Howe, 'Charles Olson: Since a Dialogue We Are', *Acts* 10 (1989), 168.
2. Lynn Keller, 'An Interview with Susan Howe', *Contemporary Literature* 36:1 (Spring 1995), 20.
3. Howe, 'Dialogue', 167.
4. Ibid., 166.
5. Ibid., 170.
6. Susan Howe, 'Where Should the Commander Be', *Writing* 19 (November 1987), 3.
7. Ibid., 6.
8. Susan Howe and Edward Foster, '*Talisman* interview', in *The Birth-mark: Unsettling the Wilderness in American Literary History* (Hanover: Wesleyan University Press, 1993), 180.
9. Ibid., 181.
10. Howe, 'Commander', 5–6.
11. Ibid., 4, citing Olson (*MP*, 421).
12. Howe, 'Dialogue', 167.
13. Ibid., 168.
14. Stephen Collis, *Through Words of Others: Susan Howe and Anarcho-Scholasticism* (Victoria, BC: ELS, 2006), 79. The poem is in fact by Olson and is re-published in *The Collected Poems of Charles Olson* (CP, 48).
15. Howe, 'Commander', 4.
16. Ibid., citing *Call Me Ishmael* (CPr, 74).
17. Howe, 'Dialogue', 169.
18. Ibid., 172.
19. Howe, 'Commander', 18.
20. Herman Melville, *Moby-Dick* (London: Penguin, 1986), 593.
21. Howe, 'Commander', 6.
22. Olson, *Call Me Ishmael* (CPr, especially 51–2).
23. Ibid., 64, cited in Howe, 'Commander', 18.
24. Olson, *Call Me Ishmael* (CPr, 105).
25. Howe, 'Commander', 18.
26. See Chapter 3 of Anthony Mellors, *Late Modernist Poetics: From Pound to Prynne* (Manchester: Manchester University Press, 2005), 90–116.
27. Sigmund Freud, *Moses and Monotheism: Three Essays* (1939), Penguin Freud Library, Vol. 13 (London, Penguin: 1990), 314, 323.

28 Melville, *Moby-Dick*, 212.
29 Philippe Lacoue-Labarthe and Jean-Luc Nancy, 'From Where is Psychoanalysis Possible?', Part II of 'The Jewish People Do Not Dream', *Journal of European Psychoanalysis* 17, Summer–Winter 2003, www.psychomedia.it/jep/number17/labarte-nancy.htm, accessed 7 February 2012. (First published *Stanford Literature Review* 8:1–2, 1991, 39–55.)
30 Freud, *Moses*, 382.
31 Lacoue-Labarthe and Nancy, 'Psychoanalysis', n.p.
32 Susan Howe, 'Commander', 7, citing *Call Me Ishmael* (*CPr*, 18).
33 Susan Howe, 'Articulation of Sound Forms in Time', in *Singularities* (Hanover: Wesleyan University Press, 1990), 17.
34 Susan Howe, *A Bibliography of the King's Book, or Eikon Basilike* (1989), *The Nonconformist's Memorial* (New York: New Directions, 1993), 50.
35 Ibid.
36 Ibid., 69.
37 Ibid., 48.
38 Susan Howe and Tom Beckett, '*The Difficulties* interview', *The Difficulties* 3:2 (1989), 21.
39 Howe, *Eikon*, 49.
40 Howe, 'Commander', 18.
41 Melville, *Moby-Dick*, 667.
42 Howe, 'Commander', 5.
43 Ibid., 6.
44 Susan Howe, 'Sorting Facts: Or, Nineteen Ways of Looking at Marker' in *Beyond Document: Essays on Nonfiction Film*, ed. Charles Warren (Hanover, NH: Wesleyan University Press, 1996), 295–343.
45 Peter Nicholls, 'Unsettling the Wilderness: Susan Howe and American History', *Contemporary Literature* 37:4 (Winter 1996), 597.
46 Howe, 'Sorting Facts', 330.
47 Howe, 'Commander', 5.
48 *Souls of the Labadie Tract* (New York: New Directions, 2007) and *That This* (New York: New Directions, 2010).
49 For a survey of the impact of Olson on women poets, see Kathleen Fraser, 'Translating the Unspeakable: Visual Poetics, as Projected through Olson's "Field" into Current Female Writing Practice' in Mary Margaret Sloan, ed., *Moving Borders: Three Decades of Innovative Writing by Women* (Jersey, NJ: Talisman, 1998), 642–54.
50 Redell Olsen, 'The Minimaus Poems', *Secure Portable Space* (Hastings: Reality Street, 2004). This section of the book follows a page of photographs of Olsen wearing Minnie Mouse ears for an outdoor performance, 74.
51 Ibid., 77.
52 Ibid., 96.
53 See David Clarke, 'The Angel of Mons', *Fortean Times*, May 2003, www.forteantimes.com/features/articles/213/the_angel_of_mons.html, accessed 7 February 2013.
54 Olsen, *Secure Portable Space*, 96.

55 Ibid, 91.
56 Ibid., 94.
57 Ibid., 89.
58 Olsen, 'the matter of cloven-poetics: or, even the title against itself', in *Formes Poetiques Contemporaines*, eds Vincent Broqua and Jean-Jacques Poucel (Paris: Double Change, 2012), 261. The text is published on Olsen's blog: http://redellolsen.co.uk/wordpress/wp-content/uploads/2012/09/Olsen-cloven-poetics2.pdf, accessed 7 February 2013.
59 Olsen, 'cloven-poetics', 262.
60 Redell Olsen, *Punk Faun* (Oakland, CA: Subpress, 2012), 92.
61 Ibid., 98.
62 Olsen, 'cloven-poetics', 260.

Section IV

History

13

The contemporaries: a reading of Charles Olson's 'The Lordly and Isolate Satyrs'

Stephen Fredman

In 1962, George Oppen ended a review of Charles Olson's books *The Distances* and *Maximus from Dogtown* with the pronouncement: 'Perhaps we should look to such poems as *The Lordly and Isolate Satyrs*, in which the voice and eye are his alone, for the best prediction of Olson's future work.'[1] To which Olson replied in a letter to William Bronk (21 December 1962): 'I thought [Oppen's] picking "The Satyrs" for a voice which was peculiarly my own, true enough.'[2] Donald Allen also singled out this poem by having it open the fourth issue of *Evergreen Review* (1958) and selected it as part of the Olson grouping to which he gave pride of place in *The New American Poetry* (1960). If the poem appears uniquely or representatively Olson's, it also locates him, through its central image of monumental motorcyclists, at the heart of the cultural moment of the late 1950s and early 1960s, a time of transition in which American social anxieties were detaching from World War II and regrouping around new forms of rebellion such as the Birth of the Cool, the Beat Movement, the Civil Rights Movement, and Rock 'n' Roll.[3] The essay that follows considers the poem both as a deeply personal meditation and as a social act of involvement in the resistant counterculture beginning to form in the United States. With antecedents in Olson's major predecessors, Herman Melville and William Carlos Williams, 'The Lordly and Isolate Satyrs' is both a visionary poem and a social document of its moment. Olson's invocation of the motorcycle club helps to situate the poem specifically within the emerging Beat Movement, where it can be compared to Allen Ginsberg's 'Howl', Robert Frank's photographs in *The Americans*, Kenneth Anger's film *Scorpio Rising*, and the social posture of cool rebellion in Hollywood movies and Pop songs of the era.

'The Lordly and Isolate Satyrs' was written in April 1956 and based on a dream. A serious reader of Freud and Jung, Olson believed that dreams supply essential psychic information that cannot be obtained by other means. The narrative voice of the poem bears the hallmark of dream transcriptions, in which, as though speaking in both the third and the first persons, the narrator witnesses and at the same time participates in the events related. As in a number of Olson's strongest poems from the late 1950s, including 'As the Dead Prey Upon Us' and 'The Librarian', 'The Lordly and Isolate Satyrs' goes beyond recounting the dream to register associations and interpretations, both personal and cultural, born from contemplation of the dream materials. It may be that what drew Oppen to the poem was Olson's expert mining of dream matter in a variety of narrative and lyrical registers, since Oppen himself had recently resumed writing poetry at the urging of a dream.[4] Not enough has been made of Olson's extensive dream work in his poetry. In fact, it would not be a gross exaggeration to say that in general outline, his poems travel between the poles of dream and scholarship. The scholarship has been traced in fine detail by George Butterick and Ralph Maud, among others, but Olson's masterly meditations on his dreams have not been accorded a similar degree of attention, nor has there been much analysis of the ways in which dreams join history, geography, mythology, and philosophy in the complex weave of Olson's poetry. I would argue that his accomplishments as dream explorer and, more broadly, as lyric poet have been obscured by an overemphasis on the epic (historical) and didactic (philosophical) Olson.

The title of 'The Lordly and Isolate Satyrs' strikes an initial lyrical note, employing a high diction that connotes nobility and classical mythology. The word 'isolate' – rather than 'isolated'– particularly calls attention to itself. It is a fairly recent word, whose first citation in the *OED* dates from 1819, and it derives most likely in Olson's usage from two of his primary sources, Melville and Williams.[5] Melville famously coined the term 'isolato' to describe the sea-faring crew in *Moby-Dick*: 'They were nearly all Islanders in the Pequod, *Isolatoes* too, I call such, not acknowledging the common continent of men, but each *Isolato* living on a separate continent of his own.'[6] The resistant attitude of self-containment that Melville depicts among the dramatis personae of the Pequod finds its way to the heart of Olson's poetics and ethics; in *The Grounding of American Poetry: Charles Olson and the Emersonian Tradition* I have argued at length for containment as Olson's characteristic poetic mode of engagement with the world.[7] Olson echoes Melville's equation of *'isolatoes'* with 'Islanders' when he declares *The Maximus Poems* addressed to the self-contained individuals he finds in his own community: 'Isolated person in Gloucester, Massachusetts, I Maximus, address you / you islands / of men and girls' (*MP*, 16). In addition to borrowing Melville's extravagant lyrical diction in 'The Lordly and Isolate Satyrs,' Olson mimics him and such predecessors as Hart Crane and Edward Dahlberg by employing this diction subversively to at once amplify and ironically deflate figures from vernacular culture; the most striking of which in Olson's poem is the 'motorcycle-club'.

Likewise concerned with resistant isolation, Williams employs high diction more sparingly than Melville. In one of his most cited poems, 'To Elsie' (1923), Williams uses the term 'isolate' twice. At the beginning of the poem he locates 'The pure products of America' who 'go crazy' in remote and in-grown communities:

> mountain folk from Kentucky
>
> or the ribbed north end of
> Jersey
> with its isolate lakes and
>
> valleys[8]

By the end of the poem, the term 'isolate' no longer refers to confinement or containment but rather to discreteness and rarity:

> It is only in isolate flecks that
> something
> is given off [.] [9]

The salvific 'something' that shines in isolate flecks seems to be an indefinable and uncontrollable vividness, occurring in a rural folk culture that resists cosmopolitan influence. Without either high culture or any 'peasant traditions to give them / character', these 'pure products of America' are left with only the images of popular culture in which to embody their imaginations.[10] The ominous and admittedly enigmatic final stanza of the poem, 'No one / to witness / and adjust, no one to drive the car', can be read in this context, thus making the point that isolate flecks of beauty, though exuberant and bearing the nation's aesthetic hopes, must founder within a popular industrial culture dominated, in the 1920s, by the automobile.[11]

If 'To Elsie' recognizes that one social response to the Machine Age can be found in the 'devil-may-care men who have taken / to railroading / out of sheer lust of adventure', 'The Lordly and Isolate Satyrs' invokes a similar response to the furious industrialization after World War II.[12] Olson memorializes the motorcycle club as a resistant social nexus newly emergent in popular culture, having his satyrs assume the guise of Marlon Brando in *The Wild One* (1953) or James Dean in *Rebel Without a Cause* (1955). The poem begins:

> The lordly and isolate satyrs—look at them come in
> on the left side of the beach
> like a motorcycle-club! And the handsomest of them,

>   the one who has a woman, driving that snazzy
> convertible
>   Wow, did you ever see even in a museum
> such a collection of boddisatvahs, the way
> they come up to their stop, each of them
> as though it was a rudder
> the way they have to sit above it
> and come to a stop on it, the monumental solidity
> of themselves, the Easter Island
> they make of the beach, the Red-headed Men
>
>   These are the Androgynes,
>   the Fathers behind the father, the Great Halves
>   (CP, 384)

Olson portrays a set of male cyclists (with only one woman, who accompanies the leader with the 'snazzy' convertible) in awe-inspiring terms, comparing them not only to ithyphallic satyrs but to monumental Asian bodhisattva sculptures, to Easter Island stone statues, to the Androgynes in Aristophanes' myth in the *Symposium* (whose splitting in half accounts for the human need to reunite with a perfect mate), to the Fathers from Freud's theory of culture as dependent on fratricide, and (further on in the poem) to angels. As 'The Lordly and Isolate Satyrs' continues, Olson also bestows on these imposing, singular figures a series of hypostasizing epithets: 'Red-headed Men', 'Great Halves', 'Themselves', 'the lonely ones', 'Source', 'The Visitors', 'Resters', and most tellingly, 'the Contemporaries' (CP, 384–7). These epithets not only point to the way these figures instantiate states of being, they also resonate with the names for mid-1950s music groups, such as The Clovers, The Four Lads, The Drifters, The Del-Vikings, and The Coasters. Finally, Olson equates the motorcyclists who show up on the Gloucester beach with sailors, comparing the way they swivel to a stop to the way a sailboat comes about in order to dock.

The tone of this opening section is characteristically Olsonian: its style of humorous overstatement, sexual provocation, and the blending of high ('lordly', 'handsomest') and vernacular ('Wow', 'snazzy') diction serves Olson's tenacious pursuit of mythical powers lying within the purview of modern life. The motorcycle club offers a ripe opportunity for the delicately balanced mythologizing the poet sees as one of his primary tasks. In fact, these satyrs could be characters in a new Homeric Hymn, on the order of the Homeric Hymn to Dionysus in which the god looks like a human boy to a gang of pirates, but once kidnapped lets loose on the ship a flow of wine, an uncontrollable growth of ivy, and a ferocious lion and bear. Olson prized the early Greek poetry of Hesiod and the

Homeric Hymns as models for the encounter of humans with elemental, untamed forces, using the title 'A Newly Discovered "Homeric" Hymn' for the poem that directly precedes 'The Lordly and Isolate Satyrs' in *The New American Poetry*. In each instance he adopts a lyrical posture of greeting and supplication with respect to the mysterious and more-than-mortal beings encountered. At the opening of 'A Newly Discovered "Homeric" Hymn' he proclaims, 'Hail and beware the dead who will talk life until you are blue / in the face' (*CP*, 363). In 'The Lordly and Isolate Satyrs' he begins one stanza with 'Hail the ambiguous Fathers' and the next stanza with 'Hail them, and watch out' (*CP*, 385). In both poems he salutes entities both familiar and dangerous, harbingers of emergent powers (the dead, the Fathers) that Olson must take account of personally and as a watchman for society at large.

In its first publication, 'The Lordly and Isolate Satyrs' itself acted as a harbinger of Olson's pivotal role in postwar American avant-garde poetry, leading off the fourth issue of *Evergreen Review*. By virtue of the journal's fame and wide circulation and the prominence of the poem in this issue, it was, in Ralph Maud's words, 'Olson's most conspicuous publication to that date' (*SL*, 273).[13] A pioneering literary quarterly published in print runs of one hundred thousand, *Evergreen Review* was launched in 1957, the year of the trial of *Howl* and the publication of *On the Road*. It presented translations of mid-century French literature and existentialist philosophy in company with the outsider American verse that its co-editor Donald Allen would soon christen as the 'New American Poetry'. In the early issues of the journal, Allen highlighted the emerging avant-garde poets and scenes he would feature in his groundbreaking anthology. The second issue, for instance, titled 'San Francisco Scene,' achieved great notoriety for its presentation of the city as a cultural capital and home to the San Francisco Renaissance and to what Kenneth Rexroth called 'the New Generation of Revolt and Our Underground Literature and Cultural Disaffiliation'; shortly to be dubbed the Beat Movement.[14] Allen was so taken with Olson's writing and sense of authority that Grove Press reprinted his first book *Call Me Ishmael* in 1958 and Allen commenced *The New American Poetry* (1960) with a generous selection of Olson's poems and began the section on poetics with his 'Projective Verse' and 'Letter to Elaine Feinstein'.[15]

Olson's prominence in the anthology has often been remarked upon, but by confining him (as Allen's groupings might lead us to do) to the scope of Black Mountain College or *The Black Mountain Review* we lose sight of the broader milieu in which he operated. When 'The Lordly and Isolate Satyrs' is seen in the context of *Evergreen Review*'s first four issues, Olson appears more simply as part of the emerging

American counterculture that would first coalesce in the 1950s and then burgeon dramatically in the 1960s. Although the heuristic labels that Allen coined to define groups in his anthology were a necessary way of situating forty-four virtually unpublished poets, the provisional terms 'Black Mountain', 'San Francisco Renaissance', 'Beat Generation', and 'New York School' have become reified as strict affiliative badges. This obscures the great degree to which poets supposedly wearing different badges met and conversed with, corresponded with, gave readings with, published with, learned from, disagreed with, and defended one another. From a sociological perspective – one prompted by attention to the mix of American poets and artists in early issues of *Evergreen Review* – it would be possible to apply a single capacious label to the poets in the Allen anthology: Beat. No matter how vociferously Olson or Robert Duncan or Frank O'Hara might seek at times to distance themselves from avowed Beats such as Ginsberg or Kerouac or Gregory Corso, they all participate in what Rexroth calls the 'revolt' against and 'disaffiliation' with dominant social, political, and sexual mores and, as Allen points out, they all adhere to 'the practices and precepts of Ezra Pound and William Carlos Williams' (to which short list of decisive precursors should be added Hart Crane, D. H. Lawrence, and surrealism).[16] In this sense Olson can be seen within the New American poets as a member of a loosely interwoven collective of countercultural practitioners.

At the same time that the first issues of *Evergreen Review*, for which Allen served as co-editor, were publishing a panoply of poets who would appear in *The New American Poetry* – Olson, Duncan, Ginsberg, O'Hara, Corso, Kerouac, Barbara Guest, Gary Snyder, Brother Antoninus (William Everson), Lawrence Ferlinghetti, Michael McClure, Jack Spicer, Philip Whalen, Robin Blaser, Paul Blackburn – the quarterly also drew attention to jazz and American art, paying close heed to recent photography. Not only do most early issues contain a portfolio of photographs, but accomplished photographic images grace the covers, including one of the San Francisco skyline by Fred Lyon as described in the 'Moloch' section of 'Howl' (second issue) and one by Hans Namuth of Jackson Pollock sitting on the running board of a disintegrating automobile (third issue). The fourth issue's cover image (Fig. 3) – a candid shot of three motorcyclists taken by the Swiss photographer Robert Frank – is clearly meant by the editor to illustrate Olson's poem. The image was titled *Newburgh, New York, 1955*, when it was published shortly thereafter in Frank's landmark book, *The Americans* (1958, 1959).[17] Alluding presumably to the photo, Olson wrote with gratitude to Allen about how well the image fits his poem: 'Did anyone tell you how it is to be put out there by another man who has covered you like your own skin?' (*SL*, 273).

3 Cover of *Evergreen Review* 1:4 (Spring 1958).

Frank drove 10,000 miles around the United States for a year on a Guggenheim fellowship, shooting over a thousand spontaneous negatives that document a new postwar America to itself and to the world – covering the country like its own skin. Like Olson, Frank seeks to create a balance between spontaneously noted features of the external world and the idiosyncratic quality of perception. In the introduction to *The Americans*, his friend Kerouac notes of Frank: 'with that little camera that he raises and snaps with one hand he sucked a sad poem right out of America onto film, taking rank among the tragic poets of the world'.[18] Frank's raw images – of racial conflict; of small-town desperation and big-city political venality; of isolated misfits, lonely jukeboxes, and endless asphalt – enact a transformation of private, un-posed moments into icons of the social dissolution and rebellious transience of postwar culture.

The emphasis on transience and rebellion can be seen in *Newburgh, New York, 1955* as well as in another photograph in *The Americans* of black motorcyclists, male and female, called *Indianapolis, 1956*. In the first image the central figure, wolfing down a hotdog, turns menacingly, as if disturbed or provoked by the photographer. In the second (Fig. 4) the couple, moulded almost into a single creature like the reunited androgyne, stares down pensively at something outside the frame. Here, Frank captures two beautiful, ineffably cool subjects in loose embrace in a segregated setting, drawing power, as Kerouac observes, from the American tragedy of race. 'Look closely / at them', Olson begs the viewer of his own segregated cyclists

> they are the unadmitted, the club of Themselves,
> weary riders, but who sit upon the landscape as the Great
> Stones. And only have fun among themselves. They are
> the lonely ones
>
> (*CP*, 385)

Best known for his enthusiastic, sometimes bombastic pronouncements, Olson devotes this passage to a poignant depiction of a rebellious and defiant but nonetheless isolated group of outsiders. The last sentence, 'They are the lonely ones', sounds again like a Pop song lyric, anticipating perhaps the chorus to Paul Anka's 'Lonely Boy' (1959): 'I'm just a lonely boy, lonely and blue / I'm all alone with nothin' to do.' Similar to Olson's casting of motorcyclists as satyrs, the Pop songs of the late 1950s and early 1960s, often supported acoustically by the Wagnerian 'Wall of Sound' constructed by Phil Spector, attempt to raise

4 Robert Frank, 'Indianapolis' (1956).

adolescent isolation to a monumental and mythical state. Frank's photos and Olson's poems take a much more worldly and grownup perspective than Anka's song; nevertheless, the poem and photos share with Ginsberg's 'Howl', Kerouac's *On the Road*, Brando and Dean films, and Pop songs addressed to restless teenagers the project of constructing a countercultural ethos out of social rebellion.

Initially, Olson represents his lonely cyclists as separate from the dreamer; they are, like the subjects of Frank's photos, cool, isolated, and self-contained. This is true both of 'the club of Themselves' and of the blond who 'was as distant as the others. She sat in her flesh too' (*CP*, 385, 386). Olson also distances them as primitive beings, who display a 'monumental solidity' and a phallic potency in their role of 'the Fathers behind the father' and 'the Sources' (*CP*, 384). Their origin is distant in space: having migrated 'they came riding in from the sea', as the goddess does in the Homeric Hymn to Aphrodite (*CP*, 385). Ultimately, though, for all their isolation, distance, and phallic potency, these beings have a direct effect upon the dreamer, bringing unimagined benefits: 'They are between us / and the ocean. And they have given us a whole new half of the beach' (*CP*, 386). Not only do they add geographical – and presumably psychic – territory, they effect a change in perception. Owing to their presence, Olson marvels, 'we saw twice as much' (*CP*, 385). With respect to both the new portion of beach and the new mode of perception, the lordly and isolate satyrs have caused a major transformation:

>   The difference is
> we are more on it. The beauty of the white of the sun's light, the
> blue the water is, and the sky, the movement on the painted lands-
> cape, the boy-town the scene was, is now pierced with angels and
> with fire. And winter's ice shall be as brilliant in its time as
> life truly is, as Nature is only the offerer, and it is we
> who look to see what the beauty is.
>
>   (*CP*, 387)

As in Blake's *Jerusalem*, the mundane world is suffused by divine presences, presences that also owe their existence to the heightened perception of the dreamer. Like Blake, Nietzsche, and Lawrence, Olson believes that, in Blake's words, 'All deities reside in the human breast.'[19] His identification with the seemingly alien and fleshly solidity of the satyrs in this strikingly lyrical passage effects a transformation in awareness both of self and of the world. The ordinary landscape 'is now pierced with angels / and with fire,' conjuring up a brilliance that is life at its most vivid, a state of heightened meaning and intensity in which he yearns to reside constantly. Ultimately, as Emerson does, Olson sees nature as the 'offerer' of such radiant moments of beauty. The rebels on wheels who bear this gift from nature are 'the Contemporaries' and they belong, he recognizes, to a vibrantly erotic experience of the present historical moment. In a climactic stanza halfway through the poem (the only one that is double-spaced) he proclaims:

> These are our counterparts, the unknown ones.
>
> They are here. We do not look upon them as invaders. Dimensionally
>
> they are larger than we—all but the woman. But we are not suddenly
>
> small. We are as we are. We don't even move, on the beach.
>
> (*CP*, 386)

Seeing 'the unknown ones' as 'our counterparts' transfixes the dreamer in an intransitive state ('We are as we are') and seems to bring the poem to an awe-struck halt. After noting, 'We don't even move', Olson comments, 'It is a stasis', and then, a few lines later, 'As of this moment, there is nothing else to report' (*CP*, 386).

In the midst of this hiatus a shift occurs: the panting cyclists who have ferried in a sense of erotic magnification suddenly forfeit their exalted status when they lose composure by breaking silence and chatting among themselves. The poet notices with disappointment 'the way their face breaks when they call across to each other,' so that 'the face / loses all containment' (*CP*, 386). As a result, 'They are not gods. They are not even stone', instead, they fall into adolescence: 'they are fifteen year old boys at the moment / they speak to each other' (*CP*, 386). Olson sums up this disturbing shift by saying, 'When they act like us / they go to pieces' (*CP*, 386). Earlier in the poem he had delineated what it means to 'act like us'. After hailing the satyrs and the increase in vision they bring ('we saw twice as much') he steps back for the first time to describe the normal people on the beach: 'We were as usual, the children were being fed pop / and potato chips, and everyone was sprawled as people are / on a beach' (*CP*, 385).

Pointing out that 'the lordly and isolate satyrs' lose the power of containment when they lapse into the state of mere mortals 'sprawled... on a beach,' Olson expresses a major tenet of his philosophy. He states it most succinctly in the second half of 'Projective Verse', which is devoted to 'the degree to which the projective involves a stance toward reality outside a poem' (*CPr*, 246). Speaking of the correct attitude toward objects, which involves the humility to regard oneself as no more than an object, Olson insists:

> It comes to this: the use of a man, by himself and thus by others, lies in how he conceives his relation to nature, that force by which he owes his somewhat small existence. If he sprawl, he shall find little to sing but himself.... But if he stays inside himself, if he is contained within his nature

as he is participant in the larger force, he will be able to listen, and his hearing through himself will give him secrets objects share.

(*CPr*, 247)

From Olson's perspective, the venal expansion of ego that bedevils human self-conception and intercourse with others, and with nature, condemns us to the flabby, pathetic posture of sprawling on a beach indulging the children in 'pop / and potato chips'. Mimicking the motorcyclists ('our counterparts') when they maintain a silent, self-contained demeanour, on the other hand, would correctly align our 'relation to nature' and allow us to perceive the 'secrets objects share'.

Throughout the poem, Olson endeavours to gauge the ways in which the 'lordly and isolate satyrs' both resemble and exceed the human beings on the beach. At times they appear like divine emanations or monumental avatars of a titanic pre-humanity. At other times, they appear to be adolescent rebels who have in their restless awkwardness joined a motorcycle club. Across this spectrum including the divine, the primitive, and the adolescent, what remains constant is a powerful erotic charge. At several points during the poem, for instance, Olson's gaze fastens on the woman who accompanies the leader. To some extent, his avid interest reduces her to a human scale that doesn't admit the added dimension of the satyrs, but she still partakes of the quality of self-containment. As a figure of beauty she is 'a dazzling blond, the new dye making her hair a delicious / streaked ash', and yet 'She was as distant as the others' without quite taking on their larger-than-life status (*CP*, 386). Olson's interest in the leader's woman could mark the phallicism in the poem as emphatically heterosexual, but the burgeoning eroticism in his treatment of the motorcyclists also spills over into homosocial and homosexual channels. Invoking Aristophanes' original humans, who had twice the limbs and organs of present humans and represented three sexes – double-male, double-female, and male-female – Olson also opens the poem explicitly to homosexuality and androgyny.

Near the beginning, after he calls the motorcyclists 'the Androgynes' and 'the Great Halves', he turns to speak in homosocial terms of three poets: the one he 'loved most', who confessed to Olson his pain 'the night he got drunk, / and I put him to bed' (Robert Creeley?); another, whose 'Sources' were snarled 'all in his mouth'; and a third who was a 'Yiddish poet / a vegetarian' with something conspicuous 'inside his pants' (Allen Ginsberg?) (*CP*, 384). Offsetting his regard for these poets and their erotic dilemmas, Olson remains fascinated by the group of phallic motorcyclists, who 'sit there, up a little, on their thing' and who sport a 'huge third leg like carborundum' (*CP*, 386, 387). As in Greek depictions of ithyphallic satyrs, Olson's hyper-masculine cyclists are inherently comic and, at least to a certain extent, queer. In this way he anticipates another trailblazing artwork focused on a motorcycle club, Kenneth Anger's 1964 film *Scorpio Rising*, in which Anger converts the fetishism and masculine high jinks of a Brooklyn motorcycle club into a homoerotic *Walpurgisnacht*, timing the scenes to coincide with twelve Pop songs of 1963.[20] Straying into queerness, Olson does not, however, embrace it wholeheartedly like Anger (whose unsuspecting cyclists had no idea they were being cast as homoerotic satyrs) or like Ginsberg in 'Howl' – which is exactly contemporaneous with 'The Lordly and Isolate Satyrs'. Although Ginsberg's 'angelheaded hipsters ... let themselves be fucked in the ass by saintly motorcyclists, and screamed with joy', Olson, while recognizing the cyclists in his poem as libidinous forces, resists merging with them physically and mentally, for they 'are our counterparts, the unknown ones. / They are here. We do not look upon them as invaders' (*CP*, 386).[21]

Ultimately, 'The Lordly and Isolate Satyrs', in its polymorphic eroticism, provides Olson with a canvas on which to imagine the beach at Gloucester as a site where elemental powers emerge from the sea. Oppen is right when he declares it a poem of Olson's 'in which the voice and eye are his alone'. The eye perceives a remarkable theophany and the voice adroitly combines expressions of awe with a late 1950s demotic speech. Giving the lie to Olson's reputation for exclamatory didacticism, this poem shows a striking, and by no means uncharacteristic, ability to mix tones and levels of diction in order to create a lyric poetry that feels at once temporally specific and open in time. Part of this ability resides in his use of the first person plural. Although the poem recounts a dream of his own, he narrates it from the standpoint of a shared experience, which the reader is invited to enter, and thus to refresh in time. In the last stanza, Olson subtly disengages from the suspended time of the satyrs and returns to quotidian life, marking how extraordinary their appearance has been:

> We stay. And watch them
> gather themselves up. We have no feeling except love. They are not
> ours. They are of another name. These are what the gods are. They
> look like us. They are only in all parts larger. But the size is
> only different. The difference is, they are not here, they are not
> on this beach in this sun which tomorrow, when we come to swim,
> will be another summer day. They can't talk to us.
>
> (*CPr*, 387)

These oneiric-mythical-prehistoric divinities reveal the splendour of life and thus inspire devotion, while yet maintaining a distance and monumentality and an inability to communicate directly with humans.

Choreographing a dance of intimacy and separation with larger-than-life beings, Olson joins artists of the postwar era in invoking motorcyclists as embodiments of irrepressible sexual energy. Unlike Beat artists such as Brando, Frank, Kerouac, and Ginsberg, though, Olson sees his bikers as elemental (if sometimes mock-heroic) actors. In this ambitious poem, he strives both to paint an appreciative portrait of the iconic motorcycle club of the late 1950s and to incorporate self-contained erotic energies from a dream into his own expanded perception of the world. Through a lyric engagement with internal and external realities, he means to be one of 'the Contemporaries'.[22]

Notes

1 *Poetry* 100:5 (1962), 332; George Oppen, *Selected Prose, Daybooks, and Papers*, ed. Stephen Cope (Berkeley: University of California Press, 2007), 27.
2 Ralph Maud, *Charles Olson's Reading: A Biography* (Carbondale: Southern Illinois University Press, 1996), 331.
3 See John Leland, *Hip: The History* (New York: HarperCollins, 2004), for an historical account of the development of the American quality of 'hipness', a quality Olson explores in this poem through the image of the motorcyclists.
4 Mary Oppen, *Meaning A Life: An Autobiography* (Santa Barbara, CA: Black Sparrow Press, 1978), 201–2.
5 Thanks to Henry Weinfield for drawing my attention to Williams as one source for the term 'isolate'.
6 Herman Melville, *Moby-Dick*, Norton Critical Edition, ed. Harrison Hayford and Hershel Parker (New York: Norton, 1967), 108.
7 Stephen Fredman, *The Grounding of American Poetry: Charles Olson and the Emersonian Tradition* (Cambridge: Cambridge University Press, 1993).
8 A. Walton Litz and Christopher MacGowan, eds, *The Collected Poems of William Carlos Williams*, Vol. I: 1909–1939 (New York: New Directions, 1986), 217.
9 Ibid., 219.
10 Ibid.
11 Ibid.
12 Ibid., 217.
13 *Evergreen Review* 1:4 (Spring 1958, copyright 1957), 5–8.
14 Kenneth Rexroth, 'San Francisco Letter', *Evergreen Review* 1:2 (Summer 1957), 5.
15 Donald Allen (ed.), *The New American Poetry, 1945–1960* (Berkeley: University of California Press, 1999), 2–39, 386–400.
16 Ibid., xi.
17 Robert Frank, *The Americans* (Paris: Robert Delpire, 1958, and New York: Grove Press, 1959).
18 Ibid., 9.

19 William Blake, *The Marriage of Heaven and Hell* (London: Oxford University Press, 1975), Plate 11.
20 Kenneth Anger, dir., *Scorpio Rising* (1964), 28 mins, colour.
21 Allen Ginsberg, *Collected Poems 1947–1997* (New York: HarperCollins, 2006), 134, 136. Another gay poet, Thom Gunn, also portrayed motorcyclists as cultural icons in 'On the Move' (1957). Using Marlon Brando in *The Wild One* as his model, Gunn sees the cyclists as representing continuous movement: 'At worse, one is in motion; and at best, / Reaching no absolute, in which to rest, / One is always nearer by not keeping still' (Thom Gunn, *Selected Poems*, ed. August Kleinzahler (New York: Farrar, Straus and Giroux, 2009), 8). Olson, contrarily, insists on their monumental solidity.
22 This essay first appeared in 'Olson @ the Century: An archival and projective reconsideration,' *Open Letter* 15:2 (Spring 2013). Thanks to the editor, Steve McCaffery, for permission to reprint.

14

Futtocks

Anthony Mellors

The ancient Sumerians, who inhabited that part of southern Mesopotamia now known as Iraq, displayed in their arts, writing, and technical and civic accomplishments the first signs of a mature civilisation. Had Charles Olson, whose obsession with human origins led him to place supreme value on Sumeria as well as the Mayan culture he researched, lived to witness the 2003 Iraq war, his deepest fears of American 'pejorocracy' would have been realised. Scant regard for cultural property meant that the Coalition forces caused serious damage to key sites such as Babylon and Ur and stood by while treasures were looted from archaeological sites and museums, among them the bull lyre from the 'Royal Cemetery' at Ur, which was stripped of its gold sheeting and precious stones and left in the car park of the Baghdad Museum.[1] Olson's 1951 essay 'The Gate and the Center' argues that Sumer is the model for polis; from the date of the first city, 3378 BC

> until date 1200BC or thereabouts, civilization had ONE CENTER, Sumer, in all directions, that this one people held such exact and superior force that all peoples around it were sustained, nourished, increased, advanced, that a city was a coherence which, for the first time since the ice, gave man the chance to join knowledge to culture and, with this weapon, shape dignities of economics and value sufficient to make daily life itself a dignity and a sufficiency.
>
> (*CPr*, 170)

Moreover, the Gilgamesh epic, in which the hero's power over his civilisation is checked by the gods, 'is an incredibly accurate myth of what happens to the best of men when they lose touch with the primordial & phallic energies & methodologies which, said this predecessor people of ours, make it possible for man, that participant thing, to take up, straight, nature's, live nature's force' (*CPr*, 173). Ralph Maud notes that an early poem by Olson, 'Tomorrow', begins 'I am Gilgamesh / an Ur world is in me / to inhabit', and we can see in this perhaps the first incarnation of Maximus, prefigured by the Babylonian poem *Enuma elish*: 'His members were enormous, he was exceedingly tall.'[2]

For Maud, the evidence from history and myth, the *muthologos*, is a prime example of what he calls the 'archaic post-modern', a term he uses to distinguish Olson's invention of postmodernism from its current meaning as 'modernism pushed to the point of alienation which allows no hauteur of identity on which to hang a coherent tale'.[3] He takes issue with Perry Anderson, who credits Olson with the first use of 'post-modern' but confines its meaning to the classical avant-garde, and also with Tom Clark, whose critical and sometimes erroneous biography of Olson is under attack throughout Maud's book, and who reads Olson's poetic as an 'oblique, discontinuous narrative' arranging archaic and contemporary elements 'like tesserae in a complex mosaic ... employing the major modernist juxtapositional mode'.[4] The problem for Maud is not that Clark ignores Olson's take-off into a kind of postmodernity, but that he refuses to acknowledge Olson's poetics as 'a coherent argument using imaged ideas'.[5] The point is that Olson's postmodernism should not be seen as *more* modernism, nor as juxtapositional, collagist, or paratactic methods going forward into the chaos of non-identity, but as 'an indispensable other on the pathway forward from the present' in the sense George Butterick gives it: 'the deeper man returns to the archaic, primordial, pre-rationalist condition, the further from modernism he advances'.[6] For Maud, postmodernism 'has been perverted from its original meaning' as a new recognition of belonging in a primordial, tribal *sensus communis*, freed from the disintegration of the modernist self. Olson drew on the 'ancient knowledge' D. H. Lawrence described in *Fantasia of the Unconscious* (Tarot as opposed to contract bridge) and anticipated 'advances in depth psychology, all the good work that has been done by attention to the soul'.[7]

Maud is no doubt aware that that term 'the soul', with its Jungian accretions, is like a red rag to a bull for the kind of postmodernist poets and critics whom he regards as straying from Olson's path. And the 'advances' in depth psychology he endorses have been renounced by these poets and critics in favour of the surreal materialism of Jacques Lacan, which Maud clearly abhors. Yet the inclusive concept of 'soul' may be little more than a humanist abstraction in the context of Olson's archaeology; and the attendant notions of coherence and belonging in a primordial realm of archetypal consciousness are problematic because they spring *from* modernism rather than providing the antidote to it. If the modernists endued their work with the symptoms of alienation, everywhere apparent, it was because they promoted a lost horizon of ethnic, tribal, racial unity in which the isolate ego is transcended by the collective force of the group, represented by totemic emblems. As

Durkheim puts it, 'when the group member feels a new life flowing within him whose intensity surprises him, he is not the dupe of an illusion.'[8] Olson evinces a liberal, but no less phallic, revision of Pound's Tradition, progressing back from classical western origins, and his ethnopoetics feeds into the contradictory impulses of late twentieth-century counter-culture, which romances collective enlightenment while becoming seduced by its Dionysian other: the tribe seeks its gods and gurus, and eventually falls prey to the corrupting force of its own subjection. The charismatic leader, representative of the gods, requires a totality of vision whether for good or ill.[9] The central problem of modern mythic culture, a culture for which myth has become reality, is that it will not work unless everyone believes. Therefore, fully realised, the polis cannot admit dissent. Donald Davie's question remains relevant here:

> [W]ho is to persuade me – and how – that the man who says he has met Artemis or turned into a tree is not dangerously self-deluded or self-intoxicated? And is this not in fact the central and unavoidable question about Pound's poetry, as about Charles Olson's and Robert Duncan's?[10]

When Olson looks for pre-classical models of polis in Mayan or Sumerian civilisation, he cherry-picks for value, ignoring the less savoury aspects of their organisation. While, for example, the Sumerians achieved a level of 'dignity' way above any previous cultural formation and – in some accounts – provided an enviable proto-democratic model for later societies, they regarded slavery as part of the natural order, just as it was for other early cultures. When Leonard Woolley excavated Ur in the 1920s, he discovered the bull lyre in one of several 'death pits' containing the remains of numerous royal attendants. Unable to find evidence of cause of death, Woolley speculated that these people had willingly sacrificed themselves by drinking poison. Recent analysis, however, shows that the retainers suffered blunt force trauma, and their corpses were preserved with cinnabar prior to burial. The souls of the departed are less important here than the soulless way they were dispatched. As Georges Roux implies in his discussion of evidence for 'democracy' in Sumeria, a tendency to sentimentalise the archaic turns speculation into fact, and 'there is no clear-cut evidence in the Sumerian tradition of a period when the city-states were ruled by collective institutions, and as far as we can go back into the past we see nothing but rulers and monarchs second only to the gods.'[11] It is precisely this kingly and godly principle, as *force*, that appeals to Olson, the 'early HUMAN KINGS' who allow us to 'see what size man can be once more capable of, once the turn of the flow of his energies that I speak of as the WILL TO COHERE is admitted' (*CPr*, 172).[12] The Sumerian kings were divinely inspired to rule over their flock like shepherds, possessed of the knowledge that 'every category of objects possessed a dynamic personality, a "will" of its own, and it was these forces immanent in nature which the gods embodied.'[13] Typically modernist, too, is Olson's insistence that coherence underpins the fragmentary work as an animistic force, which informs the will but derives from a place prior to the ego. The main difference here between Eliot's 'mythic method' and the archaic postmodern is that the latter aims to overcome the doubt and vacillation evident in the former. When Pound writes at the end of the *Cantos* –

> But the beauty is not the madness
> Tho' my errors and wrecks lie about me.
> And I am not a demigod,
>   I cannot make it cohere.
> ...
> it coheres all right
>   even if my notes do not cohere[14]

– he attests to the failure of a project Olson wants to carry forward/backward into a new coherence. The poet becomes a king whose creative energies are channelled by the gods; his *prana* is theorised in 'modern' terms through cybernetics as a self-organising system, the proprioception Olson derives from Norbert Wiener a physical and spiritual order which, Maud argues, is supported by two appositely named books by biologist Stuart A. Kauffman, *The Origins of Order* (1993) and *At Home in the Universe* (1995). But, again, what could be more modernist than the use of scientific paradigms to exemplify spiritual presentiments (e.g., Pound's 'rose in the steel dust'), the occulted version of modernity's phantasy of self-regulating systems (such as the commune and the free market)? The law of expression is the law of the organism, Olson argues in a 1951 letter to Robert Creeley, and 'both can now – had better now – be said to be mythological'.[15]

In 1951, when he was struggling with rewrites of the 'Human Universe' essay, Olson was much concerned with the question of humanism, the human and its limitations. A long letter on the Jews and mythology remained unsent, possibly because he realised that it comes dangerously close to the anti-Semitism he criticises elsewhere. The core of the letter appears to be that the Judeo-Christian tradition has given birth to the three great thinkers of the modern condition, Einstein (who turned non-Euclidean geometry into a new conception of space-time), Marx (who energised the principle of collectivity), and Freud (who revolutionised psychic and intellectual life for everyone), but that Jewish thought remains implicated in the tribal burden of ritual sacrifice, patricide, and sexual repression through the hatred of women. For Olson, this 'humanism' is a 'huge misreading of nature' because it is based on blood as the essence of life. Other traditions, such as that of 'those Africans of Frazer (the King of the Wood biz.)' or the 'Middle American Indians', knew that the source of energy stands outside the animal, in the form of the sun, 'because the Sun breeds life / that only the sun is life, in this sense, of, making it possible'. The Indians practiced sacrifice, yet:

> so far as I know, it is never father, but where the killing or cutting out of the heart is as presentation to the sun (and seems, at least as of these Indians, to be more precious, as act, when it is a young woman, not, a man, least of all, father – for Sun is father.[16]

The archaic postmodern, or post-human, would reinstate a phallic condition not based on the 'cannibalism' of the Oedipus; instead, it respects and maintains the father-figure as the source of life, like the sun itself, above merely human concerns. Humanism is an essential part of the modern life-world, but, as an earlier letter asserts, 'merely duplication of human realisms will never stretch the human system to its own reaches.'[17] It is curious, to say the least, that Olson accuses the Jews of treating women as whores but excuses the Mesoamericans of sacrificing women in the name of the father. He excuses because he wants the phallic principle to be fully mythological, and therefore to transcend the physical (human) fact of blood relations, to become by extension pure force and will. Otherwise it is difficult to make sense of the statement in a letter of 18 July 1951 which endorses the juxtapositional form of 'The Kingfishers' as 'fast enough, and final enough, also to get in the will, my will as it is human in the sense that humanism is not'.[18] The remark is part of an ongoing, elusive discussion of the problem of what Maud resolves as a coherent argument using imaged ideas but which continues to vex Olson as the fundamental issue of his poetics: is the form inwardly coherent, narrative, objective, exact, real in its 'attentions', or merely the fragments of a mosaic that might not get reconstructed? Fighting to make himself clear in the exploratory, stuttering, fragmentary epistolary form he makes his own, Olson laments the lack of narrative coherence in modern verse while insisting that the work has to project the sometimes wayward but dynamic attentions of the poet. The letters themselves perform this lack of 'fit' between apprehension and argument, the thoughts rattled out in oblique attacks, while Creeley does his damnedest to answer in kind. The 'control factor' of narration is found wanting in Rimbaud, who 'fucking well knows (who knows better) how much he *does not get in*', and Pound is called 'Cento Man' in March 1951, reprised a year or so later in a highly condensed passage that opposes the primacy of the sun to Pound's 'Cento longings'.[19] The 'cento' (Latin: 'patchwork') is an ancient form of verse constructed entirely of quotations from other works. Originally regarded as a tribute, it tends to be used nowadays as a light-verse experiment, although its procedural links with 'found' poetry make it a traditional model for paratactic composition, as for example in the work of Ashbery and Mac Low. Clearly Olson is aware that the mode of 'The Kingfishers', with its wealth of quoted material, derives from Pound, but at this point he is worried that the mythic/documentary method is antithetical to personal attention. Taken to its extreme in the cento, the juxtapositional mode would be devoid of projective energy. Hence the distress over what little Olson gleans from lines in German by Rainer Gerhardt, editor of *Fragmente*. '[G]ut für montage', writes Gerhardt, endorsing his own poetry, Olson's, and Gottfried Benn's. 'What sticks in my crop, is, this güt for montage', Olson complains, 'And so my verse is good as montage? Jesus', and can't understand how he comes to be published by an editor who appears to regard him as an enemy.[20]

Like the unresolved Pound he loves and rejects, then, Olson seems torn between modernist facture and the desire to achieve a direct poetic language that would correspond with the actuality promised by a step back to the archaic postmodern. Yet he insists that the 'mythologic, as method' (*meta hodos*, not the path itself but the way in which the path is known, the projective totality), the method derived from Eliot and Pound, 'is the only true one because, it distinguishes blood from sun, and reality from its own identical mythology, and sets sun as source and art as source'.[21] Montage, ideogram, constructivism, parataxis, juxtaposition: these are all names for, or aspects of, that method, a method that becomes increasingly insistent in *The Maximus Poems*. To renounce it would be, theoretically speaking, to reject the sun and what separates art from mere ego. But to embrace it is to risk incoherence. In 1952, Olson will define the tension as one between the psyche and the metapsyche, the personal attentions always having to obey a force that cannot be contained by the 'psychic plane' alone. The harmonious rubbing together of these planes results in the unity of the vision; yet the vision remains indirect, otherwise it would be realised only at the level of consciousness, like the poems Jack Spicer says are merely 'letters to the editor'.[22] So 'the real push asked of verse now' is 'that it put back into itself all that force which has so long been scattered in a series of proper nouns and proper narratives'.[23] In the end, coherence, as clarity, consistency, narrative, is just not Olson's thing. In spite of all the claims to system and scholarship, Olson works by way of association and accretion – and every exhilarating connection runs the risk of falling into error. Ironically, even the invention of the term 'postmodern' came about as a fortuitous side-effect of scholarly confusion: according to Clark, Olson dashed-off an eleven page letter to Yale critic Louis Martz convinced that they had both independently discovered modern Americans to be related to the Pelasgians – ancient Greek aboriginals Olson had read about in Pausanias – only to realise just before posting that Martz was referring to a Christian heretical sect known as the Pelagians. Redirecting the letter to Creeley with an extended commentary, Olson coined the term 'post-modern'.[24]

Armed with Butterick's *Guide*, the adept reader of *The Maximus Poems* is able to pull together sheets of thought and reference that would otherwise remain unspliced in Olson's vast three-masted vessel. Like all figurative vessels in fragments, *Maximus* suggests coherence while staying determinedly in pieces. Like the *Cantos*, it seems virtually unreadable without a commentary, just as the incomplete relics of Greek civilisation needed Pausanias's *Guide*. And yet the experience of reading poetry freighted with scholarly ballast seems to many readers dishonest, distracting, and somehow beside the point, especially in the case of *Maximus* which, following Olson's Herodotean notion of *'istorin*, begs the question *Is it really finding out for oneself*? When Thomas Merrill, in *The Poetry of Charles Olson*, states that the 'poems are performative moral acts that demand as much allegiance to the rigid doctrines that support them as any orthodox religion' he has at the same time to ask whether the poetry *as poetry* is 'sufficiently strong to balance the gnomic obscurities' of lines such as

>   tesserae
>   commisure
>
> (*MP*, 269)

– a complete poem, as is

>   In the harbor
>   Can 9   Num 8
>   Nun 10   Can 11
>
> (*MP*, 302)[25]

Merrill's examples are easily glossed by Butterick's *Guide*, the first representing an Olsonian variation on Pound's 'Dichtung = condensare', the 'binding together' of commisure made more poignant by its pronunciation as 'come ashore' in a 1963 reading at Vancouver (*GMP*, 421–2). The tesserae may be what Clark is thinking of when he defines Olson's poetics as a complex mosaic. The second example refers to the markings on buoys visible from Fort Point, a projection of land into Gloucester Harbor. Like Olson's Steinian 'Rose of the World' (or 'Rosa Mundi') of

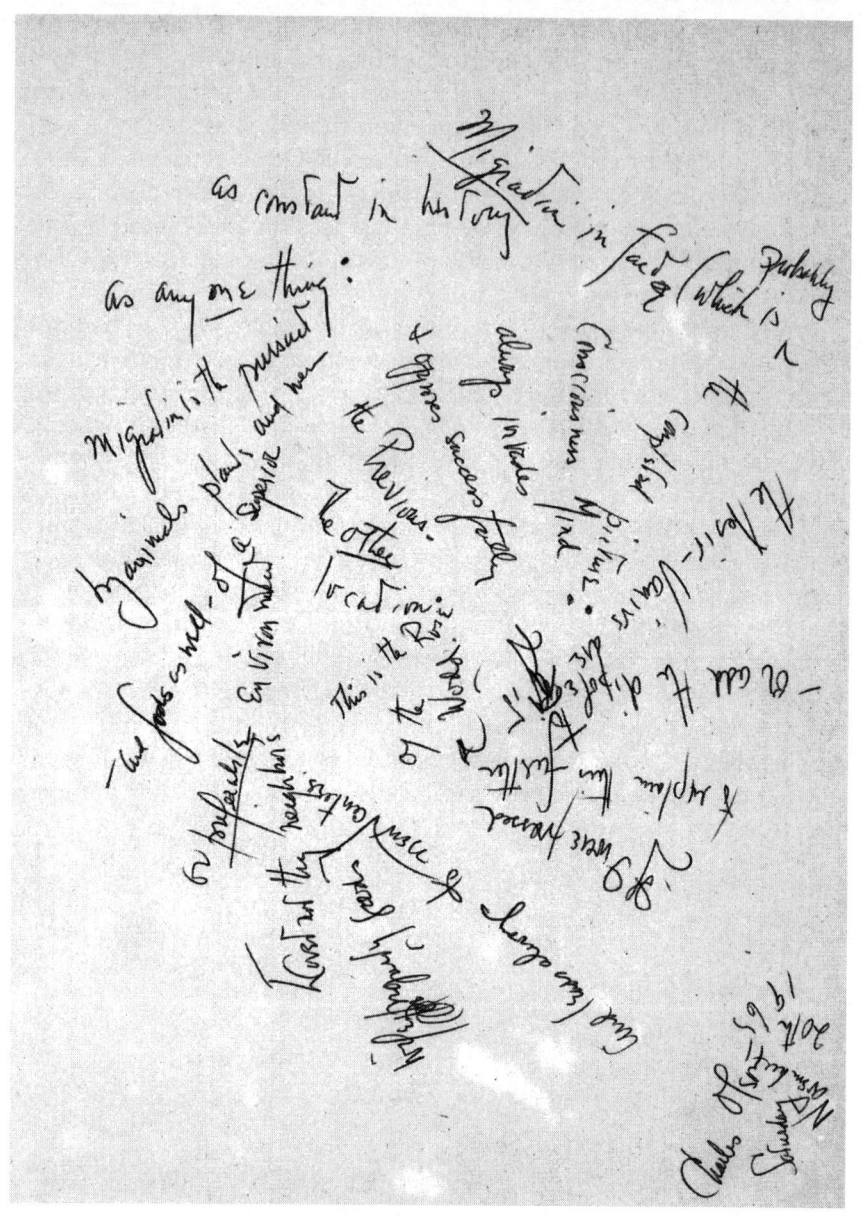

5 Charles Olson, 'Rosa Mundi' (1965).

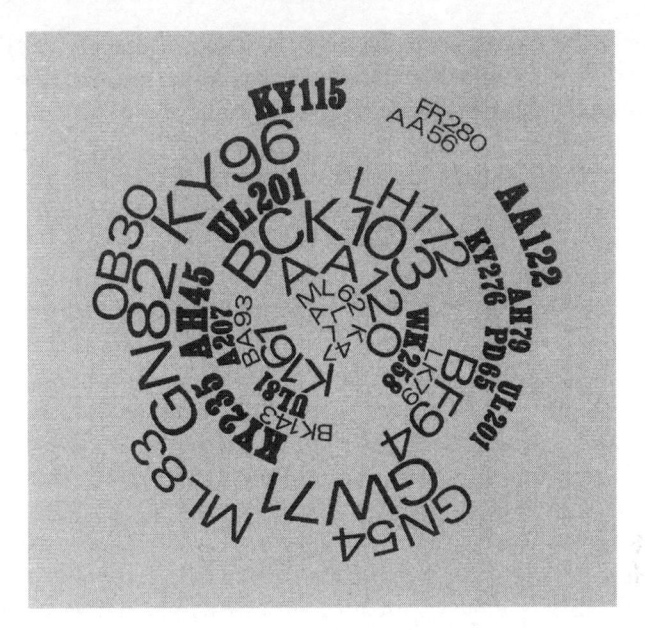

6 Ian Hamilton Finlay, 'Sea Poppy 1' (1966).

1965 (Fig. 5), it shows the influence of concrete poetry on Olson's facture, and the texts together might be said to prefigure Ian Hamilton Finlay's 'Sea Poppy' (1966) (Fig. 6).[26]

Yet there are many instances where sense is sutured or marked as incomplete or unknowable, e.g., the 1962 poem beginning 'The shape of Weymouth' and ending with:

>   unk unk
>   nescio   ballotes

'Unk' may be the unknown portions of the microfilm of port records, with which the poet was struggling, and eventually giving up on the obscurities of his source (nescio: 'I don't know') and Butterick finding himself at sea with the rest of this poem, in which conjunctions become so obscure they are subjected to tenuous biographical sense-making or ignored altogether (*MP*, 388; *GMP*, 512–15). What are the 'ballotes', previously aligned with the city of Rouen? Votes? The French word for 'bundle', or *marrube noir* (Black Horehound), an antispasmodic herb? One of the strengths of the *Maximus* poems is their negative capability in registering the act of discovery in process; this tension between Olson's thetic insistence and the provisional nature of his evidence is what gives the work its energy. If the studied incoherence of Olson's style gives him power over his readers, in that it assumes an horizon of sense that is always implicit but never reached, it displays at the same time its author's tenuous hold on authority, a gap between process and product no commentary can fill. Questioning the nature of evidence is to do more than point out gaps in scholarly knowledge, which may or may not be filled-in as more information about Olson's poetry is acquired; it is to look critically at a poetic that, in the spirit of Anaximander's indefinite *apeiron* – the *arche* as an unlimited primordial mass, perpetually yielding fresh materials – resists the suturing of gaps ('chaos') and asks that each reader discover in the text a *muthologos* or *imago mundi* set against conformity.[27] Furthermore, it is to consider how critical accounts of Olson's epic rest on key metaphors, ideas, and images which appear to govern them, as if the poetry remains accessible to a 'well-wrought urn' paradigm when in fact it disseminates the meaning of its symbols more than unifies them. From Maximus and his incarnations (Paul Bunyan, William Stevens, Gilgamesh, Bigmans, Odysseus, James Merry, etc.) to the *hominem quadratum*, stone stelae, glyphs, the Cut, the cup-hole and the Venus, a diversity of representamens form Olson's epic vision in a series of imaginative connections that whirl out centrifugally. Perhaps the most significant in terms of its circulation is the following:

> Definition: (in this instance,
> and in what others, what
> felicities?
>
> "The crooked timbers
> scarfed together to form the lower part of the compound rib are
>
> futtocks,
> we call 'em
>
> But a fylfot,
> she look like,
> who calls herself
>
> (luck

(*MP*, 44)[28]

The 'felicities' here are the supposedly organic but actually random and associative connections formed by 'scarfing' together words and images; in other words, a way of suturing materials that don't fit the application required. In this crucial example, 'futtocks', the curved timbers that make up the ribs of a ship, are scarfed to a 'fylfot', the four-footed cross also known as the *crux gammata*, tetraskelion, gammadion, and swastika. Mainwaring's *Sea-man's Dictionary* of 1644 says that futtocks should properly be called 'foote-hooks' because they are the compassing timbers, spanning the breadth of the ship, which are scarfed to the ground-timbers (see *OED*). They have no etymological link with *fylfot*, neither here nor in the *Webster's Collegiate* dictionary Butterick refers to. It is enough for Butterick that both terms appear on the same page (*GMP*, 64–5). In *Themis*, something of a primer or ur-text for Maximus, Jane Harrison explains that the Sanskrit word *swastika*, a name for wellness, applies to the *croix gammée* when it is depicted as turning in a clockwise direction. When turning anti-clockwise, it is called *sauvastika*, and means that all is not well. 'The idea is of course not confined to the East. It lives on today in Scotland, as *deisul*, "sunwise" and *widershins*. In college Combination Rooms port wine is still passed round according to the way of the Sun.'[29] And L. A. Waddell, whose work Olson was reading in 1951–2, notes that 'The Swastika form of the sun cross occurs on early Hittite and Sumerian seals and sculptures.'[30] Olson's line of thought runs from William Stevens (the ship's carpenter described in 'Letter 7' as 'the first Maximus'), to the futtocks, which bind a ship, to the fylfot, which stands for the paternal metaphor of the sun, itself leading back to the archaic values exemplified by the Sumerians and the seafaring Phoenicians Waddell believed to be the origin of the Britons. The heliotrope image (which Olson also links with the alchemical 'black chrysanthemum' or 'golden flower') is paternal because, as we have seen, the sun protects the father from sacrifice precisely by *being* the father of all things.[31] Furthermore, Stevens is identified with Olson's own father in 'Stevens Song'; both men were reduced in civic standing by the 'bosses': 'Stevens ran off / My father / stayed / & was ground down' (*MP*, 400).[32]

Olson is of course interested in the origins of the fylfot/swastika as an energised sign, not in its more recent function as Nazi heraldry. Since Charles Olson Sr. came a cropper fighting for union recognition and Ezra Pound's praise for Mussolini's union-bashing was met by Olson calling him the worst kind of Fascist, 'this filthy apologist and mouther of slogans which serve men of power', *Maximus* was hardly likely to turn into a paean to blood-and-soil politics, however sublimated.[33] Yet there is something odd about a work of the 1950s which sings of the primordial power of the swastika without a hint of irony. Disavowal, perhaps, because Olson senses that his quest for origins is similar to the obsession that led philologists, historians, and archaeologists to fuel the myths contributing to the rise of fascism. Waddell, for example, does not simply claim Phoenician origins, he argues that those origins are fundamentally Aryan. The racialist drift of nineteenth- and early twentieth-century scholarship, which remains present in the Frazerian studies of Jessie L. Weston and the Jungian criticism of Maud Bodkin, tends toward reductive archetypes of trans-cultural images. As any comparative survey of definitions of the fylfot/swastika will show, the image is far from being fixed in its symbolism: the sheer number of synonyms alone testifies to its polymorphous semiotic. In *The Migration of Symbols* (1894), Count Goblet D'Alviella solved the problem of its teeming interpretations by 'naming the image as the sign of its own unsignability'.[34] But this affirmation of its undecodable nature lent itself to the occult discourse of racial historians looking for a symbol which preserved the secret 'inner identity' of Germanic *Ursprache* and the Aryan 'root-race'. The Oriental term *swastika*, shorn of its complex cultural migration and reduced to a single, fanciful racial lineage, was used instead of the German *Hakenkreuz* as 'the sign for an image which stands for both the nostalgia of a primal loss and the yearning for a return'.[35] The Nazis did not, as some popular accounts claim, use the wrong-turning *sauvastika* as if to announce their evil intent, and when Hitler sutures the swastika into one iconic symbol it is in order to create a new mythos from an occulted heritage of 'blood'. The swastika becomes a kind of corporate logo fetishising the Aryan race and excluding the Semitic.

Olson's approach to the image hardly affirms this mythos, but it is far from deconstructing it. Instead, the chain of associations is overdetermined by the bizarre logic of his commentaries. The sun represents the father, who stands for a projective, progressive politics opposed to a mythos of blood. At the same time, because Olson identifies the Jews with a fixation on blood, the sun signifies in the traces of the Aryan mythos and therefore becomes anti-Semitic. Andrew Ross suggests that the 'doodled whirligigs' in the third volume of *The Maximus Poems* show Olson involved in a complex and contradictory troping in which 'we find both the injunction to turn under the name of the father, and the outlawed will to turn against it', with the poet unable to decide whether to turn right or left.[36] Uncertainty is a key constituent of the archaic postmodern, which, far from overcoming the poetics and politics of modernism, becomes a highly problematic reenactment of the relationship between modernist myth and ideology.

Notes

1 'The decision by adversaries to purposely target religious and cultural sites and the potential for copy-cat destruction of cultural heritage sites as a mechanism to enflame opposing forces and demoralize the population at large – last seen during the campaign in the former Yugoslavia, but perpetrated on a much larger scale in Iraq – became a factor in Coalition military strategy. The possibility of a repeat of this scenario in future conflicts cannot be ignored.' (www.cemml.colostate.edu/cultural/09476/iraq08–01enl.html);

'Ancient looted harp re-created' (http://news.bbc.co.uk/1/hi/england/shropshire/4732497.stm). See also Heather Pringle, 'Sleuthing Around the Great Death-pit' (www.lastwordonnothing.com/2011/04/29/sleuthing-around-the-great-deeath-pit).
2 Ralph Maud, '"The Kingfishers" and the Archaic Postmodern', in *Charles Olson at the Harbor* (Vancouver: Talonbooks, 2008), 135; Georges Roux, *Ancient Iraq* (Harmondsworth: Penguin, 1977), 95.
3 Maud, *Olson at the Harbor*, 133.
4 Tom Clark, *Charles Olson: The Allegory of a Poet's Life* (New York: Norton, 1991), 147.
5 Maud, *Olson at the Harbor*, 129.
6 Ibid., 133; George Butterick, 'Charles Olson and the Postmodern Advance', *Iowa Review* (Fall 1980) 4–27, 12.
7 Maud, *Olson at the Harbor*, 133, 135, 134.
8 Emile Durkheim, *Elementary Forms of Religious Life* (1915), quoted in Maud Bodkin, *Archetypal Patterns in Poetry: Psychological Studies of Imagination* (London: Oxford University Press, 1974), 277. Like Jessie L. Weston in *From Ritual to Romance* (1920), Bodkin constantly equates patterns of universal experience and their emblems with 'racial' memory. The multi-ethnic character of the line from Frazer to Jung, which translated through Olson becomes ethnopoetics, has an uneasy relationship with the racial.
9 Is Oliver Stone's *The Doors* (1991), for example, a eulogy to the psychedelic generation or a dissection of its narcissism? The answer, of course, is that it is both of these things, and the holding-together of opposites is what makes the representation mythic. It cannot accede to ideological critique because countercultural praxis has never reconciled its civic ideals with libertarianism, a condition exploited ruthlessly by neo-conservative regimes.
10 Donald Davie, *Thomas Hardy and British Poetry* (London: Routledge, 1973), 43.
11 Roux, *Ancient Iraq*, 89.
12 Quoted in conclusion by Maud, *Olson at the Harbor*, 137.
13 Roux, *Ancient Iraq*, 88.
14 Ezra Pound, *The Cantos* (London: Faber and Faber, 1975), 796.
15 Charles Olson and Robert Creeley, *The Complete Correspondence*, Vol. 6, ed. George F. Butterick (Santa Barbara: Black Sparrow Press, 1985), 73.
16 Ibid., 142.
17 Ibid., 73.
18 Ibid., 159.
19 Ibid., 42; Olson and Creeley, *Complete Correspondence*, Vol. 10, ed. Richard Blevins (Santa Rosa: Black Sparrow Press, 1996), 35, and see notes 46 and 47.
20 Olson and Creeley, *Complete Correspondence*, Vol. 6, 93.
21 Ibid., 148; Olson and Creely, *Complete Correspondence*, Vol. 10, 151–2; and see Richard Blevins's introduction to Vol. 10, xi–xii.
22 Jack Spicer, *The House That Jack Built: The Collected Lectures of Jack Spicer*, ed. Peter Gizzi (Middletown: Wesleyan University Press, 1998), 14:

'I mean, if you want to write a letter to the editor, then the thing to do is to write a letter to the editor as far as I can see. And it doesn't seem to me that's what poetry is for.'
23 Olson and Creeley, *Complete Correspondence*, Vol. 10, 42, 41.
24 Clark, *Allegory*, 208.
25 Thomas Merrill, *The Poetry of Charles Olson: A Primer* (Newark: University of Delaware Press, 1982), 214, 212–12. Merrill suggests Lawrence's morality of the blood as a paradigm for Olson's poetics. While the letters and essays of 1951-2 display an enthusiasm for Lawrence to the point of repeating his name as a mantra for the 'living fact' of *muthologos* (see *Complete Correspondence*, Vol. 10, 48), the primacy of blood over mind in this context adds extra complication to the blood/sun opposition.
26 Ian Hamilton Finlay (with Alastair Cant), 'Sea Poppy 1' (Nottingham: Tarasque Press, 1966). See also the pattern poem based on de Champlain's 1606 map of Gloucester Harbor in *The Maximus Poems*, 156, and the phallic pattern poem 'My beloved Father', 499.
27 Consider: 'Aristotle & Augustine / clearly misunderstood Anaximander / And in doing so beta'd / themselves' (*MP*, 283). The nose-thumbing undergraduate wit is left without further explanation, and Butterick refers us to an *Encyclopaedia Britannica* entry 'which would seem to have influenced Olson' (*GMP*, 405). See also W. K. C. Guthrie, *A History of Greek Philosophy. Volume 1: The Earlier Presocratics and the Pythagoreans* (Cambridge: Cambridge University Press, 1962), 72ff.
28 Amplified in 'Maximus, to himself, as of "Phoenicians"' (*MP*, 181).
29 Jane Harrison, *Themis: A Study of the Social Origins of Greek Religion* (London: Merlin Press, 1989), 526.
30 L. A Waddell, *The Phoenician Origin of Britons, Scots, and Anglo-Saxons* (London: Williams & Norgate, 1924), 298. See Olson and Creeley, *Complete Correspondence*, Vol. 6, 213, and Vol. 10, 110: 'that *mythology* – where, surely, Waddell is strong ... from Homer, first, then Herodotus, then Pausanias – last, the Sumerians – is the circle which bends the iron of their progress axis back into proper confinement.'
31 See Andrew Ross's discussion of 'Tyrian Businesses' and the pattern poems in *The Failure of Modernism: Symptoms of American Poetry* (New York: Columbia University Press, 1986), 122–8.
32 See Butterick (*GMP*, 50, 530–1), and Olson, 'The Post Office' (*CPr*, 233).
33 The exchange is recounted in E. Fuller Torrey, *The Roots of Treason: Ezra Pound and the Secrets of St Elizabeth's* (London: Sidgwick & Jackson, 1984), 225–6.
34 Malcolm Quinn, *The Swastika: Constructing the Symbol* (London: Routledge, 1994), 23.
35 Ibid., 49.
36 Ross, *The Failure of Modernism*, 124.

15

Death in life: the past in 'As the Dead Prey Upon Us'

Ben Hickman

By the mid-1950s Charles Olson had become an influential pedagogue in a burgeoning poetical counterculture. As he left Black Mountain in 1956, he had three full collections under his belt, an already voluminous publication record of expository prose including *Mayan Letters*, 'Human Universe' and the hugely important 'Projective Verse', and was exercising a more informal and direct influence on younger poets such as Robert Creeley, Cid Corman and a number of then Black Mountain students, including Ed Dorn and John Wieners. Olson's work of the period significantly developed the partly personal responses to the war and its aftermath seen in major works like 'The Kingfishers' and 'In Cold Hell, in Thicket', to give a more rhetorical and systematic account of the workings of change and human society. The immediate problems raised by the colossal failure of Western ideas manifested in the Second World War, and the apparent escalation of such failure through an expanding US imperialism, are elaborated on in the poems to become a capacious and comprehensive philosophy of the historical *per se*. By articulating a changing but ultimately changeable version of human history, Olson was also able to overcome vocational teething problems experienced in his apprenticeships to Pound, 'the snob of the West' who 'feared anything forward' and Williams, criticised as a poet who 'lets time roll him under' (*SW*, 82).[1] 'As the Dead Prey Upon Us', a 1956 poem that might be seen as the culmination of Olson's Black Mountain endeavours, is his most comprehensive articulation of this new poetics of history.

Olson's key terminological distinction in this poetics is between life and death. Early in his career, in a series of repetitions, Olson pushes and pulls these terms to create variations on the basic theme of death as the past and life as the present. 'La Préface', Olson's first mature poem, placed 'The dead in via / in vita nuova / in the way'. Though emanations from Nazi concentration camps, these dead must not be claustrophobically mourned in an indulgent navel-gazing, Olson contends, but used to open up a new time:

> The closed parenthesis reads: the dead bury the dead,
> and it is not very interesting.
> Open, the figure stands at the door, horror his
> and gone...
>
> (CP, 47)

The poem warns us that we, 'the new born', must leave these dead buried, for there are present concerns, personified in 'the Howling Babe', that must take our attention away from mere lament: 'We are born not of the buried but these unburied dead.' 'La Chute', a poem written shortly after 'La Préface', takes on the persona of Gilgamesh to raise similar questions about the role of the artist in the aftermath of death:

> ... my drum fell
> where the dead are, who
> will bring it up, my lute
> who will bring it up where it fell in the face of them
> where they are, where my lute and drum have fallen?
>
> (CP, 83)

The lute's 'fall' from 'lustiness' to death is a primordial concomitant of the poet's own crisis in the face of the aftermath of Buchenwald. The dead, that is, hinder the production of living art, inflecting it with their fallenness. This sense of contamination is most vividly described in 'At Yorktown':

> At Yorktown the church
> at Yorktown the dead
> at Yorktown the grass
> are live
>
> at York-town the earth
> piles itself in shallows,
> declares itself, like water,
> by pools and mounds
>
> (CP, 127)

Death is not to be equated with destruction, a living force in Olson's work, as 'The Kingfishers' makes clear. 'To destroy / is to start again // ... to let breath in' (CP, 189), as he declaims in one of his very first poems, 'La Torre'. In Yorktown's landscape, death is what lingers, what unnaturally continues to attach itself to life, what 'piles itself', endlessly repeating like the poem's incantatory lines. The decaying dead are anathema to the living landscape, where now 'only the flies / dawdle'. In short, 'the dead' drag us down: 'the long dead / loosen the earth, heels / sink in' (CP, 128–9).

Within these exhortations, however, Olson is nonetheless forced to account for the seductiveness of such bathos. The trace of the dead, that is, must be specified and some kind of explanation given for its continued existence. Such a project is tentatively outlined in a letter to Creeley at the time of these early poems:

> If you and I see the old deal as dead (including Confucius, say), at the same time that we admit the new is the making of our own lives & references, yet, there is bound to be a tremendous pick-up from history other than that which has been usable as reference.[2]

This superfluous but unavoidable 'pick-up' is merely resisted in most of Olson's earliest poetry, but its problematic energy, especially following the death of his mother in 1951, persists in such a manner that resistance, it seems, requires a complementary understanding.

One of Olson's most graceful poems, 'As the Dead Prey Upon Us' is crucial in this regard (*CP*, 388–95). Here, 'death in life (death itself)' is deconstructed with an intensity singling it out from almost any other Olson poem. A kind of anti-elegy, the piece urges a wakefulness, an awareness of a proper resting place for the dead that we erroneously position 'in ourselves'. Though it seeks 'peace' from the dead mother, 'As the Dead Prey Upon Us' was composed six years after the death of Mary Olson; while the inspiration for the poem seems to have come from a dream, the extrapolation from this central theme is universalising in impulse.[3] The poem's desire, in Robert Duncan's gloss, 'to be released from the grievance and ache of the mother-flesh', establishes it as a chapter in a drawn-out struggle rather than an occasional dirge.[4] Its yearning to 'grow, and act, away from / the mother' (*CP*, 431), should be read as a universal struggle between the past and the present – as about how 'the dead prey upon us' and not, as its abandoned original title 'The Mother Poem' would have suggested, merely a family drama. One implication of this universalising tendency is that 'As the Dead Prey Upon Us' should properly be read alongside Olson's 'special view of history' as a whole. It is crucial to give an account of the experience of it as aesthetic form first, however, in case we ourselves deaden Olson's thought into a static philosophy of ideas, a movement too common in commentaries on his work.

Where 'A Newly Discovered Homeric Hymn', a shorter poem written around nine months earlier, is a warning to 'Beware the dead', 'As the Dead Prey Upon Us' explores what we must do when we have inevitably become ensnared in its 'blackmail' (*CP*, 363). The poem begins with a proposition followed by an imperative that we are also invited to read as an entreaty:

As the dead prey upon us,
they are the dead in ourselves,
awake my sleeping ones, I cry out to you
disentangle the nets of being!

I pushed my car, it had been sitting so long unused.
I thought the tires looked as though they only needed air.
But suddenly the huge underbody was above me, and the rear tires
were masses of rubber and thread variously clinging together

(CP, 388)

The first question here concerns address: who are 'my sleeping ones'? The collective pronoun clearly places the addressee in the camp of the living, and yet the boundaries are blurred given that we seem to be halfway to death ourselves in our sleeping. This complication of living and dead is continued with the abrupt entrance of the car, whose exposed underbody resembles a laid-out corpse. Here, the vehicle is symbolic of the dead mother who enters immediately after: it imposes itself despite its 'long unused' lifelessness however, with a 'huge underbody' ironically 'above' Olson.

The punning phrase 'the dead souls in the living room' introduces the first revenants proper of the piece, and finesses the original confusions of living and dead. These wandering dead are in two places at once: 'in ourselves' and 'in hell'. The poem offers no heavenly habitation for the deceased, and yet its hell is peculiar, characterised above all by 'poverty' and 'tawdriness'. Though the dead notably lead a *'life in hell'*, with Olson's mother 'alive as she ever was', it is a lifeless life in which people are 'poor and doomed / to mere equipments'. This dehumanising process is emphasised by the short dream lyric in which we see a deer perversely taking on 'human possibilities'. Olson is clear such equipments are not *for use*, however, as they are followed by a long consideration of 'hindrances'. The Buddhist notion of overcoming the 'five hindrances' to meditation – sensuality, ill-will, torpor, worry and doubt – is offered as a potential solution to the shadow cast by the dead. As with the dead, the hindrances are likened to nets. Again, however, in a movement typical of Olson's use of sources to think through convictions in the moment of the poem, this solution is rejected, since 'Purity // is only an instant of being, the trammels / recur'. Indeed, Olson suggests 'perfection is hidden' *within* the hindrances themselves. This notion of freedom as constituted by its supposed hindrance is later developed in Olson's argument that 'the net' will only be overcome by setting its knots afire rather than untying them. For now, though, the trammels do indeed 'recur' with the reappearance of the mother, from whom Olson begs 'peace'. She is, however, again 'as present' as when she was alive, with a body 'as solid'. At this point Olson is forced to admit he can only find the power to achieve peace from his mother in himself: 'The nets we are entangled in. Awake, / my soul, let the power into the last wrinkle / of being, let none of the threads and rubber of the tires / be left upon the earth. Let even your mother / go' (CP, 389–91).

So far, so similar to the injunction of 'A Newly Discovered Homeric Hymn' that we 'Greet the dead in the dead man's time' (CP, 364). However, after a reminder of 'The poverty / of hell' in a movement that itself enacts a kind of jolting awake, 'As the Dead Prey Upon Us' introduces a new term: the vent. This Shelleyan 'wind', in the face of 'the ugly automobile ... the heaviness of the old house, the stuffed inner room', is offered as a force that 'lifts the sodden nets':

> The vent! You must have the vent,
> or you shall die. Which means
> never to die, the ghastliness
>
> of going, and forever
> coming back, returning
> to the instants which were not lived
>
> (CP, 391–2)

The meaning of the dead is fully described here: they are undead figures of backwardness whose net of ghastly, self-referential enclosure must be opened if the living are to become more than the mechanical repetition of 'instants which were not lived' by them but by their forbears. 'O my soul,' Olson, imploringly concludes, 'slip the cog'. This breakthrough ends an up-to-this-point frustrated first section, previously thrashing about in ideas that only reinforced the vicious circle of thinking about the dead as a means to escape their preying, or alternatively imitating their 'poverty' in the act of selfless meditation. The poet has become empowered by internalising the net – 'I am myself netted in my own being' – an act that will become crucial to his solution to the problem of the dead past (CP, 392).

Section two begins by uniting the concerns of nets and circling in the figure of the knot. Here, it is the work of 'hands' that forms the action – a significant advance on pleas to the dead mother or ascetic renunciations of living desire. This 'touch' is not content with the act of untying, which would approach the net on its own terms, but rather causes each knot to catch fire:

> The death in life (death itself)
> is endless, eternity
> is the false cause

> The knot is other wise, each topological corner
> presents itself, and no sword
> cuts it, each knot is itself its fire
>
> each knot of which the net is made
> is for the hand to untake
> the knot's making. And touch alone
>
> can turn the knot into its own flame
>
> <div align="right">(<i>CP</i>, 392–3)</div>

Unlike the dead, the knot is there for use – it is the accessible ('presents itself') counterpart to the oppressive but unrecoverable dead. Its use, however, is as fuel for fire, and Olson's self-reflexive metaphor of the knot as its 'own flame' combines a sense in which the dead net can be both consigned to its rightful place of non-existence and, in being so consumed, provide sustenance for vital existence. For though we are briefly, once again, returned to the mother, distracting Olson in a squabble with a neighbour, the poet gradually builds up to this conclusion: that 'We have only one course: // the nets which entangle us are flames'. 'The car,' at the beginning of the poem associated with the mother 'did not burn', and Olson remains tied in the indissoluble logic of the past. The lesson is that the net cannot be externalised and must be taken as ourselves, living now: 'O souls, burn / alive, burn now // that you may forever / have peace, have // what you crave'. In a double meaning expressing both the provenance and the continuance of the net, the poet urges: 'let not any they tell you / you must sleep as the net / comes through your authentic hands' (*CP*, 394).

It is the remembrance of agency, of the possibility and necessity of *doing*, that provides the 'vent' of the poem:

> all knots are a wall ready
> to be shot open by you
>
>   the nets of being
> are only eternal if you sleep as your hands
> ought to be busy. Method, method
>
> I too call on you to come
> to the aid of all men, to women most
> who know most, to woman to tell
> men to awake. Awake, men,
> awake
>
> <div align="right">(<i>CP</i>, 395)</div>

In this, the poem's crucial statement, the parameters of existence are only unchangeable if self-determination is allowed to sleep 'as your hands / ought to be busy'. This agency cannot simply be directed in any manner, but must be properly chosen by 'method'. As a way to 'slip / the cog', that is, 'method' suggests a mode of awakening in which man can be properly sovereign over his actions, over the deterministic sway of the past on the present; a way of being more than 'an ability – a machine', to quote the title of a later Olson piece. At this point Olson presents his own version of Mao's injunction, 'we must rise and act': 'Awake, men, / awake'. Though 'As the Dead Prey Upon Us' ends by returning us to the poet's personal frailties, these are presented within a framework of success, totally opposing it to the poem's beginning: the deer 'need not trouble', the mother may 'sit in happiness', and, finally, 'The automobile / has been hauled away' (*CP*, 395).

Olson's ambitious 'hauling away' had an urgency of its own in 1956, when the dominant poetry of the US was fixated on ruins, as the likes of Robert Lowell and Randall Jarrell used the past to construct historical scrapheaps, developing Eliot's reactionary 'historical sense' into a mood of full resignation at the absurdity of human history. Such glibness is not attacked in 'As the Dead Prey Upon Us', though its intention to 'disentangle' the individual from the dead family, and to articulate the present outside of mechanistic and deterministic vocabularies dependent on the past, clearly offers an alternative response to the ironic and defeatist mourning so prevalent in 'Middle Generation' verse. The project of defining the 'method' of such 'vent[ing]' is the subject of Olson's speculative prose essays, essays which in turn illuminate the motivation behind 'As the Dead Prey Upon Us'.

That Olson began this project by looking to a non-Western past is well-known. His thoughts on the Maya in his 1951 essay, 'Human Universe', though tinged with a peculiar kind of orientalism, give rise to a crucial methodological conviction:

> [A] people different from himself — they will be the subject of historians' studies or tourists' curiosity, and be let go at that, no matter how much they may disclose values he and his kind, you would think, could make use of. I have found, for example, that the hieroglyphs of the Maya disclose a placement of themselves toward nature of enormous contradiction to ourselves, and yet I am not aware that any of the possible usages of this difference has been allowed to seep into present society... [Such history is offered] as decoration of knowledge upon some Christian and therefore eternal and holy neck. It is unbearable what knowledge of the past has become.
>
> (*CPr*, 163)

Creeley opposed Olson to a defeatist history in which 'you're stuck in some inexorable manner and it grinds you out, you're always too late because it all happened last year'.[5] Here, Olson contends that we must look beyond the temporal imperialism of absorbing all past culture into the familiar categories of our own. Rather than opening self-knowledge through the appreciation of different ways of thinking, the 'tourists' curiosity' hangs all history on an 'eternal and holy neck'. Its 'use' as difference, therefore, is lost in favour of a decoration to further enforce existing values. Olson's underlying conviction, of course, is that the US itself must strive to be different, to go beyond a continuing tradition that to him seemed intent on re-living the Roman Empire, European colonialism and the Second World War all in one. In a letter of the same year, Olson tells Vincent Ferrini: 'when traditions go, the DISCONTINUOUS becomes the greener place'.[6]

Olson's most important prose work, *The Special View of History*, would systematise this attack on continuity. Though, as we will see shortly, Olson's sense of such a power is most fully expressed – indeed, enacted – in his own concrete acts of cultural intervention and communal constitution at Black Mountain, where he wrote the essay as a series of talks in 1956, his effort to 'repossess [man] of his dynamic' at the conceptual level forms a usefully distilled background to some of the wider project's motivations (though we should not, of course, conceive of the latter as literally preceding the other in Olson's development). *The Special View of History*, though itself an event that Olson performed at Black Mountain and around California, is Olson's most abstract and speculative meditation on the nature of the subject within the becoming of history. The work bases its notion of the discontinuous 'event' on a reading of A. N. Whitehead, whose 'cell-theory of actuality' rested on the idea that continuity was something achieved by entities after their existence had first been secured in discontinuity; the idea of a 'next occasion' in a supposed continuum being only meaningful as such by the 'introduction of novelty'.[7] Olson develops such a notion in the essay, summed up in its central but paradoxical statement, 'MAN IS A CONTINUOUS CHANGE IN TIME'.[8] He also significantly broadened the issue by reading the apparently given 'continuity of becoming' politically as a ruse by which any action on the part of the subject will seem futile.[9] In effect, Olson poses a sense of agency in discontinuity: 'the irresistible is usually only that which hasn't been resisted'.[10] Asking, 'What are we to do but break the egg of history, and get outside', Olson answers with the 'act' of humans, here analogous to Whitehead's 'electrons' but with a distinct sense that continuity is an *issue* for man, against an unchanging 'history' that merely grinds him down.[11]

Here we are returned explicitly to the question of constitutive power. Olson's contention is that history is 'what [man] does'.[12] 'History,' he asserts, 'is the *function* of any one of us': we act upon history, rather than vice versa, in Olson's special view.[13] In a crucial pun, Olson terms such action the 'actual', which is alone 'determinative'.[14] 'Man has the context of his own species for his self or he is a pseudo creature,' Olson writes, and within his notion of the human subject is an acknowledged post-humanism which allies his thought with more contemporary theories of revolutionary politics.[15]

The French Maoist philosopher Alain Badiou can help translate some of Olson's only apparently vague assertions regarding man and action, into the vocabulary of 'social action' that Olson had announced as a poetic concern at the very start of his career. Badiou's subject is tied up with his theory of the Event, which closely echoes Olson's 'act' as radically discontinuous. Indeed, for Badiou the event *is* an event because of its 'impossibility' in relation to the logics it displaces; it is a 'totally ab-normal' void in the structure of being.[16] This status as an absence gives the event a quality that allows it, like no other phenomenon, to be *chosen* by subjects, who in the act of this decision are constituted as such. For Badiou the subject is not given, but 'becomes' through the act of choosing and instituting the Event, what he more ambiguously calls a *fidelity* to the event. Thus in his attempt to renew the notion of agency in the wake of poststructuralism, Badiou denies the category of subjecthood to any human lacking a precise, and probably revolutionary, social agency. Olson, likewise, criticises the 'old cosmology', or rationalism, as a deadening of man's potential: 'Man is simply filling an empty space. Which turns quickly by collapse into man is skin and flesh surrounding a void as well. It is the counsel of despair.'[17] Olson's notion of man as 'An active', on the other hand, opens the notion of the human up to the prospect of a future, as opposed to limiting him to a past made to seem necessary and consummate by humanism or 'what we have had'.[18] The being of the subject for Olson is what he does (though not, as we shall see, without limit). 'Man is. He acts'. The two are identical and cannot, one suspects, exist apart for Olson in the true sense: 'Actual wilful man,' he writes, 'has to do something about himself.'[19]

The immediate objection to such assertive self-determination, is that it simply repeats romantic ideals of the transcendent ego. To break the 'egg of history' could be taken to imply an escape from it entirely. That such a reading would be a mistake can be shown in two ways: first, by reading *The Special View* back to the context from which it emerges, and second, by reading Olson's own counter to such romantic soul-making in his concept of the 'limit'. For the first, we can trace Olson's conception of action as a question of social participation back to his earliest essays. 'Human Universe', for example, bemoans how:

> The notion of fun comes to displace work as what we are here for...
> Spectatorism crowds out participation as the condition of culture.... All
> individual energy and ingenuity is bought off—at a suggestion box or the
> cinema. Passivity conquers all. Even war and peace die (to be displaced
> by world government?) and man reverts to only two of his components,
> inertia and gas.
>
> (CPr, 159)

Spectatorism and passivity are equated with representative and indeed global totalitarian government, where work and energy – what Olson would later call 'action' – are 'bought off'. The consequence of inaction, he suggests, is domination, as in this later *Origin* letter:

> the spectatorism which both capitalism and communism breed—breed it as surely as absentee ownership... doth breed it, separating men from action surely as—as a leadership—these two identities limit production, or regulate it, in that monstrous phrase which turns all things toward creation's opposite, destruction.[20]

Absentee ownership is, of course, an issue for Olson for many reasons, not least of which is its role in destroying the link between community and place, but here it represents the absence of power in the people who are subject to it. The important 1953 *Maximus* poem, 'Letter 23', would more particularly pit itself 'against nascent capitalism except as it stays the individual adventurer and the worker on share – against all sliding statism, ownership getting in to, the community as, Chamber of Commerce, or theocracy; or City Manager': an announcement that explicitly ties the acting subject ('individual adventurer') with the communal constituency ('worker on share') (*MP*, 105).

Charles Bernstein has criticised 'Olson's refusal to accept the limits of knowledge'.[21] As a post-humanist of sorts, and distinguished from Bernstein by a belief in change, it seems Olson does indeed refuse to set such limits. There are other limits in Olson, however. 'Limits,' he writes, 'are what any of us / are inside of.' Creeley qualifies this statement, reporting his mistake in taking 'such "limits" to be a frustration of possibility rather than the literal possibility they in fact must provoke.'[22] *Special View* makes a crucial distinction between two types of acting in similar terms:

> one gets two sorts of will, a will of power or a will of achievement. The first one is the one in which the will collapses back to the subjective understanding — tries to make it by asserting the self as character. The second makes it by non-asserting the self as self. In other words the riddle is that the true self is not the asserting function but an obeying one, that the actionable is *larger* than the individual and so can be obeyed to.[23]

Stephen Fredman has claimed that Olsonian limit serves as a means to 'combat the pervasive American belief in unlimited possibilities'.

This needs serious qualification, however, since Fredman also ties this combat with a resistance to change in Olson.[24] The American belief in unlimited possibilities is emphatically personified for Olson at the start of his career in the figure of Ahab. Olson's Ahab, the pure subjectivity seeking exclusive power through force of self-will, is the ultimate ungrounded figure: without origin, without community, without place, without limit. His anti-social egotism, however, is itself a limit in historical terms; as Olson grandly declares in *Call Me Ishmael*, he is the end of the project of Western Man, of humanism.

The true action or will, on the other hand, acknowledges the limits of 'the self as character', obeying the wider context of what is 'actionable'. This figure moves from a conventional humanist conception of the freedom *from* to the Hegelian notion of freedom *to*, as Creeley recognised: in attending to the larger grounding and limits of the individual, one achieves a true self, and truly acts. There must be an 'END of individual responsible only to himself' represented by Ahab' (*CPr*, 105). In this, man is responsible to 'history', conceived as 'the confidence of limit as a man is caught in the assumption and power of change' – a richly ambiguous statement on a par with Marx's, '*Men make their own history*, but they do not make it as they please'.[25] Man is caught in the power of change, that is, but he must also assume that power, and institute change through action. This action is neither the negation of history nor resignation to its apparent determinism; it is, as 'As the Dead Prey Upon Us' tells us, the application of 'method', of a special view of history in which we 'awake' ourselves and historical process simultaneously. The 'nets of being' are limits, but they need not be escaped or transcended, but rather fired up, transformed and made transformative. In itself a performance in how we might 'slip the cog', Olson's poem is the enactment of this transformation. Its dramatisation of a mind thinking itself simultaneously through, out of, and awake from the deadening effects of a culture obsessed with repeating its past represents one of the key articulations of Olson's radical projective poetics.

Notes

1 Catherine Seelye (ed.), *Charles Olson and Ezra Pound: An Encounter at St Elizabeths* (New York: Grossman, 1975), 53, 83.
2 Charles Olson, *Mayan Letters*, ed. Robert Creeley (London: Jonathan Cape, 1968), 5–6.
3 Michael Rumaker, *Black Mountain Days* (Asheville: Black Mountain Press, 2003), 175.
4 Robert Duncan, *The H. D. Book*, ed. Michael Boughn and Victor Coleman (Berkeley: University of California Press, 2011), 218.

5 Quoted in Charles Olson, *The Special View of History*, ed. Ann Charters (Berkeley: Oyez, 1970), 12.
6 Olson, letter in *Origin I* (Spring 1951), 6.
7 Alfred North Whitehead, *Process and Reality: An Essay in Cosmology*, Corrected Edition, eds David Ray Griffin and Donald W. Sherburne (New York: Free Press, 1978), 290.
8 Olson, *The Special View*, 33.
9 Whitehead, *Process and Reality*, 68.
10 Olson, *The Special View*, 18.
11 Ibid., 26.
12 Ibid.
13 Ibid., 17.
14 Ibid., 34.
15 Ibid., 25.
16 Alain Badiou, *Peut-on penser la politique?* (Paris: Seuil, 1985), 78; Badiou, *Being and Event*, trans. Oliver Feltham (London: Continuum, 2011), 507.
17 Olson, *The Special View*, 47–8.
18 Olson, *Mayan Letters*, 67.
19 Olson, *The Special View*, 58.
20 Olson, *Letters for Origin*, ed. Albert Glover (London: Cape Goliard Press, 1969), 103.
21 Charles Bernstein, *Content's Dream* (Los Angeles: Sun & Moon Press, 1986), 328.
22 Robert Creeley, *A Quick Graph: Collected Notes and Essays*, ed. Donald Allen (San Francisco: Four Seasons Foundation, 1970), 71.
23 Olson, *The Special View*, 45.
24 Stephen Fredman, *The Grounding of American Poetry: Charles Olson and the Emersonian Tradition* (Cambridge: Cambridge University Press, 1993), 38.
25 Olson, *The Special View*, 26.

16

'To Gerhardt, There, Among Europe's Things of Which He Has Written Us in His "Brief an Creeley und Olson"': Olson on history, in dialogue

Sarah Posman

In 1954 Charles Olson wrote a short review of Ernst Robert Curtius' *European Literature and the Latin Middle Ages*. I take this review as my prompt to sketch Olson's understanding of history, and the ways in which his American historical stance related to his sense of European historicism, 'the historism [...] plaguing all Europeans' as the review has it.[1] Reading Olson in his role of poet-historian implies that we not only take into account the intellectual debate he touches on but also explore the ways in which his poetry responds to that debate. My focus in this essay is the early 1950s transatlantic poetic exchange between Olson and Rainer Maria Gerhardt, a German poet, Pound translator and editor of the literary magazine *fragmente*.

It was Gerhardt, Olson tells us in the review, who introduced him to Curtius. In 1951 Gerhardt wrote a poetic letter to Robert Creeley and Olson, the 'Brief an Creeley und Olson' or 'Letter to Creeley and Olson', to which Olson replied with the poem 'To Gerhardt, There, Among Europe's Things of Which He Has Written Us in His "Brief an Creeley und Olson"'.[2] 'To Gerhardt', as Paul Christensen and Thomas Merrill have noted, is an authoritative poem.[3] The poet we encounter here is convinced of his case: Gerhardt, despite his best intentions and fascination with America, is stuck in a European mode of writing, which gets writers tangled up in discourse instead of setting them in contact with reality. Ironically, in other words, Gerhardt's European method alienates him from his European situation. Olson is not, however, in a hostile mood. He urges Gerhardt to respond, wants him to write back in 'simplicities' that are his own.[4] Gerhardt, unfortunately, didn't ever 'come back / under [his] own / steam' (*CP*, 218). Upon hearing of Gerhardt's suicide in 1954, Olson wrote the funeral poem 'The Death of Europe' in which he laments the fact that the German poet, 'the first of Europe [he] could have words with', didn't manage to escape a

European take on tradition, a European intellectualism,[5] and in so doing appreciate the energy of his time and place, something the American writers he so admired did know how to get across:

> (O, Rainer,
> you should have ridden your bike
> across the Atlantic instead of your mind,
> that bothered itself too much
> with how we were hanging on
> to the horse's tail, fared, fared
> we who had Sam Houston, not
> Ulysses
>
> (CP, 309, 313)

In what follows, I outline Olson's American response to Curtius and Gerhardt's European stance, and conclude by observing ways in which Olson's American poetics converges with, rather than opposes, European debates on the past and how to write it.

Curtius' *Europäische Literatur und lateinisches Mittelalter* came out in Germany in 1948 and was translated into English in 1953. The book presents 'Latinity' as the binding force in a European literary tradition and calls for an historical concept of Europe, as opposed to a Europe dismembered into geographical fragments. Curtius wanted his readers to see European literature as a 'whole', spanning twenty-six centuries from Homer to Goethe.[6] He also wanted them to think about their relation to the past and builds in a reflection on the humanities and their methods. His answer to the question 'how to study literature' lies in a combination of history and philology, as a 'technique to unravel [texts]'.[7] To a certain extent, Curtius' wish to reinvigorate the study of literature via history tallies with Olson's concern for history. Just as Olson approaches history, with Herodotus, as a journey of finding out for oneself, Curtius stresses experience over textbook knowledge. 'To see European literature as a whole,' he writes, 'is possible only after one has acquired citizenship in every period from Homer to Goethe.'[8] Less vehemently than Olson's aversion to logic and classification – which in 'Human Universe' the poet considered tools bequeathed by the Greeks that, by the twentieth century, have become habits of thought 'absolutely interfere[ing]' with action – Curtius nonetheless criticizes the discipline of literary history and the 'catalogue-like knowledge of facts' by which it proceeds (*CPr*, 156).[9] Instead of mining the literary past for facts and details, he proposes that literary scholars engage in a 'phenomenology of literature'.[10] By his account, the future of historical inquiry lies in a renewal of the bond between poetry and history, in a stress on 'a poetic form of presentation'.[11] In this regard Curtius refers to the

French vitalist philosopher Henri Bergson as the only contemporary philosopher to have tackled the problem of the creative imagination. It is Bergson, Curtius asserts, who has shown that the fiction-making function, the human drive to 'make myths, stories, poems', is necessary to life.[12] In 'The Gate and the Center', Olson likewise stressed the link between life and story-making, calling for a reinvigoration of 'the POINT & PURPOSE of [...] the act of myth' (*CPr*, 172).

Despite the parallel concern for creative experience, and the sympathy Olson felt towards Gerhardt and Curtius, Olson couldn't laud *European Literature and the Latin Middle Ages*.[13] 'I should have known,' he reflects in the review, 'I had sniffed typology in Gerhardt's longish poem, "Brief an Creeley und Olson"' (*CPr*, 339). He had loved feeding on the scope of the book but found fault with the scholar's desire to 'develop analytical methods, that is, methods which will "decompose" the material (after the fashion of chemistry with its reagents) and make its structures visible.'[14] In the grip of science and religion, Curtius' grand project, by Olson's account, fails to coin a stance that could steer historical reflection in a new direction, away from the modernist system builders Curtius aligns with: Ernst Troeltsch, Arnold J. Toynbee and, among other writers, T. S. Eliot. To the German philologist's claim that 'specialization has thus opened the way to a new universalization', the American poet responds that 'it just damn well ain't true' (*CPr*, 341). Picking up Curtius' reference to Bergson, furthermore, Olson warns against history by way of soothing stories: 'It is not the Beast we are in danger from. It is, the Beauty. Bergson was wrong. Or half-right. The fabulation function is man's uniqueness. But when he uses it to make the Bauble?' (*CPr*, 340) No, Olson decides '[i]t better be Walter Prescott Webb you use as backfire to check this book'. As an American, Webb knows 'that where tales are today is not in stories but in things, in Colt, revolvers' (*CPr*, 339, 341).

For all its 'political and hortatory' vigour, its claims on what is (half) wrong and right, and its desire to lure '[Curtius] and Gerhardt, and all Europeans' into escaping the European tradition they cling to and make it to the great plains, the review fails to set up a dialogue with the Europeans it pities or to elaborate on the potential of the fiction-making function (*CPr*, 341). In the penultimate paragraph Olson all but throws in the towel:

> I better stop. I can see I am not going to do what Blackburn insists I can't: think. That is, I ought to do two things: (1) elucidate what history is, in the face of the historism now plaguing all Europeans, and so the world, by proselytizing from that center; and (2) expose the 'phenomenology of literature' Curtius thinks he is arriving at through such a 'science of European literature' as he takes the present book to be.
>
> (*CPr*, 341)

Although Olson adds that '[i]t would be easy to do both', those issues in fact occupied him for much of his life. Claims on the nature of history, on literature and on experience are not lacking from his prose writings. As instances in a dynamic engaging with the question of how to position oneself in relation to the past, those statements make for usable entries into his project. In Olson's scheme, nevertheless, it's up to activity – energy, movement – more than declaration, to elucidate. To see Olson's *poiein,* his story-making, in action, in other words, we need to turn to his poetry.

Olson's remark that he 'had sniffed typology in Gerhardt's longish poem, "Brief an Creeley und Olson"', echoes his correspondence with Robert Creeley. Creeley is the one who brought Olson and Gerhardt in contact with each other, and in the letters the two American friends exchanged in 1951 Creeley translated as much as he felt up to of Gerhardt's letters. A letter by Creeley from 12 January enthusiastically reports on Gerhardt that '[h]e is really behind it moves'.[15] Creeley is also critical, however, of Gerhardt's tendency to uphold a theory of poetry that doesn't correspond to his practice. On Gerhardt's distinction between poetic form and content, Creeley writes:

> A damn shame. Breaking the thing to look at it, forget to pull it back, to its only state (possible). I much suspect that a good deal of it, the talk, is talking around a gig, he may very well demonstrate very damn different 'principles,' concerning, in the writing itself. (Do germans, then, really, ALL: classify???) It's very damn odd – the intelligence that can assert that a poem IS integral unit & then treat of 'form' & 'content' as tho they had no such relation/ or were externally joined. A bug.[16]

When the 'Brief an Creeley und Olson' reached Creeley in February 1951 he wrote Olson that he thought it 'pretty damn good', despite its heavy leaning on Ezra Pound.[17] Gerhardt's poetic letter breathes Pound's influence through quotations, in hooking together poetry and the places ('syntax over the rooftops of Parma') as well as forces ('the shock of the poem / or the theory of finance') that have shaped the modern world, and when it calls to the masters of western poetry (Virgil, Dante) from a contemporary, ruinous Europe ('Siena Verdun Monte Cassino Narvik Stavanger Murmansk Mostar Cambrai Garmisch Partenkirchen Minsk Moscow Berlin Rotterdam').[18] The poem's 'whirl of time', announced in the first of its 'montages', moreover, echoes Pound's intention in *Guide to Kulchur* to break with neat evolutionary schemes and understand the past 'NOT [...] in chronological sequence [...] but [...] by ripples and spirals eddying out from us and from our own time'.[19] In his letter, Creeley promises to send Olson a translation and includes an onset, of which the first couple of lines read:

> 12/12...
> corydon, in the 7ᵗʰ eclogue
>   nymphae, noster amo, liberthrides, aut mihi Carmen
>   quale meo codro concedite
>   travel drowns out the dead
> but Francesca   not in the clouds of dante
>   not in the steps [really: degrees –
>   gradations] of heaven
>   7 heavens
> the heathen number
> Francesca   not heart of the tongue
> & the syntax held in muck
> of piddling floods   the shore
>   noster amo
>   & to forget aesthetic considerations
> the usual, & to be in the speech ²⁰

Creeley concludes his letter by praising Gerhardt for 'stand[ing] in a position TO MOVE'.²¹ In his reply, Olson shares Creeley's admiration for Gerhardt and 'agree[s] we need push him, forward: no language is excuse for impeding that kind of moving'.²²

In 'To Gerhardt,' then, Olson wants to persuade Gerhardt to move beyond what he refers to in 'Human Universe' as logos or discourse, language by which one sets oneself apart from the world in order to discriminate, analyse and classify. The German poet should think through his intention to 'be into the speech', and approach language as 'shout (tongue)' (*CPr*, 155). Where Gerhardt's Corydon figure triggers a summoning of the benchmarks of western culture (Virgil and Dante in Creeley's translation; Virgil, Parma, Erasmus, the Jesuits and Dante in Heider and Jalowetz's), Olson starts his poem with a roaming, ungentle 'Bear-son', miles away from any city of wisdom, but looking to America:

> so pawed,
> by this long last Bear-son
>   with no crockery broken,
>   but no smile in my mouth
>   June 28ᵗʰ, '51, on this horst
>   on the Heat Equator, a mediterranean sea
>   to the east, and north
>   what saves America from desert, waters
>   and thus rain-bearing winds,
>   by subsidence, salt waters
>   (*CP*, 212)

Although Olson invites Gerhardt to America, the poet will need to do more than incorporate America into his poetry. Location is not the solution: 'place / as a force is a lie. / or at most a small truth', and neither does it suffice for Gerhardt to import American poetry (*CP*, 214). Where Gerhardt writes:

> In old Europe
> translate Pound
> and Williams
> attempt
> these vocables in a way
> still unknown here [23]

Olson responds: 'Nor with the power of American vocables / would I arm you in Kansas, when you come' (*CP*, 215–16). Instead of looking to Pound, who incorporates the canon of European intellectual and cultural tradition into his (largely negative) vision of America, Gerhardt should embrace his present: 'I am giving you a present / For you forget (forgetting / is much more your problem / than you know, right-handed one' (*CP*, 216).

Olson's rebuking of Pound in 'To Gerhardt' has been commented on by a number of critics.[24] Interestingly, Christopher Beach, in outlining Olson's relationship to Pound's approach to history, stresses that 'Olson would doubtless have associated Curtius's stance with that of Pound.'[25] Like Curtius, Pound approaches history by staging the treasure chamber of the European past as a source of inspiration for a bleak-looking present. Pound's 'ripples and spirals eddying out from us' may be well-made, but he still moves too much 'inside the Western box'; that is, though his writings shake up our take on the directions of history – for Olson *Guide to Kulchur* 'razzledazzles History' – they ultimately work to conserve rather predictable relations (stories about great men) in a predictable framework (broadly speaking, Curtius' 'twenty-six centuries').[26] Gerhardt's frame of reference, Creeley was happy to see, opens up from Virgil and Dante to Babylonian deities ('Tamuz, En-lil, all the lads' he reports in his letter).[27] By montage 4, moreover, Gerhardt critically pauses at his own method:

> somehow we remain empty
> not fully bailed out by this
> method [28]

Even so, for Olson, Gerhardt's method remains too faithful to a modernist reassembling, to an ordering of discursive elements into a new whole that 'sniff[s] of typology'. To Gerhardt's attempt to ground his poem in life, via an allusion to Pound's *Cantos* – 'but Dante will not let us live / always the fields to be harvested / always the same sky above the bent-over backs / earth burdened'[29] – Olson responds: 'as though it were true / they cared a damn / for his conversation' (*CP*, 215).

In order for Gerhardt to be a poet for whom storytelling is, once again, 'a form of human experience itself', Olson suggests he make contact with a past in which stories functioned as physical responses to worldly phenomena.[30] Faced with Gerhardt's letter, Olson cannot 'talk of method ... / as though it were a dance / of rains, or schmerz' (*CP*, 215). Both the mythical act and the deep-felt pain of Gerhardt's moment of writing – what Olson thinks should be at the heart of his 'Letter' – are missing from his poem. Much as Olson mocks Pound's historical position in 'A Lustrum for You, E. P.' ('You wanted to be historic, Yorick'), he finds that there is something tragicomic about Gerhardt's project that intends to tackle history yet concerns itself with words and monuments – 'words as signs worn / like a toupee on the head of a Poe cast / in plaster' – instead of things and life (*CP*, 38, 215). Olson wants to persuade Gerhardt to turn his back on twenty-six centuries of European literature ('You are not / Telemachus') and accept the 'present' he gives him (*CP*, 218). This present is a concrete object, 'a rod of mountain ash', that should enable Gerhardt to find access to a memory that binds him to his primitive, 'beastly' forebears, a memory arrived at via long-lost songs rather than (only) literary dexterity:

> It is a rod of mountain ash I give you, Rainer Maria Gerhardt,
> instead of any other thing, in order that you may also be
> left-handed, as he was, your Grandfather,
> whom you have all forgotten, have even lost the song of, how
> he was to be addressed:
>
>> 'Great man,
>> in climbing up the tree,
>> broke his leg.'
>
> (*CP*, 217)

In addition to an object via which the twentieth century ('the present') opens up to the distant past, Olson's gift is an invitation:

> Or come here
> where we will welcome you
> with nothing but what is, with
> no useful allusions, with no birds
> but those we stone, nothing to eat
> but ourselves, no end and no beginning, I assure you, yet
> not at all primitive, living as we do in a space we do not need to contrive
>
> (*CP*, 219)

Olson wrote 'To Gerhardt' in Campeche, Mexico but these lines do not only invite Gerhardt to appreciate Mayan culture. 'Here' also refers to the zone of poetry as history Olson is trying to create, a place emptied of what he finds superfluous in Gerhardt's poem (and in Pound). Olson has on offer 'nothing but what is'. No 'useful allusions', then, by which to claim one's position in relation to the Homer-Goethe lineage. Olson presents a community that may not shy from violence yet, paradoxically, is not primitive since there is little need for a crafty 'making it new'. Olson wants to be without Pound's 'fatherhood' ('Let you pray to him, we say / who are without such fatherhood') and live in a community which feeds on itself, on its primal 'fabulatory function' that enables it to reinvigorate rather than to move away from its direct relationship to its environment (*CP*, 219). For Olson this community of writers is American – Webb and Melville, not Curtius – yet the direct, materialist historical sensation Olson values is hardly an American prerogative. In this respect, Curtius' reference to Bergson is not random. On the continent, Bergson's vitalist project had given rise to a new understanding of experience, a pure contact with an ever-changing reality through an all-encompassing memory.

In his letters to Creeley Olson mocks vitalism, the philosophy of life Bergson is often associated with.[31] According to Olson:

> VITALISM   sounds like, looks like, is:
> detergents, &
> ramashamamurti[32]

And yet, in *The Special View of History* Olson tells us that we shouldn't look upon history as either a sequence of events, fate, or something we are 'making' but as life.[33] History amounts to energy to be spent and the term may even be used 'promiscuously with life'.[34] The only problem with the word 'life', Olson explains, is that 'it means what nature offers, not what man DOES'.[35] Olson's stance is alien to a passive vitalism in which some kind of mystical life force takes care of all development. He wanted to feel life and history by writing back to it. Life, we read in 'Human Universe' is kinetic and 'there is only one thing you can do about kinetic, re-enact it.... Art does not seek to describe but to enact' (*CPr*, 155). Nevertheless, Olson's concern for 'what man DOES' can be seen to build on an understanding of time as continuous, creative movement that Bergson made popular.[36] In 'Equal, That Is, to the Real Itself' Olson stresses how in the nineteenth century 'an idea shook loose' (*CPr*, 121) He credits nineteenth-century mathematicians Bolyai and Lobatsjevski but above all Georg Friedrich Bernhard Riemann with opening our eyes to the continuous aspect of reality – to the fact that reality is 'without interruption' (*CPr*, 122). Riemann's work, Gilles Deleuze argues, plays an important role in Bergson's understanding of experience, which is always an experience of time and which the philosopher calls duration. For Deleuze, Bergson's use of the word 'multiplicity' draws on Riemann's distinction between discrete multiplicities, determined by the number of their elements, and continuous multiplicities, determined by the phenomena unfolding in them or the forces acting in them.[37] Whereas the former, in Olson's words, correspond to 'the old system and includes discourse, language as it had been since Socrates', it is 'the continuous' one that is 'more true' (*CPr*, 121). Bergson, Deleuze points out, was the philosopher who drew Riemann's mathematical discussion of multiplicities into the sphere of experience, making the continuous multiplicity the function of duration.

Throughout his oeuvre Bergson searches for ways by which to gain access to this qualitative multiplicity that is duration. In his scheme we live alienated from this pure experience of time because we are trained to think of time as something that is infinitely divisible rather than continuous and because we lack the means to express the ever-changing impressions that make up experience, language being a bland system of conventions. In his early *Laughter* (1900) the philosopher nevertheless turns to literary language as the means to make duration felt. He calls on the poets to conjure up 'certain rhythms of life and breath that are closer to man than his inmost feelings, being the living law – varying with each individual – of his enthusiasm and despair, his hopes and regrets'.[38] Rhythms of life and breath that open up a stale discourse to the flux and change that constitutes reality, inner and outer, are in a sense also what Olson calls for in 'Projective Verse' and what he summons Gerhardt to hear via the ancestral songs he inserts in 'To Gerhardt'. Yet breath alone does not undo the hold of discourse.[39] A second answer Bergson provides concerns the fiction-making function, which he elaborates on in *The Two Sources of Morality and Religion* (1932). At the core of this book is the idea of an open morality and a corresponding dynamic religion. Whereas a closed morality, for Bergson, is concerned with social cohesion and preservation, and to that end proceeds by rigid rules, an open morality stands for a pluralist constellation in which there is free and creative reflection. In such an organization, individuals are able to enter into myriads of open relations with their world and each other – Olson's open field poetics is not far off. The fiction-making function Bergson discusses does not in itself warrant an open society. Quite to the contrary, when 'society makes itself obeyed it is thanks to the story-telling function'.[40] We want to conform – yet not all of us do, all the time. By contrast, Bergson points to a force which he calls 'creative emotion', an emotion which corrupts the instinct to conform and compels us to create ('We have no choice'), plunging us into duration.[41] Here an open society, configured as a continuous multiplicity, comes into view. For Bergson such an encounter with duration always implies a recalibrating of our present, via affective memory – via, in 'To Gerhardt', one's grandparents' melodies ('your Grandfather, / whom you have all forgotten, have even lost the song of') (*CP*, 217).

Bergson's protagonists in *The Two Sources of Morality and Religion*, those who know how to breathe creative emotion into the fiction-making function, are, however, not quite the most worldly of citizens. The philosopher's heroes are saints and mystics and the creative emotion they experience flows into them from Nature, not historical reality. This explains the appeal of the book to Curtius, whose project comes with a Christian message of unity – hence Olson's 'Bauble' comment in his review. But Bergson led to more intellectual activity than the somewhat anachronistic masterpiece of a German philologist. Walter Benjamin, whose notion of *Erfahrung* echoes Bergson's understanding of experience, set out to reconfigure the Bergsonist notion of duration by grafting it onto historical reality, onto 'what man DOES'. For duration to be immanent to materiality and practice, it must be configured as something that transforms with human history and structures of experience – concretely, for Benjamin, creativity in new modes of technology and new forms of social organization. In his own writing Benjamin aimed for a direct mode of history by experimenting with a montage technique. On his *Arcades Project* he wrote: 'Method of this project: literary montage. I needn't *say* anything. Merely show. I shall purloin no valuables, appropriate no ingenious formulations. But the rags, the refuse – these I will not inventory but allow, in the only way possible, to come into their own: by making use of them.'[42] Gerhardt's montages, which Olson counters by way of 'speech, made up of particulars only', are far more in line with Pound's ingeniously formulated ones than with Benjamin's, and it's not my point to weld Olson to Bergson or Benjamin.[43] Only in some Bergsonist open society, in which there is no talk about world wars or death, can we imagine Olson, Gerhardt and Benjamin, riding their bikes across the Atlantic and having words with each other. What I've wanted to point out, rather, is that the concern for a poetic mode of history writing that knows how to convey particulars, what Gerhardt admired in American poetry – Olson and Creeley, building on Pound – and what Olson claimed for American writing, is not alien to, but part of, the continental debate on history and history writing.

Notes

1. Charles Olson, 'Robert Ernst Curtius', (*CPr*, 341).
2. Interestingly, there are different versions of Gerhardt's poetic letter. The text printed in the 2007 collected writings of Rainer Maria Gerhardt, *Umkreisung: Das Gesamtwerk,* edited by Uwe Pörksen, with Franz Josef Knape and Yong-Mi Quester (Wallstein Verlag) is that of the 1952 *Umkreisung* edition. It consists of three parts: I. montage, II. montage, III. brief. The English translation by Werner Heider and Joanna Jalowetz, published in *Origin* 4 (Winter 1951–2) consists of 6 montages. Since the opening lines in Creeley's partial translation don't keep track with Heider and Jalowetz' version I assume the 'Brief' Gerhardt sent to Creeley is not the source text used for the *Origin* translations.
3. Paul Christensen, *Charles Olson: Call Him Ishmael* (Austin: University of Texas Press, 1979), 109; Thomas F. Merrill, *The Poetry of Charles Olson: A Primer* (Newark and London: University of Delaware Press and Associated University Presses, 1982), 113.
4. Charles Olson, 'To Gerhardt, There, Among Europe's Things of Which He Has Written Us in His "Brief an Creeley und Olson"' (*CP*, 220).
5. Despite Olson's materialist stance, this an ironic reproach, given Olson's reputation of 'scholar poet'.
6. Ernst Robert Curtius, *European Literature and the Latin Middle Ages*, translated by Willard R. Trask (Princeton: Princeton University Press, 1953), 6, 12.
7. Curtius, *European Literature and the Latin Middle Ages*, 15.
8. Ibid., 12.
9. Ibid., 15.
10. Ibid., ix.
11. Ibid., 8.
12. Ibid.
13. Curtius had made a favourable remark on Olson in his review of *fragmente* #1 which incorporated a translation of Olson's 'The Praises'.
14. Curtius, *European Literature and the Latin Middle Ages*, 15.
15. Charles Olson and Robert Creeley, *The Complete Correspondence*, Vol. 4, ed. George F. Butterick (Santa Barbara: Black Sparrow Press, 1980), 109.
16. Ibid., 109.
17. Ibid., 125.
18. Rainer Maria Gerhardt, 'Letter for Creeley and Olson', trans. Werner Heider and Joanna Jalowetz, *Origin* 4 (Winter 1951–2), 187.
19. Ibid., 187; Ezra Pound, *Guide to Kulchur* (London: Peter Owen, 1978), 60.
20. Olson and Creeley, *Complete Correspondence*, Vol. 4, 126.
21. Ibid., 127.
22. Ibid., 131.
23. Gerhardt, 'Letter for Creeley and Olson', 191.
24. See Christopher Beach, *ABC of Influence: Ezra Pound and the Remaking of American Poetic Tradition* (Berkeley: University of California Press, 1992).
25. Ibid., 94.

26 Olson, 'Mayan Letters', (*SW*, 129).
27 Olson and Creeley, *Complete Correspondence*, Vol. 4, 126, 125.
28 Gerhardt, 'Letter for Creeley and Olson', 190.
29 Ibid., 191.
30 Charles Olson, *The Special View of History*, ed. Ann Charters (Berkeley: Oyez, 1970), 20.
31 On Bergson and vitalism, see Frederick Burwick and Paul Douglass (eds), *The Crisis in Modernism: Bergson and the Vitalist Controversy* (Cambridge and New York: Cambridge University Press, 1992).
32 Olson and Creeley, *Complete Correspondence*, Vol. 4, 43.
33 Olson, *The Special View*, 17.
34 Ibid., 18.
35 Ibid., 28.
36 On Bergson's influence on American culture see Tom Quirk, *Bergson and American Culture: The Worlds of Willa Cather and Wallace Stevens* (Chapel Hill and London: University of North Carolina Press, 1990).
37 Gilles Deleuze, *Bergsonism* (New York: Zone Books, 1991), 39–40.
38 Henri Bergson, *Laughter: An Essay on the Meaning of the Comic*, trans. by C. S. H. Brereton and F. Rothwell (København, Los Angeles and Saint Paul: Green Integer, 1999), 141.
39 In Bergson's philosophical trajectory duration is first discussed in terms of inner experience in *Time and Free Will: An Essay on the Immediate Data of Consciousness* (1889), yet by *Creative Evolution* (1907) bears on (impersonal) life.
40 Deleuze, *Bergsonism*, 109.
41 Ibid., 110.
42 Walter Benjamin, *The Arcades Project*, ed. Rolf Tiedemann, trans. Howard Eiland and Kevin McLaughlin (Cambridge, Mass.: Belknap Press, 1999), 460 ('Convolute N').
43 That said, an interesting link between Olson and Bergson is C. G. Jung, whom Olson admired. On Bergson and Jung, see for example: Pete A. Y. Gunter, 'Bergson and Jung,' *Journal of the History of Ideas* 43 (1982), 635–52.

17

'Moving among my particulars': the 'negative dialectics' of *The Maximus Poems*

Tim Woods

Riven by striking tensions and fissures, *The Maximus Poems* is nevertheless an optimistic narrative of adventure and edification, a journey of the modern spirit that is preoccupied with the possibility of its own structure and being. Indeed, Olson's very line structures constantly defy the laws of grammar as they test the ontological imagination beyond its conventional boundaries. The 'sentences' begin with subjects that frequently appear interchangeable with their objects, or to pivot on verbs that are swiftly negated or inverted in supporting clauses. When 'is' is the verb at the core of any claim, it rarely shoulders the familiar burden of predication. Instead, it becomes transitive in an unfamiliar and challenging sense, affirming the inherent movement in 'being', disrupting the ontological assumptions that ordinary language lulls us into making (as Wittgenstein makes clear in his *Philosophical Investigations*).

In its focus on human subjectivity, *The Maximus Poems* must be *read* to have its meaning enacted. Like the grammatical subject, the human is never simply and immediately there. As soon as one gets a grammatical indication of one's location, one travels forth and becomes something different from what one was when the initial knowledge was gained. The poems require and effect the imaginative identification of the reader with the travelling subject so that reading becomes a poetically instructive form of travel. Whether journeying literally or metaphorically through texts, myths, or narratives, it is only through inquiry and experience of existence as a *practical action*, that Olson's subject may seek consciousness of the 'self':

> the voyage *out*
> is the voyage
> *in*.[1]

Travelling away, moving to the external, into exile, is thus paradoxically conceived of as a means of 'coming home'.

The rhetorical inversion in the Olson line, as well as the narrative structure of the poems as a whole, conveys the elusive nature of both the grammatical and human subject. The reading needs to be *silent*, since this holds different performances in balance better than reading aloud, which has to select just one. Against the compulsion to fix the grammatical subject into a univocal and static signifier, Olson's sentences indicate that the subject can only be understood in their movement. When Olson's sentences suggest that substance is a subject, the 'is' carries the weight of 'becomes', where becoming is not a unilinear but a cyclical process. One reads the lines incorrectly if one relies on the ontological assumptions of unilinear reading, for the copula is a nodal point of the interpenetration of 'substance' and 'subject'. Each *is* itself only to the extent that it is *for* the other because, just as Hegel does, Olson conceives of self-identity to the extent that it is mediated through what is different. To read the lines 'correctly' would mean to read them cyclically, bringing to bear the variety of partial meanings permitted on any given reading. It is not just that substance is being clarified, or that the subject is being defined, but the very meaning of the copula is itself a locus of movement and plurivocity.

The grammatical subject is, therefore, never self-identical, but is always and only itself in its reflexive movement. The line does not consist of grammatical elements that reflect or indicate corresponding ontological entities. The line calls to be taken as a whole ('Write like ... a sentence was a complete thought. Make any sentence a complete thot'), and in turn indicates the wider context in which it can be taken.[2] But the way in which this context is 'indicated' is less referential than rhetorical. Olson's lines attempt to *enact* the meanings they convey; they show that what 'is' only 'is' to the extent that it is *enacted*. Olsonian lines are read with difficulty, for their meaning is not immediately given or known; they call to be reread, with different intonations and grammatical emphases. The lines rhetorically call attention to themselves, preventing a straightforward reading and forcing a consideration of the *way* things are said as essential to *what* is said. The lines mime their own struggle, deflection, resistance and engagement with thought and objects: we read:

> the contingent motion of
> each line as it
> moves with – or against –
> the whole – working
> particularly out of its immediacy.[3]

The discrete and static words on the page deceive one only momentarily into thinking that discrete and static meanings will be released by our reading. Olson acknowledges to Cid Corman that, 'I have a damn irritating style of punctuation and placements ... I do it gravely, as part of, my method, believing that, resistance must be a part of style if, it is part of the feeling'.[4] It is quite evident from reading Olson's correspondence with Cid Corman during the establishment of the magazine *Origin*, that he was (almost pedantically) particular about spacing, fonts, and indentations.[5] The materiality and typography of the writing is as important as the content. If one refuses to give up the expectation that linearly arranged univocal meanings will unfold from the words at hand, one will find Olson confusing, unwieldy, unnecessarily dense and opaque. But if one questions the presumptions of prevailing ideologies, one will experience the incessant movement of the line that constitutes its meaning.

Olson and Adorno

Since Olson's poetic defies our expectations of a linear and definite philosophical presentation, it initially obstructs (no one reads Olson quickly); but once we have reflected upon the assumptions from which Olson wants to release us, the rhetoric bares the irreducibly multiple meanings which continuously determine and shape each other. The multiplicity of meanings is not static, according to Olson, but is in the essence of becoming, of movement itself. In reading for multiple meanings, for plurivocity, ambiguity, and metaphor in the general sense, one experiences concretely the alteration of reality in the inherent dialectical thinking.

In the opening to *The Origin of German Tragic Drama* (1925), Walter Benjamin defends the loose form of his treatise, with its digressive, non-deductive mode of reasoning, and its lack of purposeful and coherent organization, on the grounds that the representation of truth best emerges from an 'immersion in the most minute details of subject-matter'.[6] He adds:

> Representation as digression – such is the methodological nature of the treatise. The absence of an uninterrupted purposeful structure is its primary characteristic. Tirelessly the process of thinking makes new beginnings, returning in a roundabout way to its original subject. This continual pausing for breath is the mode most proper to the process of contemplation ... the art of interruption in contrast to the chain of deduction; the tenacity of the essay in contrast to the single gesture of the fragment; the repetition of themes in contrast to shallow universalism; the fullness of concentrated positivity in contrast to the negation of polemic.[7]

Benjamin considered dialectical mediation with its telos of sublation (*Aufhebung*) as an artificially unifying notion, since no totality exists. He eschewed empirical philosophy's 'acquisition of knowledge' through inductive generalisation, which he regarded as a subjective synthesis of reality. Benjamin's methodology replaced such an idealist approach and was based on the notion of the 'mosaic' or the 'constellation', wherein concrete objects were able to maintain their integrity in the face of conceptualising logic.

Writing to Cid Corman in October 1950, on the character which the impending magazine *Origin* should adopt, Olson summarised several preoccupations of his early writing, which have marked affinities with Benjamin's thoughts:

A GRAPH:
    ENERGY   vs   humanism
  non-deductive   vs   deduc (educ, polituck, cultchuk
NATURE TAKES NOTHING BUT LEAPS worseus progress,
                                                          accumulation,
  (de Broglie brothers)   succession, tradition
art as the wedge of the
    WHOLE FRONT   (god help us)   vs   art as culture.[8]

Here is Olson's polemical challenge to the claustrophobia in poetry established by the 'traditional' humanist poets and critics: the reorganisation of temporal and spatial categories necessary to mount a philosophical and poetic thrust against the dominant aesthetic ideology; the attack against a stultifying rationality and logic of classification; and the notion of art as an activity of social *processes* rather than as the product of an élitist culture based on some eclectic principles of aesthetics, 'the whole dull business of CULTURE'.[9] Olson's emphasis is firmly on the need to refrain from qualitative judgements, in the effort to analyse the workings of language and the constituent factors in art: 'we are not here either to praise or to bury BUT TO EXAMINE what's around, that is of USE, not that, we admire'.[10]

Olson's desire to maintain discriminations and differences in a commodifying world which elides distinctions, has a specific affinity with Adorno's methodological effort. Adapting Benjamin's ideas, Adorno's critique of non-dialectical thinking was levelled at the manner in which the conceptual or general is mistaken for 'truth' rather than merely another mode of thought. While focussing on particularity and recognising that conceptuality cannot be dismissed, Adorno utilises clusters of concepts, continuous combinations and arrangements of words which Adorno called 'constellations'.[11] Thus, ideas could remain empirical and self-contained, but because they are discontinuous with each other in constellations, gain something 'more'. The three principles upon which Buck-Morss discerns Adorno's 'constellations' are constructed (differentiation, non-identity, active transformation), are also evident in Olson's ideas.[12] Buck-Morss argues that the principle of differentiation is the articulation of nuances which pin-point the concrete, qualitative differences between apparently similar phenomena. As such, phenomenal elements have no absolute value, no constant meaning, if taken out of the context of their particular manifestations. Hence, constellations are an effort to preserve 'difference in unity', or to hold apart the seemingly identical.

'Dialectics is the consistent sense of non-identity', wrote Adorno.[13] Similarly, Olson's poetics persistently strive after what is left out of the picture by conceptualisation, that non-identical element. Just as Adorno argues that it is the marginalia of philosophy which is important, so *The Maximus Poems* stresses that it is the marginalia of history which is central to historical understanding. Olson's attempt to describe 'the hinges of civilisation to be put back on the door'[14] has a parallel with Adorno's definition of 'negative dialectics': 'To change this direction of conceptuality, to give it a turn toward nonidentity, is the hinge of negative dialectics'.[15] In both cases, there is an attempt to rethink the relations between subjects and the world in such a way that the methodology and poetics become a means to allow civilisation to move freely. Both writers desire to turn the conceptual subsumption of the non-conceptual back on itself – into a reflection of its very operation – to show that the revelation of objects in conceptualisation is also actually a concealment. According to Adorno, '[Philosophy] must strive, by way of the concept, to transcend the concept'; it must dismantle the coercive logical character of its own course by the contradictions of that very logic.[16] Similarly, by way of the journey through histories, Olson incorporates what has been lost by particular models of history, and rejects history as a singular, linear progression of a set of self-fulfilling actions. Just as Adorno interprets the identity principle as a deferral or displacement of identity,[17] so Olson considers that identification always embodies an otherness. Adorno argues that, 'As a sense of nonidentity through identity, dialectics is not only an advancing process but a retrograde one at the same time. To this extent, the picture of the circle describes it correctly. The concept's unfoldment is also a reaching back'.[18] Olson's affinities with this mode of thinking are clear. The reiteration of the need to reach back to 'other' texts, narratives, ideas, ways of seeing, in order to advance, is a major element of Olson's awareness of the circularity of dialectical progression. The unfolding of one narrative/history/event necessitates the exclusion of others, and Olson's methodology (literally 'path after') is to focus attention on those cultures (Sumerian, Hittite, Hopi Indian), discourses (mythology, alchemy) and modes of thinking (psychobiology, the *I Ching* and Synchrony) marginalised by such histories. Adorno's language of demythologising, liberating, and subverting, has its parallel in Olson's discourse: he speaks of the need for the 'hinges' of the twentieth century to be 'released from both the 18th' and the 'inadequate rationalizing after Locke and Descartes'; for a 'freshening of syntax'; to 'wake up the time spans and materials lying behind Hesiod, so that they can seem freer than they have'.[19]

If differentiation leads to the breaking apart of the apparently identical, Buck-Morss argues that non-identity is then the juxtaposition of the apparently unrelated and the dissimilar.[20] The assumption underlying this procedure is 'that reality was itself contradictory that its elements formed no harmonious whole'.[21] The work of art cannot reflect the world as content, but can only act as a negative witness. Its value in contesting the world lies in the integrity of its denial of the world, its registration of the contradictions in its own material, giving evidence of the world in which it is situated. The correspondence between the text and the social formation exists as an *inverse* relation.

As a recognition of the discontinuous and contradictory, it is just such an inverse relation that Olson presents in *The Maximus Poems*:

> Now all things
> are true by inverse.
>
> (MP, 51)

On these grounds, Olson explores the disjunction between the text and the social formation in which it is created. Describing what would make a good magazine, Olson states that 'such a deal takes *composing* ... composing by discontinuity, non-deduction, field, fragment, grit & vulgarity, that, at root, can make a magazine, today, fresh ... there is composing – juxtaposition, correlation, interaction'.[22] Similarly, Olson's poetics attempt to reveal truth as contradictory through the juxtaposition of extremes, rather than by eliminating contradictions as untrue. For this reason, Olson retains his factual errors in the text of the poem as he progresses, puzzling over problems and unexplained questions. One example might be the problems encountered in the attempt to establish the familial lineages of the settlers in the Dogtown settlement. In the poem 'DECEMBER, 1960', Olson unquestioningly mentions the family relations between Josselyn and Cammock (*MP*, 195); but later, Olson shows himself pondering over 'the question who is / Goodwoman Josselyn? Margaret Cammock?' (*MP*, 463).[23] Olson's poems are thus *compositions*. Like Louis Zukofsky's 'A', Olson's sentences develop like musical themes: they break apart and turn in on themselves in a continuing helix of variations. The phenomena of these compositions are perceived as 'overdetermined' so that their contradictory complexity

The 'negative dialectics' of The Maximus Poems 239

needs to be disentangled through interpretation. But there is never an affirmation, or 'final cadence'. The contradictions are explored, picked apart, unravelled; they are not resolved.

In representing an object within a constellation, cognitive interpretation for Olson and Adorno does more than merely record the object's genesis as a natural process. It aims to reveal or release a suppressed energy:

> Such immanent universality of the individual is *objective* as *sedimented history* ... Becoming aware of the constellation in which a thing stands is tantamount to deciphering the constellation which, having come to be, it bears within it. Cognition of the object in its constellation is cognition of the process stored in the object.[24]

In a letter to Robert Creeley, Olson reinforces this idea of constellation as *the* methodological technique:

>   CONJUNCTION & DISPLACEMENT, the sense of, C&D, D&C, etc etc. Is verse.
>   Is quite another thing than time.
>   Is buildings. Is
>
> des ign.
>   Is – for our trade –
>   THE DISJUNCT, language
>
> in order to occupy space, *be* object (it being so hugely as intervals TIME) has to be thrown around, re-assembled, in order that it speak, the man whose interstices it is the re-make of.[25]

Olson reinforces this as the poetic methodology of *The Maximus Poems* in a short two-word 'poem': 'tesserae / commissure' (*MP*, 269). Butterick cites Olson's explanation of the word 'tesserae' as '"the little pieces that are used in making a mosaic ... all those pieces of stone and glass and color" and "commissure" as meaning "bound together"'.[26] Composition by mosaic also urges a cognitive procedure which arises from specific attention to the object's *dynamic* situation in the world, rather than allowing predetermined arrangements to dictate the appearance of the object.

Olson's interest in dynamic relationships is manifested in a preoccupation with dialectics throughout his writings.[27] Complaining about the stranglehold of Socrates over the style of discourse, Olson states 'I have not, for so many years, been engaged in dialectic, for nothing'.[28] In another letter to Cid Corman, Olson states that a 'finished' work finds itself defined as such only in a dialectic with 'the so-called un-finished'.[29] Closure always holds tensions which open up. The urgency in the writing derives from the continuous insistence on the writing re-enacting the *process* of cognition, a 'RE ENACTMENT OF, / the going reality'.[30] The specificity of the particular is constantly maintained as the yard-stick of the universal: 'man as common has to be restored by way of you or me as particular'; 'grab hold, first (in order to accomplish the common), by DOCUMENTATION → the specific'; 'you must cease to think of a poem as anything but an expression of THAT WITH WHICH YOU ARE A SPECIALIST – which has to be, if it is a poem, YR SELF, YR THINGS, no one else's, nothing else but that you are sure of'.[31] Writing about the success of certain New England writers who re-established an American spirit in poetry in the early fifties, Olson says 'they have exposed the local by demonstrating that the particular is a syntax which is universal, and that it cannot be discovered except locally, in the sense that any humanism *is* as well place as it is the person'.[32] Olson is clearly aware of the way in which universalising tendencies can lead to commodification and reification and writes in his essay 'Human Universe' that abstraction from experiences, 'comes out a demonstration, a separating out, an act of classification, and all I know is, it is not there, it has turned false' (*CPr*, 157). In this case, Olson is describing an epistemological process which always carries an 'untruth': whilst purporting to establish the facts, abstraction from reality only gives priority to the conceptual. Olson's invocations of Keats' notion of Negative Capability and Heisenberg's Uncertainty Principle in 'Human Universe' are equally attempts to reveal or release the 'non-identical' for knowledge. When Keats speaks of '*Negative Capability*, that is when man is capable of being in uncertainties, Mysteries, doubts, without any irritable reaching after fact and reason', Olson argues that Keats is 'unfixing' things.[33] That is, Keats recognizes what Olson calls 'the unadmitted further half of the truth' (*SVH*, 42) and what Adorno calls cognition of the non-identical.[34] Such a re-introduction of dialectics into the perception of the world, is for Olson (and Adorno) a corrective to the misconceived static and reified universe. Implicitly rejecting much of the empirical philosophical tradition upon which Pound founded his language theories, Olson invokes the Hegelian dialectical tradition (which includes the subsequent variety of Marxist reformulations of the dialectic) in support of his concepts of language in *The Special View of History*.[35] Both Hegel and Olson cite their philosophical roots in the theories of flux and movement posited by Heraclitus: both oppose dialectics (*kinesis*) to *stasis* (or as Marxists have reformulated it, reification) in language. Olson's poetics is a struggle to reintegrate *kinesis* with human perception, as a means to preserving subjective activity in objective experience: 'There is only one thing you can do about the kinetic, reenact it. Which is why the man said, he who possesses rhythm possesses the universe.... Art does not seek to describe but to reenact' (*CPr*, 162). As Olson clearly sees, the divorce of the artist from his activity leads to the pressing question: 'Can one restate man in any way to repossess him of his dynamic?' (*CPr*, 160).

Olson's attack on the logic of Greek classification is bound up with his strategies to de-reify history and explode preconceived models of temporality. He wrote to Corman that it is 'the refreshment of values so far as history goes, that I am after'.[36] Olson argues that one must escape from the 'historical' frame of thought 'that there is truth, and that evidence can bring it forth ... it is right here that logic and classification most strongly work against verse and prose'.[37] In its place, Olson urges:

> that there is any time except
> that one time which matters, YOUR OWN
> (the LIE of history is that a man can find or take any relevance out
> of the infinite times of other men except as he pegs the whole thing
> on *his* time: and i don't mean times, that sociological lie, I mean
> *your* TEMPI – mine,
> in short, all that TIME IS, is RHYTHM
> (and there is no way of knowing any rhythm OTHER THAN YOUR
> OWN, than BY your own.[38]

Olson calls for self-reflection about historical perspective and the need to 'start thinking in NON-HISTORICAL ways – to start substituting the art of STORY for the non-art but logic of HISTORY'.[39] This substitution of narrative for the logic of classification of facts is an attempt to blast open the concept of time-continuum imposed by chronological and factual accounts of history. It is designed to make historians masters of their materials, reflexively acknowledging the past as a discursive construct of the present (and hence subject to ideological bias). Olson would appear to be even more radical, in that he denies any general history – he emphasises that there is not even a present ('times, that sociological lie') but rather '*your* TEMPI' – suggesting a sort of intersubjectivity that exceeds any generalised subject of history. History appears not as a series of successive acts, but as the 'eternal presence' of the single act perpetually reconstructed. What happened in the past, never escapes subjective representation. Olson states in *The Special View of History*:

> there are TWO stances. Always are. It isn't a question of fiction versus knowing. 'Lies' are necessary in both – that is the HIMagination. *At no point outside a fiction can one be sure.*
> What did happen? Two alternatives: make it up; or try to find out. Both are necessary. We inherit an either-or, from the split of science and fiction (my italics).[40]

One inherits a set of reified choices which derive from an artificial separation of discourse. Olson maintains that neither the discourse of fiction or science in isolation can effectively present an adequate representation of history. Undoing 'the LIE of history' necessitates the introduction of a 'nowness', a temporality centred on the rhythm of a specific, active, social subject. The precursor of such an idea is once again Walter Benjamin:

> Historicism contents itself with establishing a causal connection between various moments in history. But no fact that is a cause is for that very reason historical. It became historical posthumously, as it were, through events that may be separated from it by thousands of years. A historian who takes this as his point of departure stops telling the sequence of events like the beads of a rosary. Instead, he grasps the constellation which his own era has formed with a definite earlier one. Thus he establishes a conception of the present as the 'time of the now' which is shot through with the chips of Messianic time.[41]

It is a sense of time as pregnant with meaning, rather than merely the passing of time; it is the moment of disruption or crisis within the smooth flow of continuity. The necessity for refusing to reduce the present to a mere repetition of the past, rests in the liberation of the present from the conformism about to overpower and strait-jacket it.[42] He introduces some form of '*Jetztzeit*' as a means to breaking open the illusion of an unbroken linear development in history.

A new ethic of perception

Olson's refusal to submit to an homogenised temporality, stems from his recognition that an homogeneous history is barren and arid. Reaching for new representations at every moment in his writing, necessitates the practice of a new ethic of perception, an 'ALTERNATIVE TO THE EGO-POSITION'.[43] In 'LETTER 9' of *The Maximus Poems*, there is a struggle with language and the process of representation, to allow the sensation of the moment to carry the verse. Olson takes a sheer delight in moments of realisation: many of his poems are records of the process of his dawning awareness of something, a direct emotional reaction to events, rather than emotion recollected in tranquillity. The poem attempts to suspend reflection in favour of a spontaneous reaction to the beauty of a perception:

>   I, dazzled
> as one is, until one discovers
> there is no other issue than
> the moment of

> the pleasure of
> this plum,
> these things
> which don't carry their end any further than
> their reality in
> themselves
>
> (*MP*, 46).

At moments like this, the Olsonian project can seem almost Poundian, to see the object as 'it really is' in itself, with no conceptual or linguistic interference. These attitudes of Olson's can seem naïve (although as many poets and critics attest, the attitude is very American in its passion for directness of access – Olson's plum here seems related to the ones that the Williams persona took from the icebox in 'This is just to say'). Yet the dazzlement is also abstract, because it is a *reflection* on the immediate. The self-identity grasped here is only momentary (and illusory), since he shifts quickly away from focussing purely on the object. The third section of this poem is a perspective of the harbour stretching out in front of the subject, a panorama of the different hues and shades of the visible colours. However, it is recognised that this view is constructed:

> As of myself
> I'd pose it,
> today,
> as Alfred at Ashdown, a wild boar
> (*aprino more*, Asser says)
>
> (*MP*, 47).

The subject seems to suggest that it is 'reality-in-itself' that is being perceived, and yet there is the ironic recognition that the subject constructs the panorama. In *Aesthetic Theory*, Adorno continually highlights this oscillation between delineating the object (and controlling it), only to find that it has slipped beyond one's grasp, or that it is not what one assumed it to be: 'The work of art is both a process and an instant. Its objectification, while a necessary condition of aesthetic autonomy, is also a petrifying tendency. The more the social labour embodied in an art work becomes objectified and organized, the more it sounds empty and alien to the work'.[44] Olson's allusion to Alfred suggests some form of conquering aesthetic, an aesthetic which is violent, forceful and domineering. Gone is 'reality-in-itself' in this analogy, since an aggressive representative desire is introduced. Gone too, is the desire for an object untouched by any lyrical interference by the ego – the subject is very much in evidence here! This is an example of Olson's talk about seizing the world, fashioning it as one wants it rather than as one receives it.[45] He presents this mode of representation as contrasting directly with another mode: Alfred's aggression 'versus / my own wrists and all my joints, versus speech's connectives, versus the tasks' (*MP*, 47). This latter approach which involves the body in writing and conceives of cognition and language as an extension of the body, is analogous to the mode of writing which allows the purity of plums to stand forth in their own self-contained reality:

>   Flowers, like I say.
>   And I feel that way,
>   that the likeness is to nature's,
>   not to these tempestuous
>   events,
>   that those self-acts which have no end no more than their own
>   are more as plums are
>   than they are as Alfreds
>   who so advance
>   men's affairs
>
> (*MP*, 47–8).

The poem thus deals with the oscillation between 'self-acts' and mediated representations. The priority of the object is placed against an epistemological position which places importance on the subject in the process of cognition. The poem charts the paradox in which a focus on outward reflections on objects brings one back to the self and the role of the constitutive subject. This becomes evident in the final section of 'LETTER 9':

>   I measure my song,
>   measure the sources of my song,
>   measure me, measure
>   my forces
>
> (*MP*, 48).

The syntax presents a complex dialectic of the subject and object, an interrelationship between the poem and the producer, in which all types of measurement occur. The subject and the object measure each other: 'I' measures the 'song' and the 'song' measures 'me'. In the final analysis, the language of the poem enforces a continual re-evaluation of measurement, as well as the object of that measurement.

Olson thus reintroduces what according to him has been omitted from the process of writing since the Greeks formalised the perceptive process into a static record of an abstract object: motion, and above all, attention to the *process* of perception. Writing of Melville's representation of the cognitive act in *Moby-Dick*, Olson makes this point clearly in 'Equal, That Is, to the Real Itself': 'Melville couldn't abuse object as symbol does by depreciating it in favour of the subject. Or let image lose its relational force by transferring its occurrence as allegory does. He was already aware of the complementarity of each of two pairs of how we know and present the image – & object, and action & subject' (*CPr*, 121). For Olson, seeing does not lead to an abstract object: it is an imitative re-enactment of the process of 'coming-to-know'. Writing is a seeing, and a seeing is a contestation with the objects in the world. In his 'Letter to Elaine Feinstein', Olson comments that an image is locked into a specific form of seeing:

> Comparison. Thus representation was never off the dead-spot of description. Nothing was *happening* as of the poem itself – ding and zing or something. It was referential to reality. And that a p. poor crawling actuarial "real" – good enough to keep banks and insurance companies, plus mediocre governments etc
>
> (*CPr*, 251).

Olson wants writing to be an *engagement* with the object perceived, not just a 'description'. Olson's sarcastic dismissal of the 'thing-in-itself' ('ding and zing or something'), clearly indicates his contempt for an abstracted objectivity divorced from that 'relational force' so well preserved in Melville's prose.

However, 'comparison' and 'description' here might well compare with Adorno's concept of 'mimesis' rather than with 'imitation'. This parallel between Olson and Adorno continues in their similar approach to the object. Adorno's approach to the crisis in representation consists in bypassing the conventional understanding of mimesis as representation or imitation. Instead, as Michael Cahn has clearly and forcefully demonstrated, Adorno takes 'mimesis' to be a process of making oneself similar to the environment and in it 'the outside serves as a mould onto which the inside *moulds itself*.'[46] However, as Cahn points out, this does not imply, as the translator of Adorno's work thinks, that 'mimesis imitates the environment'.[47] Cahn shows that Adorno distinguishes between 'identification with' (i.e. a mimicry which is part of survival) and 'identification of' (which is a conceptual, repressive disfigurement of the object). Adorno is quite clearly conscious of the uneasy ambiguity between mimesis and imitation; (i) imitation might mean/ designate (the production of) a thing-like copy, but equally it might refer to (ii) the activity of a subject which models *itself* according to a given prototype. The first meaning is the bad manifestation of 'imitation', and only the second one may be termed 'mimesis.' As Adorno makes clear in *The Dialectic of Enlightenment*, his conception of the subject is one where there is an involved attitude in the process of imitation as an adaptive 'identifying with' which is guided by the logic (Logik) of the object. Essentially Adorno insists upon the early Greek meaning of *mimêsis*, 'impersonating by dancing or acting', which plays an important role in Adorno's understanding of the concept: 'All art, above all music, is kindred to drama'.[48] Olson equally argues that drama is a pre-eminent model for the understanding of art. Cahn argues that in rejecting 'imitation as being controlled and imprisoned by the visual, the order of the *eidos* and *theorein*', and replacing this with the kinetic, Adorno resorts to the 'original' meaning of 'mimesis': 'For him, making *oneself* similar to an Other, is the condition of the possibility of the less fundamental production of a copy, and this explains why he grants priority to mimesis and at the same time insists that it comprise imitation as one of its aspects.'[49]

However, mimesis as an adapting and correlating behaviour does not presuppose a clear line of demarcation between subject and object, or inner and outer, the two poles between which mimesis mediates, because it is understood as 'an attitude towards reality prior to the fixed opposition of subject and object'.[50] The key point about mimesis is that as a correlative function, it is set against rationality as an integrative and stabilising factor. Quoting *Aesthetic Theory*, 'Rationality without mimesis negates itself', Cahn argues that emptied of any mimetic element, for Adorno rationality becomes completely severed from the objects it pretends to grasp. Mimesis is thus the corrective to abstract rationality: 'With the advancement of Enlightenment the mimetic dimension, being threatened with extinction, finds a last refuge in art, where its forgotten truth, the memory of magic and mimicry as the condition of the possibility of rationality, is virtually neutralised'.[51] Adorno seeks to reactivate this 'forgotten truth', to bring back this forgetting which has reified the object, to inject the mimetic back into the rational.

Olson is clearly also interested in mimesis, and in terms similar to those of Adorno. Again and again in his letters to Cid Corman, Olson stresses the importance of mimesis in writing as a 'RE ENACTMENT OF, / the going reality'; the 'GETTING IN THE GOING ENERGY OF THIS PRESENT'; 'THE PRESENT GOING REALITY IS THE ONLY SUCH SOIL'; the need 'to do with a process of *fronting* to the *whole* front of reality *as it now presents itself*'.[52] In 'Projective Verse', a certain mimetic impulse underlies his concept of 'Objectism.' Olson continually pushes for a mimetic return to the process of writing:

> The objects which occur at every given moment of composition (of recognition, we can call it) are, can be, must be treated exactly as they do occur therein and not by any ideas or preconceptions from outside the poem, must be handled as a series of objects in field in such a way that a series

of tensions (which they also are) are made to *hold*, and to hold exactly inside the content and the context of the poem which has forced itself, through the poet and them, into being.

(*CPr*, 243–4)

This mimesis is conceived of as a corrective to the installation of the subject as the centre of the perceptive process. Adorno's conception of the 'priority of the object' is primarily directed against an epistemological tradition which increasingly placed importance on the subject in the process of cognition, which eventually led to the subject becoming the sole legitimate ground of cognition. Olson similarly directs his call for the priority of the object against a poetic tradition which has blurred the cognitive dialectic between subject and object in favour of the subject's superiority, to the point where this now dominant anthropocentricism necessitates an 'ALTERNATIVE TO THE EGOPOSITION'.[53] But Olson recognises that the subject cannot be banished altogether, since this will merely lead to a situation where *mimesis* without *rationality* negates itself. What is needed is an aesthetic position which attempts to reintroduce the lack to supplement and reinforce the dominant.

Writing for Olson is kinaesthetic: it is an attempt to break through the veil of objectivity in the modern world, to become a mimesis of action. Olson wants language to enact the process of perception. For this reason, he constantly inveighs against any acceptance of those 'assumptions which are part of, or coloured by "Western" or "Christian" history' and 'our assumptions abt taste and "the aesthetics of" any art (as proceeding fr, the Greeks, & first formulated significantly by Aristotle, and Longinus, etc.'[54] In their place he wants the 'kinetics of contemporary physics' and the '*graphic*'.[55] Any simple acceptance of preconceived aesthetic styles or standards, would be a submission to the ideology of 'linear progress' in a reified world of abstraction and identification, and consequently, a succumbing to one's alienation from production to an 'actuarial "real"'. The struggle with a rationality based on the logic of identification and similarity, is that of exposing 'the false face' of the illusion of a totalising perception:

> (you see, it has not been sufficiently observed, particularly in our own time, that reason & the art of comparison are a stage which man must master, but, are not what our world takes them to be, final discipline: they wear the false face. For beyond them is direct perception and contraries, which dispose of argument. But such a movement forward is very difficult for a rational society to comprehend, implying, as it does, a circular concept of life. That is, the harmony of the universe is not logical, or, better, is post- or supra-logical. As is the order of any created things.[56]

Laying the grounds here for his seminal essay 'Human Universe', Olson goes on to say that 'I have fed as much on a remark of Blake's as on single remark of any man: Oppositions are not true contraries'.[57] The importance of the contrary in Olson's attempt to outline a different form of argument approaches a somewhat Hegelian formulation, in which contraries exist as dialectical constituents in a process of production. Olson perceives through Blake that whereas oppositions lack the interactive dimension of dialectical relationships, contraries produce transformations. Objects exist in these relations; they do not have some *a priori* existential ontology as a totality.

Insisting on those particulars

Olson's attacks on rationality and the imposition of an applied order on the objective world produce an increasing source of tension within *The Maximus Poems*, since the poems progressively seem to deny this. Despite his frequent focus on chance and aleatorical indeterminacy[58] and Jung's philosophical conception of synchronicity and acausality (see Olson's allusions to Jung's essay 'Synchronicity: An Acausal Connecting Principle'[59]), the denial of a fundamental totality to existence is something about which Olson remains ambivalent. For at the moments of dealing with the metaphysical texts of alchemists and his flirtations with Jungian archetypal thought, Olson seems to accept their holistic proposals in his search for alternative philosophies concerning the problematics of space, time and causality.[60] This runs contrary to Olson's challenge to the traces of humanist totality in non-dialectical thinking. Olson's contradictory attitude to totalising thought suggests that his poetics resist any impositions of an unriven continuity. If a definition of rationality denotes a Weberian adherence to a rule, as opposed to acting on impulse or at random, the concept of synchronicity directly challenges this. Synchronicity challenges rationality as a consistency in linking our thoughts or statements, creating a logical order of premise moving to conclusion. It also challenges the consistency of linking our actions, or the creation of the efficient order of means to ends. The systematisation and rationalisation of belief as the elimination of particular judgements which cannot be subsumed under a more general judgement, is persistently challenged by Olson's insistence on particulars; and it is what attracts him to this challenge to conceptual thinking occasioned by a 'negative dialectics'.

Notes

1 Charles Olson, *Letters for Origin 1950–1956*, ed. Albert Glover (London: Cape Goliard, 1969), 128.
2 Ibid., 120.
3 Ibid., 85.
4 Ibid., 40.
5 See for example, Olson, *Letters for Origin*, 39–40.
6 Walter Benjamin, *The Origin of German Tragic Drama*, trans. John Osborne (London: Verso, 1985), 29.
7 Benjamin, *Origin*, 28, 32.
8 Olson, *Letters for Origin*, 11.
9 Ibid., 10.
10 Ibid., 10–11.
11 See Theodor W. Adorno, *Negative Dialectics*, trans. E. B. Ashton (London: Routledge and Kegan Paul, 1973), 162–6.
12 Susan Buck-Morss, *The Origin of Negative Dialectics: Theodor W. Adorno, Walter Benjamin, and the Frankfurt Institute* (Brighton: Harvester, 1977), 98.
13 Adorno, *Negative Dialectics*, 5.
14 Charles Olson, 'the hinges of civilization to be put back on the door', in George F. Butterick (ed.), *Additional Prose: A Bibliography on America, Proprioception, & Other Notes & Essays* (Bolinas, CA: Four Seasons Foundation, 1974), 25.
15 Adorno, *Negative Dialectics*, 12.
16 Ibid.
17 '"A" is to be what is not yet' (Adorno, *Negative Dialectics*, 150).
18 Ibid., 157.
19 Charles Olson, 'A Work', in *Additional Prose*, 33.
20 Buck-Morss, *Origin*, 99.
21 Ibid., 100.
22 Olson, *Letters for Origin*, 12.
23 See further poems (*MP*, 463, 590–1), and Butterick, *A Guide to The Maximus Poems of Charles Olson* (*GMP*, 595) for notes on this issue.
24 Adorno, *Negative Dialectics*, 163.
25 Charles Olson and Robert Creeley, *The Complete Correspondence*, Vol. 2, ed. George Butterick (Santa Barbara and Santa Rosa CA: Black Sparrow Press, 1983), 66–7.
26 Quoted from Olson's reading at Goddard College and cited in Butterick, *Guide* (*GMP*, 382); see Butterick's additional notes on this notion of bonding disparate materials, particularly his references to Jung's *Aion*.
27 Olson stresses the role of *dialexis* in pre-Aristotelian discourse as an example of the energy discharged with knowledge, and appears to act like an alternating electric current, in which the discharge of energy sets the will and the mind up as violent initiators of action: 'It would seem to me that this is because the most missing understanding of what they did do is *dialexis*, at

whatever date that word even might have come to have the meaning of an actual action of dialogue: *dialectical* does mean one to one, and an immediate discharge of mental engagement in which the will and the mind are like aggressive motor actions, and are complimentary in that they do compliment the other person engaged, as though there was a one-to-one possible, as though the conversation was between us and a meeting of minds was possible. It is socializing, and relational'. (Quoted from Olson's reading at Goddard College and cited in Butterick, *GMP*, 54.)

28 Olson, *Letters for Origin*, 33.
29 Ibid., 5.
30 Ibid., 10, 6–8.
31 Ibid., 81–2, 119.
32 Ibid., 127.
33 John Keats, Letter to George and Tom Keats, 21, 27(?) December, 1817, in *Letters of John Keats*, ed. Robert Gittings (Oxford: Oxford University Press, 1970), 43. This extract is quoted as the epigraph to Charles Olson's lecture given at Black Mountain College in 1956, printed in Charles Olson, *The Special View of History*, ed. Ann Charters (Berkeley: Oyez, 1970).
34 Olson, *Special View*, 42.
35 Olson almost certainly studied Hegel at Harvard, and his use of Hermann Weyl's mathematical philosophy also rests on the latter's interest and research in German Idealist philosophy.
36 Olson, *Letters for Origin*, 29.
37 Ibid., 83.
38 Ibid.
39 Ibid.
40 Olson, *The Special View*, 20.
41 Walter Benjamin, 'Theses on the Philosophy of History', in *Illuminations*, ed. Hannah Arendt (London: Fontana, 1973), 265.
42 This insistence on overcoming the pressure of conformism exerted by Tradition, extends to resisting the strait-jacketing of traditional rhythms as well. In *Letters for Origin* (84–5), Olson rails against Corman's use of the pentameter as a 'declared base (which becomes a strait jacket)' in an echo of Pound's injunction to 'compose in sequence of the musical phrase, not in sequence of a metronome', from 'A Retrospect', in *Literary Essays of Ezra Pound*, ed. T. S. Eliot (London: Faber, 1954), 3; and Louis Zukofsky's similar injunction '[The poet] does not measure with handbook, and is not a pendulum', in Louis Zukofsky, 'A Statement for Poetry', in *Prepositions* (London: Rapp and Carroll, 1967), 31. The requirement is to work from the particular ('YR RYTHYM') rather than the dominant mode or pattern.
43 Charles Olson, *Mayan Letters* (London: Cape, 1968), 29.
44 Theodor W. Adorno, *Aesthetic Theory*, Gretel Adorno and Rolf Tiedemann (eds), trans. C. Lenhardt (London: Routledge and Kegan Paul, 1984), 147.
45 Olson speaks of this appropriating aspect as a manner of 'taking the Earth as a *One* – by the old law that a one is only so if it produces one. This would be, then, if you talk a Causal Mythology, the simplicity of the principle

"that which exists through itself is what is called meaning" – will be that one produces a one. The Earth, then, is conceivably a knowable, a seizable, a single, and *your* thing'. Charles Olson, *Causal Mythology*, ed. Donald Allen (San Francisco, CA: Four Seasons Foundation, 1969), 5.

46 Michael Cahn, 'Subversive Mimesis: Theodor W. Adorno and the Modern Impasse of Critique', in M. Sparisou (ed.), *Mimesis in Contemporary Theory: An Interdisciplinary Approach* (Philadelphia: Benjamins, 1984), 27–64.
47 Theodor W. Adorno and Max Horkheimer, *The Dialectic of Enlightenment*, trans. John Cumming (London: Verso, 1979), 187.
48 Theodor W. Adorno, *Minima Moralia: Reflections from Damaged Life*, trans. E. F. N. Jephcott (London: Verso, 2006), 174.
49 Cahn, 'Subversive Mimesis', 34.
50 Adorno, *Aesthetic Theory*, 80.
51 Cahn, 'Subversive Mimesis', 36.
52 Olson, *Letters for Origin*, 10, 8, 6, 5.
53 Olson, *Mayan Letters*, 29.
54 Olson, *Letters for Origin*, 51.
55 Ibid.
56 Ibid., 54.
57 Ibid. Olson refers to this notion of Blake's on several occasions: see the letter to Robert Creeley, 8 March, 1951 (*SW*, 86); and 'This Is Yeats Speaking' (*CPr*, 143). One might quote additional statements from William Blake, *Complete Writings* (ed.) Geoffrey Keynes (Oxford: Oxford University Press, 1969) of equal interest: 'Without contraries is no progression', 149; 'Contraries are positives, a negation is not a contrary', 518; and 'Negations are not contraries; Contraries mutually exist', 639.
58 See Olson, *The Special View*, 48.
59 'JUST AS MORNING TWILIGHT AND THE GULLS, GLOUCESTER, MAY 1966, THE FULL FLOWER MOON' (*MP*, 520); and see Carl Jung, 'Synchronicity: An Acausal Connecting Principle', in *The Structure and Dynamics of the Psyche*, trans. R. F. C. Hull, *The Collected Works of C. G. Jung*, 20 vols, second edn (London: Routledge and Kegan Paul, 1957–1979), Vol. 8, 530.
60 Olson clearly became strongly interested in Jung's work on archetypes, myth, alchemy and symbolism and many sections of *The Maximus Poems* are organised around Jung's ideas. One of Olson's central texts, 'The Secret of the Black Chrysanthemum', is based on the Jungian symbol of the 'golden flower'; see *Olson: The Journal of the Charles Olson Archive* 3 (Spring 1975), 64–81.

18

A note on Charles Olson's 'The Kingfishers'

Charles Bernstein

'The Kingfishers' is both thrilling and exasperating, inspiring and challenging.[1] The date of its composition has become as emblematic as anything in the poem: 1949. Just four years after the bombing of Hiroshima, just four years after the gates of Auschwitz were broken open and the unfathomable lies of what happened there were revealed, the same year as Mao's forces triumphed in China (Olson's 'La lumiere de l'aurore est devant nous. Nous devons nous lever et agir' ['The light of dawn is before us. We must arise and act.'] is from Mao) (*CP*, 87). Sixty-five years later, we are still confronted with the dogged question at the heart of this poem, 'shall you uncover honey / where maggots are?', a line that has the status of Adorno's questioning of the possibility of lyric poetry in the wake of the 'final solution' (the systematic extermination process) (*CP*, 93). Is our Western heritage salvageable?

A stirring, iconic voice rises up in this poem, one phrase tumbling upon the next, hectoring, charged, bursting through the dead silence and complacency often associated with this proto Cold War moment in US history. Olson's rhetorical power is a blast against conformity, against the postwar methodology of 'prosperity' through repression. 'What pudor pejorocracy affronts': our decency, if we still have it, in the human dethronement of that moment, 1949 (or 2014), is offended by the worsening rule of government (*CP*, 92). And Olson breaks beyond 'the Western box' with his opening, signal, invocation of Heraclitus: all is change, stasis is Thanatos (a death wish). And so the poem enacts this very Heraclitian change/movement/dynamic/parataxis; it invokes a poetics of dynamic movement, where each phrase takes on new meaning in new contexts. One thought is overlaid on another, a veritable palimpsest, like they say.

I've read the poem many times over the years and I still don't follow it, I keep diving back in for more. You can never step into the same poem twice (to conflate Olson and Heraclitus). The poem is a bracing test of nonlinear reading because it quickly loses the reader trying diligently to 'follow,' since it demands another approach, one that doesn't follow the leader but the *lieder*. Guy Davenport calls the poem as a whole an ideogram, marking its unmistakable, and not entirely happy, Poundian lineage. The poem is weighted/freighted by those Poundian need-to-know (or do you?) uncited references, as for example the appropriations from Prescott's *History of the Conquest of Mexico* ('the priests ... rush in among the people,' 'of green feathers feet, beaks and eyes / of gold') (*CP*, 89, 88).

And at or near the centre, 'I thought of the E on the stone'. This is not Frank O'Hara referring casually and without consequence to graffiti on Second Avenue but an allusion to the inscrutable inscription on the Stone at Delphi. But this is the weight that for Olson we cannot cast off: of the enigma of our cultural histories, which form us and from which we are formed. We are not one but many, and from the many threads the fabric of our possible lives will be woven. Do we weave it or let it be woven for us? Will dawn follow this dark night?

We come late to a world that we feel, less and less, is of our making: we are estranged from that which we feel we are, by right of nature, familiar; as if our own hand was not part of our body, or our own society no longer a polis, no longer 'ours' (to extend a fragment of Hekalitus quoted by Olson in his *Special View of History*).[2]

Near the end, Olson quotes a couplet from Rimbaud's *Season in Hell* ('Alchemy of the Word'): 'si j'ai du goût, ce n'est guères / que pour la terre et les pierres' ('I only find within my bones / A taste for eating earth and stones', as Paul Schmidt translates it) (*CP*, 92).[3] Rimbaud, Heraklitus, Mao, Prescott, Delphi are, for Olson, points outside the deadness that inscribes 'us' in the 'West' in the wake of the war. They are stones with which we might build a new world, word by word; but they are also the weights of that other demonic world (of which the New World is not innocent). This dead-mid-century poem marks a liminal moment between a controlled Poundian montage (ideogram) and the possibility for a more open-ended collage that might come after.

'The Kingfishers'' acknowledgment of the crisis for Western culture in the wake of the war is the postmodern turn, where the call of the poet is so much bird feed. 'The kingfishers! / who cares / for their feathers / now?' (*CP*, 86). As Jack Spicer would say a decade later, 'No / One listens to poetry.'[4]

Notes

1 The first version of this piece was published as 'A note on Charles Olson's "The Kingfishers"' for Arkaddi Dragomoshchenko's translation in *Sibila: Poesia e Critica Literària*, http://sibila.com.br/english/a-note-on-charles-olsons-the-kingfishers-for-arkaddis-dragomoschenkos-translation/3099, posted 21 August 2009, accessed 16 May 2014, reprinted by kind permission of the author.
2 Charles Olson, *The Special View of History*, ed. Ann Charters (Berkeley: Oyez, 1970), epigraph and 27.
3 Paul Schmidt, *Arthur Rimbaud: Complete Works* (New York: Harper Perennial Modern Classics, 2000), 234.
4 Jack Spicer, *My Vocabulary Did This To Me: The Collected Poetry of Jack Spicer*, eds Peter Gizzi and Kevin Killian (Middletown, Connecticut: Wesleyan University Press, 2008), 372.

Section V

Space

19

Transcultural projectivism in Charles Olson's 'The Kingfishers' and Clifford Possum Tjapaltjarri's *Warlugulong*

Peter Minter

Literal depth

Whenever I think about Charles Olson's *projectivism* I start out with a visual apparition. Instead of reckoning first with words or language or a language-based grammar of some kind, I see a material apparatus hanging in an imagined space. This apparatus has a plastic, tangible shape, and buoyancy, somewhat like a mobile or constellation hanging in the air as if formed by the condensation of kinetic energy within a field of appearance in my mind.[1] Its appearance is shaped by a choreographic modelling of the projective impulse, an archetype of an eruption of energy that is aroused by the attention of cognition and materialised as an aesthetic object in a moment of *poiesis*. This projective form springs forth with substance and shape. Like a mobile, it is a set of points in space marked by gestural and rhetorical density, and like a constellation it is the articulation of those points in a web of relation, movement and attachment. It is also moving, a momentum creating vectors of spatialisation and materialisation. Its movement is always contingent and emergent, rarely descriptive.

It is only after fabricating this apparatus in my imagination that I actually begin to read Olson's poems, as if their words, lines, pitch and ideation are only available to me once I have properly manufactured a reading machine of the right calibration and fidelity. This doesn't occur discursively or reductively; the emergence of projective form does not involve the accumulation or elimination of poetic substance. Rather, I end up with a technology that can detect and transmit new orders of reality. It functions somewhat like a wildly arranged antenna that takes the shape of the signal it receives, solidification occurring along emergent patterns of cybernetic intensification, a vehicle for the plastic and semantic materialisation of *poiesis*.

In 'A Bibliography on America for Ed Dorn' Olson cites Alfred North Whitehead's 'we should start from the notion of actuality as in its essence a process.'² Likewise, the projective form I imagine is actualised in a rendering of process, an unfolding and synthesis of sensation and historical information. Whitehead goes on to write that:

> this process involves a physical side which is the perishing of the past as it transforms itself into a new creation. It also involves the mental side which is the Soul entertaining ideas.
>
> The Soul thereby by synthesis creates a new fact which is the Appearance woven out of the old and the new—a compound of reception and anticipation, which in its turn passes into the future.[3]

The 'physical side' and the 'mental side' coalesce to form a 'compound of reception and anticipation', a fact of 'Appearance' in which the material cosmos coheres with cognition and culture in the process of *poiesis*. The projective structure is both immediately sensational and immediately genealogical, an event appearing simultaneously along vectors of interiority and exteriority. We might say that, both *despite* being and *because* it is a projection of the imagination, my fabrication of a projective form is a substantiation of a narrative of the history of the present.[4] As Olson writes in 'Proprioception', the projective form appears *literally* as historical 'depth' projected within and through corporeality:

> the 'body' itself as, by movement of its own tissues, giving the data of, depth ... *movement* or *action* is 'home'. Neither the Unconscious nor Projection ... have a home unless the DEPTH implicit in physical being—built in space-time specifics, and moving (by movement of 'its own')—is asserted, or found-out as such.[5]

Movement through the material cosmos and historical space-time produces a corporeal home 'woven out of the old and the new—a compound of reception and anticipation.'

In this essay I propose that projectivism's corporealisation of history, which has its vanishing point in the genealogical depth of the interiority of the body (individual and collective) and its biophysical and linguistic materialisations, shares a *poethical* gestalt with Australian Aboriginal art. Readings of Olson's mid-twentieth century revisionism and postmodernism have often focused upon his ambitious, post-Poundian reach for a Mesoamerican, Mayan symbolic archaeology as a restorative to what he perceived to be a (postwar) crisis in Western ontology and representability. Between 1949 and the mid-1950s Olson was propelled by a recuperative fervour for a contemporary *muthologos* and for Mayan hieroglyphs, both of which are considered in detail below. I aim to complement this critical milieu by reading Olson's projectivist aesthetic for its transcultural antipodean promise, and claim that Olson's projection of an enabling 'archaic postmodern' mythos has compelling corollaries in the poetics of Aboriginal art objects.[6]

My use of *poethics* here is of course indebted to Joan Retallack's foundational thesis in her essay *The Poethical Wager*, in which ethics and aesthetics coalesce along radically classical contours:

> Every poetics is a consequential form of life. Any making of forms out of language (poesis) is a practice with a discernible character (ethos) .... this hybrid [is a] frank and unholy union of modernist and postmodernist questions joined to the Aristotelian concern for the link between an individual and public ethos.[7]

Ethos as 'character' is to know the 'nature' of something, its 'stance toward reality' as Olson might say (*CPr*, 246). Retallack's poethics fuses 'making' and 'nature' to yield *ethos* as a foundational substratum to *poiesis* – ethics precedes ontology, as Emmanuel Levinas reminds us in *Otherwise than Being: Or, Beyond Essence*.[8] We come into being amidst others. As we shall see, Aboriginal paintings similarly assume a projective gestalt in which a foundational ethos (the Dreaming and cultural law) precedes but is simultaneously materialised in the action of the painting and its substantiation of Country, its 'nature' and 'character'.[9] With this in mind, in the following I will present a discussion of a major modern Aboriginal artwork, and a congruous reading of Olson's postmodern projectivist exemplar, 'The Kingfishers' (1949). Following Retallack's poethical example, we can broadly group these correlations under two main headings: the poetic and the ethical. The poetic includes questions of medium, genre and mode, content, form and production. The ethical includes archives of character, genealogies of cultural memory, histories of the present. Together they tell us something about the *nature* of being-in-nature. Looked at separately, they provide us with useful conceptual tools for making a transcultural comparison of two very different cultural spheres.

'I hunt amongst stones'

Discourse on contemporary Australian Aboriginal art was revolutionised in 1998 by the publication of *Aboriginal Art* by visual anthropologist and cultural theorist Howard Morphy. Morphy writes that:

> Aboriginal paintings are maps of land. It is necessary, however, to define precisely what is meant by a 'map' in this context ... [F]rom an Aboriginal perspective the land itself is a sign system. ... Aboriginal paintings can only be fully understood as maps once it is realised that the criterion for inclusion is not topographical but mythological and conceptual; paintings are thus representations of the totemic geography.[10]

From an Aboriginal perspective, the land is already a sign system because it was implicitly encultured at the moment of its creation in the Dreamtime. 'The Dreamtime' and the 'Dreaming' describe a dimension that is spatially and symbolically contiguous with quotidian reality while being pre-historical and continuous with the future. The term is not a straightforward translation of an Aboriginal word, but was rather invented in 1896 by anthropologists Baldwin Spencer and F. J. Gillen, who took the Central Australian Arrernte word *altyerrenge* (commonly 'Alcheringa', meaning 'belonging to dreams') to denote a complex set of transhistorical mythological and religious concepts.[11] The Dreamtime is the source of Morphy's 'totemic geography', fabricated by ancestral beings who emerged from the earth and whose actions produced the natural landscape and all its cultural attributes. Signs of their production are everywhere, simultaneously embedded in the material landscape and in narrative and song:

> Every action of the ancestral beings had a consequence on the form of the landscape. The places where they emerged from the earth became waterholes or the entrances to caves; where they walked, watercourses flowed; and trees grew where they stuck their digging sticks in the ground ... where they died hills formed in the shape of their bodies, or lakes formed from pools of their blood. Over time the features of the earth began to take shape, and as long as the ancestral beings lived on the surface of the earth they modified its form little by little.[12]

Ancestral beings created humans, moulded either from their bodies or from the earth itself. In the Lake Eyre (Diyari) myth, the first humans appear half-formed in the mud, and then dry out in the sun 'until they gained the strength to disperse across the landscape.'[13] Likewise, and perhaps most significantly for our immediate concerns, they created language, song, ceremony and law. Indeed, as Morphy underlines, they created art, the 'songs, dances, paintings, ceremonies and sacred objects' which record significant and transformative events in their lives and journeys.[14]

From an Aboriginal perspective, the landscape is therefore considered to be a composition of encoded narratives that are recalled and reiterated in moments of poiesis, such as in paintings (on bark, the body or canvas), stories or ceremony. As W. E. H. Stanner famously wrote in 1962, '[t]he Aborigine moves, not in a landscape, but in a humanized realm saturated with meaning.'[15] Rather than simply exhibiting topographies in a conventionally empirical or picturesque manner, Aboriginal artworks represent nodes of cosmological and semiotic intensity that were created in the Dreaming, are still present today and indeed are substantially present in the objective artwork itself. They are visible in paintings and in oral or performed narratives of Country. As Morphy writes:

> rather than being topographical representations of landforms, Aboriginal paintings are conceptual representations which influence the way in which landscape is understood. When Aboriginal paintings do represent features of landscape, they depict them not in their topographical relations to one another but in relation to their mythological significance.[16]

Aboriginal paintings actualise an aesthetics of the 'history of the present'. They begin from an irrefutable set of actualities: the emergence of the lived cosmos in the Dreaming, the contiguous emergence of language and painting and song and ceremony as materialisations of an ancestral poethics, and the present-moment expression of the *ethos* of a place, the genealogy of its character or nature. In a sense the artworks are simultaneously genealogical and concrete, as both substance and a history of substance. As such they are generically projective, insofar that they represent *and actualise* the fusion of the proprioceptive senses and the kinetic flow of semiotic intensity.

One of the most important Australian paintings of the twentieth century is Clifford Possum Tjapaltjarri's *Warlugulong* (1977) (Fig. 7).[17] This work is an exemplary instance of the acrylic 'dot' painting style that emerged in the early 1970s at Papunya, an Aboriginal community in the western desert of the Northern Territory. Clifford Possum Tjapaltjarri was one of the first generation of Papunya artists, a movement now known as Papunya Tula that succeeded in transforming Aboriginal art practice. For the first time Aboriginal art was produced using synthetic paints and canvas rather than ochres, bark, sand or the body. This radical adjustment in materials and media underpinned the unfurling of Aboriginal art into galleries and the international art market.[18] *Warlugulong* is an epic composition of nine Dreamings centred around the creation of an originary mythic bushfire by the ancestral being Lungkata. The work palimpsests a set of Dreamings from across a vast geography, including, for instance, groups of dancing women, tracks of walking emus, rock wallaby men, goanna men and dingoes and their associated Dreaming stories.[19] To return to Morphy's sense that Aboriginal paintings are maps of totemic geographies, *Warlugulong* exhibits an archetypal synthesis of Aboriginal Dreaming and a cartographic logos in which *ethos* and *topos* are materially and historically actualised.

The nucleus of a projective reading of *Warlugulong* can be found in its plastic corporealisation of the 'nature' of the artist's Country in its material, historical and poetic dimensions, its 'stance toward reality'. Looked at first as a painting per se, the work is a material artefact made

7 Clifford Possum Tjapaltjarri, *Warlugulong* (1977).

of synthetic polymer paint on canvas. It's perhaps not surprising that when the painting was purchased at auction in 2007 by the National Gallery of Australia it was widely compared with the gallery's notorious purchase of Jackson Pollock's *Blue Poles* in 1973. Ron Radford, the director of the gallery, was reported to say at the time that *Warlugulong* 'is to dot painting what *Blue Poles* is to American Art'.[20] Not unlike Pollock's reduction of classical scale, perspective and depth to the projective actualisation of the action of the body, Possum Tjapaltjarri's painting (painted, like Pollock's, with the canvas on the ground) emerges at the confluence of the body of the painter and site of expression. Morphy emphasises the manner in which Possum Tjapaltjarri, while painting different intensities of the 'totemic geography', moved:

> around [the painting] ... reorienting the relationship between features according to their present position and focus ... there are various twists in geographic perspective in order to incorporate mythological perspectives ... [and it] is in the nature of such maps that multiple perspectives are superimposed on one another and that there are differences in scale.[21]

The scale of the body is made central to the creative procedure. I will discuss below how Possum Tjapaltjarri's actualisation of the metamorphosis of spatial, historical and mythological perspective has its poetic corollary in the postmodernist 'will to change' in Olson's 'The Kingfishers'. In *Warlugulong* the plastic form of the painting is produced by the corporealisation of intensities of lyrical history, both in the movement and action in the mode of production, and in the painting's polysemous manifestations of the Dreaming. The work takes on a form that is an extension of the body and of the physical topologies of the Dreamtime.

Alongside the consideration of materials and form and formation, the projective gestalt of *Warlugulong* also hinges on the substantiation of Law (and lore) in Country and its immediate expression in the artwork. In the same manner that the actions of ancestral beings in the Dreamtime created a 'totemic geography', they also simultaneously created law and language. Law and language are properties of Dreaming and Country and emerge through both natural features in the environment and human artefacts like artworks, ceremony and song. In moments of expression such as the reiteration of ceremonial stories in song or dance or painting, the law and language are made present and sustained. It's in this sense that *Warlugulong* also presents an *ethos* of place, its topology of 'character' and 'nature'. In concert with its material corporealisation of the Dreaming, the painting's actualisation of a pre-ontological ethical dimension (in the Levinasian sense) is intrinsic to its projective poiesis. Essentially, the *ethos* of the 'totemic geography' is manifest in its substantiation of dimensions of co-relation and habitation. More than just caring for or appealing to Country, an *ethos* of Country calls upon histories of 'character' as they appear within networks of connection, interdependence and signification. Much about this has been written elsewhere.[22] Not unlike Olson's *Maximus*, the epic character or 'persona' of *Warlugulong* is produced in 'obey[ing] the figures of / the present dance' and its genealogies of meaning as they are reproduced and reiterated (*MP*, 5). From an Aboriginal perspective, the 'nature' of a place is not simply a function of ecosystem or aspect. It is a contemporary iteration of a history of the present, a *poethics* that synthesises ancient semiotic geographies and landscapes of 'character' as they are expressed in the present. As cultural theorist Stephen Muecke explains, 'an ethical disposition is induced into subjects via a place, without didacticism or intentions to "do good". This could be an unexpected version of the posthumanism some have been looking for in contemporary philosophical thought.'[23]

'What does not change / is the will to change'

With some stretch of the imagination, Charles Olson could have been a fabulous Aborigine, his kingfisher not unlike the walking emus, rock wallabies or dingoes. Wanting to 'hunt among stones', Olson announced in 'The Kingfishers' a pugnacious rejection of 'the biases of westernism, of greekism' which by the middle of the twentieth century had in Olson's mind devolved into a culture of alienation, industrial-technologism and atomic war.[24] Ralph Maud writes about Olson's 'mood of antagonism' toward T. S. Eliot's desolate 'Fisher King' of *The Waste Land*, his adversarial repudiation of a culture of estrangement and death and espousal of reinvented primal life in which 'one must go *back* before the Greek philosophers, and *out* into still living primitive societies'.[25] For Olson, the disintegration of the Cartesian ego demanded, poetically at least, a vigorous exposition of a regenerative compositional principle. Against the bleakness of the Holocaust and Hiroshima, 'The Kingfishers' marks the beginning of Olson's radical reassertion of the value of the intact 'human figure as part of [the] universe of things'.[26] It is also poethically paradigmatic of a projective transfiguration of material nature, proprioceptive cognition and corporealised cultural history that can be transculturally and transhistorically correlated with Aboriginal art.

'The Kingfishers' essentially seeks a thorough reintegration of the psyche and the cosmos. The poem opens with Olson's translation of Heraclitus's Fragment 23 (via Plotinus *Enneads* IV.viii.1: metaballon anapaute (*metaballon anapaute*), 'change alone is unchanging') and embarks upon breaking through the sclerotic poetics of the west to actualise a mode of *poiesis* that restores legitimacy to 'the human universe'.[27] At the heart of 'The Kingfishers', and of projectivism more generally, is a call to rehabilitate the modern by recuperating a primal mode of sentience in which the body and sensation, cognition, language and history are poetically substantiated. Olson wants us to 'get back, in order to get on', to 'resurrect primal values that have been driven out of sight by the alienating force of European civilisation.'[28] As 'archaeologist of morning' his legendary tack was south into Mesoamerica and the archaeological ruins of the pre-Columbian Mayan cultures found in the Yucatan Peninsular, Mexico and Guatemala.[29] Although Olson's first expedition to Yucatan occurred in 1950, the year after he wrote 'The Kingfishers', the poem proleptically presents an assemblage of figures that were to become pivotal to his 'post-modern ... post-humanist ... post-historic ... going live present ... "Beautiful Thing"'.[30] Much has been written already on the poem's key tropes – the alluring feathers ('the kingfishers' feathers were wealth'); the movement through a crack in the ruins; Plutarch's 'E on the stone'; the light of dawn and Mao's Far East communist revolution; nesting and transcendentally rising forth from foul 'rejectamenta'; the fecundity of the Mayan legacy; 'uncover[ing] honey / where maggots are' (*CP*, 86, 87, 93).[31] For our purposes, and following Paul Christensen's affirmation that the poem is 'a model of the projectivist poetic executed successfully', I return to the poethical nexus between genealogies of *poiesis* and *ethos*.[32]

At the forefront of Olson's enterprise is to actualise a *poiesis* that can repair Western culture's separation of *logos* and the life of the mind and reason from the wellspring of proprioceptive experience and mythological invention. As Robert Creeley made clear in his introduction to *Mayan Letters*, Olson had for some time been 'moving in this direction, back to a point of origin ... to break with the too simple westernisms of a "greek culture"':

> Yucatan made the occasion present in a way that it had not been before. The alternative to a generalizing humanism ... that there had been and *could* be a civilization anterior to that which he had come from ... The problem was, to give form, again, to what the Maya had been – to restore the 'history' which they were. For in the Maya was the looked-for content: a *reality* which is 'wholly formal without loss of intimate spaces ... the persistence of both organism *and* will (human)'.[33]

Olson's reach toward Yucatan is aligned with his pursuit of a pre-Platonic anteriority to the alienating *logos* of the west, a time when *mythos* and *logos* were undifferentiated. In his *Maximus* poem 'Letter 23', Olson isolates the abstraction of the *logos* to Pindar (c. 522–443 BC) and Plato (c. 428–328 BC), and employs a pivotal term in his restorative project, the *muthologos*:

> ... *muthologos* has lost such ground since Pindar
>
> ... "Poesy
> steals away men's judgment
> by her *muthoi*" (taking this crack
> at Homer's sweet-versing)
>
> "and a blind heart
> is most men's portions." Plato
>
> allowed this divisive
> thought to stand, agreeing
>
> that *muthos*
> is false. *Logos*
> isn't—was facts
>
> (MP, 104)

As George F. Butterick shows in *A Guide to the Maximus Poems of Charles Olson*, Olson is reiterating an argument presented in James Thomson's 1935 *The Art of the Logos: On the traditional stories of the ancient Greeks* (GMP, 145–6).[34] Thomson writes that the first to distinguish between Muthos and Logos was Pindar. 'Surely marvels are many,' he says, 'and methinks in part *Muthoi* adorned with cunning fictions beyond the true Logos do deceive the minds of men':

> Here, Muthos, the false Story, is contrasted with Logos, the true.... It is from this usage that 'myth' has come to mean ... 'a fictitious narrative'. ... Even Plato, one is rather surprised to learn, makes no distinction between the words in his ordinary use of them. It is only when the need arises to discriminate between the false Story and the true, between imagination ... and demonstrable fact, that he follows Pindar and calls the false a Muthos. Yet the converse did not hold, and in normal usage Logos did not mean a true story. It means simply a Story.
>
> (GMP, 145–6)

In their more ancient senses, *logos* and *mythos* were interchangeable, and could *both* be considered 'fictional' or 'mythological' depending on the mode of the discourse itself. Indeed, Thomson writes that:

> Logos did not originally mean 'word' or 'reason', or anything but merely 'what is said' ... the question of truth or falsehood did not arise ... a Muthos was a Logos, and a Logos a Muthos. They were two names for the same thing.[35]

More recent scholarship concurs. Critical and cultural theorist Laurent Milesi agrees that, as elements in a philosophy of *poiesis*, *muthos* and *logos* were:

> two complementary activities, usually attuned to each other 'in accordance with nature' in order to express ... myth. If logopoeia came to designate, as it were, an artistic 'speech act' which could be directly reflective of nature, the *muthos* or thing spoken, uttered or 'acted' by the mouth, had its ... correspondence in ... the thing done or enacted.[36]

In a manner that is analogous to Possum Tjapaltjarri's creation of a 'totemic geography' in painting, by moving around the canvas and shifting the scales of narrative and history according to location, perspective and memory, 'The Kingfishers' synthesises nodes of experience, ideation and historical depth within the projective gestalt of the poem. Both artworks produce a projective *muthologos* in which *mythos* and *logos* create a narrative substance where proprioceptive sensation in the present moment is fused with a genealogy or archaeology of locality and its lived archive. As we saw in *Warlugulong*, Olson's *muthologos* collapses time and space to produce an *ethos* of spatialised embodiment which mitigates the 'egotistical sublime' of the West (*CPr*, 239). A central image in 'The Kingfishers' is the 'E on the stone', a primal inscription which signals Olson's enthusiasm for Mayan hieroglyphs as synecdoches for a corporealised *muthologos*. The 'E on the stone' is perhaps both the 'symbol that Plutarch had found on the omphalos stone at the temple of Delphi'[37] and, according to Carol Kyle, a Mayan astronomical sign described by the great ethnographer of Mesoamerica, J. Eric Thompson, whose *Maya Hieroglyphic Writing* (1950) is listed in Olson's bibliography in *Mayan Letters*.[38]

Hieroglyphs had Olson's full attention from the late 1940s into the 1950s. In his pioneering essay 'Human Universe' (1951) he writes that the Mayans:

> invented a system of written record, now called hieroglyphs, which on its very face, is verse, the signs were so clearly and densely chosen that, cut in stone, they retain the power of the objects of which they are the images.
> (*CPr*, 159)

Here Olson could equally be describing the projective poethics of the painting *Warlugulong*. In the same year that he composed 'Human Universe', Olson wrote in a Fulbright application that 'the study of a "hieroglyphic" language [is] a valuable core to investigating morphology of culture ... a fresh ground for a concept of "humanism"' (*SL*, 145–6). This 'stance toward reality' was further echoed in another application for support also written in 1951:

Mayan 'writing', just because it is a hieroglyphic system in between the pictographic and the abstract (neither was it any longer merely representational nor had it yet become phonetic) is peculiarly intricated to the plastic arts, is inextricable from the arts of its own recording (sculpture primarily, and brush-painting), in fact, because of the very special use the Maya made of their written stones (the religious purpose their recording of the movements of time and the planets seems to have served), writing, in this very important instance (important not only historically but also dynamically in terms of its use in cultures today), can rightly be comprehended only, in its full purport, as a plastic art.[39]

Thus we have come full-circle. Olson's *muthologos*, which collapses the flawed Platonic separation between *mythos* and *logos*, can be aligned with his sense of the hieroglyph as 'plastic art'. Just as I began by imagining the projective as a plastic form emergent at the confluence of the proprioceptive and the semantic, Olson projects the hieroglyphic as a synthesis of the material and the representational. Perhaps the entire poem 'The Kingfishers' can be read as a single hieroglyph, its shifts in historical and spatial scale echoing the semiotic gestalt of an action painting. Finally, as I discussed in my reading of *Warlugulong*, both Olson's projectivism and Aboriginal art share the actualisation of genealogies of poethical substance. What is actualised is both the plastic medium and the *ethos* or 'character' of its location, its 'nature' in the present and as it has been forever iterated.

The Will to Cohere

Olson's quest to establish the cosmological roots of projectivism in a radically anterior *muthologos* may have enjoyed an excursion to the antipodes. Australian Aboriginal cultures have been intact for tens of thousands of years, their modes of expression actualising a real-time proprioceptive account of the Dreaming, its 'totemic geographies' and its lawful 'character' in Dreamtime story, song and art. Clifford Possum Tjapaltjarri's *Warlugulong* and the paintings of Papunya Tula, and indeed the great oeuvre of Aboriginal art more generally, succeed (among many other things) in substantiating a poiesis that synthesises the Dreaming, its emergence and manifestation in space and time, and the contemporary lived experience of its *ethos* and genealogy. Not unlike Olson's poethics in 'The Kingfishers' and his sense of the potential in the hieroglyph, Aboriginal art is contiguous with the body, the breath, perception and ideation

> ... precisely as intimate as verse is. Is, in fact, verse. Is their verse. And comes into existence, obeys the same laws that, the coming into existence, the persisting of verse, does.[40]

At the conclusion of his essay, 'Charles Olson's Archaic Postmodern', Ralph Maud reminds us of Olson's 1951 essay 'The Gate and the Center'. Writing on ancient Sumerian exemplars, Olson is eager for:

> the WILL TO COHERE ... The proposition is a simple one ... energy is larger than man, but therefore, if he taps it as it is in himself, his uses of himself are EXTENSIBLE in human directions & degree
>
> (CPr, 172)

I began this essay by bringing to mind the trope of the mobile, a moving archetype of densities of form and animation. As we have seen, the will to *co-here* is the condensation of lived kinetic energy, constellations of sensation, cognition and semiotic density calibrating the emergence of an articulated self. 'The Kingfishers' fly above *Warlugulong*, the morning sun gold on their wings.

Notes

1 On 'the *kinetics* of the thing' see Charles Olson, 'Projective Verse' (*CPr*, 240).
2 Charles Olson, 'A Bibliography on America for Ed Dorn', *Additional Prose: A Bibliography on America, Proprioception & Other Notes & Essays*, ed. George F. Butterick (Bolinas: Four Seasons Foundation, 1974), citing Alfred North Whitehead *Adventures of Ideas* (Cambridge: Cambridge University Press, 1943), 355.
3 Whitehead, *Adventures of Ideas*, 355.
4 Michel Foucault, *Discipline and Punish: The Birth of the Prison* (New York: Vintage Books, 1995), 31.
5 Olson, *Additional Prose*, 18.
6 Ralph Maud, 'Charles Olson's Archaic Postmodern', *Looking for Oneself: Contributions to the study of Charles Olson, Minutes of the Charles Olson Society* 42 (September 2001), http://charlesolson.org/Files/archaic1.htm, accessed 16 May 2014.
7 Joan Retallack, *The Poethical Wager* (Berkeley: University of California Press, 2003), 11.
8 Emmanuel Lévinas, *Otherwise Than Being: Or, Beyond Essence* (Hague: Boston, Hingham, MA: M. Nijhoff, 1991).
9 On the Aboriginal Australian term 'Country', see Deborah Bird Rose, *Nourishing Terrains: Australian Aboriginal Views of Landscape and Wilderness* (Canberra: Australian Heritage Commission), www.environment.gov.au/heritage/ahc/publications/commission/books/pubs/nourishing-terrains.pdf.
10 Howard Morphy, *Aboriginal Art* (London: Phaidon Press, 1998), 103, 106.
11 Sir Spencer Baldwin and Francis James Gillen, *The Native Tribes of Central Australia*. (London: Macmillan & Co., 1899). While there are numerous other words in Aboriginal languages to denote The Dreaming, *Alcheringa*

has become common following W. E. H. Stanner, 'The Dreaming (1953)', *White Man Got No Dreaming: Essays, 1938–1973* (Canberra: Australian National University Press) and Jerome Rothenberg and Dennis Tedlock, *Alcheringa*, 9 vols (New York: Jerome Rothenberg & Dennis Tedlock, Stony Brook Poetics Foundation, 1970).

12 Morphy, *Aboriginal Art*, 69.
13 Ibid., 73.
14 Ibid., 84.
15 W. E. H. Stanner, *White Man Got No Dreaming*, 131.
16 Morphy, *Aboriginal Art*, 103.
17 Clifford Possum Tjapaltjarri, *Warlugulong*, 1977, National Gallery of Australia, Canberra, synthetic polymer paint on canvas, http://artsearch.nga.gov.au/Detail-LRG.cfm?IRN=167409, accessed 16 May 2014.
18 On the emergence and history of the Papunya Tula art movement, see Geoffrey Bardon, *Papunya Tula: Art of the Western Desert* (Ringwood, Vic.: McPhee Gribble, 1991); Hetti Perkins, Hannah Fink and Art Gallery of New South Wales., *Papunya Tula: Genesis & Genius* (Sydney: Art Gallery of New South Wales, 2000); and Judith Ryan and Philip Batty, *Tjukurrtjanu: Origins of Western Desert Art* (Melbourne, Vic.: National Gallery of Victoria, 2011). On Clifford Possum Tjapaltjarri, see Vivian Johnson, *The Art of Clifford Possum Tjapaltjarri* (Sydney, 1994).
19 See Possum Tjapaltjarri, *Warlugulong*, 'The main subject of the painting is Lungkata's punishment of his two sons who did not share their catch of kangaroo with their father, as is customary. The skeletons of the two boys are depicted in the atmospheric effect of charred earth, smoke and ash on the right. [The] Dreamings include a group of women from Aileron dancing across the land, represented by their footprints in the top right running laterally across the canvas. Below these are the tracks of a large group of Emus returning to Napperby (the artist's homeland). The footprints of the Mala or Rock Wallaby Men, travelling north from the area around present-day Port Augusta (in South Australia), can be seen in the vertical line of wallaby tracks to the left of centre. Further to the left are the tracks left by the legendary Chase of the Goanna Men. And the tracks of the Tjangala and Nungurrayi Dingoes travelling to Warrabri appear along the left edge of the painting. The footprints of a Tjungurrayi man who attempted to steal sacred objects run laterally along the lower edge towards a skeleton in the lower left, indicating the man's fate. A family travelling to Ngama is represented by their footprints aligned vertically in the right third of the canvas, while the tracks of Upambura the Possum Man run along the meandering white and yellow lines that provide the compositional structure of the painting.'
20 Sebastian Smee, 'NGA Acquires a New Blue Poles', *The Australian*, 26 July 2007, 11.
21 Morphy, *Aboriginal Art*, 106.
22 See, for instance, Rose, *Nourishing Terrains: Australian Aboriginal Views of Landscape and Wilderness*, and Deborah Bird Rose, *Reports from a Wild*

Country: *Ethics for Decolonisation* (Sydney: University of New South Wales Press, 2004).
23 Stephen Muecke, *Ancient and Modern: Time, Culture and Indigenous Philosophy* (Sydney: University of NSW, 2004), 90.
24 Charles Olson, *Mayan Letters*, Cape Editions, 17 (London: Cape, 1968), 48.
25 Ralph Maud, *What Does Not Change: The Significance of Charles Olson's 'The Kingfishers'* (London: Associated University Presses, 1998), 24.
26 Olson, *Mayan Letters*, 69.
27 Guy Davenport, 'Scholia and Conjectures for "The Kingfishers"', *The Geography of the Imagination: Forty Essays* (San Francisco: North Point Press, 1981), 89.
28 Charles Olson, 'The Gate and the Center', (*CPr*, 168); and M. L. Rosenthal, *The New Poets: American and British Poetry since World War II* (New York: Oxford University Press, 1967), 164, cited in Maud, *What Does Not Change*, 24.
29 Charles Olson, *Archaeologist of Morning* (London: Cape Goliard, 1970).
30 Charles Olson, 'The Present Is Prologue', Olson, *Additional Prose*, 207.
31 Sources include Charles Bernstein, 'A Note on Charles Olson's "The Kingfishers" for Arkaddi Dragomoschenko's Translation', *Sibila: Poesia e Critica Literària* http://sibila.com.br/english/a-note-on-charles-olsons-the-kingfishers-for-arkaddis-dragomoschenkos-translation/3099, accessed 16 May 2014 and reprinted in this volume; George F. Butterick, 'Charles Olson's "The Kingfishers" and the Poetics of Change', *American Poetry* 6:2, 1989; Davenport, 'Scholia and Conjectures for "The Kingfishers"'; Carol Kyle, 'The Mesoamerican Cultural Past and Charles Olson's The Kingfishers,' *Alcheringa* New Series 1.2; Maud, *What Does Not Change*, among others.
32 Paul Christensen, *Charles Olson, Call Him Ishmael* (Austin: University of Texas Press, 1979), 98.
33 Robert Creeley, 'Preface to the First Edition (1953)', *Mayan Letters*, 5–6.
34 Butterick refers us to Olson's source, J. A. K. Thomson, *The Art of the Logos. [on the Traditional Stories of the Ancient Greeks.]* (London: George Allen & Unwin, 1935), 18–19.
35 Thomson, *The Art of the Logos*, 17, 19, cited in Butterick (*GMP*, 146).
36 Laurent Milesi, 'From Logos to Muthos: The Philosophy of Pound's and Olson's Mythopoetics', *Avant-Post: The Avant-Garde under 'Post-' Conditions*, ed. Louis Armand (Prague: Litteraria Pragensia), 223–4.
37 Christensen, *Call Him Ishmael*, 96.
38 John Eric Sidney Thompson, *Maya Hieroglyphic Writing: Introduction* (Washington: Carnegie Institution of Washington, 1950), 237, cited in Kyle, 'The Mesoamerican Cultural Past and Charles Olson's the Kingfishers', 71.
39 Charles Olson, 'Project (1951): "The Art of the Language of Mayan Glyphs",' *Alcheringa* 1:5, 95.
40 Olson, *Mayan Letters*, 43.

20

The view from Gloucester: Open Field Poetics and the politics of movement

David Herd

'The thing we are now in'

When Donald Allen began to conceive the framework for the anthology he came to call *The New American Poetry*, he had it in mind to include recent work by senior modernists and their immediate successors: Williams, H. D., cummings, Moore, Pound, Stevens, Rexroth, Patchen, Zukofsky. Taking advice from trusted contemporaries, he first put the plan to Robert Creeley, who supported the idea. Charles Olson took a different view:

> I wldnt myself add either of these two units: either the 'aunties' or the grandpas. If the thing we are now in is it is just in its own character, and there isn't one of us who isn't bound together in that way, than by any of those older connections. In fact those connections strike me as smudging the point; 1950 on ...[1]

One can't discount an awareness of reputation in this statement. Allen wrote to Olson in 1957, by which time he had published a series of significant shorter poems, had largely completed the first volume of *The Maximus Poems*, and in 'Projective Verse', 'Human Universe' and the seminars subsequently known as *The Special View of History* had gone further than any contemporary to establish a new poetics. Much more than Creeley, Olson was himself, by 1957, a senior figure. He had no need for antecedents.

Such self-aggrandizing motives notwithstanding, however, Olson's letter advising Allen made a substantive critical point.[2] What they (Olson, Allen and the new generation of poets) were now 'in', Olson insisted, had its 'own character' and whatever that moment was it was more binding on contemporaries than any connections to the literary past, however recent. Olson's phrasing is itself characteristic, presenting, in its string of monosyllables ('now in is it is just') a circumstance the parameters of which are extremely difficult to discern but which are nonetheless binding on those who find themselves so situated. In its double effect of uncertainty and collectivity, this could be taken as the premise for any number of early Olson poems, including 'The Kingfishers' and 'In Cold Hell, in Thicket'. There is, in other words, an axiom at work in Olson's letter to Allen. The present moment is distinct unto itself and such sense of collectivity that can subsequently emerge must set out to register that fact. What he wanted to insist on was a new beginning, and he gave a date: 1950 on.

1950 was the year Olson himself published 'Projective Verse' in *Poetry New York*. A number of other documents from around that time, poems and essays, relate to that inaugural statement of open field poetics in their insistence on the need of new beginnings. The short prose statement 'Resistance', written for Jean Riboud in 1949 and published in Vincent Ferrini's Gloucester-based magazine *Four Winds* in 1953, is one such. As Olson writes:

> When man is reduced to so much fat for soap, superphosphate for soil, fillings and shoes for sale, he has, to begin again, one answer, one point of resistance only to such fragmentation, one organized ground, a ground he comes to by a way the precise contrary of the cross, of spirit in the old sense, in old mouths. It is his own physiology he is forced to arrive at.
> (CPr, 174)[3]

I refer to 'The Resistance' to recall that for Olson, whatever else his poetic project had to answer to, right there at the beginning was the fact of the concentration camps. This is not just to make the historical point that among his contemporaries Olson was unusual in his readiness to respond to this fact. The point, rather, is that from the beginning his work set itself the task of arriving at figures and forms that would both acknowledge the reality and implications of the camps and would also enable thought to move beyond them. Two figures emerge at the outset: 'physiology' and 'resistance'. Such had been the fragmentation of the human form that the body itself, human physiology, must be re-asserted. He had begun to re-assert it already in *Call Me Ishmael*, where his account of the story of the whale ship Essex graphically recovered the details of human suffering and abandonment that lay behind Melville's novel.[4] The term 'Resistance' has two meanings. It refers to the French Resistance, of course, in which Riboud had been active, but it also sets up a field of relations, the kind of field Olson was beginning to explore as he contemplated 'Projective Verse', resistance in its physical sense signifying 'the impeding effect exerted by one material thing on another'. The point is not just, then, that in this text which asserts the need for new beginnings Olson writes in horror at the fact of the camps, but that as he does so he begins to form the frameworks that would underpin his poetics: a field of relations in which bodies stand their ground.

In *A Charles Olson Reader* Ralph Maud couples 'The Resistance' with Olson's 1948 poem 'La Préface'. 'La Préface' is significant, again, not (simply) for the tone of its response to the Corrado Cagli Buchenwald drawings which are its source; what matters, rather, is the way Olson begins to figure that response. Written a year before 'The Kingfishers', it is the first poem in which statements are set down according to the impulses he would formulate as open field poetics, lines and phrases being so placed as to hold their position visually on the page. It is an aesthetic departure he identifies explicitly with the revelations of the camps, the poem's unidentified speaker observing '"My name is NO RACE" address / Buchenwald new Altamira cave' (CP, 46). Altamira is the northern Spanish cave in which prehistoric paintings were first found. By analogy, what we are dealing with in Olson's post-Buchenwald poem is a new, perhaps foundational aesthetic, the fundamental element of which, as Olson makes clear, is space. As the poem says:

> Put war away with time, come into space.
> It was May, precise date, 1940. I had air my lungs could breathe.
> He talked, via stones   a stick   sea rock   a hand of earth.
> It is now, precise, repeat. I talk of Bigmans organs
> he, look, the lines! are polytopes.
>
> (CP, 46)

'La Préface' is important in Olson's career because it arrives at elements that would endure throughout his work. He is among stones already, as he would be in 'The Kingfishers', he is attentive to the act of breathing, as he would be in 'Projective Verse', and in 'Bigmans' he was forming the outline of the persona who would become 'Maximus'. Most significantly, though, Olson establishes the primacy of 'space' to this new poetic, presenting the human body (figured as 'polytopes') in space as a necessary resistance to the obliterations of war.

Among the various names Olson gave the aesthetic he was looking to inaugurate in 'The Resistance' and 'La Préface', one was the name 'postmodern'.[5] As various commentators have observed, and as Miriam Nichols has rigorously documented, Olson's sense of the 'postmodern' quickly came to be displaced in the 1970s and 1980s, largely by versions of the term that were grounded in the scepticism of deconstructive theory.[6] The argument here is that from the vantage point of 2014, Olson's postmodernism, his sense of 'the thing we are now in', has come, or should come, to seem variously pertinent again. Taken up as they are with the business of a Massachusetts fishing town, *The Maximus Poems* can seem remote from the concerns of these early statements. They aren't though. What one finds in Olson's epic is a necessary working through of frames and figures that have their origin in his first articulations of the post-Buchenwald world in which he found himself. I say necessary because it is only in the scale of *Maximus* that Olson is able to overcome tensions and contradictions that both fuelled and bedevilled his statements of poetics. What he establishes in his epic poem is the centrality of considerations of the polis to the postwar period. Taken from the Greek for city state, 'polis' is an entirely key term for Olson. What it comes to stand for in his writing is the question of how political belonging should be formulated and re-thought. What he evolves in the writing of *The Maximus Poems* are forms of thought that speak directly to the states of political exclusion and exception that were the legacy of the Second World War, and that have once again become definitive of where we find ourselves.

Poetics

How to read Olson's statements of poetics is a difficult question. Such is the vitality and seeming authority of his essays that they have quite often occluded the poems themselves. This is partly an effect of scale: easier to read 'Projective Verse' than to read *Maximus*; to get Olson from his taxing but nonetheless pithy manifesto and then to accommodate the poems through that lens. The problem with such a procedure is that one quickly finds oneself in contradictions. The manifesto is at odds with itself, or at very least doesn't resolve itself; it is difficult to square with the claims of subsequent statements, for instance *The Special View of History*; it cannot be thought to provide a trouble free entry into the poems. Which is to say that 'Projective Verse', like all of Olson's essays, is not a guide. It does not hold that vantage. What it constitutes, rather, is a necessary element of the process, a thinking through (and aloud) that is continuous with the poems themselves.

These caveats notwithstanding, as a thinking through of the complex of issues he found himself faced with at the beginning of his career, Olson's manifesto is nonetheless a remarkable statement in which, for all the authority of the presentation, not the least part of the interest lies in its irresolution. One could reasonably analyse the document into three main elements: the body (in its fundamental physiology), space (in the form of the open field itself), and movement (in the form of kinetics). One way to read the manifesto is as a series of reconfigurations of these elements in various registers, as repeated efforts to satisfy the urgencies of the present moment. To give an example, offered early on:

> From the moment he ventures into FIELD COMPOSITION – puts himself in the open – he can go by no track other than the one the poem under hand declares, for itself.
>
> (*CPr*, 240)

Composition is a body (the poet himself) moving or being moved through space. It is hardly the last word on the subject of how a poem is written, but Olson's priorities are clearly established.

As a statement of purpose, the manifesto has proved least enduring as it figures the human form itself. Olson's claim that the breath is the determinant of prosody can't hold good; one can't in any meaningful sense square the spaces on the page with the passage or duration of the poet's breath. What the insistence on the breath does underline, as Olson insists, is that there is 'a man in it', that the poetry is informed by an acute sense of the finitude of the human form. By contrast, his articulation of the space of the poem as a set of relations between its elements is subtle and far-reaching. Thus:

> every element in an open poem (the syllable, the line, as well as the image, the sound, the sense) must be taken up as participants in the kinetic of the poem just as solidly as we are accustomed to take what we call the objects of reality.
>
> (*CPr*, 243)

From which it follows that, as Olson needs a multi-claused sentence to say:

> The objects which occur at every given moment of composition (of recognition, we can call it) are, can be, must be treated exactly as they do occur therein and not by any ideas or preconceptions outside the poem, must be handled as a series of objects in field in such a way that a series of tensions (which they also are) are made to *hold*, and to hold exactly inside the content and the context of the poem which has forced itself, through the poet and them, into being.
>
> (*CPr*, 243–4)

Although, as Olson acknowledges, this attention to the poem's 'elements' signals a debt to Pound's Imagist manifesto, it is also true that nobody had previously described a poem like this. If 1950 is a beginning, and if the work that understands itself as dating from that moment is addressing a new set of realities, it is in such complex articulations of space that the new poetic is to be found. As Peter Middleton argues elsewhere in this volume, one language informing that articulation is the language of contemporary physics, enabling Olson to think in terms of the particles of the poem. There is another language also, though, the language of 'recognition' and 'participants'. 'Projective Verse' is not

Open Field Poetics and the politics of movement 277

a political statement so one should not force a politics upon it. What one can say, though, is that Olson is seeking an articulation of space according to which nothing is left out, in which everything is granted 'recognition'. That's what the open field poem is: a space of recognition, a framework in which all participants are acknowledged as such.

The question is, how to square such an image of the space of the poem with his express desire that it also articulate movement, kinetics. The shift from the term 'elements' to the term 'participants' helps here. Just as later, in *The Special View*, Olson will insist on the value of *'istorin*, on finding out for oneself, so here he imagines a space governed by the dynamism of participation. There is also, however, the language of holding. In the open field poem the tensions that constitute it are made to '*hold*, and to hold exactly' (Olson's emphasis). Or as he puts it a paragraph later, the poem's objects will 'keep ... their proper confusions' (*CPr*, 244). This takes us to a central tension in Olson. The language of 'holding' and 'keeping' is consonant with the language of 'recognition'. It proposes a poetry governed by an impulse to register objects as and where they stand. This is the poem's resistance. What the language of 'holding' and 'keeping' is not so consonant with is the manifesto's drive to movement, its insistence on 'kinetics'. It is not a tension Olson resolves in 'Projective Verse' and so he continues to think it through. *The Special View of History* is one such re-thinking.

In the seminars Olson led in 1956 at Black Mountain, he presented both a complication and a loosening of the terms that 'The Resistance' and 'Projective Verse' had set out. Olson's preoccupation in those seminars was defined by the epigraph from Heraclitus with which the published text is prefaced: 'Man is estranged from that with which he is most familiar'. What 'that' refers to is man himself (to take the gender non-neutral term Olson uses), or rather, man's physicality. What man is most estranged from, in other words, is the physical condition that constitutes the limit – Olson speaks also of the circumference – of his understanding. For those keeping up with Olson's thought in this period, the idea of the limit would not have been unfamiliar. In the second part of 'Projective Verse', the poet is precisely characterised in terms of the degree to which he limits himself:

> If he sprawl, he shall find little to sing but himself .... if he is contained within his nature as he is participant in the larger force, he will be able to listen, and his hearing through himself will give him secrets objects share.
> (*CPr*, 247)[7]

Crucially, here, we have not stepped away from the discourse of common physicality that Olson presented in 'The Resistance'. The 'containment' of 'Projective Verse', like the 'limit' of *The Special View of History*, addresses what Olson was calling human nature in 1947, the human universe in 1952, and, in the seminars themselves, in 1956, the species. As he puts it in *The Special View*: 'Man has the context of his own species for his self, or he is a pseudo creature'.[8] The new element in *The Special View* is what Olson calls 'emplacedness'. There is not exactly a contradiction here: 'emplacedness' is, as Olson sees it, the way we are limited. Or rather, we cannot grasp our limitations unless we grasp our contingency upon place. Where the tension emerges is in the next move, the move that takes an argument which is good for the species into an argument about politics. The claim is this:

> History is the new localism, a polis to replace the one which was lost in various stages all over the world from 490 BC on.[9]

Of the various Olsonian claims presented so far, this is the one that fits most readily with what has generally come to be thought of as his practice. What the new localism means, in practice, is Olson's research in the archive of the Gloucester historical society. Such an insistence on localism, and especially the localism of archival work itself, is consistent with the emphasis in 'Projective Verse' on 'holding' and 'keeping'. It is difficult to reconcile, however, with the emphasis on movement, the re-emergence of which tension (between the language of 'holding' and the language of 'kinetics') requires us to address the 'view' itself; the view of *The Special View*.

I have coupled *The Special View of History* with 'Projective Verse' because they complicate one another in significant ways. In the transcripts of the seminars, but especially the section called 'The View', Olson again articulates the historical priorities of his present moment. It was necessary to re-visit the polis because organised politics had manifestly failed. It was necessary to emphasise a shared and fragile physicality because what that failure amounted to was a refusal to register a commonality of condition. The move that was not necessary, I suggest, is the shift from a contingent physicality to an insistence on the new localism. The way Olson gets to that position is via the view. It is in the view, as Olson sees it, 'emplaced' as it is, that our limitation most fully presents itself. The consequence is that a poetics which had insisted (still insists, at times, in the seminars themselves) on the human universe, on the language of species and shared physicality, comes suddenly to be emphasising a local variant.

The appeal of *The Special View of History* in the context of Olson's writing as a whole is that it can straighten things out. It can allow his epic to be accounted for in terms of its relation to a particular place and can allow the angle of the epic's vision to be identified with Maximus. In a way that 'Projective Verse' is not, it can be positioned as a guide to the poem. The problem is that in settling on the specifics of the view, Olson didn't register the degree to which he had entered into contradiction with his earlier pronouncements. How, one might ask, can the subjectivism of the view be related to the 'objectism' (the image of the person as object among objects) he so insisted on in 'Projective Verse' (*CPr*, 247). Likewise, what has happened, in all this emphasis on the specificity and stability of the single view, to the question of movement? At which point, I want to suggest, what we have reached is a limit of expository prose, that tensions which go unresolved in 'Projective Verse' and which seem unobserved in *The Special View of History*, remain entirely live in the project of Olson's ongoing poem. It is through its response to that network of tensions, I want to suggest, that *The Maximus Poems* formulates its polis. Briefly though, I want to deviate into a different discourse, to recall what was, and remains, at stake.

Exception

Miriam Nichols' overarching literary historical argument in *Radical Affections* is that criticism turned away from Olson too quickly, that writing didn't learn all that it might have from him because the shift of intellectual ground towards a deconstructive postmodernism rendered him too abruptly marginal. My argument, as corollary, is that as we read Olson now it is his postwar sense of the postmodern that more accurately characterises the moment we are living through. One basis for this claim, a way of thinking about the contemporary moment that Olson chimes with, is Giorgio Agamben's account of the state of exception. The way to make the argument, however, is through Agamben's precursor, and Olson's contemporary, Hannah Arendt.

In 1950, the year of 'Projective Verse', Arendt published *The Origins of Totalitarianism*. The purpose of the book was to trace the origins of Totalitarian government back through the gradual consolidation of the idea of the nation as the defining political entity of the modern age. As she outlined her intention in her preface, the book:

> was written ... to discover the hidden mechanics by which all traditional elements of our political and spiritual world were dissolved into a conglomeration where everything seems to have lost specific value, and has become unrecognisable for human comprehension, unusable for human purpose.[10]

Like the Olson of 'Projective Verse', as Arendt contemplated the origins and the implications of the Second World War, what she sought was a discourse which registered collective specificity. Like Olson, she considered an insistence on such specific values as a form of resistance. 'Human dignity,' as she put it, needed 'a new guarantee', 'a political principle' which might register shared vulnerabilities.[11]

The real interest of setting Arendt alongside Olson, however, is not that they arrived at a common idiom in the immediate aftermath of the war but that for Arendt, as for Olson, what that idiom necessarily led to was a re-consideration of the polis. Revising *The Origins of Totalitarianism* for publication as a second edition in 1958, Arendt added a chapter entitled 'The Decline of the Nation State and the End of the Rights of Man', the point of which was to explore the postwar legacy of the thinking that had produced totalitarianism. What Arendt observed was a reality in which 'the nation-state was no longer capable of facing the major political issues of the time'.[12] This was the consequence of the series of complex historical interactions that had made mainstream race thinking possible, and which, following totalitarianism's reinforcement, was the real consequence of the Second World War. The name for that consequence was 'statelessness'. For Arendt, 'statelessness' was 'the newest mass phenomenon in contemporary history' and 'stateless persons' were 'the most symptomatic group in contemporary politics'.[13] What they were symptomatic 'of' was a failure in modern political organization. For complex and evolving reasons, the modern political state had become, by the early part of the Twentieth Century, synonymous with the idea of nation. The consequence of this was that citizenship came to be identified with national affiliation. Simply put, to fall outside of one national jurisdiction was to fall outside of all jurisdictions. Only in the modern environment, with its 'completely organized humanity', 'could the loss of home and political status become identical with an expulsion from humanity altogether':

> Before this, what we must call a 'human right' today would have been thought of as a general characteristic of the human condition.... Only the loss of a polity itself expels him from humanity.[14]

Arendt is of interest now in part because Agamben has revived her. Really what that means, though, is that the realities Arendt was looking to account for in the period after the Second World War have come to seem pressing again. To set those realities out, Arendt's question, in 1957, was: where does the person who falls outside a given polity, for whatever reason, come to rest? What Arendt was talking about was what Agamben has come to term the state of exception; that state in which a person is outside the law but subject to the law's force; the territory of exclusion in which human rights should, in theory, operate, but in which, in practice, a person's vulnerability is re-exposed.[15]

This comes back to Olson in significant ways. What Agamben's ongoing inquiry into biopolitics and the state of exception has helped us to register is that we are once again living in an environment in which the relation between the polis and human vulnerability is one we are obliged to contemplate. In other words, the primary discourses out of which Olson generated his postmodern poetics now seem not remote but uncomfortably current. What he established was a set of questions which, as the question of the polis has once again becoming pressing, it is important to revisit. And what really needs to be revisited, in this context, is Olson's 'view' itself, or rather, the way, in his writing, view and polis intersect. The implication of *The Special View of History* is that locality, the specifics of a given place, is a necessary restriction on the human view. This takes us, again, to the question of movement. To so insist, as he does in the seminars, that a person's view is underwritten by their relation to the materiality of a given polis would seem to leave little room for kinetics. What one finds in *The Maximus Poems*, however, are forms of articulation that allow one to think through participation in the polis otherwise, forms of articulation that allow, crucially, for circulation.

Olson's crossings

In its ongoing provisionality, as an aspect of its sense of process, *The Maximus Poems* makes a number of attempts to define, or configure, the polis. The first attempt is made as early as 'Letter 3', and finds Olson/Maximus in belligerent mood:

> As the people of the earth are now, Gloucester
> is heterogeneous, and so can know polis
> not as localism, not the mu-sick (the trick
> of corporations, newspapers, slick magazines, movie houses,
> the ships, even the wharves, absentee-owned
>
> they whine to my people, these entertainers, sellers
>
> they play upon their bigotries (upon their fears
>
> (*MP*, 14)

Heterogeneous as Gloucester is (as the people of the earth are) it can understand polis in ways that do not revert to localism. Such an understanding could, in fact, be taken to be the task or substance of the poem, since the 'localism' that is to be resisted is identified as the product of various corporate forms of culture. This generates a nice complexity, that the bigotries and fears which constitute 'localism' are themselves generated by absentee interests: newspapers, movie houses. For those actually in Gloucester, including the poet and his persona, a different image of the polis is possible. The question for the poem is how to articulate that image.

Heterogeneity is a necessary but by no means sufficient condition of the kind of polis Olson wants ultimately to propose. Speaking later in Letter 3 against those same corporate interests, Olson observes that 'slaver / would keep you off the sea, would keep you local, / my Nova Scotians, / Newfoundlanders, / Sicilianos, / Isolatos' (*MP*, 16). The phrasing is ambiguous: do the regional groupings constitute localism, or, in their heterogeneity, stand out against it? Either could be true, and since that is the case then heterogeneity is not, in itself, a sufficient response to the limitations of localism. What really matters, as Olson/Maximus observes, is that the corporations would seek to keep people 'off the sea'. Or as he puts it a little earlier, addressing himself to the 'Root person in root place', what such a person needs to be told about is 'the condition of the under-water, the cut-water of anyone' (*MP*, 16).

Still the best critical commentary on what Olson calls, here, 'the condition of the under-water', is Jeremy Prynne's lecture on *The Maximus Poems* delivered at Simon Fraser University in 1971. First published in *Iron* magazine, and reprinted in the *Minutes of the Charles Olson Society* in April 1999, the objective of Prynne's lecture was to communicate a sense of the scale of Olson's poem as a whole. It is to the point, therefore, that (as he reports) Prynne re-read *Maximus* volumes one and two the night before he lectured. As much as anybody could be said to, as Prynne stood up to speak to the Simon Fraser audience he did so with the whole of Olson's poem in mind. From which basis he offered three key observations. The first is that Olson's poem is 'in the condition of something which is not lyric', which is to say that it is in the condition of epic.[16] The second point is that what the poem takes in, from the vantage point of Gloucester, is what Prynne repeatedly calls the 'curve' of the whole (whether the whole is taken to be the earth, or even the cosmos). Prynne's third point is that in communicating the relation of people to that curve, what the poem primarily communicates is the movement across space, that it is one of the 'great epic performances that can carry across that distance'.[17] The signal achievement of Prynne's lecture is that in a single delivery it recalls *Maximus* to the discourses of species, space, physiology and movement that were critical to Olson as he began to formulate his poetics. Crucial to that re-positioning of the poem is Prynne's sense of the poem's view. The fact that it is not in the condition of lyric means that it is not conditioned by the view of a given speaker. Maximus articulates the poem for Olson, but the poem's view, as Prynne wants to insist, is not limited to that of its governing persona.

In the context of this essay, the question arising is how Prynne's account of the scope of the poem intersects with Olson's stated ambition to articulate a polis which is not understood as localism. The answer, I want to suggest, has to do with the figure of the curve. To state this plainly, from the outset of his career, as he began to contemplate the historical circumstances in which he found himself, Olson's thought was characterised by the figure of the curve. An early instance of this figuring is offered by his poem 'The Moebius Strip', with its fascination for the movement of Moebius's continuous loop. More significantly, that same loop becomes critical to the process of understanding articulated by 'The Kingfishers', where, as he memorably reports, 'the feed-back proves, the feed-back is / the law' (*CP*, 89). The law, the law of the poem that is, is figured according to the continuous loop of interaction issued by feedback. Writ large, which is to say across the scale of *The Maximus Poems*, what that continuous curve of articulation becomes is the poem's repeated gesture of chiasmus.[18]

To take a prominent instance, consider the beguiling closing section of 'Maximus, at Tyre and at Boston', the full extent of which reads:

> that we are only
> as we find out we are
>
> (*MP*, 99)

Poised as it is at the end of a poem which switches historical locations, Olson's phrasing across the line-break issues in many resonances, many forms of feedback. To paraphrase the statement itself, what we are told is that it is in the act of discovery that we become ourselves, that in research we find ourselves anew in the object of our thought. The figure for this mode of understanding is thus appropriately chiasmus, affording the mirrored positioning of the phrase 'we are'. Olson poems often end like this, an enigmatic (if not explicitly chiasmatic) phrasing feeding us back into the processes of the poem. It is the larger resonances that matter, though. Once we hear the chiasmus at work in the basic mode of inquiry, the finding out that is the act of what Olson calls *'istorin*, then we see that in this case the poem's title itself is a feedback loop; 'Maximus, at Tyre and at Boston' describes a state of doubling and historical interaction that results in reflection and continuous re-animation. What we are given to understand, in other words, is that this is in no sense the work of a single view, but of views constantly engaging one another. Another chiastic moment, from 'Maximus, to Gloucester', underscores this point:

> Gloucester can view
> those men
> who saw her
> first
>
> (*MP*, 111)

This moment in the text proceeds a lovely cummings-like sonnet in which John White and his party of fourteen men, of whom eleven are known (making 'twenty-two eyes'), first see and are altered by Gloucester. Hence the first line break in the short passage quoted, Olson's prosody apposing 'Gloucester' to the 'men / who saw her / first', objects among objects in the open field of the poem. The point, though, here, is not to read individual moments of the poem, but to catch the drift of the whole. Thus it is the principle of participating views that necessitates the constant supply of documents, because the documents are consistently reflecting upon one another. What the poem must avoid above all is the situation Stephen Higginson finds at Marblehead, Cape Ann and Portsmouth in 1795: 'No noise. // And no discussion' (*MP*, 80). No chiasmus; no feedback.

No polis, real or imagined, historical or poetic, is beyond feedback. That is, I would want to suggest, part of Olson's point – that we argue, that we participate – but it is also emphatically true that his image of the polis was limited. As Rachel Blau DuPlessis observes in her chapter in this volume, in Olson's epic of human labour there is little or no evidence of women's work. That omission must be underlined, made the subject of critique and annotation. My point here, however, has to do with human movement, the claim being that as he re-imagined the polis in the aftermath of the war, what he sought were forms of thought that pictured and permitted what he called kinetics. This cuts against the localism, the seeming 'emplacedeness' of the poem, but it equally speaks to the work's larger images and trajectories: to the great image of geological migration (provided by Wegener and Wilson) that appeared on the cover of the Fulcrum edition of *Maximus Poems IV, V, VI*; to the fact that the Olson family drama was fundamentally one of arrival.

What Olson could achieve on the scale of *The Maximus Poems*, that he couldn't achieve within the limitations of discursive prose, was an image of the polis as a series of crossings. The crossing is there, as Prynne insists, in the scale of the whole, in the curve of the poem's migration, out and back. It is there, also, in the poem's method, and its imagery of interaction, each object being constantly engaged in and by a field of other objects. Continuous as it is with 'Projective Verse', and with that manifesto's sense of the situation in which it found itself,

The Maximus Poems offers a form of thought which can help us with the thing we are in now: an image of the polis to which the crossing is axiomatic.

Notes

1 Donald Allen (ed.), *The New American Poetry, 1945–1960* (Berkeley, Los Angeles, London: University of California Press, 1999), 448.
2 For a detailed account of Allen's preparation, see Alan Golding, 'The New American Poetry Revisited, Again', *Contemporary Literature* XXXIX:2, 180–211.
3 Publication details of 'The Resistance' are given by Ralph Maud in *A Charles Olson Reader* (Manchester: Carcanet, 2005), 3–4, 213.
4 For a consideration of the physiology of *Call Me Ishmael*, see David Herd, '"From him only will the old State-secret Come": What Charles Olson Imagined', *English*, 59:227, 375–95.
5 For Olson's first use of the term (20 August 1951), see Charles Olson and Robert Creeley, *The Complete Correspondence*, Vol. 7, ed. George Butterick (California: Black Sparrow, 1987), 15.
6 See Miriam Nichols, *Radical Affections: Essays on the Poetics of Outside* (Tuscaloosa, AL: The University of Alabama Press, 2010), 2–5.
7 For the strongest account of the way 'limit' informs Olson's poetic, see Stephen Fredman, *The Grounding of American Poetry: Charles Olson and the Emersonian Tradition* (Cambridge: Cambridge University Press, 1993).
8 Charles Olson, *The Special View of History*, ed. Ann Charters (Berkeley: Oyez, 1970), 25.
9 Ibid.
10 Hannah Arendt, *The Origins of Totalitarianism* (London: George Allen and Unwin Ltd, 1967), xxx.
11 Ibid., xxxi.
12 Ibid., 261.
13 Ibid., 277.
14 Ibid., 297.
15 Giorgio Agamben, *State of Exception*, tr. Kevin Attell (Chicago and London: The University of Chicago Press, 2005), 1–4.
16 J. H. Prynne, 'On *Maximus IV, V, VI*', *Minutes of the Charles Olson Society* 28 (April 1999), 3.
17 Ibid., 6.
18 With reference to various different intellectual contexts, a number of scholars have noted the chiasmatic quality of Olson's thought. See, in particular, Nichols, *Radical Affections*, 6–7.

21

Why Olson did ballet: the pedagogical avant-gardism of Massine

Karlien van den Beukel

In the summer of 1951, Charles Olson returned from Yucátan to teach at Black Mountain. Within days, there was a crisis. A favourite student of Olson's, Nick Cernovich, taught in dance by Katherine Litz, performed a solo which sparked huge interest at the College. Immediately after the event, Olson wrote to his correspondent Robert Creeley:

> My boy Cernovich did for us all his newest dance ... a St Francis. But that doesn't matter. All birds and creatures including the human are, here, left inside the organism of his body in motion. And it is something. The real biz.[1]

Olson was very moved; 'tears, almost out'. Yet the title stuck in his craw. The title of the dance elevated a Christian saint; apostasy to the 'Human Universe' lectures Olson was in the very throws of delivering to the College. After the performance he told Cernovich to get the 'St Francis title to hell and gone'.

That did not go down well. An indignant Olson wrote to Creeley that the 'fucking supercilious' student had gone and attack[ed]the sun-moon narrative of HU [Human Universe]' and while he was at it, had also taken 'a side-swipe' at Olson's poems.[2] Black Mountain colleague and friend, Ben Shahn, supported the student, allegedly intervening with 'I violently disagree' as Olson struck out at the St Francis title.

The solo was based on St Francis of Assisi's poem 'Hymn to the Sun'. Cernovich had danced poems before, notably Olson's 'Pacific Lament' the previous year, but, through his New York friendship with Merce Cunningham, may have learnt of the source for this solo from dance circles.

Olson's reaction took up an entire '8–pager' to Creeley. In the letter, Olson, to whom 'reality is implicitly mythological', assails the origin of blood sacrifice in Abrahamic religions – ad hominem, directed at the Jewish Shahn – in order to celebrate solar worship.[3] It then occurs to Olson that solar worship in ancient Mayan civilisation – the 'Human Universe' source – also involved blood sacrifice, the victim human: 'the cutting out of the heart is as presentation to the sun'.[4] The letter was withheld from Creeley, and later repeatedly referred to as 'the stake or fetish' letter.[5]

The flare-up around Cernovich's dance appears to have been driven by Olson's jealous desire for poetry acolytes. The literary scholar Alan Golding has identified Olson's teaching method as in 'a Poundian tradition of pedagogical avant-gardism'.[6] The idealised trope for this pedagogy – 'sacred knowledge' of poetry is enigmatically conveyed among a homosocial 'coterie audience of initiates' – is the Pythogorean Brotherhood, a trope which is also ciphered into 'Applause', the poem written for Cernovich after his 'St Francis' dance.[7]

While Golding argues Olson 'furthered' Poundian pedagogy by 'locating that pedagogy within an experimental academic institution', at the time it was shown up as problematic, not least by other teaching practices within Black Mountain. Some days after the 'St Francis' dance, Katherine Litz performed Olson's poem 'Glyphs' in college assembly as *The Glyph*, a dance in which she struggles about in a closed sack. Olson exhorted it was a signature piece of abstract kinesis; students enjoyed it as a topical skit. The poet Ed Dorn, also a student at Black Mountain in the summer of 1951, has remarked that:

> [Olson's] great conflict as a teacher was democracy. He got his method from his predecessors, Pound, Eliot, and they were all such fascists. The method was the problem, all knowledge is elite.[8]

The observation is that Olson himself is conflicted on his pedagogic method: a crisis that particularly emerges after the 'St Francis' dance. 'The fetish letter' contained, in his words, 'dangerous passages', where in the poem 'Applause', we find a recurrence of the blood sacrifice motif:

> you show a heart ...
>   to be offered
> to any diorite knife of priest or fool
> until it knows how young it is, how strong...
>   (CP, 229)

The symbolically violent glyph-wielding 'priest or fool', the Poundian pedagogue, is self-reflexively destabilised. 'Applause' (later retitled 'A Man Who Is Not St Francis'), then, offers a dialogic conversation, but also turns to dance as a teaching. In its wake, Olson looks more widely to dance collaborative practice as a pedagogic method. At Black Mountain, modern dance, as Katherine Litz taught it, was based in improvised practice, requiring 'the self-reflexive dramatization of the creative process.'[9] Olson, drawing on his own formative education in dance, begins composing dance plays – *King of the Wood, The Born*

Dancer and *Apollonius of Tyana* – for students (both male and female) to perform at the College. Olson's teaching thus becomes projected into a collaborative practice where the interpretative study of the plays would generate poetic knowledges even as the dance performance would be creatively engendered by the body of Black Mountain students themselves.

The dance, of course, is generative of 'sacred knowledges' in the 'Poundian tradition'. The ontological radiance of the dancer is powerfully configured in high modernist poetics.[10] Pound in 1946, had confided esoteric mysteries to Olson: of the Russian ballerina Astafieva – her 'spermatopyros' dance: 'come down from Byzantium, the making of the seed of life, it turning into fire';[11] of Yeats, and of T. S. Eliot, who had seen Massine as the luminous manifestation of the poetics of impersonality: 'the great dancer ... of the Russian School ... is ... a vital flame, that impersonal and if you like, inhuman force'.[12]

The avatar redux – Olson on Cernovich: 'he dances with a knowledge of the sun'[13] – radiates, summons up the knowledge of the poets in early modernism. In subject matter, the adapted dance plays – *King of the Wood* (Frazer), *Apollonius of Tyana* (G. R. S. Mead) *The Born Dancer* (Nijinsky) – draw on early modernist sources (anthropology, theosophy, Ballets Russes) even as the dance poetics of modernism is radically reinterpreted.

It was Olson's prompt, 'I told him of my premier and what I had done with Massine and Platoff', which sparked off Pound's recollection.[14] Olson himself is reprompted by Cernovich, the man who is not St Francis. Actually, it was Marc Platoff who was St Francis – and in the apotheosis 'Hymn to the Sun' – in the Massine Hindemith ballet *St Francis* in 1940, the year Olson was a company dancer in the Ballet Russe de Monte Carlo.[15]

During the late 1930s, Olson had been remarkably educated in dance by Massine himself, acquiring inside knowledge of the choreographic practice of narrative ballet in the Ballet Russe. The mysteries, plain journeyman work. It can be seen in the scope of register in his dance plays – from light comic sketches to major innovative work – patterned on that of 1930s Ballet Russe repertory. The production notes in the dance plays also evidence Olson's working knowledge of theatre dance. In *The Born Dancer* – 'a ballet' – he gives instructions on how to revive dance roles from Diaghilev-era choreographed ballets, while also gnomically reprising some figures of 1930s dance political history.

Massine's pedagogical avant-gardism, then, may be a significant precedent for Olson's teaching in the dance plays. The difficulty is that Massine's democratisation of ballet not only diverges considerably from, but is also erased by the very modernist aesthetic ideology that had drawn attention to him as an exemplary luminary. That Massine took (a not *danse d'ecole* material) Olson under his wing may be a case in point. Thus, it is through the poet's own formative experiences that we may best gain insight into Massine's pedagogy.

Olson first learnt of ballet by reading Lincoln Kirstein's *Hound & Horn*. Kirstein's master narrative of classical dance, structured on T. S. Eliot's 'Tradition and the Individual Talent', grandly swept from the ballet's origins in the royal courts of Europe to Massine as one of the great innovative choreographers in *danse d'ecole*. As ballet was still exclusively a European high art theatre form, it was only in 1936, when the international Ballet Russe de Monte Carlo toured the United States, that Olson first saw ballet performed.

Following the company by railway from Boston, to Providence, to Worcester, he absorbed ballet repertory by attending every local performance. Somewhere along the way, he befriended Marc Platoff, whose name was Russified when he'd joined the Ballet Russe as the company's first American dancer in Seattle the year before. Platoff introduced Olson to the Ballet Russe's artistic director, Massine, who 'was not only a dancer, not only a choreographer, but also a teacher'.[16]

Massine's teaching, for all its informal contingencies, would have been anticipated as academic dance scholarship. Primed by his *Hound & Horn* reading, Olson would have regarded the imperial ballet-trained Massine as the embodiment of the autotelic discipline of ballet: 'the whole of the literature' is felt in 'the bones', making for the 'acute' consciousness of 'contemporaneity'.[17] The materiality of dance, residing in physical gesture, is accessed by kinetic memory. Edwin Denby remarked in a contemporaneous review: '[Massine] is an encyclopedia of ballet, character, speciality, period, and even of formulas from modern German dancing.'[18]

When Massine taught Olson, however, he began by drawing out habitus – environment, history, literature and everyday social practice – in the students:

> In his talks with us, he wanted us to tell him all we could about America – Melville, Whitman, Mark Twain, about our history, our rivers, our mountains, whatever we were proud of, all we could tell him. In turn, he taught us about painting and music, about movement and form and silence and repose.[19]

Place, for the dancer, is 'his given, as a first fact'.[20] The dancers connect into 'what is native to themselves, even the places, heroes and gods local to their neighborhoods', where the dance could take any scope, the residual rhythm is telling.[21] The retrospective implies that this very fluid conversational exchange informs the primacy of the local in Olson's later poetics.

In 1940, Massine asked for Olson to be given a Ballet Russe company contract. This extended his education into performance practice. After several weeks rehearsing with the company, Olson premiered in a surrealist costume by Chanel in the Freudian dreamscape *Bachannale* at the Boston Opera House. Platoff was in the lead, a Dalí the backdrop. Denby, reviewing Massine's *Bacchanale,* noted the ballet 'was a kind of charade',[22] a cryptic game or a ceremonial pretence, where Olson's own untitled role – variously reported as 'a dreaming giant',[23] 'a tree',[24] and even 'he said he carried a spear'[25] – seems an enigmatic cipher Massine choreographed into the ballet. The movement Massine choreographed for Olson was 'to amble on ... and lie down full length on the stage for a time'.[26]

This movement – repeated by Tyana in *Apollonius* – is not in the idiom of classic ballet.[27] This is significant, not because it would single out the figurante, but, rather, because it is reflective of the diverse range of dance backgrounds of the *Bachannale* principal dancers around him: Platoff was trained in American modern dance; Frederic Franklin had started out with Josephine Baker at the Casino de Paris, the Indonesian-born Nini Theliade joined the company after appearing in Reinhardt's film *Midsummer Night's Dream.*

Edwin Denby observed: 'Massine deserves the greatest praise for the company he has chosen'.[28] Yet this diversity, if expressed in ballet performance, is a complete anathema to the ideology of the formal aesthetic of dance classicism. The classic technique, *danse d'ecole,* as Lincoln Kirstein had emphasised, was rigorously maintained by the Russian School of Imperial Ballet. 'The developed classical ballet is a powerful modern weapon articulated by its amplification of an ancient language.'[29] Kirstein had launched his own 'academy' with the imperial ballet-trained Balanchine in New York in 1935, in order to achieve 'a similar consistent discipline for the native American stock'.[30]

Even as Kirstein was promoting 'unity' of classic technique to form a national ballet, Massine was interested in 'diversity' of dance in ballet. His ballets, then, were not invariably choreographed in the classic idiom. *St Francis* (1938), notably, was choreographed in the modern dance idiom. The idea for the ballet – St Francis's 'Hymn to the Sun' celebrates the sanctity of all life – had been the composer's, Hindemith, whose work was banned in the Third Reich. In choreographing *St Francis*, Massine set the title role on Marc Platoff – who had been taught the Martha Graham technique in Seattle – where Massine then first danced the role in public performance. 'Unorthodox in subject matter, elevated in tone, and revolutionary in its choreographic procedure', the ballet was particularly appreciated in America, where modern dance flourished natively as high art form.[31]

By 1940, when Marc Platoff danced the title role in performance, the war had broken out. The Ballet Russe was now stranded in the United States. The new ballets the company produced would necessarily be for an American audience. Massine's 1934 *Union Pacific*, with a libretto by Archibald MacLeish, had been the first international ballet with an American story and dance idiom, while in 1939, Platoff, by now a principal dancer, was invited to choreograph the Ballet Russe's first American-produced ballet, *Ghost Town*. Platoff's retrospective memoir too illuminates the significance of habitus in Massine's method, but then also, the difficulties Massine himself had, away from Europe.[32] Americans – composers, librettists, artists – would need to do collaborative dance production. In giving Olson a company contract in 1940, it may be that Massine intuited a poet, with the scale of a *Moby-Dick* libretto in him, but who needed more experience in dance production. In the event, that potential would never be realised within the Ballet Russe itself.[33]

The war had provided leverage to Lincoln Kirstein's project and he persuaded major financial and critical backers to shift their capital from the stranded Ballet Russe into his own New York Balanchine-directed ballet company. The choreographic work was indisputably powerful. By 1942, even Ballet Russe management were in secret negotiation with Kirstein to get the Balanchine works into their repertory.[34] Massine, sidelined, resigned from the company. His ballets were immediately dropped from repertory, never revived since. Balanchine's work, what Kirstein called 'the ore of immediate lyric truth,' came to define 'American ballet': the formal aesthetic of abstract neoclassicism.[35]

'The dance, to key it: it is a wide investigation into the local, the occasional, what you may even call the ceremonial.'[36] Massine's teaching, the poet's own formative experiences of it in the 1930s, then, is central to the dance philosophy in *Apollonius of Tyana*. This dance play is the most important of the plays that Olson was writing in 1951, as he sought to move his Black Mountain College teaching from Poundian pedagogy into dance collaborative production. True, Massine's choreography of Olson's 'premier' ('how to dance / sitting down') is an enigmatic initiate ritual of the highest order, but it does have its wits about it. A spirit of democracy seems to return to Olson. After the withheld 'fetish letter' on the St Francis dance, Olson writes to Creeley:

> I had promised Nick I would do a work with him this summer, and this week, together we had worked out this idea – it is a use of Apollonius of Tyana.[37]

The sources for all Olson's 1951 dance plays come from early modernist knowledges (Pound's Apollonius in Canto XCIV, itself sourced in the theosophical study by G. R. S. Mead). Apollonius, however, first appears in the poem 'Applause' ('A Man Who Is Not St. Francis') addressed to Nick Cernovich:

> no prayer
> except as prayer is solely as we speak to one another and are heard
> as he listens who is clean of slaughter and of pantomime...
> the beauty here
> is methodological
>
> (CP, 228)

The prayer line alludes to the only words directly attributable to Apollonius of Tyana himself, as cited in Mead.[38] The idea for the dance play *Apollonius*, then, comes after Cernovich's 'Hymn to the Sun' dance, which sparks off the idea of Apollonius, whose spiritual teaching can be identified with by the dancer, yet offers a radical model beyond the blood sacrifice of 'Christism' (and ancient Mayan civilisation).

'Together we had worked out this idea.' In the dance play, then, Nick Cernovich was to dance the title role, Apollonius, and Olson 'to be Tyana, the word or speaking part.'[39] Just as Massine set the title role of 'St Francis' on Platoff, so Olson sets the title role of 'Apollonius' on Cernovich. Apollonius is, of course, completely embodied in the textual narrative; that is, in Olson's 'word part'. Yet Apollonius is envisioned as a dancer and, specifically, Cervonich's 'Hymn to the Sun' dance ('not mimesis but kinesis ... is its base') would be the impetus for creating live performance.[40] While there was the discussion of a collaboration, these dance plays were actually not produced at Black Mountain. In the poem 'Applause' ('A Man Who Is Not St Francis') there is reference to dance:

> it does not matter; each of us
> has to clear himself of his own materials, to resist
> an overfondness for his source, for title
> drawn by any other court of deed than he himself
>
> It comes to this, to the simplest: are the appearances not
> what it is, is it not exactly what it looks like?
>
> (CP, 226)

So what exactly does the 'Hymn to the Sun' dance look like? The simplest: do it to know. Yet this is a reflective issue; immediately concerned with Cernovich's practice, where dance historical perspectives may recover the dance. At the time, there was also another observer to this dance, Katherine Litz, and Olson writes:

She takes the Cernovich dance as too pantomimic (which tells me, she doesn't yet know, the kinetic accomplishment, when she sees it) is, that, it is almost art, is, too poised.[41]

Litz's own dance practice was based in pure movement, the physical properties of the body signifying the meaning of its own materiality.[42] She apparently saw Cernovich's dance as 'too pantomimic', so mimetically expressive of a dramatic narrative, the life of the saint. In seeing it as 'almost art, is, too poised', Litz may be recalling the Graham technique which the 1938 Massine ballet *St Francis* was based on. For Olson, that ballet was the memory through which Cernovich's dance is observed as 'kinetic accomplishment'. If we turn to Paul Hindemith's notes on the final scene, the apotheosis, of the Massine Hindemith ballet *St Francis*, we find that:

> Here all symbolic personifications of heavenly and earthly existence mingle in the course of the different variations through which the six-measure theme of the passacaglia is transformed.[43]

Compare this to Olson on Cernovich's dance: 'All birds and creatures including the human are, here, left inside the organism of his body in motion.' The later 'Hymn to the Sun' dance allows for the visual memory of the apotheosis in the earlier Massine *St Francis* ballet.

Edwin Denby, a detractor of this ballet, observed: 'St Francis seems ... a parody of an illuminated Book of Hours ... with a grand finale of anthroposophic chorus girls.'[44] To the cold pragmatic eye, then, the ballet is pantomiming a devotional literary work. Interestingly, theosophy is manifested in the Byzantine expressionist modern dance of the choric production line. Critics who noted that the ballet was 'revolutionary in its choreographic procedure' observe the apotheosis as 'the hands of the dancers seem to leave their bodies, mute, like birds taking flight'.[45] This also observes mimesis, but it construes that the working masses – 'the hands' – rise up in the faith of the sanctity of life. The dramatic narrative ballet then, conveyed complex meaning through mimesis. For Olson, the 'mingling' of 'the symbolic personifications of heavenly and earthly existence' would be also associated with the dance in modernist poetics. Consider, for example, T. S. Eliot's 'The Death of St. Narcissus' (1915), a poem in which the saint undergoes three incarnations – 'tree' to 'fish' to 'girl' – where each is caught, a 'continual self-sacrifice': 'So he became a dancer to God.' In the lines from 'Applause':

> But what I see is no such thing, no sacred ring achieved, no mixing
> with any other thing, nor man, fish, god or beast
>
> (CP, 228)

The kinetic dance, then, necessarily cannot be mediated in metaphoric language: or, to cite Yeats on the dancer in 'Byzantium': 'Those images that yet / Fresh images beget'. In Olson's writing of Cernovich's dance, kinesis is worked through into the poetics:

> Your knowing
> is of an order of the blood permitting
> breath to blow back any feathers of a bird without worrying
> how he speaks, the wading man to note without identification
> the consensual fish which swims in the shallow water like his feet,
> to kneel to pick raspberries in the difficult place that woods are....
>
> (CP, 228)

The dance is an ecological meditation. Through dance kinesis – the modern dance as taught at Black Mountain – the dance poetics of modernism are radically reinterpreted. The place is very far removed from the Ballet Russe, but then it was Massine who wanted 'us to tell him all we could about ... our rivers, our mountains, all we could tell him.'

Notes

1 Letter July 15, 1951, in Charles Olson and Robert Creeley, *The Complete Correspondence* Vol.6, ed. George Butterick (Santa Barbara: Black Sparrow Press, 1985), 137.
2 Ibid, 139–40.
3 Ibid, 145.
4 Ibid, 142.
5 The 'stake or fetish' appears in a letter dated 17 July 1951. Olson and Creeley, *Correspondence*, Vol. 6, 147. In a letter dated 22 July 1951, Olson wrote to Creeley: 'It's beginning to be historic, isn't it, that document!! which, still, none one has seen but me! not even you!!!)' (Olson and Creeley, *Correspondence*, Vol.6, 177).
6 Alan Golding, 'From Pound to Olson: the avant-garde poet as pedagogue', *Journal of Modern Literature* 34:1, 2010, 86–106.
7 Ibid., 98.
8 Quoted in Tom Clark, *Charles Olson: The Allegory of a Poet's Life* (Berkeley: North Atlantic Books, 2000), 209.
9 Daniel Belgrad, *The Culture of Spontaneity: Improvisation and the Arts in Postwar America* (Chicago: University of Chicago Press, 1999), 159.
10 See Frank Kermode, *Romantic Image* (London: Routledge and Kegan Paul, 1957).
11 Catharine Seelye (ed.), *Charles Olson and Ezra Pound: An Encounter at St Elizabeths* (New York: Grossman, 1975), 79.
12 T. S. Eliot, 'Four Elizabethan Dramatists. 1. A Preface', *Criterion* II (Feb. 1924), 115–23. For a fuller account of Eliot and Massine, see Terri A. Mester, *Movement and Modernism: Yeats, Eliot, Lawrence, Williams and*

Early Twentieth Century Dance (Fayetteville: University of Arkansas Press, 1997), 74–6.
13 Letter 15 July 1951, Olson and Creeley, *Correspondence*, Vol. 6, 147.
14 Seelye (ed.), *An Encounter at St Elizabeths*), 79.
15 Massine was principal dancer and choreographer in Diaghilev's Ballets Russes (1909–29). For an account, see Lynn Garafola, *Diaghilev's Ballets Russes* (Oxford: Oxford University Press, 1989). In the diaspora of the company after the Diaghilev era, Massine became principal dancer and choreographer in de Basil's Ballets Russes de Monte Carlo (1932–8). The company split, and thereafter, Denham managed the Ballet Russe de Monte Carlo with Massine as artistic director (1938–42), while de Basil formed the Original Ballet Russe. See the documentary film *Ballets Russes* (2006) directed by Dayna Goldfine and Dan Geller (New York: Zeitgeist Films) for the 1930s 'Ballet Russe' era, with interviews of surviving principal dancers (including Marc Platoff) of the Ballet Russe de Monte Carlo. For a detailed analysis of Massine's ballets, see Leslie Norton, *Léonide Massine and the Twentieth Century Ballet* (Jefferson: McFarland, 2004). In the essay, I have followed Edwin Denby's convention of using 'Ballet Russe' when referring to the 1930s companies formed after the diaspora of the Diaghilev era 'Ballets Russes'.
16 John Finch, 'Dancer and Clerk', *The Massachusetts Review* 12:1 (Winter 1971), 34–40. As Olson's fellow traveller to the Ballet Russe, John Finch's retrospective is the major first-hand account of Olson in the ballet.
17 T. S. Eliot, 'Tradition and the Individual Talent', *Selected Essays* (London: Faber and Faber, 1932), 14.
18 Edwin Denby, Review for *Modern Music* (Nov–Dec 1936), in *Dance Writings*, ed. Robert Cornfield and William MacKay (London: Dance Books, 1986), 40.
19 Finch, 'Dancer and Clerk', 37–8.
20 Charles Olson, *Apollonius of Tyana* in *The Fiery Hunt and Other Plays*, ed. George Butterick (Bolinas: Four Seasons Foundation, 1977), 72.
21 Olson, *The Fiery Hunt*, 75.
22 Denby, Review for *Modern Music* (Oct–Nov 1939), *Dance Writings*, 60.
23 'Massine rehearsed Charlie in the part. He was to amble on, taller than a dream giant' (Finch, 'Dancer and Clerk', 38).
24 'Olson told the editor in conversation in 1968 he was dressed as a tree' (George Butterick, 'Introduction', *The Fiery Hunt*, xxi).
25 Olson told Connie Wilcock and her sister in 1940 that 'he had signed up for the Ballet Russe because he wanted the experience of meeting ballet personnel and of knowing life backstage.' Afterward, he told them: 'He was a member of the chorus and carried a spear!' Jane Atherton, 'Memories of Charles Olson', *Minutes of the Charles Olson Society* 31 and 32, September 1999.
26 Finch, 'Dancer and Clerk', 38.
27 'Tyana swings to easy reclining position, indolent, you may say, lying like a confident thing, on one elbow, and watching all the movements of the dancer' (Olson, *The Fiery Hunt*, 58).

28 Denby, 'Massine and the New Monte Carlo', Review for *Modern Music* (Nov–Dec 1938), *Dance Writings*, 51.
29 Lincoln Kirstein, *Dance: A Short History of Theatrical Classical Dancing* (New York: G.P. Putnam, 1935), 327.
30 Ibid., 325.
31 John Martin, *New York Times* (October 1938) cited in Vincente García-Márquez, *Massine: A Biography* (London: Nick Hern, 1996), 266.
32 Marc Platt (aka Marc Platoff) and Renée Renouf, '"Ghost Town" Revisited: A Memoir of Producing an American Ballet for the Ballet Russe de Monte Carlo', *Dance Chronicle* 24:2 (2001), 147–92.
33 Olson's first dance play, *The Fiery Hunt* (1948), based on *Moby-Dick*, was commissioned by Erick Hawkins for the Martha Graham Company but never produced.
34 For different accounts see García-Márquez, *Massine*, 289, 306–7; Martin Duberman, *The Worlds of Lincoln Kirstein* (Evanston: Northwestern University Press, 2008), 371–2.
35 Kirstein, *Dance*, 327.
36 Olson, *The Fiery Hunt*, 69
37 Letter 22 July 1951, Olson and Creeley, *Correspondence*, Vol. 6, 178.
38 'We men should ask the best of beings through the best thing in us, for what is good – I mean by means of mind, for mind needs no material things to make its prayer.' Apollonius cited in G. R. S. Mead, *Apollonius of Tyana: The Philosopher Explorer and Social Reformer of the First Century AD* (London and Benarcs: Theosophical Publishing Society, 1901), 46.
39 Letter 27 July 1951, Olson to Creeley, *Correspondence*, Vol. 6, 210.
40 Olson, *The Fiery Hunt*, 73.
41 Letter 15 July 1951, Olson and Creeley, *Correspondence*, Vol. 6, 146.
42 Belgrad, *Culture of Spontaneity*, 159.
43 Cited in *Boston Symphony Orchesta Concert Programs*, Seventy-First Season (1951–2), 502.
44 Denby, 'Massine and the New Monte Carlo', Review for *Modern Music* (Nov–Dec 1938), *Dance Writings*, 53.
45 Cited in García-Márquez, *Massine*, 266.

22

On the back of the elephant: riding with Charles Olson

Iain Sinclair

I have a theory by which I try, but fail, to live: which is that at this stage in life I don't want to go anywhere I can't walk.[1] This presented problems when I was exploring America, which I've been doing for a book I've been working on, and which I'll be drawing into this discourse; a book called *American Smoke: Journeys to the End of the Light*. What it's about is the fact that when I began, when I was firing up my first enthusiasms in the early 1960s, I was captured by the figure of Charles Olson and the whole Black Mountain School of writers. Earlier, as a schoolboy, I'd become engrossed in Kerouac, by way of a chance gift of that gaudy paperback original, *Maggie Cassidy*. I hadn't appreciated that these legendary beings lived a short drive away from each other in that same early-settled corner of the New World. Lowell and Gloucester are geographically close, working cities engaged in very different kinds of work: one a mill town on a powerful river, the Merrimack, and the other a historically important fishing port.

The two figures, alive and dead, haunted me. I think now of the title of a late poem by Ed Dorn, 'The Deceased are the Travellers Among Us', and as an extension of that provocative notion, a phrase from *The Undiscovered Country* by Carl Watkins, 'The soul in purgatory was a traveller passing through, not a permanent resident.'[2] Olson and Kerouac would argue over the implications of residence and mobility, the great American neurosis about the daunting scale of the place where they found themselves, between Atlantic Ocean and the always difficult but seductive draw of the West. I was fascinated by the notion of the bad journey, towards Mexico or Alaska, volcano or ghost town from the Californian gold rush. So I kept returning to that little mustard-yellow booklet put out in England by Cape Goliard Press in 1966: *West*.[3] 'Men are only known in memory,' Olson says (*CP*, 595). At the conclusion of the adventure of any expedition, physical or in language, there must be a resolving image. In this Olson poem, it's a beauty:

>   one lone Indian
> fishing in the river at the bottom of
> the Barranca del cobre
>
> (CP, 600)

The mentoring by our elected forefathers is significant. In 1975, through my own small press, I published a book called *Lud Heat*.[4] Here, at the time of a period of employment as a gardener in the riverside reaches of East London, was my crude attempt to register an allegiance to Olson. The book opens with a tag from Yeats, 'The living can assist the imagination of the dead',[5] which became my working credo. I was cutting the grass around Hawksmoor churches and plotting alignments between significant London buildings, seeing the streams of history as a plurality rather than as a series of laminated notice-boards copy-written by hacks for the benefit of dubious political and sub-civic entities.

I should make it clear at the start of this discussion that I'm guided by Olsonian principles, which is to say I'm going to digress, professionally, by intention, one image following directly on the heels of another. But, unlike Olson, I won't go on for four hours or four days, that's the only difference. Draw breath and strike out, sink or swim. Follow the figure of the dance, as David Herd has identified it: between the force fields of physiology and geo-politics.[6]

London's an odd place just now, and coming onto the road, to find my way to Canterbury, is launching into another hallucinatory trip. Keeping an eye on traffic, on stalled civil engineering projects, and rehearsing what I might, usefully, say, I listened to a CD provided by Colin Still. It was a CD of Black Mountain poet Ed Dorn and he's reading *Idaho Out*. So here you have a beatific superimposition of English roads and the madness of escaping traffic and warnings of winds as you cross the bridge over the Medway, and, at the same time, this *live* voice with its astringent and witty take on the politics of being in America. And again, it's worth remarking, the recordings were made by English enthusiasts. The book from which the readings are taken is published in London by Dr Stuart Montgomery's very useful Fulcrum Press. 'History has always seemed to me lying right on the table,' Dorn says.[7] Here are poems about the inauguration of Johnson, poems about the landscape of Idaho, the Shoshone, all of these things in play. Howard Hughes appearing in *Gunslinger*. It's disorientating to know that you can be following the classic English pilgrimage route to Canterbury voiced by a kindly ghost sitting alongside you, recalling his days venturing into Kent. 'Slightly disappointed,' Dorn wrote, 'from thence to Croydon.' There were once proper transatlantic bridges on offer. In the 1960s, we were fortunate that writers like Dorn and Tom Clark were based in Colchester at Essex University; poets like Andrew Crozier and John Temple were going to Buffalo; there were proper exchanges.

My instinct, having worked through that engagement with local sub-cultures and topographies, and the tramp around London's orbital motorway, was to step right away and in my old age, my biblical allotment of years rapidly approaching, to go back – or to make an imaginative return, if such a thing is possible, to the sites I had been reading about in fugitive magazines and booklets. Gloucester, Massachusetts, was as fabulous as Homer's Troy; it was a familiar mystery not an achievable bus stop. Now, by the accident of launching out on a new book, I was there. *Physically*. In October rain. I was staying in a writer's hut that had formerly been occupied by the poet Vincent Ferrini, the person to whom Olson addresses the *Maximus* sequence by way of an impassioned correspondence. 'Write to me,' he ordered, 'and tell me how my streets are' (*SL*, 106). Already he is laying claim to the territory of the poem. He's not even in Gloucester, the first *Maximus* poems are coming out of Black Mountain College. Ferrini is embedded in the fishing town, he's working as a picture framer. I think his marriage has broken up. He's lodged in a small roadside hut, a step away from the harbour. For a couple of weeks, I must live with this man's leather hat on the wall, with all of his books and CDs, with the actual heat and smell of his presence; how the guy moved through the tight space, how he slept on this bed and went over to the kitchen and the bathroom. There were also a lot of photographs and blackboard scribblings related to Olson, so I experience a double hit that is overwhelming. The ghosts do argue: the rough demotic of the street and the high cast of Olson's ever-expanding mythology. Under a low roof, in a site of complete specificity, the starry ceiling of Olson's over-reach is present. The *sound* of those Camel cigarettes, as Dorn reports, being whaled at a gulp.

And then I realized that what Olson was working toward was the idea of the chart: if you saw the room where he lived in Gloucester, in Fort Square, the wall was covered with maps, poems, false starts, picture postcards. Prompts and potentialities. Dead ends. A demonstration, before his own eyes, of the theory of open field poetics. The sifting of hard evidence. You have to make the jump back to Kerouac, his notebooks, the scroll he produced for *On the Road* (exhibited recently in the British Library). An enormous teletype roll, taped together, no paragraph breaks, real names for characters. This relic is a virtual road; a map of simultaneity with everything happening at once, like a Chinese painting from the museum in Seattle. A form of paper cinema much closer to Kerouac's primary intention than the recent fancy travelogue by Walter Salles, that abortive and posthumous translation of the big book. Blocks of hot type become a flowing river. There is no room to fake anything. The dynamic carries you tight against the margin. Kerouac starts firing out ellipses like Céline, to keep up – in a way approved by Olson – with the pace of thought. The author disappears into the text. Publication aborts the purity of the original form and brings a level of fame and intrusion that Kerouac is incapable of handling. He dies of celebrity, a few inches from a 24-hour TV set in Florida retirement, before he reaches the age of fifty. In his mother's house.

I have to start by trying to shape this Gloucester interlude as a classic Olsonian journey, a push out from the shore and then a turn back to land. If the two movements of *The Maximus Poems* are that: the first volume, looking at the sea, dedicated to the 'figure of outward', Robert Creeley, and examining the economics of the fishing trade; then the second sweep coming back into Gloucester itself, the condition of coast having an ambiguous status, between the infinity of ocean and the density of the land and its histories.

I want to say something about Dogtown, which is this area behind the settlement of Gloucester, now a scatter of glacial erratics mixed with the ruins of the original villages, the cellar holes and debris of an attempt to dig in. An extraordinary and haunting place, of which I formed no true picture from my earlier reading. *American Smoke* is about a halting excursion into my own youth, my enthusiasms, my invented geographies. And the figures who inhabit those places.

I start where I want to finish. And I'll give you the key. I want to read that Olson poem, 'MAXIMUS FROM DOGTOWN – II' which comes from *Maximus IV, V, VI*. I think what is important to have in mind is what Jeremy Prynne talked about in a lecture in 1971 at Simon Fraser University; it stops you short, the idea that *Maximus* is a simple poem coming from a complicated man. How does he put it? 'The poem is simple, but the life it came out of, and the pre-occupations that surround it, immeasurably dense and confused and packed with a kind of fertile obscurity.'[8] And the notion really is that life, as the thing that we're given, that ribbon of being, is an allegory – which is how Tom Clark pitches it in his biography of Olson. A large and potent myth. A novel using the elements of a man's history creatively, balancing research against memory and improvisation. With all the attendant risks. Olson quotes this from Keats: 'Man's life of any worth is a continuous allegory'. He's actively looking for the metaphor and he's also paying his respects, his love, to the place where he happens to have come to ground. This is 'MAXIMUS FROM DOGTOWN – II', just hold it as a chart of things that we will try to connect up later.

        the Sea – turn yr Back on

> the Sea, go inland, to
> Dogtown: the Harbor
>
> the shore the City
> are now
> shitty, as the Nation
>
> is – the World
> tomorrow
>
> (*MP*, 179)

And again that later passage:

> the greater the water you add
> the greater the decomposition
> so long as the agent is protein
> the carbon of four is the corners
>
> in stately motion to sing in high bitch voices the fables
> of wood and stone and man and woman loved
>
> and loving in the snow
> and sun
> > the weather
>
> > on Dogtown
> > is protogonic but the other side of heaven
> > is Ocean
>
> (*MP*, 180)

That is so strong and so direct in its terms. You can see how Olson loves signs and shapes, how he responds to Mayan glyphs, spends time in Yucatan trying to find a language that's also a mark of energy. Olson contrives his theory of what he calls 'Projective Verse' as a strike at the physicality of writing which is also a measured defence of his own practice. Kerouac composes, in a sort of neighbourly rivalry, his own *Essentials of Spontaneous Prose*: you must not revise or self-censor. Let it pour, image following image, through the draw of breath. Although, when I was in the Harry Ransom Humanities Research Center in Austin, Texas, I saw Kerouac's work journal at the time of the composition of *On the Road*, from the late 1940s, and he's counting how many words he's done a day and he's revising and agonising and weighing up, even though the actual composition when it comes is a great rush – fuelled, as it apparently was, by copious infusions of caffeine. There is that kind of remorseless, look-no-hands, surging torrential aspect to it. Kerouac feels that he must try to incorporate *everything*. He's noticing and connecting and digressing and consciously repeating himself, building up a rhythm: like and utterly unlike Olson. Olson said at one point that Kerouac was the finest writer in America. And Kerouac for his part was jealous of Olson's scholarship, his academic status, the fact that this large man has been able to take on the town of Gloucester and create a mythology of place in a way that Jack wants to do with Lowell but never quite pulls off. Kerouac, through sentiment, and sensory recall, is closer to someone like Dylan Thomas. His recasting of Lowell in *Dr Sax* is a haunted memoir of childhood, in which the industrial town is personalised, made into a sump of origin and immigration and gothic shadows.

What Olson thinks of as history is the amniotic fluid through which he's swimming and struggling. He is a person who, unlike Kerouac, has been positioned in the body of political life of America. He starts out teaching at Harvard. He actually tutors the Kennedy boys and finds Jack dim. He can't see what they're doing there, I mean they turn up at Harvard with manservants. They do a little swimming and hire somebody to fudge their term papers. Then Olson is in Washington working for the Democrats: he knows how the system operates. And, when he's in Washington, he takes the opportunity to visit the disgraced Ezra Pound who is locked away in the asylum at St Elizabeth's for all those years. He makes regular visits and debates the form and reach of the modernist epic: how far back you need to go, beyond the Greeks. More significantly, and this is the breaking point, there is the collision with Pound's rancid prejudices. And then Olson goes down to Florida where he's spending time in a property once occupied by Ernest Hemingway. He's writing his book on Melville and *Moby-Dick*, *Call Me Ishmael*, which uses some spectacular original research. He digs out the volumes that were in Melville's library, he deciphers annotations. He makes a number of major discoveries. And, by way of this activity, is invited to meet John Huston in Hollywood, to hold discussions about a potential *Moby-Dick* film. Huston is quite enthusiastic and they get as far as floating a model whale in the studio tank. Unfortunately, it keeps sinking. Jack Warner, who's on holiday in the south of France, comes back and says, 'Kill the fucking fish'. And that was the end of that. Seven years later *Moby-Dick* does get made, but now the screenplay is by Ray Bradbury, the science fiction writer, and Olson is gone. Olson is connected in all these ways.

The push is towards Sacramento, and the idea of the West, the gold fields. 'I was writing,' Olson said, 'about the distance / between Sacramento / and the old old West' (*CP*, 600). Which was, as he read it, one of the crucial American themes or stories. So it's not just the Gloucester voyage of the fishing fleets and the colonists, out into ocean, there's the push west; the fact of unknowable space.

In the mid-60s, Olson comes to London with the notion of getting himself to Dorchester, in the West Country, to research John White and the impetus behind the founding of the settlement in Gloucester. He wanted to look at mercantile records in the museum. This is where the Olson biography intersects, in a very accidental way, with my own: he was staying in the house of a wealthy patron of the arts, a lively and interesting woman called Panna Grady. She had taken this house on Hanover Terrace, alongside Regent's Park. Olson, a former lover, had been upstairs for several months, beached and restless. Now Allen Ginsberg and his small entourage occupied the summerhouse. In July 1967, I turned up at the door, a very youthful and innocent figure, to ask Ginsberg if he would be part of a film I'd been commissioned to do about the Dialectics of Liberation at the Roundhouse in Camden. I'm having this preliminary conversation with no knowledge of Olson's relation with the house and with Panna Grady. I don't find that out until much later. I only set eyes on Olson one time, in the Queen Elizabeth Hall, where he's reading with Stephen Spender and Auden and all those people, and he refuses to go down onto the stage. He is sitting up in the audience, and he happens to sit right alongside me. The person next to me says, 'You can't leave him in the aisle, give him your chair.' So I get up. We only exchange two or three words: that was our only engagement in this life. And of course he is led down to the stage, reluctantly, and he reads. He doesn't like this reading because it is too formal, not open-ended. He stumbles and starts a number of times.

While he's with Panna Grady in London, he has conversations with Ginsberg, and also with Burroughs, who visits the Hanover Terrace house. There is a tremendous interchange of energies, a testing of ideas. Olson says that history's over, because he has come to that point. He's using the term postmodernism before anyone else – but it's not that ironic thing, like eggcups on TV studio roofs. It's not the modernism of Pound and Eliot; he's gone beyond that. Ginsberg and the Beats are fascinated. What Olson is proposing is another form of activity called *'istorin*, which is what you can find for yourself: the history of any event is how you came to this room, how you think, what you bring with you, all of that. Ginsberg gave me his understanding of those conversations with Olson:

> Olson declared that history was ended – in the sense that what we know of history is only what we know of images left behind. Those images were an abstraction from the actual event, so history was just another poem, as interpreted by those poets, some of them bum poets, who happened to be around. And now there has been a change of consciousness – to include *event* as part of the abstraction of history. And electronic eavesdropping equipment, now in its primitive stage, will ultimately develop

so that anybody can tune in on the president, can get into his bathroom through laser beams. Which means that all secrets are out.[9]

So there we were with Charles Olson and his special sense of history, spreading right out, infiltrating English culture – and at the same time as this, extraordinarily, the English poet who is our leading Olsonian of the period, and who is supplying Olson with research materials and helping with the editing and sourcing of *Maximus*, Jeremy Prynne, was actually in Olson's flat in Fort Square in Gloucester. He's writing poems on Olson's typewriter. So you have fertile conjunctions going on without anybody being really aware of it. The visit to Olson is a rite of passage for young English poets of a particular dispensation. But, spiritually, emotionally, Olson is in a winter decline. He's back in Gloucester but the world around him has changed, and continues to change; the fishing industry is in decline, the economic bite is already visible. Can audiences be found for the great poem of place he's struggling to deliver?

Ed Dorn has this beautiful statement: 'Only writers are real.' Of course I agree, completely, and I think the world is dividing into zones where writers are real because they have been condemned by some Faustian contract into brokering discriminations of love in the world – while other enclosed and invaded zones are given over to politicians promoting non-human entities, CGI terrains fit only for cyber-people. The public men are so smooth, they've trained themselves to absorb consensus, the opinions of others. They have no morality of their own, beyond immediate gratification. They are weeping and apologising for everything that's nothing to do with them, anything that's happened twenty or thirty years ago. They'll apologise for the War of the Roses and the Black Death but ignore Iraq and Afghanistan.

Olson is locked away in his cabin in Gloucester, in Fort Square; a community of Sicilian fisherman looking out over a working harbour. It is a period of limbo for both men, Olson and Kerouac, and for America, when they do, finally, contrive a meeting.

> Olson was avid for conversation, the audience that Kerouac could never be. They held the door open and Jack crawled from the car. There were newspapers spread up the slippery steps, a welcome mat for a literary cardinal. The Lowell writer was trampling over one of those sneering Boston reviews and he took it as an intended insult. The night never picked up. Olson had been known to keep young poets, across from England, probably Cambridge, trapped for forty-eight hours while he pounded them with metaphors, poetry and truth. He finished the bottle. He dry swallowed psilocybin buttons from the cache Leary gave him, a container the size of one of those old-fashioned confectioner's jars. Pink pills: peanuts. Sweaty excitement fed by the evident intelligence and attentive respect of the

willing victim, now groggy, green-white, punchdrunk. He sucked them dry, husked them, striding to the window, then back across the steamy room, temperature cranked to tropical hothouse by the blue flare of the gas stove. Shirt soaked. Gripping the rim of the table. That mesmerising voice seemed to come now from all corners of the room at once as the formerly-young man crawls towards the distant exit, the dangerous steps. 'The world has moved,' he reported, 'in another context, on.'[10]

What Olson learnt above everything else was his own sort of negative capability: to be able to live in your flaws and with your flaws. But he didn't do what William Carlos Williams, one of the modernist figures he most admired, wanted him to do: he called his great work *The Maximus Poems* and not *Gloucester*, in the way that Williams called his book *Paterson*. Williams missed the point. Olson chose the figure of Maximus because he was completely taken by the idea of size and scale; he wanted something bigger than life, a figure he could relate to Gilgamesh and Samson, to Odysseus and the idea of the eternal voyage. They were all questing for verifiable evidence, combing records and charts, to underpin Homer, Hesiod and Herodotus. They wanted to know what Venetian sailors were reporting, as eyewitnesses, of unexplored coastlines. The nature of the Homeric voyage is that it is made from fits and starts; it goes out, it stops, it halts, it winds back, it picks up at another point in the narrative, it trespasses into the land of the dead – and then, finally, it is permitted to return home: this great arc of homecoming that is the shape Prynne refers to in his talk at Simon Fraser. He says that *Maximus* is made from two movements, both leading to the revelation that the curvature of the universe is love. All of these late-modernist projects are, at base, about that.

I'm going to round off now by getting to the rocks of Dogtown. I have to get to those rocks. We've had the first movement to the sea and out. Now we must come behind the city to the place of rocks. I really had no sense of it until I got there and began to walk among those tracks and boulders. Dogtown is a labyrinth, you get lost in no time at all. It's a place to wander and to disappear. Carved into the rocks are texts. One of Olson's most striking *Maximus* figures is James Merry, the handsome sailor who wrestles with a young bull. By accident or design, in the middle of my wanderings, I came upon that stone.

> To have a destination, I settled on the clearing where the handsome sailor, James Merry, fought a young bull, and was gored, tossed, trampled. Self-sacrificed to his own vanity. And drunkenness. An episode of great fascination for Charles Olson, who addresses it in the Dogtown poems of *Maximus*. 'The bios / of nature in this / park of eternal / events.'
>
> Now, with trails branching off, left and right, I found myself in the place

I needed to be. Green-white lichen on a stone beside the path. Letters cut, shallow declivities repainted in red: JAS. MERRY DIED SEPTEMBER 1892. The confirmation of the poem, first read so many years ago, so far away; as myth or fable, like the *Mabinogion*, now fact. I stood in the clearing with its alien grass, like hair or mattress stuffing, summoning the sound of the bull.

When Olson came to Dogtown with Sanders, he was wrecked, afloat on bourbon and the leftovers of the Leary experiment in his medicine cupboard, a fistful of psilocybin 'peanuts' and a bottle of LSD. 'Twenty *million* micrograms,' Sanders said. 'Enough for Manhattan.' Olson creeps along in a battered station wagon, ferrying the boys to the Panna Grady house. Sanders (a classicist) envisions him as Poseidon. That greasy sailor's mane held in place with a rubber band. Ed is downloading, through involuntary chemical rushes, the Lovecraft nightmare of Gloucester's inhabitants as part-fish; mutating in front of his bulging red-rimmed eyes. Cold blooded Puritan creatures with gills-in-the-throat. Ocean returnees, reverse evolutionists. The future recorder, through *The Family*, of the Charles Manson dune buggy madness, wanders off into the serpentine trails of Dogtown; where he is found and rescued by the police in the early hours of the morning. He is wearing his stage outfit, an all-red suit.[11]

It was a voyage, an amazing voyage for me. A year ago, coming into it, coming off the back of my own cod-Homeric voyage, the absurdity of taking a swan pedalo from Hastings, the swan lake by the funfair, round to Rye, then by river to the Medway, from the Medway to the Thames, then back to London. So this was kind of a lunatic English homage to the Olsonian voyage I am trying to describe, the over-reach. And it was always in my mind that as soon as I came ashore, I would be heading off to Gloucester. It took four weeks to reach the mouth of the River Lea and it was the perfect preparation.

And then, quite suddenly, I'm in the Writer's Center, this roadside shack in Gloucester, and there is a DVD, a film that Vincent Ferrini's nephew, Henry, made about Olson. It's got John Malkovich reading sections from *Maximus*, all kinds of strange connections, but the real punch arrives at the end as one of the extra features. Olson, quite roughly documented, in the Fort Square room, reading the poem I read to you at the beginning. And this was absolutely mesmerising and lifted everything from the theoretical pitch I'm making to a different register. You witness the man, the energy of him as he grasps his own poem; the practical demonstration of projective verse, the full body reading. I'll finish just with a couple of lines on that:

> The only way to properly experience Olson was to watch one of the extra features on Henry Ferrini's DVD. The poet, caught sweatily close, mammal head lolling and rocking, reads 'The Cow of Dogtown' from

Maximus IV, V, VI. I could have attempted this without leaving Hackney. But having absorbed a little of the weather of place, the poet's performance hit with new force. In his Fort Square apartment, up against a wall of maps and photographs, Olson is, absolutely, in flow of inspiration. The balletic precision in the waving and signalling of arms as he conducts this torrent of words, at varying pace, cigarette stub pinched flat between finger and thumb. I never witnessed such a thing, such naked delivery. The gathering together of geological particulars, and the processing of technical terms into the energy field of the poem, was what I wanted from Gloucester.

Nothing more than that, he taught us how to read. The gossip of slack biography is impertinence. The man lives in language. He knows just how to end a passage, arms flung wide, as he brings 'Maximus, from Dogtown – II' into harbour. What is broken and fragmentary on the page coheres. A secret formula. 'Heart to be turned to Black / Stone / is the Throne of Creation.' The other side of heaven, for Charles Olson, after Dogtown, is the ocean. I play Ferrini's film again. And again. And again. I love the way Olson says *carbon*.[12]

Notes

1 This essay is based on the text of a talk given at the University of Kent, 16 October 2012.
2 Carl Watkins, *The Undiscovered Country: Journeys Among the Dead* (London: Bodley Head, 2013), 18.
3 Charles Olson, *West* (London: Cape Goliard Press, 1966).
4 Iain Sinclair, *Lud Heat: A Book of the Dead Hamlets* (London: Albion Village Press, 1975).
5 Ibid., 15.
6 See David Herd, 'From him only will the old State-secret come: what Charles Olson Imagined', *English* 59 (227), 375–95.
7 Edward Dorn, *Idaho Out* (London: Fulcrum Press, 1965), 3.
8 J. H. Prynne, 'On *Maximus IV, V, VI*', *Minutes of the Charles Olson Society* 28 (April 1999), 2.
9 Iain Sinclair, *American Smoke: Journeys to the End of the Light* (London: Hamish Hamilton, 2013), 119.
10 Ibid., 50–1.
11 Ibid., 67–8.
12 Ibid., 71–2.

23

Charles Olson's first poem

Ralph Maud

'Purgatory Blind' is probably what Charles Olson is referring to in a letter to Robert Creeley as 'the very 1st po-em', adding that it was written in Gloucester on the Annisquam River [1] – that is, the early draft (before it got its title), the first six lines of which we have known from George Butterick's transcription of them, published in his *Guide To the Maximus Poems of Charles Olson*:

> Between the river and the sea I
>   sit writing,
> The Annisquam and the Atlantic
> My boundaries, and all between
> The moors of doubt and self-
>   mistrust maintaining
> A perilous structure of landness
>   against the flood
> Of northern war and native
>   smug content.[2]

(*GMP*, 126)

The poet helps to pin down the date when he later reminisces: 'Wrote my first poems / and an essay on myth / at Kent Circle' (*MP*, 299). A letter to Waldo Frank from Gloucester, 25 March 1940, dates the completion of the essay on myth and thus the poem:

> And yesterday I knocked off after 25,000 words and that section on myth was done, one of those wonderful strides we strike once in a while ... Gloucester is breath stealing: sunned and wind, its color suddenly open to my eyes after the drab of N.Y. Yesterday I walked against a bitter wind miles along the coast alone with the gulls.

(*SL*, 29)

In the same letter he describes the boarding house at 3 Essex Avenue (on Kent Circle), the Annisquam River to the east and Gloucester Harbor (the Atlantic) to the south:

> I am living in a house which sits on a jut of land between the river, which ebbs and floods under my eye out the east window and the sea which moves and pushes and breaks against the window to the south. I don't know when I have been so open to life here.

The optimism of the letter is rather at odds with the above six lines, and with 'Purgatory Blind' as revised.[3]

The revision took place in a mood described in a later letter to Waldo Frank, sent from Stage Fort, 24 September 1940:

> In May when I finished a long section on Mardi and myth and the Pacific, I felt wrong. I had lost my method, unknowingly. I have had to find it again, and like the trance upon the sea these September days have I been. I have stayed on in this room in a purgatory blind.

So the draft poem is picked up, is revised, and gets its title in a mood of stasis.

It is eight years later that Olson recalls for Edward Dahlberg and Caresse Crosby the passage from which he took the phrase. In Keats's 'Epistle to John Hamilton Reynolds' he found: 'Lost in sort of Purgatory blind, / Cannot refer to any standard law / Of either earth or heaven' (SL, 84, 86). Olson presumably felt the meaning of 'blind' as a concealed place of waiting was appropriate to his condition and the draft as he then revised it.

However, the early ending is a different matter and comes right out of the poet's vigorous walk along Cape Ann's coastline:[4]

> Over all the gulls, white, hungry and gray
> Insisting, in flight or rest, their toughness upon us, human,
> Wingless and restless, hungry as well for more than
>   ravage, food, flight
> Asking only warmth and peace and exaction each to each.
> Today the waters of sea sky and river o'erwhelm the
>   fragile land of us
> And force us upward where there is no life
> Antaeus torn from the ground by Hercules.
> We shall down to strength only by spirit.
> We can be gulls only by other wings than those of flight
> Wings of warmth and tenderness
> Covering one another
> Huddled close and near upon this earth
> Between the crick and sea
> The moor.

The warmer humanity of these early lines, mirroring a youthful achievement in completing a difficult essay on myth, contrasts with the series of enigmatic questions of the revised printed poem. It is the draft rather than the revision which offers a better and more accurate candidate for consideration as Olson's first poem.

Notes

1 Letter from Charles Olson to Robert Creeley, 28 November 1951, in Charles Olson and Robert Creeley, *The Complete Correspondence* Vol 8., ed. George Butterick (Santa Barbara: Black Sparrow Press, 1987), 192.
2 The lines are transcribed from Olson's notebook '#4 Cambridge & N.Y. Winter–Spring 1940', Box 42, Charles Olson Research Collection, Archives and Special Collections at the Thomas J. Dodd Research Center, University of Connecticut Libraries.
3 'Purgatory Blind' (as revised) was printed by George Butterick as the first poem of *The Collected Poems* (*CP*, 3), from a typescript, Box 17, Folder 654, Charles Olson Research Collection, Archives and Special Collections at the Thomas J. Dodd Research Center, University of Connecticut Libraries.
4 These fourteen lines follow the six quoted above from Olson's notebook '#4 Cambridge and N.Y. Winter-Spring 1940', Box 42, Charles Olson Research Collection, and are printed here for the first time. Copyright University of Connecticut Libraries. Used with permission.

Bibliography

Works by Charles Olson

Olson, Charles, *Call Me Ishmael*, New York, Reynal and Hitchcock, 1947.
Olson, Charles, *Y & X*, Washington DC, Black Sun Press, 1949.
Olson, Charles, *Charles Olson Reading at Berkeley*, transcribed by Zoe Brown, San Francisco, Coyote Press, 1966.
Olson, Charles, *Selected Writings*, ed. and intro. Robert Creeley, New York, New Directions, 1966.
Olson, Charles, *West*, London, Cape Goliard Press, 1966.
Olson, Charles, *Mayan Letters*, ed. Robert Creeley, London, Jonathan Cape, 1968.
Olson, Charles, *Causal Mythology*, ed. Donald Allen, San Francisco, Four Seasons, 1969.
Olson, Charles, *Letters for Origin*, ed. Albert Glover, London, Cape Goliard, 1969.
Olson, Charles, *Archaeologist of Morning*, London, Cape Goliard Press, 1970.
Olson, Charles, *The Special View of History*, ed. Ann Charters, Berkeley, Oyez, 1970.
Olson, Charles, 'Project (1951): "The Art of the Language of Mayan Glyphs"', *Alcheringa* 1:5 (1973).
Olson, Charles, *Additional Prose: A Bibliography on America, Proprioception & Other Notes & Essays*, ed. George Butterick, Bolinas, Four Seasons Foundation, 1974.
Olson, Charles, *Charles Olson reads from Maximus Poems IV, V, VI*, Folkways Records, 1975.
Olson, Charles, 'Notes and uncollected *Maximus* Materials', *OLSON: The Journal of the Olson Archives* 5 (Spring 1976).
Olson, Charles, *The Fiery Hunt and Other Plays*, ed. and intr. George Butterick, Bolinas, Four Seasons Foundation, 1977.
Olson, Charles, 'Journal of Swordfishing Cruise on the *Doris M. Hawes*' [1936] in *OLSON: The Journal of the Olson Archives* 7 (Spring 1977).
Olson, Charles, 'A Letter to the Faculty of Black Mountain College', *OLSON: The Journal of the Olson Archives* 8 (Fall 1977).
Olson, Charles, *Muthologos: The Collected Lectures and Interviews*, in two volumes, ed. George Butterick, Bolinas, Four Seasons Foundation, 1979.

Olson, Charles and Creeley, Robert, *The Complete Correspondence*, Volumes 1–10, ed. George Butterick (1–8), Richard Blevins (9 and 10), Santa Barbara, Black Sparrow Press, 1980–96.
Olson, Charles, *The Maximus Poems*, ed. George Butterick, Berkeley, Los Angeles & London, University of California Press, 1983.
Olson, Charles, *Charles Olson & Cid Corman: Complete Correspondence 1950–1964*, Vol. 1, ed. George Evans, Orono, ME, National Poetry Foundation, 1987.
Olson, Charles, *The Collected Poems of Charles Olson (excluding the Maximus poems)*, ed. George Butterick, Berkeley, Los Angeles & London, University of California Press, 1997.
Olson, Charles, *Collected Prose*, ed. Donald Allen and Benjamin Friedlander, intro. Robert Creeley, Berkeley, Los Angeles & London, University of California Press, 1997.
Olson, Charles and Boldereff, Frances, *A Modern Correspondence*, ed. Ralph Maud and Sharon Thesen, Hanover: Wesleyan University Press, 1999.
Olson, Charles, *Selected Letters*, ed. Ralph Maud, Berkeley, Los Angeles & London, University of California Press, 2000.
Olson, Charles, *Muthologos: Lectures and Interviews*, revised second edition, ed. Ralph Maud, Vancouver, Talonbooks, 2010.

Works by other writers

Adorno, Theodor W., *Negative Dialectics*, trans. E. B. Ashton, London, Routledge and Kegan Paul, 1973.
Adorno, Theodor W., and Horkheimer, Max, *The Dialectic of Enlightenment*, trans. John Cumming, London, Verso, 1979.
Adorno, Theodor W., *Aesthetic Theory*, ed. Gretel Adorno and Rolf Tiedemann, trans. C. Lenhardt, London, Routledge and Kegan Paul, 1984.
Adorno, Theodor W., *Minima Moralia: Reflections from Damaged Life*, trans. E. F. N. Jephcott, London, Verso, 2006.
Agamben, Giorgio, *Homo Sacer*, Stanford, CA, University of Stanford Press, 1995.
Agamben, Giorgio, *State of Exception*, Chicago and London, University of Chicago Press, 2005.
Agamben, Giorgio, *The Kingdom and the Glory: For a Theological Genealogy of Economy and Government*, Stanford, CA, University of Stanford Press, 2011.
Allen, Donald (ed.), *The New American Poetry, 1945–1960*, Berkeley & London, University of California Press, 1999.
Arendt, Hannah, *The Origins of Totalitarianism*, London, George Allen and Unwin Ltd, 1967.
Badiou, Alain, *Peut-on penser la politique?*, Paris, Seuil, 1985.
Badiou, Alain, *Being and Event*, trans. Oliver Feltham, London, Continuum, 2011.

Ballets Russes (2006), documentary film directed by Dayna Goldfine and Dan Geller, New York, Zeitgeist Films.
Bardon, Geoffrey, *Papunya Tula: Art of the Western Desert*, Ringwood, Vic., McPhee Gribble, 1991.
Barnett, Lincoln, 'J. Robert Oppenheimer', *Life* (10 October, 1949).
Barry, Kevin (ed.), *James Joyce: Occasional, Critical, and Political Writing*, Oxford, Oxford World's Classics, 2000.
Beach, Christopher, *ABC of Influence: Ezra Pound and the Remaking of American Poetic Tradition*, Berkeley, University of California Press, 1992.
Belgrad, Daniel, *The Culture of Spontaneity: Improvisation and the Arts in Postwar America*, Chicago, University of Chicago Press, 1999.
Benjamin, Walter, *Illuminations*, ed. Hannah Arendt, New York, Schocken Books, 1969.
Benjamin, Walter, *The Origin of German Tragic Drama*, trans. John Osborne, London, Verso, 1985.
Benjamin, Walter, *The Arcades Project*, ed. Rolf Tiedemann, trans. Howard Eiland and Kevin McLaughlin, Cambridge, Mass, Belknap Press, 1999.
Bergson, Henri, *Laughter: An Essay on the Meaning of the Comic*, trans. C. S. H. Brereton and F. Rothwell, København, Los Angeles and Saint Paul, Green Integer, 1999.
Berry, Eleanor, 'The Emergence of Charles Olson Prosody of the Page Space', *Journal of English Linguistics* 31:1 (March 2002).
Blackburn, Paul, *The Parallel Voyages*, intro. Clayton Eshleman, ed. Edith Jarolim, illus. Ellen McMahon, Tucson, Arizona, SUN-gemini Press, 1987.
Blake, William, *The Marriage of Heaven and Hell*, London, Oxford University Press, 1975.
Blaser, Robin, *The Fire: Collected Essays of Robin Blaser*, ed. Miriam Nichols, Berkeley, University of California Press, 2006
Blau DuPlessis, Rachel, *Purple Passages: Pound, Eliot, Zukofsky, Olson, Creeley and the Ends of Patriarchal Poetry*, Iowa City, University of Iowa Press, 2012.
Bodkin, Maud, *Archetypal Patterns in Poetry: Psychological Studies of Imagination*, London, Oxford University Press, 1974.
Boer, Charles, *Charles Olson in Connecticut*, Chicago, Swallow Press, 1975.
Boldereff, Frances, *Reading Finnegans Wake*, Woodward, Penn., Classic Non-Fiction, 1959.
Boldereff, Frances, *Hermes to His Son Thoth: Being Joyce's Use of Giordano Bruno in Finnegans Wake*, Woodward, Penn., Classic Non-Fiction Library, 1968.
Bradford, William, *Bradford's History of Plymouth Plantation 1606–1646*, ed. William T. David, New York: Barnes & Noble, Inc. 1946
Bram, Shahar, *Charles Olson and Alfred North Whitehead*, trans. Batya Stein, Lewisburg, Bucknell University Press, 2004.
Brandom, Robert, *Articulating Reasons: An Introduction to Inferentialism*, Cambridge, Mass., Harvard University Press, 2000.
Brownjohn, Alan, 'Alan Brownjohn Remembers Peter Porter', *TLS*, 22 February 2012.

Buck-Morss, Susan, *The Origin of Negative Dialectics: Theodor W. Adorno, Walter Benjamin, and the Frankfurt Institute*, Brighton, Harvester, 1977.

Bunting, Basil, *The Complete Poems*, Oxford, Oxford University Press, 1977.

Burwick, Frederick and Douglass, Paul (eds), *The Crisis in Modernism: Bergson and the Vitalist Controversy*, Cambridge and New York, Cambridge University Press, 1992.

Butterick, George, *A Guide to the Maximus Poems of Charles Olson*, Berkeley, University of California Press, 1980.

Butterick, George, 'Charles Olson and the Postmodern Advance', Iowa Review (Fall, 1980).

Butterick, George, *Editing The Maximus Poems: Supplementary Notes*, Storrs, University of Connecticut Library, 1983.

Butterick, George, 'Charles Olson's "The Kingfishers" and the Poetics of Change', *American Poetry* 6:2 (1989).

Byrd, Don, 'The Possibility of Measure in *Maximus*', boundary 2 2.1/2 (Autumn 1973–Winter 1974).

Byrd, Don, *Charles Olson's Maximus*, Urbana, University of Illinois Press, 1980.

Cahn, Michael, 'Subversive Mimesis: Theodor W. Adorno and the Modern Impasse of Critique', in M. Sparisou (ed.), *Mimesis in Contemporary Theory: An Interdisciplinary Approach*, Philadelphia, Benjamins, 1984.

Charters, Ann, *Olson/Melville: A Study in Affinity*, Berkeley, Oyez, 1968.

Christensen, Paul, *Charles Olson, Call Him Ishmael*, Austin, University of Texas Press, 1979.

Clark, Tom, *Charles Olson: The Allegory of a Poet's Life*, Berkeley, North Atlantic Books, 2000.

Clarke, David, 'The Angel of Mons', *Fortean Times*, May 2003, online text www.forteantimes.com/features/articles/213/the_angel_of_mons.html.

Collis, Stephen, *Through Words of Others: Susan Howe and Anarcho-Scholasticism*, Victoria, BC, ELS, 2006.

Collis, Steve, *Dispatches from the Occupation: A History of Change*, Vancouver, Talonbooks, 2012.

Coolidge, Clark, 'Notes Taken in Classes Conducted by Charles Olson at Vancouver, August 1963' in *OLSON: The Journal of the Charles Olson Archives* 4 (Fall 1975).

Creeley, Robert, 'Preface to the First Edition (1953)', *Mayan Letters*, London, Cape editions, 1968.

Curtius, Ernst Robert, *European Literature and the Latin Middle Ages*, translated by Willard R. Trask, Princeton, Princeton University Press, 1953.

Davenport, Guy, *The Geography of the Imagination: Forty Essays*, San Francisco, North Point Press, 1981.

Davidson, Michael, '"By ear, he sd": Audio-Tapes and Contemporary Criticism', *Credences* 1:1 (1981), 105–20.

Davidson, Michael, *On the Outskirts of Form: Practicing Cultural Poetics*, Middletown, CT., Wesleyan University Press, 2011.

Davie, Donald, *Thomas Hardy and British Poetry*, London, Routledge, 1973.

Davie, Donald, *The Poet in the Imaginary Museum*, ed. Barry Alpert, Manchester, Carcanet Press, 1977.
Deleuze, Gilles, *Bergsonism*, New York, Zone Books, 1991.
Denbow, Jeremy, *Season in Hell: An English Translation from the French*, Lincoln, NE, iUniverse, Inc, 2004.
Denby, Edwin, *Dance Writings*, ed., Robert Cornfield and William MacKay, London, Dance Books, 1986.
Dobran, Ryan, 'Introduction', *Glossator* 2 (2010).
Dolar, Mladen, *A Voice and Nothing More*, Cambridge, MA, MIT Press, 2006.
Dorn, Ed, *Idaho Out*, London, Fulcrum Press, 1965.
Drucker, Joanna, *Figuring the Word: Essays on Books, Writing, and Visual Poetics*, New York, Granary Books, 1998.
Duberman, Martin, *The Worlds of Lincoln Kirstein*, Evanston, Northwestern University Press, 2008.
Duncan, Robert, *The H. D. Book*, ed. Michael Boughn and Victor Coleman, Berkeley, University of California Press, 2011.
Einstein, Albert, *The Meaning of Relativity*, trans. Edwin Plimpton Adams, London, Methuen, 1922.
Einstein, Albert and Infeld, Leopold, *The Evolution of Physics*, Cambridge, Cambridge University Press, 1947.
Einstein, Albert, *Relativity: the Special and the General Theory: A Popular Exposition*, trans. Robert W. Lawson, London, Routledge, 1993.
Eliot, T. S., *Selected Essays*, London, Faber and Faber, 1932.
Eliot, T. S., *Collected Poems 1909–1962*, London, Faber and Faber, 1986.
Ellingham, Lewis, and Killian, Kevin, *Poet, Be Like God: Jack Spicer and the San Francisco Renaissance*, Hanover, Wesleyan University Press, 1998.
Evans, Amy and Zamir, Shamoon (eds), *The Unruly Garden: Robert Duncan and Eric Mottram: Letters and Essays*, Oxford, Peter Lang, 2007.
Finch, John, 'Dancer and Clerk', *The Massachusetts Review* 12:1 (Winter, 1971).
Fisher, Allen, *Place*, Hastings, Reality Street, 2005.
Fitterman, Robert and Place, Vanessa, 'From *Notes on Conceptualisms*', www.uglyducklingpresse.org/wp-content/uploads/2013/07/Notes_free.pdf
Forrest-Thomson, Veronica, *Poetic Artifice: A Theory of Twentieth-century Poetry*, Manchester, Manchester University Press, 1978.
Foucault, Michel, *Discipline and Punish: The Birth of the Prison*, New York, Vintage Books, 1995.
Frank, Robert, *The Americans*, Paris, Robert Delpire, 1958 and New York, Grove Press, 1959.
Fraser, Kathleen, *Translating the Unspeakable: Poetry and the Innovative Necessity*, Tuscaloosa, AL, University of Alabama Press, 2000.
Fredman, Stephen, *The Grounding of American Poetry: Charles Olson and the Emersonian Tradition*, Cambridge, Cambridge University Press, 1993.
Freer, Lyndsey M (ed.), *Edward Dorn: Charles Olson Memorial Lectures*, New York, CUNY, Lost and Found series, 2012.
Freud, Sigmund, *Moses and Monotheism: Three Essays*, London, Penguin Freud Library, 1939.

Garafola, Lynn, *Diaghilev's Ballets Russes*, Oxford, Oxford Univeristy Press, 1989.
Garafola, Lynn, 'Lincoln Kirstein, Modern Dance, and the Left: The Genesis of an American Ballet', *Dance Research: The Journal of the Society for Dance Research* 23:1 (2005).
García-Márquez, Vincente, *Massine: A Biography*, London, Nick Hern, 1996.
Gerhardt, Rainer Maria, 'Letter for Creeley and Olson', translated by Werner Heider and Joanna Jalowetz, *Origin* 4 (Winter 1951–2).
Ginsberg, Allen, *Collected Poems 1947–1997*, New York, HarperCollins, 2006.
Golding, Alan, 'From Pound to Olson: the avant-garde poet as pedagogue', *Journal of Modern Literature* 34:1, 2010.
Golding, Alan, 'The New American Poetry Revisited, Again', *Contemporary Literature* XXXIX 2.
Graves, Robert, *The White Goddess: A Historic Grammar of Poetic Myth*, enlarged edn, New York, Farrar, Straus and Giroux, 1966.
Gunn, Thom, *Selected Poems*, ed. August Kleinzahler, New York, Farrar, Straus and Giroux, 2009.
Gunter, Pete A. Y., 'Bergson and Jung', *Journal of the History of Ideas* 43 (1982)
Halden-Sullivan, Judith, *The Topology of Being: The Poetics of Charles Olson*, New York, Peter Lang, 1991.
Halsey, Alan, and Selerie, Gavin, *Days of '49*, Sheffield, West House Books, 1999.
Hampson, Robert, *Seaport*, Exeter, Shearsman Books, 2008.
Hampson, Robert and Montgomery, Will, 'Innovations in Poetry' in Peter Brooker, Andrzej Gasiorek and Andrew Thacker (eds), *The Oxford Handbook of Modernisms*, Oxford, Oxford University Press, 2010.
Harrison, Jane, *Themis: A Study of the Social Origins of Greek Religion*, London, Merlin Press, 1989.
Herd, David, 'From him only will the old State-secret come: what Charles Olson Imagined', *English* 59 (227).
Hesiod, *The Homeric Hymns and Homerica*, trans. Hugh G. Evelyn-White, London, William Heinneman, Cambridge, Harvard University Press, 1950.
Hodgkiss, Peter, 'Chris Torrance interviewed by Peter Hodgkiss', *Poetry Information* 18 (Winter/Spring 1977–8).
Hoeynck, Josuha S., *Poetic Cosmologies: Black Mountain Poetry and Process Philosophy*, Ann Arbor, Proquest, 2008.
Howe, Susan, *My Emily Dickinson*, Berkeley, CA, North Atlantic Books, 1985.
Howe, Susan, 'Where Should the Commander Be', *Writing* 19 (November 1987).
Howe, Susan, 'Charles Olson: Since a Dialogue We Are', *Acts* 10 (1989).
Howe, Susan, *The Birth-mark: Unsettling the Wilderness in American Literary History*, Hanover, Wesleyan University Press, 1993.
Howe, Susan, 'Sorting Facts: Or, Nineteen Ways of Looking at Marker', in Charles Warren (ed.), *Beyond Document: Essays on Nonfiction Film*, Hanover, NH, Wesleyan University Press, 1996.
Howe, Susan, *The Nonconformist's Memorial*, New York, New Directions, 1999.
Howe, Susan, *Souls of the Labadie Tract*, New York, New Directions, 2007.
Howe, Susan, *That This*, New York, New Directions, 2010.

Jaussen, Paul, 'Charles Olson Keeps House: Rewriting John Smith for Contemporary America', *Journal of Modern Literature* 34:1 (Fall 2010), 107–24.
Johnson, Vivien, *The Art of Clifford Possum Tjapaltjarri*, East Roseville, NSW, Gordon and Breach Arts International, 1994.
Jung, Carl, 'Synchronicity: An Acausal Connecting Principle', in *The Structure and Dynamics of the Psyche*, trans. R. F. C. Hull, *The Collected Works of C. G. Jung*, Vol. 8, second edn, London, Routledge and Kegan Paul, 1985.
Katz, Daniel, *The Poetry of Jack Spicer*, Edinburgh, Edinburgh University Press, 2013.
Keats, John, *Letters of John Keats*, ed. Robert Gittings, Oxford, Oxford University Press, 1970.
Keller, Lyn, 'An Interview with Susan Howe', *Contemporary Literature* 36:1 (Spring 1995).
Kermode, Frank, *Romantic Image*, London, Routledge and Kegan Paul, 1957.
Kirstein, Lincoln, *Dance: A Short History of Theatrical Classical Dancing*, New York, G. P. Putnam, 1935.
Kyle, Carol, 'The Mesoamerican Cultural Past and Charles Olson's the Kingfishers', *Alcheringa* New Series 1:2 (1975).
Lacoue-Labarthe, Philipe and Nancy, Jean-Luc, 'From Where is Psychoanalysis Possible?' (Part II of 'The Jewish People Do Not Dream'), *Journal of European Psychoanalysis* 17 (Summer–Winter 2003).
Lévinas, Emmanuel, *Otherwise Than Being: Or, Beyond Essence*, Hague, Boston, Hingham, MA, M. Nijhoff, 1991.
March, Robert H., *Physics for Poets*, New York, McGraw Hill, 1970.
Marshak, Robert E., 'The Nuclear Force', *Scientific American* 202 (March, 1960).
Marx, Karl, and Engels, Frederick, *Selected Works in One Volume*, London, Lawrence and Wishart, 1980.
Maud, Ralph (ed.), *Charles Olson's Reading: A Biography*, Carbondale, Edwardsville, Southern Illinois University Press, 1996.
Maud, Ralph, *What Does Not Change: The Significance of Charles Olson's 'The Kingfishers'*, London, Associated University Presses, 1998.
Maud, Ralph, 'Charles Olson's Archaic Postmodern', *Looking for Oneself: Contributions to the study of Charles Olson, Minutes of the Charles Olson Society* 42 (September 2001), http://charlesolson.org/Files/archaic1.htm.
Maud, Ralph (ed.), *A Charles Olson Reader*, Manchester, Carcanet Press, 2005.
Maud, Ralph, *Charles Olson at the Harbor*, Vancouver, Talonbooks, 2008.
Mead, G. R. S., *Apollonius of Tyana: The Philosopher Explorer and Social Reformer of the First Century AD*, 1901, http://gnosis.org/library/grs-mead/apollonius/apollonius_mead_17.htm
Melville, Herman, *Moby-Dick*, with an introduction and notes by David Herd, Ware, Wordsworth, 2001.
Mellors, Anthony, *Late Modernist Poetics: From Pound to Prynne*, Manchester, Manchester University Press, 2005.
Merrill, Thomas, *The Poetry of Charles Olson: A Primer*, Newark, University of Delaware Press, 1982.

Mester, Terri A., *Movement and Modernism: Yeats, Eliot, Lawrence, Williams and Early Twentieth Century Dance*, Fayetteville, The University of Arkansas Press, 1997.

Middleton, Peter, 'Charles Olson: A Short History', *Parataxis* 10 (2001)

Middleton, Peter, 'Open Oppen: Linguistic fragmentation and the poetic proposition', *Textual Practice* 24:4 (2010).

Milesi, Laurent, 'From Logos to Muthos: The Philosophy of Pound's and Olson's Mythopoetics', in Louis Armand (ed.), *Avant-Post: The Avant-Garde under 'Post-' Conditions*, Prague, Litteraria Pragensia, 2006.

Mill, John Stuart, 'Thoughts on Poetry and its Varieties', *Dissertations and Discussions*, Vol. 1 London, Longmans, 1867.

Miller, Jr, James E., *The American Quest for a Supreme Fiction*, Cambridge, Cambridge University Press, 1979.

Montgomery, Will, *The Poetry of Susan Howe: History, Theology, Authority*, London, Palgrave, 2010.

Moravcsik, Michael J., 'High Energy Physics: An informal report of the Rochester Conference', *Physics Today* 12:10 (October 1959).

Morphy, Howard, *Aboriginal Art*, London, Phaidon Press, 1998.

Mottram, Eric, 'Poets from North East England interviewed by Eric Mottram' in *Poetry Information* 18, Winter/Spring 1977–8.

Muecke, Stephen, *Ancient & Modern: Time, Culture and Indigenous Philosophy*, Sydney, University of NSW, 2004.

Mulford, Wendy, *The East Anglia Sequence*, Peterborough, Spectacular Diseases, 1998.

Nicholls, Peter, 'Unsettling the Wilderness: Susan Howe and American History', *Contemporary Literature* 37:4 (Winter 1996).

Nichols, Miriam, *Radical Affections: Essays on the Poetics of Outside*, Tuscaloosa, AL, University of Alabama Press, 2010.

Norton, Leslie, *Léonide Massine and the Twentieth Century Ballet*, Jefferson, McFarland, 2004.

Olsen, Redell, *Secure Portable Space*, Hastings, Reality Street, 2004.

Olsen, Redell, *Punk Faun*, Oakland, CA, Subpress, 2012.

Olsen, Redell, 'the matter of cloven-poetics: or, even the title against itself', in Vincent Broqua and Jean-Jacques Poucel (eds), *Formes Poétiques Contemporaines*, Paris, Double Change, 2012.

Pattison, Neil, Pattison, Reitha, Roberts, Luke (eds), *Certain Prose of The English Intelligencer*, Cambridge, Mountain Press, 2012.

Perkins, Hetti, Hannah Fink, and Art Gallery of New South Wales, *Papunya Tula: Genesis & Genius*, Sydney, Art Gallery of New South Wales, 2000.

Platt, Marc (aka Marc Platoff) and Renée Renouf, '"Ghost Town" Revisited: A Memoir of Producing an American Ballet for the Ballet Russe de Monte Carlo', *Dance Chronicle*, 24:2 (2001), .

Pokorny, Julius, *Indogermanisches etymologisches Wörterbuch, Indo-European Etymological Dictionary*, Francke Verlag, 1959.

Pound, Ezra, *Guide to Kulchur*, London, Peter Owen, 1966.

Pound, Ezra, *Literary Essays of Ezra Pound*, ed. T. S. Eliot, New York, New Directions, 1968.
Pound, Ezra, *The Cantos*, London, Faber and Faber, 1975.
Pound, Ezra, *Personæ: The Shorter Poems of Ezra Pound*, London, Faber and Faber, 2001.
Presley, Frances, *Paravane; New and Selected Poems 1996–2003*, Cambridge, Salt Publishing, 2004.
Prynne, J. H., 'Charles Olson, Maximus Poems IV, V, VI' in *The Park* 4, 5 (Summer 1969).
Prynne, J. H., 'On *Maximus IV, V, VI*', *Minutes of the Charles Olson Society* 28 (April 1999).
Quinn, Malcolm, *The Swastika: Constructing the Symbol*, London, Routledge, 1994.
Quirk, Tom, *Bergson and American Culture: The Worlds of Willa Cather and Wallace Stevens*, Chapel Hill and London, University of North Carolina Press, 1990.
Raworth, Tom, 'Tom Raworth: An Interview' in *Vort* 1 (1972).
Retallack, Joan, *The Poethical Wager*, Berkeley, University of California Press, 2003.
Rexroth, Kenneth, 'San Francisco Letter', *Evergreen Review* 1:2 (Summer 1957).
Reynolds, Nancy and Malcolm McCormick, *No Fixed Points: Dance in Twentieth Century*, New Haven, Yale University Press, 2003.
Riddel, Joseph, 'Decentering the Image: The "Project" of "American" Poetics?', in Josué V. Harari (ed.) *Textual Strategies: Perspectives in Post-Structuralist Criticism*, Ithaca, Cornell University Press, 1979.
Riley, Peter, *Excavations*, Hastings, Reality Street, 2004.
Rose, Deborah Bird, *Nourishing Terrains: Australian Aboriginal Views of Landscape and Wilderness*, 1996.
Rose, Deborah, *Reports from a Wild Country: Ethics for Decolonisation*, Sydney, University of New South Wales Press, 2004.
Rosenthal, M. L., *The New Poets: American and British Poetry since World War II*, New York, Oxford University Press, 1967.
Ross, Andrew, *The Failure of Modernism: Symptoms of American Poetry*, New York, Columbia University Press, 1986.
Rothenberg, Jerome, and Dennis Tedlock, *Alcheringa*, 9 vols, Jerome Rothenberg & Dennis Tedlock, New York, Stony Brook Poetics Foundation, 1970.
Rother, James, 'Charles Olson's *The Distances* [1960]: A Retrospective Essay'. *Contemporary Poetry Review* (200), 10 July 2012, http://www.cprw.com/Rother/olson.htm
Roux, Georges, *Ancient Iraq*, Harmondsworth, Penguin, 1977.
Rumaker, Michael, *Black Mountain Days*, Asheville, Black Mountain Press, 2003.
Ryan, Judith, and Philip Batty, *Tjukurrtjanu: Origins of Western Desert Art*, Melbourne, Vic., National Gallery of Victoria, 2011.
Schmidt, Paul, *Arthur Rimbaud: Complete Works*, New York, Harper Perennial Modern Classics, 2000.

Scully, Maurice, *livelihood*, Bray, County Wicklow, Wild Honey Press, 2004.
Seelye, Catherine (ed.), *Charles Olson and Ezra Pound: An Encounter at St Elizabeth*, New York, Grossman/Viking, 1975.
Selerie, Gavin, *To Let Words Swim into the Soul: An anniversary tribute to the art of Charles Olson*, London, Binnacle Press, 1980.
Selerie, Gavin (ed.), *The Riverside Interviews 1: Allen Ginsberg*, London, Binnacle Press, 1980.
Selerie, Gavin (ed.), *The Riverside Interviews 6: Tom McGrath*, London, Binnacle Press, 1983.
Selerie, Gavin, *Azimuth*, London, Binnacle Press, 1984.
Selerie, Gavin, *Roxy*, Hay-on-Wye, West House Books, 1996.
Selerie, Gavin, *Le Fanu's Ghost*, Hereford, Five Seasons Press, 2006.
Shaw, Lytle, *Fieldworks: From Place to Site in Postwar Poetics*, Tuscaloosa, AL, The University of Alabama Press, 2013.
Silliman, Ron, *The New Sentence*, New York, Roof Books, 1987.
Silliman, Ron, 'Un-seen, ur-new: The history of the longpoem and "The Collage Poems of Drafts"', *Jacket* 2 (14 December 2011), http://jacket2.org/article/un-scene-ur-new.
Sinclair, Iain, *The Kodak Mantra Diaries*, London, Albion Village Press, 1971.
Sinclair, Iain, *Lud Heat: A Book of the Dead Hamlets*, London, Albion Village Press, 1975.
Sinclair, Iain, *Ghost Milk: Calling Time on the Grand Project*, London, Hamish Hamilton, 2011.
Sinclair, Iain, *American Smoke: Journeys to the End of the Light*, London, Hamish Hamilton, 2013.
Skelt, Peterjon (ed.), *Prospect into Breath: Interviews with North and South Writers*, Twickenham & Wakefield: North and South, 1991.
Smee, Sebastian, 'NGA Acquires a New Blue Poles', *The Australian*, 26 July 2007, 11.
Spencer, Baldwin Sir, and Francis James Gillen, *The Native Tribes of Central Australia*, London, Macmillan & Co., 1899.
Spicer, Jack, *The House that Jack Built: The Collected Lectures of Jack Spicer*, ed. with an Afterword by Peter Gizzi, Middletown, Wesleyan University Press, 1998.
Spicer, Jack, *My Vocabulary Did This To Me: The Collected Poetry of Jack Spicer*, ed. Peter Gizzi and Kevin Killian, Middletown, Wesleyan University Press, 2008.
Stanner, W. E. H., *White Man Got No Dreaming: Essays, 1938–1973*, Canberra, Australian National University Press, 1979.
Stein, Charles, *The Secret of the Black Chrysanthemum*, Barrytown, Station Hill, 1979.
Stephens, Paul, 'Human University: Charles Olson and the Embodiment of Information', *Paideuma* 39 (2012).
Stone, Oliver, *The Doors* (1991), film, USA, Columbia Pictures.
Tarlo, Harriet, 'Radical Landscapes: experiment and environment in contemporary poetry', *Jacket* 32 (April 2007).

Thompson, John Eric Sidney, *Maya Hieroglyphic Writing; Introduction*, Washington, Carnegie Institution of Washington, 1950.

Thomson, J. A. K., *The Art of the Logos [on the Traditional Stories of the Ancient Greeks.]*, London, George Allen & Unwin, 1935.

Torrey, E. Fuller, *The Roots of Treason: Ezra Pound and the Secrets of St. Elizabeth's*, London, Sidgwick & Jackson, 1984.

Troan, John, 'Science Reporting—Today and Tomorrow', *Science* 131:3408 (22 April 1960).

Vickers, Daniel, *Farmers & Fishermen: Two Centuries of Work in Essex County, Massachusetts, 1630–1850*, Chapel Hill, University of North Carolina Press, 1994.

Von Hallberg, Robert, *Charles Olson: The Scholar's Art*, Cambridge, Mass, London, Harvard University Press, 1978.

Waddell, L. A., *The Phoenician Origin of Britons, Scots, and Anglo-Saxons*, London, Williams & Norgate, 1924.

Watkins, Carl, *The Undiscovered Country: Journeys Among the Dead*, London, Bodley Head, 2013.

Weyl, Hermann, *Principles of Mathematics and Natural Sciences*, trans. Olaf Helmer, Princeton, Princeton University Press, 1949.

Whitehead, Alfred North, *Adventures of Ideas*, Cambridge, Cambridge University Press, 1933.

Whitehead, Alfred North, *Process and Reality: An Essay in Cosmology*, London: Cambridge University Press, 1929. Corrected Edition. eds David Ray Griffin and Donald W. Sherburne, New York, Free Press/Macmillan Publishing Co. Inc., 1978.

Wiener, Norbert, *Cybernetics: Or Control and Communication in the Animal and the Machine*, Cambridge, MA, MIT Press, 1948.

Wild, Jeff, 'Charles Olson's Maximus: A Polis of Attention and Dialogue', *Olson Now*, Michael Kelleher and Ammiel Alcalay (eds), available at http://epc.buffalo.edu/authors/olson/blog/wild.pdf

Williams, Jonathan, *The Loco Logodaedalist in Situ*, London, Cape Goliard, 1971.

Williams, William Carlos, *The Collected Poems of William Carlos Williams*, Vol. I: 1909–1939, ed. A. Walton Litz and Christopher MacGowan, New York, New Directions, 1986.

Žižek, Slavoj, *On Belief*, London, Routledge, 2001.

Zukofsky, Louis, *Prepositions*, London, Rapp and Carroll, 1967.

Index of writings by Charles Olson

'3rd letter on Georges, unwritten' 136
'A Bibliography on America for Ed Dorn' 135, 139
'a Plantation a beginning' 128
'ABCs' 89
'ABCs (3–for Rimbaud)' 60
'An Ode on Nativity' 115–16
Apollonius of Tyana 288, 291–2
Archaeologist of Morning 115, 265
'As the Dead Prey Upon Us' 17–18, 48, 182, Chapter 15 *passim*

'Ballad for Americans' 89

Call Me Ishmael 1, 29, 32, 55–6, 113, 115, 117, 128, 149–50, 159, 163, 164–70, 185, 219, 273, 302
'Causal Mythology' 89, 250 n.45,
'Credo' 92

'For Sappho, Back' 157

'Help Me, Venus, You Who Led Me On' 157
'Human Universe' 12, 26, 27, 38, 52, 54, 91, 92, 198, 209, 215, 217–18, 222, 225, 228, 240, 248, 267, 272, 286

'I, Maximus of Gloucester, to You' 157
'In Cold Hell, in Thicket' 15, Chapter 4 *passim*, 103–7, 110, 114, 129, 157, 159, 209, 273

King of the Wood 287–8

'Letter 22' 48
'Letter for Melville 1951' 89
'Letter to Elaine Feinstein' 1, 28, 114, 151, 185, 245
Letters for Origin 115

'Maximus, at Tyre and at Boston' 283
'Maximus, to Gloucester: Letter 2' 9
'Maximus, to Gloucester, Letter 27 [withheld]' 44, 110
Maximus, from Dogtown 181
'Maximus, from Dogtown—I' 61
'Maximus, from Dogtown—II' 28, 61, 300
'Maximus, to Gloucester: Letter 15' 16, Chapter 7 *passim*, 120
Mayan Letters 129, 130, 140, 209, 265, 267

'Projective Verse' 1, 2–3, 10, 11, 14–15, 18, 26, 38, 40, 41–2, 59–60, 62, 65, 78, 79, 80, 82, 84, 89, 91, 97, 98, 105–6, 113, 127, 140, 149, 151–5, 157, 170, 185, 190, 209, 229, 246, Chapter 20 *passim*, 301

'Quantity in Verse, and Shakespeare's Late Plays' 121

'The Advantage' 153, 157

Index of writings by Charles Olson

The Born Dancer 288
The Distances 181
'The Gate and the Center' 159, 195, 223, 269, 271
'The Kingfishers' 1, 3–6, 18, 83, 85, 103–4, 106–7, 120, 129, 130, 153, 155, 156, 199–200, 209, 210, Chapter 18 *passim*, Chapter 19 *passim*, 273–4, 283
'The Librarian' 48, 120, 182
'The Lordly and Isolate Satyrs' 17, Chapter 13 *passim*
The Maximus Poems 3, 4, 8, 9, 10, 18, 19, Chapter 1 *passim*, 44, 48, 53, 57, 61, 91, 110, 111–12, 114–15, 116, 127, 128, Chapter 10 *passim*, 149, 151, 155, 156, 182, 200, 206, Chapter 17 *passim*, 272, 274–5, 279, 281–5, 300, 305, 308
The Special View of History 4, 5, 8, 27, 52, 216, 228, 240, 241, 272, 275, 277, 278–9, 281
'The Twist' 48, 49, 120,
'These Days' 157

West 115, 297

Y & X 1, 64, 156

Index

Adorno, Theodor W. 18, 235–42, 243, 245–8, 252, 312
Agamben, Giorgio 13, 21n.24, 279–81
Allen, Donald 1–2, 7, 10, 17, 20 n.5, 120, 181, 185–6, 272–3
  New American Poetry, The 7, 10, 120, 181, 185, 186, 272
Anger, Kenneth 181, 192
Arendt, Hannah 12, 13, 279–81
Aristophanes 184, 191
Aristotle 47, 59, 247

Ballet Russe 288–94
Baraka, Amiri (LeRoi Jones) 8, 10, 12, 121
Beat generation / movement / poetry 120, 181, 185, 186, 193, 303
Benjamin, Walter 35, 230,
Bergson, Henri 18, 222–3, 228–30
Berkeley Poetry Conference (July 1965) 78, 89
Black Mountain College 1, 8, 14, 19, 39, 40, 49, 52, 103, 106, 107, 114, 118, 131, 185, 186, 209, 216, 277, 286, 287–8, 291–2, 294, 297, 298, 299
Blackburn, Paul 8, 14, 15–16, Chapter 7 *passim*, 186, 223
Blake, William 150, 154, 189, 248
Blaser, Robin 26, 49, 77–8, 186
Boer, Charles 115, 135
Boldereff, Frances 1, 10, 16, 64, Chapter 11 *passim*

Brando, Marlon 183, 189, 193
Butterick, George F. 10, 15–16, 17, 19, 29, 92, 99–100, 111, 121, 135, 155, 158, 164–5, 182, 196, 201–5, 266, 308
Byrd, Don 53–4, 93

Caedmon recordings 103–4, 106–7
Cagli, Corrado 1, 64, 274
Cahn, Michael 245–6
Cape Goliard Press *see* Goliard Press
Cernovich, Nick 286–8, 292–4
Charters, Ann 55–6, 121
Clark, Tom 10, 64, 118, 196, 298, 300
Clayre, Alasdair 116–17
Clifford Possum Tjapaltjarri 18, Chapter 19 *passim*, 262, 270 n.18
Corman, Cid 10, 33–4, 92–3, 121, 209, 234–5, 236, 239, 241, 246
Crane, Hart 182–3, 186
Creeley, Robert 1–2, 6–7, 10, 11, 16, 28, 103, 107, 111, 121, 129, 139, 141, 149, 152, 159–60, 191, 198, 199, 201, 209, 211, 215, 218–19, Chapter 16 *passim*, 239, 265, 272, 286–7, 291–2, 300, 308
Crozier, Andrew 10, 114, 131, 299

Dahlberg, Edward 10, 152, 159, 183, 309
Dante 15, 65, 68–9, 86, 168, 224–6

Davidson, Michael 84, 143
Davie, Donald 127, 131–2, 197
Deleuze, Gilles 228–9
Denby, Edwin 289–90, 293
Dorn, Edward 28, 44, 115, 118, 120–1, 131–2, 135, 139–41, 209, 257–8, 287, 297–9, 304
Duncan, Robert 48, 77, 97, 111–12, 113, 186, 197, 211

Einstein, Albert 57–60, 198
Eliot, T. S. 4, 15, 45, 46–7, 65–6, 68–72, 129, 152–3, 198, 200, 215, 223, 264, 287, 288, 289, 293, 303
Emerson, Ralph Waldo 189–90
Essex University 115, 298–9
Evergreen Review 10, 17, 181, 185–7, *187*

Ferrini, Vincent 96, 128, 155–6, 216, 273, 299, 306, 307
Finlay, Ian Hamilton, 'Sea Poppy 1' (1966) 202–3, *203*
Fisher, Allen 12, 43, 117, 199, 122–3
Frank, Robert 17, 181, 186, 188, *188*
Fredman, Stephen 4, 13, 17, 218–19
Freud, Sigmund 143, 167–9, 181, 184, 198, 290
Friedlander, Benjamin 10, 14, 135, 146
Fulcrum Press 284, 298

Gerhardt, Rainer Maria 18, 200, Chapter 16 *passim*
Gilgamesh 150, 195–6, 204, 210, 305
Ginsberg, Allen 17, 48, 115, 181, 185–6, 189, 191–3, 304
Goethe, Johann Wolfgang von 38, 222, 228
Goliard Press / Cape Goliard Press 10, 115, 297
Grady, Panna 115, 303, 305–6

Hall, Barry 10, 115

Harvard University 1, 114, 250, 302
Hegel 219, 234, 240, 248
Heraclitus / Heraklitus 4, 54, 240, 252, 253, 264–5, 277
Herodotus 4, 111, 142–3, 222, 305
Hesiod 31, 57, 59, 61, 184–5, 238, 305
hieroglyphs 129, 215, 258, 267
Homer 167–8, 184–5, 189, 222, 228, 299, 305–6
Howe, Susan 17, 117, 149, Chapter 12 *passim*

'*istorin* 4, 17, 20 n.10, 44, 54, 142, 201, 277, 283, 303–4

Jones, LeRoi *see* Baraka, Amiri
Jung, Carl 27, 49, 107, 157–8, 167, 181–2, 196, 205–6, 248

Keats, John 27, 116–17, 240, 300, 309
Kerouac, Jack 48, 185, 186–9, 193, 297, 299–302, 304
Kirstein, Lincoln 289–91
Kramer, Samuel Noah 150, 156

Lawrence, D. H. 130, 156, 186, 189, 196
Litz, Katherine 286, 287, 292–3
Livesay, Dorothy 80–1, 84

Mac Low, Jackson 44, 200
MacSweeney, Barry 116, 119
Mao Zedong 5, 130, 215, 252, 253, 265
Marx, Karl 4, 143, 198, 219, 240
Maud, Ralph 7, 10, 13, 19, 44, 52, 121, 149–50, 159, 182, 185, 195–9, 264, 269, 274
Mayan civilisation 7, 26, 130, 141–2, 158, 195, 197, 227, 258, 265–8, 286, 292, 301
Melville, Herman 1, 2, 17, 19, 28, 55–6, 113, 115, 128, 154, 163–4, 166–7, 168, 170–1, 181–3,

228, 244–5, 273, 289, 302
Moby-Dick 1, 56, 113, 128, 140, 291, 296 n.33, 302
modernism / modernists 1–2, 4, 17, 116, 118, 121, 139, 163, 171, 172, 196, 198–200, 206, 223, 226, 259, 272, 288–9, 292–4, 302–3, 305

New American Poetry, The, see Allen, Donald
New Testament 144, 167
Newton, Isaac 57–9
Nichols, Miriam 11–12, 13, 14, 47, 61, 274, 279

O'Hara, Frank 17, 186, 253
Odyssey / Odysseus 137, 204, 305
Olsen, Redell 17, 119–20, Chapter 12 *passim*

Plato / Platonism 27, 45, 47, 54, 265–6, 268
Platoff, Marc 288–92
Plutarch 156, 265, 267
'polis' 12, 13, 14, 16, 18–19, 25, 28, 34, 41, 110, 137–40, 145, 172–3, 195, 197, 253, 275, 278–85
Pollock, Jackson 186, 263
postmodernism 2, 12, 34, 36, 139, 151, 196, 198–201, 206, 253, 258–9, 263, 265, 269, 274, 275, 279–81, 279, 303
Pound, Ezra 1, 17, 25, 38, 60, 64, 79–80, 85, 86, 104, 108, 116, 118, 127–8, 130, 131, 136, 144, 149, 152–3, 186, 197–201, 205, 209, 221, 224, 226–8, 230, 240, 253, 258, 272, 276, 287–8, 291–2, 302, 303
Prospect 10, 114, 127, 128, 131
Prynne, J. H. 10, 12, 98, 99, 114, 117, 118, 119, 127–8, 131, 282–4, 300, 304, 305

Rexroth, Kenneth 185, 186, 272
Riemann, Georg Friedrich Bernhard 56, 228–9
Rimbaud, Arthur 6, 11, 60, 82–3, 199, 253
Ross, Andrew 53–4, 206

San Francisco 77–8, 80, 185–6
Second World War 3, 10, 12, 181, 183, 209, 216, 275, 279–80
Shakespeare, William 113, 121, 165, 166, 169
Silliman, Ron 82, 84, 145
Simon Fraser University 10, 282, 300
Sinclair, Iain 12, 13, 19, 115–16, 119
Snyder, Gary 43, 118, 186
Spicer, Jack 15, Chapter 5 *passim*, 186, 200, 253

Temple, John 122, 299
Thesen, Sharon 149–50, 151, 159
Turnbull, Gael 10, 113–14, 131

Vancouver conference 7, 77, 79–80, 84, 120, 123, 126 n.54, 201
Virgil 224, 225, 226
von Hallberg, Robert 25–6, 34, 68, 93

White, John 128, 284, 303
Whitehead, Alfred North 26–7, 44, 47–9, 53, 57–8, 111–12, 117, 216, 257–8
Whitman, Walt 153–4, 170, 289
Williams, William Carlos 9, 181, 186, 305

Yeats, W. B. 38, 78, 150, 288, 294, 298
Yucatan, Mexico 128–9, 141, 142, 143, 265, 286, 301

Zukofsky, Louis 89, 139, 144, 238–9, 250 n.42, 27